D0505937

Shakespeare Revealed

Also by René Weis

The Yellow Cross: The Story of the Last Cathars 1290–1329
Criminal Justice: The True Story of Edith Thompson

Edited by René Weis

Henry IV Part 2
John Webster: 'The Duchess of Malfi' and Other Plays
King Lear: A Parallel Text Edition

Shakespeare Revealed

A Biography

RENÉ WEIS

JOHN MURRAY

© René Weis 2007

First published in Great Britain in 2007 by John Murray (Publishers)
A division of Hodder Headline

The right of René Weis to be identified as the Author of the Work
has been asserted by him in accordance with the Copyright, Designs
and Patents Act 1988.

1

A CIP catalogue record for this title is available
from the British Library

ISBN 978-0-7195-6418-5

Typeset in Bembo by M Rules

Printed and bound by Clays Ltd, St Ives plc

Hodder Headline policy is to use papers that are natural, renewable
and recyclable products and made from wood grown in sustainable
forests. The logging and manufacturing processes are expected to
conform to the environmental regulations of the country of origin.

John Murray (Publishers)
338 Euston Road
London NW1 3BH

To the memory of
Edith Graydon
25.XII.1893–9.I.1923

Contents

Illustrations

Acknowledgements

During the writing of this book I have incurred a number of debts which it is a pleasure to acknowledge. I am grateful to Robert Bearman and his staff at the Shakespeare Birthplace Trust Record Office in Henley Street whose expertise in the collections held in trust there made all the difference. The pioneering work on the Stratford records by archivists at the Birthplace Trust is as groundbreaking today as it was eighty years ago. I must thank the chief guides at Hall's Croft, Nash house, the Birthplace, Anne Hathaway's cottage, and Mary Arden's house for their erudition and enthusiasm. Their ability to conjure up Shakespeare for visitors is impressive, as Jim Shapiro and I discovered late one cold autumn afternoon in Wilmcote. I must thank him for his encouragement and for instructing me, somewhere on the road between Snitterfield and Norton Lindsey, to trust my instincts on topography and not to be unduly intimidated by Schoenbaum. His own recent book on the year 1599 has already established itself as a classic, a master lesson in how to write about moments in Shakespeare's life.

In Stratford I was privileged to enjoy the company of Stanley Wells and Paul Edmondson of the Education Department of the Shakespeare Birthplace Trust on many occasions. They were generous to a fault with their time and expertise. I particularly remember spending time with them one summer's evening in the chancel of Holy Trinity, pondering the layout of the Shakespeare graves, inspecting the misericords and taking instruction from Nigel Penn about Shakespeare's church. Paul kindly invited me to a conference in Charlecote in the great hall of that same country house where the young Shakespeare may have been arraigned by Sir Thomas Lucy, while Russell Jackson asked me to chair a seminar on biography at the Shakespeare Institute. At the Bath Literary Festival I appeared along-side a number of distinguished writers and scholars who impressed on me the importance of the sectarian divide in the England of Shakespeare's time. It was a privilege to share my interest in John Gerard of the Society of Jesus with Gerard Kilroy, whose devotion to the memory of Edmund Campion made me realize that the first Elizabethan age endures not just because of Shakespeare.

Anthony West patiently answered queries about the history of the Shakespeare folios after 1623. His two Oxford volumes on the First Folio offer a fascinating survey for the kind of detective work on Folio trails that may yet lead us back to Shakespeare's friends in the King's Men, or even to Lady Elizabeth Barnard, the poet's grand-daughter. Gabriel Egan responded to my queries about Shakespeare's theatres with the exemplary thoroughness of his entries in *The Oxford Companion to Shakespeare*. Michael Wood has been an inspir-ation ever since his riveting programmes about the Trojan War set new standards for understanding the past as a real place which echoes in timeless landscapes. In his recent quest for Shakespeare he trans-ports us back into the poet's world with flair, enthusiasm, and intellectual rigour.

My students at UCL have been a constant source of pleasure and friendship. Alison Thorne and Marinella Salari, made possible a visit to the *università degli studi di Perugia* to lecture on Shakespeare's life and work. My greatest intellectual debt is to my friend and colleague Henry Woudhuysen, who was once more the most generous of men with his peerless erudition, time, and library. When I was a graduate student Ross Woodman of the University of Western Ontario in Canada gave me his copy of the original Scolar Press edition of Samuel Schoenbaum's *William Shakespeare: A Documentary Life*. Ever since then I have wanted to write on Shakespeare's life. On retiring from UCL Keith Walker left me his set of Geoffrey Bullough's eight-volume *Narrative and Dramatic Sources of Shakespeare*. Bullough's work was my constant companion during the research for this book, as were my fond memories of Keith. Peter Swaab urged me to consider that Shakespeare's works could not possibly be divorced from his life, while Nathalie Jacoby caused me to hone my views on Shakespeare's London. In Foster Court in the 1970s David Daniell, the Arden Shakespeare editor of *Julius Caesar* and the world's leading authority on William Tyndale, father of the English Bible, offered some of the most cutting-edge teaching of Shakespeare in the country. For this and for much else I want to thank him. Over the years I have accumulated broader intellectual debts to a number of colleagues at UCL, particularly to Rosemary Ashton, Mark Ford, Helen Hackett, Philip Horne, Dan Jacobson, Danny Karlin, Tim Langley, Kathy Metzenthin, Karl Miller, Neil Rennie, John Sutherland, David Trotter, and Sarah Wintle. I am grateful to David Scott Kastan of Columbia for his friendship and guidance, and to George Walton Williams for the most scintillating table talk on Shakespeare since Coleridge.

During the writing of this book I worked with two singularly benign deans. It is a pleasure to thank Gerard O'Daly and Jane Fenoulhet of UCL for all their help and good will, and also Michael Worton for his selfless hard work and friendship. UCL once again backed me and granted me extra leave towards completing this book. John Allen of the UCL library readily tendered sound advice spiced up with literary parodies and John Spiers was, as ever, a mine of information. It is a pleasure again to record a debt to Emmanuel Le Roy Ladurie for responding so instructively to my queries about the weather during Shakespeare's lifetime. His recently published *Histoire humaine et comparée du climat* appeared in time for me to consult on the crops and wet summers of the 1590s and on the frosts of the early seventeenth century. There can never have been a more opportune moment for writing on '*le climat*'; it is hard to imagine anyone doing it nearly as well as Le Roy Ladurie.

Sarah Lee took photographs for me in Shakespeare's home county which also happens to be hers. I want to thank her for the pleasure of her company during our visits to Warwickshire and for her outstanding work. James Hutchinson alerted me to ways in which beggars in *King Lear* may connect back into Shakespeare's real world. I must thank two outstanding former research students, Tom Rutter and Chris Laoutaris, from whom I learnt more than I could ever teach them. Kate Mossman came to my rescue over the King's Men and on many occasions shared with me her incomparable literary gifts.

On 2 February 2002 Emmanuel Bock treated me to *Twelfth Night* in the glorious Middle Temple hall on the four hundreth anniversary of the play's performance there, while the stellar Josepha Jacobson made possible dinner with her lawyer peers in the same. Here Shakespeare's cousin Greene once sat as did John Marston and his father. So did John Manningham, whose racy anecdote about Shakespeare's sex life may have had its origin in after-dinner table talk right here. Shakespeare almost certainly performed in Middle Temple and was probably gossiped about in it. In 2006 Geoffrey Gower-Kerslake entertained me in another great hall, that of Gray's Inn. There, staring down at us from the wall behind the dais of benchers and judges, were portraits of Robert Cecil and of Henry Wriothesley, Third Earl of Southampton, as he looked in later life. The picture records the date 1587 when the young Southampton first joined Gray's Inn. In this very hall which, unlike the one at Middle Temple, escaped the Blitz unharmed, Shakespeare's *The Comedy of Errors* was performed on 28 December 1594. The title turned out to be peculiarly fitting since that night's proceedings descended into anarchy. A note of wry humour echoes beneath the chronicler's remark that with the play 'that night was begun, and continued to the end, in nothing but confusion and errors, whereupon it was ever afterwards called *The Night of Errors*'.

Philippe and Pascale Delarche afforded me the chance to work quietly on the book in Pernand-Vergelesses and John Snelson of the Royal Opera House Covent Garden caused me to think again about *Macbeth*, *Romeo and Juliet*, and *The Tempest* when I needed to do so most.

It gives me special pleasure to thank Matthew Roberts and Emma Page-Roberts for their friendship, encouragement and generosity.

I wish to thank everyone involved in the publication of the book at John Murray, and particularly Martin Collins, Roland Philipps, Christopher Phipps, Liz Robinson, Nick de Somogyi, Caroline Westmore, and Rowan Yapp.

ACKNOWLEDGEMENTS

Bill Hamilton of A. M. Heath & Co once again gave me much of his precious time and was always calm, steady, and kind.

But most of all I want to thank Jean. This book is also for her.

René Weis
UCL
11 November 2006

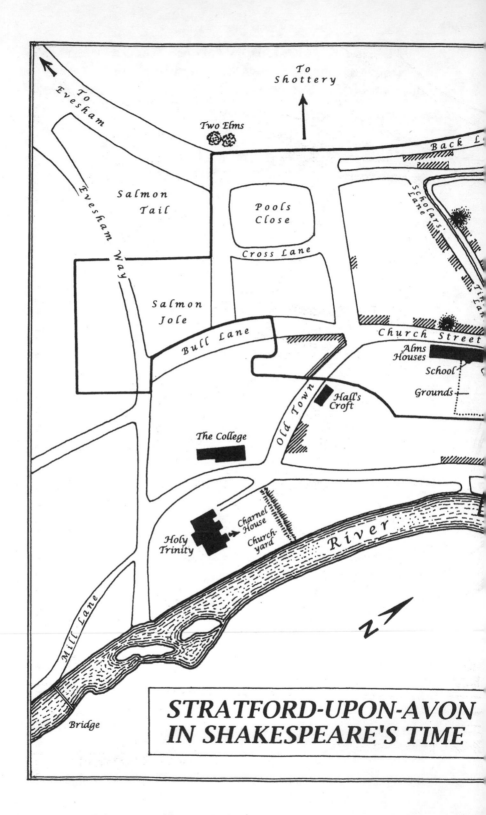

STRATFORD-UPON-AVON
IN SHAKESPEARE'S TIME

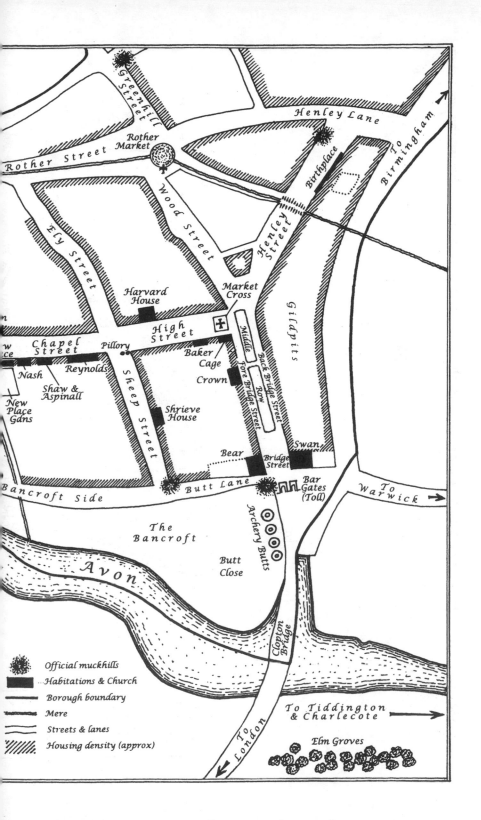

Greenhill Street

Henley Lane

To Birmingham

Rother Street

Rother Market

Birthplace

Wood Street

Henley Street

Ely Street

Gildpits

Harvard House

Market Cross

High Street

Chapel Street

Pillory

Middle

Baker

Back Bridge Street

Cage

Fore Bridge Street

Row

Nash

Reynolds

Crown

Shaw & Aspinall

New Place Gdns

Sheep Street

Shrieve House

Swan

Bear

Bridge Street

Bar Gates (Toll)

Bancroft Side

Butt Lane

To Warwick

The Bancroft

Archery Butts

Butt Close

A v o n

Clopton Bridge

Official muckhills

Habitations & Church

Borough boundary

Mere

Streets & lanes

Housing density (approx)

To London

To Tiddington & Charlecote

Elm Groves

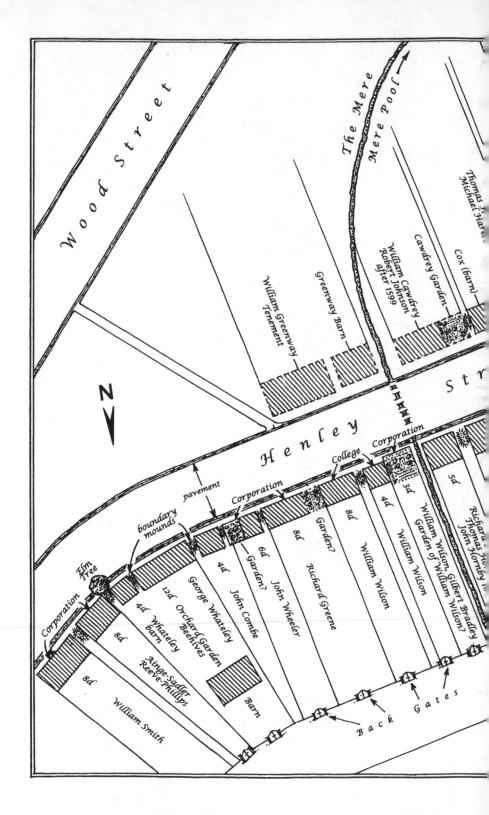

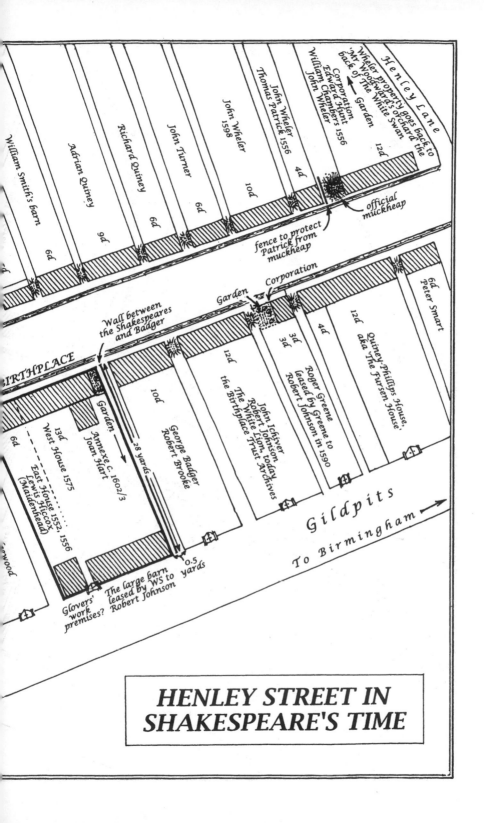

Henley Lane

Wheler property goes back to
Mr Woodward's orchard the
back of The White Swan

Corporation
Edward Hunt
William Chambers 1556
John Wheler

John Wheler
1598

John Wheler
Thomas Patrick 1556

John Turner

Richard Quiney

Adrian Quiney

William Smith's barn

↑ Garden

12d

4d

10d

6d

6d

9d

6d

official
muckheap

fence to protect
Patrick from
muckheap

Garden

Corporation

6d
Peter Smart

12d

Quiney-Phillips House,
aka 'The Tursen House'

4d

3d

Roger Greene
leased by Greene to
Robert Johnson in 1590

3d

John Ichiver
Robert Johnson
The White Lion, today
the Birthplace Trust Archives

12d

Wall between
the Shakespeares
and Badger

BIRTHPLACE

Garden →

← 28 yards →

10d

George Badger
Robert Brooke

Annexe c. 1602/3
Joan Hart

13d
West House 1575
....
East House 1552, 1556
Lewis Hiccox
(Maidenhead)

6d

Glovers'
work
premises?

The large barn
leased by WS to
Robert Johnson

0.5
yards

Gildpits

To Birmingham →

HENLEY STREET IN SHAKESPEARE'S TIME

Prologue

A T SOME POINT in the late 1580s a young married glover from Stratford-upon-Avon set out for London and became the greatest playwright of all time. He left behind his wife and their three small children, his mother, his father, his brothers and sister, and his friends. People from his kind of background did not do that kind of thing, but William Shakespeare was never one to conform to rules. In a relatively short time he made a fortune from writing plays and poems. The professional London theatre was barely ten years old when he arrived, but this was a date with destiny. Shakespeare's dramatic talent was incomparable. None of his contemporaries could match it, and no one has since. This is such a familiar idea that it is easy to forget quite how strange it must have been for someone to become rich from the proceeds of public entertainment. The scale of Shakespeare's achievement has made it seem almost too good to be true, its scope apparently beyond a mere glover turned playwright with at best a humble local grammar school education. There is undoubtedly a mysterious dimension to Shakespeare's range and to his exceptional verbal facility. He had the largest vocabulary of anyone who has ever written in English, and perfect dramatic timing. His moral and imaginative sympathy lift him right out of his period, making him as contemporary today as he was a contemporary of Spenser, Marlowe, and Jonson. That he is in some ways larger than life is undeniable, but then so is all genius. It is no more possible to explain the secret of Shakespeare's talent than it is to account for Mozart's gifts. Only Shakespeare ever knew what it was that enabled him to write the way he did.

There is one character in the later plays with whom Shakespeare is commonly identified: Prospero in *The Tempest*, the last play Shakespeare wrote without collaboration. Prospero sees himself as a magician whose art allows him to conjure up entire worlds of men and women, to lord it over their lives, and even to resurrect them from death. Whatever else he may or may not have thought, Shakespeare did not take a modest view of his own gifts and achievements, and even if Prospero is not Shakespeare and the Milan to which Prospero wishes to retire is not Stratford-upon-Avon, the links between Shakespeare's life and his works may be far closer than is commonly assumed. This book aims to show just how deep these connections really are, and to demonstrate that the plays and poems contain important clues not only to Shakespeare's inner life but also about real, tangible, external events.

A cumulative amount of circumstantial evidence demonstrates beyond doubt that Shakespeare responded in his work to events from his life. In a sense of course that is self-evidently the case as far as his own feelings are concerned. His King Lear could hardly have raged on the heath unless Shakespeare himself had known extreme anger and frustration and the urge to vent it against the elements and the world at large. That does not mean that he tore off his clothes on a heath in Warwickshire, or that he had three daughters, of whom two were conspiring against him while the third, his youngest, was trying to save his life and sanity. Shakespeare was no more King of England than he was a prince of Denmark, a middle-aged black man consumed by love and jealousy and rendered vulnerable to treachery by his race, or a Jewish financier seeking revenge on Christians for putting him out of business or spitting on him. The echoes that bounce across the boundary between life and art are much subtler, but are there to be caught by those who listen. Shakespeare may not have had three daughters, but he did have two. If it were to emerge that at just the time *King Lear* was being written there were tensions in Shakespeare's household and events in his sexual life that might have helped shape the plot of the play, they should not be ignored: to do so would be to fly in the face of common sense.

The most thought-provoking remark ever on the convergence of Shakespeare's life and works belongs to the poet John Keats, one of Shakespeare's most assiduous and intelligent readers. In a letter of 1819 he wrote that 'A man's life of any worth is a continual allegory – and very few eyes can see the mystery of his life . . . Shakespeare led a life of Allegory: his works are the comments on it.' For Keats, Shakespeare's life and his plays and poems were inextricably linked in ways that were mutually reflective and illuminating, merging to form a secret history – the history this book sets out to decode. Keats's near contemporary William Wordsworth, author of an epic autobiographical poem, suggested that the *Sonnets* were the key with which Shakespeare had unlocked his heart. Shakespeare lived and breathed theatre, composing countless iambic pentameters, memorizing lines, acting in his own plays and in those written by fellow dramatists, while at the same time reading widely in the classics and in English and Roman history. He mostly wrote as the mood took him. The intensity of his plays derives from an imaginative struggle to come to terms with the eternal human issues of love, life, and death. One of his greatest works, perhaps the most famous tragedy in the world, he called *Hamlet* after his own dead son. To try to detach the plays and poems from the life of their author is as counter-intuitive as it would be to seek to separate him from the national history of his era.

Shakespeare lived emphatically in history and no one has ever doubted that this left a deep imprint on his work. When he was born, the recent Protestant revolution had put the English Bible at the core of the national culture. If it had not been for the Reformation Shakespeare would not have read the scriptures, he might not have gone to school, and he might never have left Stratford. On the other hand nor would he have lived in a country in which the slaughter of innocent people for their beliefs was a matter of public spectacle, the town of his birth might well have been more harmonious, and he might have slept more quietly in his bed. He would have attended the same mass as every other good Catholic of Stratford-upon-Avon and the England of his forebears would also have been his spiritual inheritance. Their history and his would have been identical – Catholic, and European.

The Shakespeare story begins and ends in a Midlands market town. He always thought of it as home, and he returned to it at the age of thirty-three. It must have marked him more than any other place in his life, including the glittering big city where he made his fortune. His family and his roots were all here. To know Shakespeare's Stratford intimately is a prerequisite for forming a mental picture of the child who became the man. Had Shakespeare never written anything at all, he would only ever have been a witty and resourceful glover living in Henley Street. He would probably have featured in the annals of Stratford as a hard-working businessman, might have joined the council, and might have become mayor. His horizons would have been much more circumscribed, he would not have hobnobbed with the top people in London. There would probably have been no extra-marital affairs – and above all no outlet for the pressure-cooker that was his imagination, what Wordsworth called 'the hiding places of man's power'. Few passages in Shakespeare's plays and poems better render his own sense of the creative inner self than Richard II's soliloquy in the dungeon of Pomfret Castle. The king is alone and abandoned, without realm, or crown, or human company. His boon companions, those parasites who poisoned his mind, the infamous 'caterpillars of the Commonwealth', are all gone. His world has contracted to his prison cell, and in his despair he decides to people it from within his own head: 'My brain I'll prove the female to my soul, / My soul the father'. Between them, these two will engender a parallel universe, a 'little world' just like the world itself. Inside his head Richard is lord of all he surveys and freely weaves in and out of whichever role takes his fancy, whether king or beggar. The fact that out of all the characters Shakespeare created it should have been a gay king who put into words the inner mechanisms of the imagination may not be a coincidence. Like Richard II he imagined worlds within worlds, and as with Richard so there are question marks hanging over Shakespeare's sexuality. Before his brain and soul could unite Shakespeare needed to give them sustenance and this he did with an impressive amount of reading. He could never have done this if he had stayed in Stratford, even though his Stratford education provided him with the key to unlock the portals that led to Ovid, Virgil, Horace, Cicero, Plautus, and Terence. His years in the grammar school had given him the classics and equipped him with a superb command of rhetoric.

Shakespeare and his family left their mark on Stratford-upon-Avon in many different ways. Stories about him started to circulate in the town in his lifetime, continuing after his death and during the lives of his daughters and granddaughter. The material reality of sixteenth-century Stratford was Shakespeare's habitat. This was the physical space that the greatest writer of all time inhabited, and eventually he himself became his home town's favourite object of folklore. Moreover, Stratford stories about Shakespeare have a way, sooner or later, of turning out to be true, or very nearly so.

I

Stratford, 1564: Birth of a Genius

WILLIAM SHAKESPEARE DIED 391 years ago. After his death his younger contemporary Ben Jonson wrote about him that he

> loved the man and do honour his memory, on this side idolatry, as much as any. He was indeed honest and of an open and free nature; had an excellent fancy; brave notions, and gentle expressions wherein he flowed with that facility that sometime it was necessary he should be stopped . . . His wit was in his own power, would the rule of it had been so too.

Jonson is a great witness, trenchant, steeped in theatre, and never fawning. This tribute provides a convenient starting point. He is talking about 'the man', but almost at once conflates the man with the poet and playwright. Jonson did not distinguish categorically between the man and the work. The two go together, and the main reason for writing a biography of Shakespeare at all is those plays and poems that have given untold pleasure to people the world over since they were first written between 1590 and 1613. If there is such a thing as a window into the soul of the subject, as in one of his sonnets Shakespeare suggested there was, his plays and poems are the subject of his soul.

Jonson has the advantage of having known Shakespeare well. He anticipated that his friend Will Shakespeare would in the judgement of posterity outshine Jonson himself and all his contemporaries, that he would be ranked with Ovid, Virgil, Horace, and Homer and ultimately above them all. It was Jonson who best captured Shakespeare's legacy: in his elegy in the first Folio of 1623 he apostrophized his friend as the 'soul of the age' and the 'wonder of our stage' before, finally, claiming that Shakespeare 'was not of an age, but for all time'.

He was both, and this book will show how deep are the traces left by his age and his own life in his plays which have proven to be every bit as timeless as Jonson predicted. In the 1623 Folio Jonson also authenticated the celebrated egg-headed depiction of Shakespeare by Martin Droeshout. It has not pleased the many, but it is a true likeness and, in Jonson's judgement, not a bad one at that. On the facing page is Jonson's address 'To the Reader':

> This figure that thou here seest put,
> It was for gentle Shakespeare cut,
> Wherein the graver had a strife
> With nature to outdo the life.
> O could he have but drawn his wit
> As well in brass, as he has hit
> His face, the print would then surpass
> All that was ever writ in brass.
> But since he cannot, reader, look
> Not on his picture but his book.
>
> B[en] J[onson]

It is comforting for the Shakespeare biographer to have this testimony, to know what Shakespeare looked like, to be told by Shakespeare's friend Ben Jonson that the artist 'hit' Shakespeare's face to the life. Very few past lives from Shakespeare's sort of background afford this luxury. In addition to the Folio frontispiece there is one other authenticated representation of Shakespeare, the famous bust in the chancel of the Church of the Holy Trinity in Stratford, erected during the lifetime of Shakespeare's sister Joan, his widow and his daughters. It was in place by the time the first Folio was published in 1623.

Shakespeare spent much of his life in the provincial Warwickshire town of his birth. Stratford-upon-Avon was a backwater compared to London, but it was not therefore backward, nor was it small. Since the 1490s it had been linked to the south of the country by an imposing stone bridge across the river Avon. It is known now as Clopton Bridge, after its builder, the Stratford benefactor Sir Hugh Clopton, but in Shakespeare's day it was the 'great bridge', 'Stratford Bridge', or the 'stone bridge', renowned throughout the region and well looked after by the corporation. Shakespeare's works are impregnated by his county and place of birth, Warwickshire. His imagination was steeped in the local countryside as surely as William Wordsworth's was in the lakes and mountains of Cumbria. In his choice of images Shakespeare frequently returns to his origins at home. This is as true of the painful, figurative English landscape of *King Lear* as it is of that so very Warwickshire-like magic wood in *A Midsummer Night's Dream*. Shakespeare never bought property in London during his years of working there but, after 1597, chose instead to base himself in a huge and comfortable new house in Stratford-upon-Avon. Though London was the scene of his great triumphs, and where he kept company with the good, the true, and the reckless, he was only ever a lodger there.

The outline of the Stratford that Shakespeare knew remains largely intact. At the southern edge of the town, in splendid isolation on the Avon, sits the Church of the Holy Trinity, providing one of the most cherished silhouettes in all rural England, as evocative as the paintings of Constable. A mediaeval priory and township once surrounded it, hence the name 'Old Town', by which the area was already known in Shakespeare's time. Old Town Lane still links Holy Trinity with the Bancroft, the old common on the Avon.

The other place of worship in the town was the Gild Chapel of the Holy Cross, opposite there once stood the largest house in town, bought by Shakespeare in the 1590s. He and his family would have heard the din of its bells every day and every night, but Virginia Woolf was wrong when she wrote, 'And when the clock struck, that was the sound that Shakespeare heard'.[1] The large bell in the tower of the Gild Chapel dates only from 1633. Shakespeare never heard it, but his daughters did. On the outside the chapel looked the same then as it does now, and as it did before the Reformation, but William was born just too late to see its interior in its Catholic glory. His father was the borough chamberlain who paid for the mandatory Protestant vandalism of its mural paintings: 'Item paid for defacing images in the chapel 2 shillings, 10 January 1564'. Two hundred and forty years later the wonderful frescoes in the Gild Chapel began to bleed through the whitewash. Then they started to fade, and now, another two hundred years on, they have almost entirely disappeared. Copies reveal what they looked like. South of the Gild Chapel is the King's

New School, named after Edward VI. The core of this late mediaeval grammar school still exists, its long classrooms on the ground and first floor spaces that Shakespeare must have known well. One of its inside chambers, to the left of the staircase, at the south-eastern end of the building, served as the town council's meeting room. Adjacent to the school another surviving set of timbered fifteenth-century buildings bulges out into the pavement, the Stratford almshouses.

Shakespeare was baptized in Holy Trinity on Wednesday 26 April 1564.[2] The spring of 1564 was a bad time to be born, because plague was on its way – within three months of Shakespeare's birth the Register of Holy Trinity ominously records '*hic incepit pestis*' – 'here the plague started'.[3] Though not overcrowded and congested like London and other big cities in which the plague spread like wild-fire, provincial towns were not immune. One effect of the plague was that the number of Stratford baptisms dropped by half, from more than eighty in 1562 and 1563 to thirty-nine in 1564 – twenty-five boys, of whom William was one, and fourteen girls.

In any case this must have been an anxious time for Shakespeare's parents John Shakespeare and Mary Arden. William was their third child and the first boy. Two girls, Joan and Margaret, had preceded him, but neither had lived for more than a few months. Joan was baptised on 15 September 1558 and died, it seems, not long afterwards. It took her parents four years to produce another daughter, Margaret, and she only lived for a few short months. The two girls were named after Mary Arden's sisters, but there were no Williams in either the Shakespeare or Arden families, so the boy was presumably named after a neighbour or a friend, or someone who was both. It was a common baptismal name in Elizabethan Stratford and it is usually taken for granted that the haberdasher William Smith of Henley Street stood as Shakespeare's godfather. He and John Shakespeare were both corporation 'chamberlains' at the time of William's birth in April 1564, in which office they were charged with keeping the accounts of the borough for that year, itemizing all revenues and expenses. William Smith called his own son John, perhaps reciprocating the godfathering compliment. The two men certainly lived for fifty years in the same street in the same town.[4]

But it is just as likely that William Tyler rather than William Smith was Shakespeare's godfather. Tyler was a butcher with premises on the south-east side of Sheep Street near the Bancroft (roughly opposite the present 'Cordelia' cottage). He was a few years older than John Shakespeare and had a son named Richard, born in the autumn of 1566. This Richard Tyler is remembered in the first draft of Shakespeare's will, crossed out in the final version, and may also be linked to the naming of one of Shakespeare's daughters.

John and Mary Shakespeare had a fourth child, another boy, Gilbert, born in 1566 and probably named after the glover Gilbert Bradley who lived three doors east of John Shakespeare in Henley Street. Gilbert was followed by a second Joan in 1569, and two years later by another girl, named Anne after her mother's sister Agnes (Agnes and Anne were interchangeable). Another son was baptized Richard on 11 March 1574, named after his grandfather Richard Shakespeare from the nearby village of Snitterfield. John's and Mary's last child was another boy, Edmund, baptized on 3 May 1580 when Will was 16, Gilbert 14, Joan 11, and Richard 6.

The name Edmund was rare in sixteenth-century Stratford, and there were no Edmunds in the immediate Arden and Shakespeare families, so the odds are that this child was named after Edmund Lambert from Barton-on-the-Heath, husband of Mary Arden's sister Joan. Yet there is also the possibility that it was connected with Edmund Campion, in 1580 already revered in recusant circles, and martyred the following year. There were undoubtedly those who were named after him. One was the Jesuit William Weston, who called himself William Edmunds to honour his friend Campion, with whom he had been at Oxford. He spent many years incarcerated at Wisbech in Cambridgeshire and in the Tower of London and was eventually released into exile on the verge of blindness, becoming a saint to his followers. The civil war waged for the souls of the English people between Catholics and Protestants was the deepest spiritual and political reality of the time, and inevitably affected Shakespeare and his family. Since William Shakespeare, Edmund Campion, William 'Edmunds' Weston, Edmund Shakespeare, and Edmund 'the bastard' Gloucester in *King Lear* all interleave in this story, it will be as well to be aware of another man who was born in the same year as Shakespeare. John Gerard was better born than the poet and joined the Society of Jesus at a time when to do so and then to return to

England was tantamount to committing suicide. He did just that, and suffered accordingly. There was a certain dash about Gerard, the tall Jesuit Hotspur who converted Penelope Rich (née Devereux), sister of the mercurial Earl of Essex and the object of the most acclaimed sonnet cycle of the age, Sidney's *Astrophil and Stella*. He happened also to be a master of disguises, and also a wonderful writer and autobiographer. A close friend was a priest who found his way into Shakespeare's *Macbeth*, Father Henry Garnett. Shakespeare's and Gerard's lives ran on parallel tracks in the England of the period: the one, Shakespeare, inside the tent even if perhaps only just, the other, Gerard, militantly outside and thus exposed fully to the vengeful savagery of the Elizabethan state. Gerard's autobiography offers the most intimate, immediate, and intensely lived account of the years and of the country that Shakespeare inhabited.

Mary Arden was still a spinster when her father Robert Arden of Wilmcote made his will on 24 November 1556. Since little Joan was born in September 1558, Mary and John probably wed in the summer or autumn of 1557. Assuming that she was around eighteen during her first pregnancy in 1558, this would place her birth in 1540. John seems to have been her senior by some ten years, because he was renting property in Henley Street by 1552, when he must have been in his early twenties after a full seven-year apprenticeship as a glover – clearly a hard worker, to be able to set up on his own. He had spent his youth in his yeoman father Richard's home in the village of Snitterfield, some three miles north-east of Stratford. 'Snitterfield' means 'open land haunted by snipe', and the landscape resembles a bowl of rolling fields – perfect for farming. As a young man John must have helped out his father in the family's fields, among them those which lay beyond the church on the right-hand side of the road to Luscombe and Norton Lindsey. These fields were known as Burman and Redhill, and in the 1590s Shakespeare's uncle Henry was fined for not maintaining a drainage ditch between them. Today a housing estate sits on fields that were once tilled by Shakespeares.

Sixteenth-century local records make it possible to identify Richard Shakespeare's farm or 'messuage' with certainty, for it derived from a property sold in 1504 to Mary Arden's grandfather, Thomas Arden of Wilmcote: 'one messuage and eighty acres of land at Snitterfield, the messuage being situated between the tenement of William Palmer and a lane called Maryes Lane, and extending in length from the King's highway to a small rivulet.'5 The 'rivulet' is the Bell Brook, which meanders along today's School Road through the lower village towards the Green, 'Maryes lane' corresponds to Bell Lane, and the 'King's highway' is Church Road. The property that now straddles the south corner of Bell Lane and Church Road occupies the site of Shakespeare's grandfather's house. Whenever William Shakespeare visited Snitterfield to see his aunt and uncle, he must have passed this very spot. His roots were right here. In due course the Shakespeare farm and its substantial lands rolling down all the way to Bell Brook reverted to the Ardens, who had retained the freehold, and were bequeathed to Mary Arden's brother-in-law Edmund Lambert.

How it was that John Shakespeare of Snitterfield turned up in Stratford as a glover is not known, but he was a restless spirit on the make, and make it big he did at first, and not just with gloving: he was also trading in wool on a lucrative scale, and not always wholly legally – it was close enough to racketeering for him to attract his own personal government surveillance agent, whose reports on him survive in the National Archives in Kew. In October 1556 John Shakespeare acquired the eastern wing of what is now known as the Birthplace from Edward West, as well as a house of a similar size in Greenhill Street from George Turnor, probably related to the John Turnor who lived across the road from the Shakespeares in Henley Street. John Shakespeare was becoming a man of substance, and a serious property-owner. He had proven himself to be an astute businessman and artisan. He was on the up and he was ready to marry, and marry he did. Mary Arden was not quite the boss's daughter, but she was as good as, given the relationship between his father and hers, and she stood to inherit considerable property in Wilmcote from her father. In 1557 John and Mary Shakespeare embarked on married life in the Henley Street house.

Twenty-two years separate the Shakespeares' first-born daughter Joan and the last baby, Edmund. What did Will Shakespeare, fifteen at the time of Edmund's arrival, make of his pregnant and ageing mother? The physical rituals of childbirth were inescapably raw, real, and unavoidable. Usually a cabal of women would gather around the woman who was giving birth, in the woman's home. There was no escaping the pain and the screaming, and everyone, men, women, and children knew what was going on, as much outside in the street as inside.

Such elemental facts of life would have helped shape Shakespeare's imagination as much as anything. Though mothers do not feature nearly as prominently in his plays as fathers, he certainly knew a great deal about motherhood, and a mother's 'pains', as he put it, were never far from his mind. While the statute which forbade women to act on stage made it harder to play mothers than fathers, daughters than sons, the impressive number of daughters in Shakespeare's plays – in the teeth of this practical difficulty – underlines the emotional hold that this particular bond had over Shakespeare, and mothers are nevertheless given a powerful voice. There is a tense moment towards the end of *Richard II* when young Aumerle is forced by his father York to reveal his treachery to the usurper king Bolingbroke, Henry IV. Without a moment's hesitation the aged father decides to report his son's treason to the king, in the full knowledge that this will mean certain death to him. The boy's mother, the Duchess, protests vehemently:

> Why, York, what wilt thou do?
> Wilt thou not hide the trespass of thine own?
> Have we more sons, or are we like to have?
> Is not my teeming date drunk up with time?
> And wilt thou pluck my fair son from mine age,
> And rob me of a happy mother's name?
> Is he not like thee, is he not thine own?

When he refuses to heed her pleas she interjects, 'Hadst thou groaned for him / As I have done, thou wouldst be more pitiful.' Here a mother's sufferings and child-rearing are granted considerable moral authority. The Duchess knows how hard it is to create life, and it is this knowledge that makes her value it so much more intensely. Earlier in the same play King Richard's Queen had called the bearer of bad news, Sir Henry Green, the 'midwife to my woe'. Her soul, she claimed, had 'brought forth her prodigy, / And I, a gasping new-delivered mother, / Have woe to woe, sorrow to sorrow joined.' from his earliest years Shakespeare knew exactly what 'a gasping new-delivered mother' was like.

Illegitimacy and a mother's desire to bear her baby in a different faith were the main reasons for concealing a birth from public knowledge – yet by its nature giving birth was an event it was almost impossible to hide. In the 1550s the local burghers of Stratford were fined time and again by the town council for sheltering expectant mothers from outside the parish, the borough records apparently a moving testimony to repeated acts of kindness to strangers. It may be that even the most hard-hearted of citizens melted at the thought of a heavily pregnant and vulnerable woman – but for the most part such philanthropy was connected with recusancy.

Eleven years before Shakespeare's birth the heads of four families were convicted in Stratford and fined by the manorial court or court leet for receiving into their homes 'women strangers', known as 'inmakers' or 'inmates', who were 'brought to bed of children contrary to the order of the last leet court'. The fines available ranged between 20 shillings and £4, although the fines actually levied were much lower. Because such illegal lodgers or transients, whether Catholic or not, might become a burden on the local public purse, a raft of legislation dealt with getting rid of inmates who were not registered with the borough. Their presence meant that the corporation was not entirely in control of its residents. In the autocratic state that was Tudor England the free movement of people was restricted by means of stringent laws against so-called vagabonds. The immense hardships this caused some of the most unfortunate in society were later powerfully evoked by Shakespeare's Poor Tom in *King Lear*.

In 1556 the shepherd John Cox was fined fourpence for 'receiving a woman great with child'. Cox was a Henley Street fixture whom Shakespeare knew all his life because he lived opposite his home until the Cox house was destroyed by fire in 1594. His neighbour on the same south side of Henley Street was William Cawdrey. He headed a clan of die-hard Catholics, and the fact that Cox sheltered a woman might suggest that he shared his neighbour Cawdrey's faith. With a family named Badger the Cawdreys and Coxes formed a Catholic cluster near John Shakespeare in the middle of Henley Street; at the top of the street was another, of Cloptons, Reeves, Sadlers, Ainges, and

Whateleys. In 1557 Richard Reeve, a tenant of the Cloptons who were the godfathers of all things popish in Stratford, was punished for shielding an inmate, as were the Whateleys next door: their Catholic credentials were impeccable. They might have been expected to thrive during the period 1554–7, when the militantly Catholic Mary was on the throne, yet this was just the period when the Stratford manorial courts were particularly exercised by clandestine births. The Midlands might have been in spiritual ferment, but it seemed the borough of Stratford at least was determined to avoid becoming a Catholic enclave.

From the Catholic point of view, the need to fend for themselves in this way felt by Catholic women epitomized Protestant inhumanity. Thirty years later, at the height of the anti-Catholic hysteria that marked the Armada year of 1588, the Jesuit Henry Garnett complained to his superiors in Rome that

> A certain woman with child, when her time of delivery drew near, travelled to another county where she might have her child. Catholics have to do this, for if they give birth in their own house the question always arises as to where the child is to be baptized . . . It is a crime punishable at law for a mother to give birth to a child and not to have it baptized [by the minister], or for her to move about in public before she has been childed by him. So by chance it happened that this woman, after a short labour, gave birth in an open field by the road, without any other woman present; and then she carried her infant son at the breast to the house of a neighbouring [Catholic] lady.[6]

As mayor, on Sundays, John Shakespeare was escorted with his family from his home in Henley Street to his mayoral pew at the very front of Holy Trinity, wearing red robes and his alderman's ring. William later recalled the alderman's ring on his father's finger. Henley Street was full of children and several of the best families of the town lived here. William would have played with them in a child's world of gardens and orchards.

Mary and John Shakespeare must have run a mostly happy home, accounting for the potent sense of family – his own family, solid, sound and secure – that runs through Shakespeare's plays. Unlike others among his Stratford contemporaries, he never left the town permanently, presumably from a yearning to be close to his family, his mother and father as much as his wife and children. Shakespeare's instinct for nature was fostered and honed during childhood, and the seeds of his immense linguistic range were sown during these early years. Shakespeare's experiences as a child would have involved helping his parents with chores around the house, lending a hand in the stables and out in the fields, and pruning and harvesting the fruit trees in the family's orchards in Stratford, Snitterfield, and Hampton Lucy, learning from his parents and grandparents the names of flowers, birds, and animals. He listened and remembered, useful mental exercise for the future actor and writer who would commit lines to memory at short notice while all the time writing them for others and himself too. The extent to which the flora and fauna, the very folk memory of Warwickshire, find their way into Shakespeare's works at every juncture is unmistakable. It is one thing to read about the dive-dapper 'peering through a wave', and ducking in when 'being looked on' – in *Venus and Adonis* – but to spot a little grebe or dive-dapper on a pond or in a still corner of the Avon enhances the imaginative life of the image. The only way Shakespeare could have learnt to keep ducks apart from grebes, to know that one of the dive-dapper's characteristics was its extreme shyness, was through patient bird-watching on the river, through living close to nature in a way that is increasingly rare today.

2

William Shakespeare's Schooldays: *c.*1570–9

A S A FORMER mayor John Shakespeare could send his eldest son to the local grammar school for free. Free school education from the age of five or six was a privilege, and John Shakespeare would have appreciated that knowledge meant power, that being able to read and write would be a huge asset to a glover. The school records have disappeared, but it is inconceivable that William went to one further afield, and his plays demonstrate an easy familiarity with the classic grammar school syllabus. Nicholas Rowe, born fifty-eight years after Shakespeare's death, wrote in 1709 that Shakespeare's father

> had bred him, 'tis true, for some time at a free-school where 'tis probable he acquired that little Latin he was master of; but the narrowness of his circumstances and the want of his assistance at home forced his father to withdraw him from thence and unhappily prevented his further proficiency in that language – upon his leaving school, he seems to have given entirely into that way of living which his father proposed to him.

According to Rowe, Shakespeare was forced to leave school before he reached fifteen, the normal school-leaving age for someone going full term. Quite when this was cannot be determined, but Shakespeare's knowledge of the classics and of rhetoric is such that he can scarcely have left much before 1579 when, it seems, his father first hit rough waters.

Though John Shakespeare himself signed with a cross sometimes, at other times with a pair of compasses, this does not necessarily mean that he could not write; he had after all kept the corporation accounts for the years 1563 and 1564. At the very least it is highly likely that he and other members of his family could read. Whatever the wider national spread of literacy, William Shakespeare clearly assumed that craftsmen like weavers, carpenters, joiners, tinkers, tailors and bellows-menders – to mention only the so-called 'rude mechanicals' in *A Midsummer Night's Dream* – could read and, in the case of at least one of them, Peter Quince the carpenter, write as well. As Bottom the weaver puts it on waking up from his wonderful dream about the queen of fairies, 'I will get Peter Quince to write a ballad of this dream.' These were, in the words of the master of ceremonies of the Athenian court, 'Hard-handed men that work in Athens here, / Which never laboured in their minds till now.' They were perhaps not strong on punctuation – his misplacing of stops and commas is what turns Quince's prologue into an egregious, supremely artful farce – but it is of course Shakespeare's punctuation which delivers the brilliant double-entendres of the speech. He was clearly never bottom of the class. There are true illiterates in the plays, as for example the Capulet servant in *Romeo and Juliet* who is dispatched to deliver the invitations to the Capulet ball that night, but cannot do so because he is unable to read the addresses on his piece of paper. He protests, comically: 'It is written that the shoemaker should meddle with his yard and the tailor with his last, the fisher with his pencil and the painter with his nets; but I am sent to find those persons whose names are here writ, and can never find what names the writing person hath here writ. I must to the learned.' Enter to him Benvolio and Romeo. When the servant asks Romeo whether he 'can read anything you see', Romeo replies, 'Ay, if I know the letters and the language.' The man who wrote these lines at the age of thirty-one knew not only more words than anyone ever in the English language but would also master French and had some Italian too.

Like other such schools in the country Stratford Grammar, or the King's New School as it was now known, subjected its charges to a tough regime. From 6 a.m., when school started with prayers, it was five long hours before a lunch break from eleven to one. Little William undoubtedly went home then, returning at one for another five hours. In the darkness of winter the hours contracted to seven to eleven and one to four. The masters of Elizabethan schools were quick to flog their charges, but the glover's son had, it seems, mostly fond memories of his schooldays, even if he was also intimidated by them. He returned to them repeatedly in his writings. The most famous reference of all occurs in Jaques' speech 'All the world's a stage' in *As You Like It*:

> At first the infant,
> Mewling and puking in the nurse's arms,
> Then the whining schoolboy, with his satchel
> And shining morning face, creeping like snail
> Unwillingly to school.

It seems clear that Shakespeare experienced school just like anyone else, a sense further borne out by Romeo's claim outside Juliet's window that 'Love goes toward love as schoolboys from their books, / But love from love towards school with heavy looks.' His lines need not necessarily describe his own experience as a reluctant little boy at school in the early 1570s: by the time he embarked on *As You Like It* he was 35 and would have seen his own brothers, also entitled to a free education there, go to school. Later, during his returns to Stratford, he would have watched Hamnet do the same. But of course it is more tempting to think that he must be writing about himself here, of little Will with his satchel making his way to school while wishing himself home again with his parents. Childhood anxiety about school is as recognizable in the cameo as the little boy's 'shining morning face', spruced up by an affectionate mother perhaps just as unwilling to send him off as he was to depart.

The journey from Henley Street to the school in Church Street takes barely ten minutes. For approximately half the year the streets of Stratford would have been dark at six or seven in the morning, but also far less deserted at that time than they are in the twenty-first century. People rose with the sun, often rather earlier and the lanes of the Elizabethan town would have been busy from well before dawn. Nor, obviously, was Will Shakespeare the only child in Stratford to go to school. Others would have joined him on this daily calvary, including the son of his putative godfather, William Smith, Jr, whom he might have picked up just before turning into High Street. The Ainges, the bakers who were neighbours of the Smiths near the top end of Henley Street, probably had children at school too, supposing they could afford it. And there were Whateley children, from that distinguished family of glovers, whittawers (specialist white leather tanners), and town councillors, who lived one door down from the Ainges towards the Shakespeares. These Elizabethan boys were the first generation to go to school the way children still do today.

Among the young scholars was probably one Robert Debdale, from a recusant family in Shottery; many years later Shakespeare read a vicious diatribe against Debdale and his fellow Jesuits in a text that became an important source for *King Lear*. Another Catholic boy at the school was about a year and a half younger than Shakespeare, son of Alderman Rafe Cawdrey, a major player in the town, who had family connections in Henley Street through his father 'old William Cawdrey'. The boy, George Cawdrey, eventually joined the English Seminary in Rheims and became a priest. Then there was Richard Field, the son of a tanner, two and a half years older than Shakespeare. Strong bonds were forged at school then as now, and in the case of Shakespeare and Field it was one that seems to have lasted throughout their lives. Both men fetched up in the metropolis, and Field printed Shakespeare's two long poems. Unlike Shakespeare, he never returned permanently to Stratford, but it is likely enough that the two men occasionally made the journey back to Warwickshire together. In those pre-industrial times men and women from the same area or the same town remained closely loyal to one another. There is, as will become clear, plenty of evidence to this effect regarding Stratfordians in London.

The Fields lived in Bridge Street, and if Richard did join the boys coming from Henley Street on the walk to school it would have been at Market Cross, which they all had to pass on their way to Church Street. Its clock tower rang out the hour. On Thursday market days the stall holders, particularly those who, like Shakespeare's father, were among the privileged licensed to sell by the Cross, would have been setting out their wares from well before 6 a.m. when the schoolboys passed. Quite how precious those early ties of friendship were to Shakespeare can be gleaned from *Julius Caesar*, when the noblest of all his heroes, Brutus, evokes the memory of shared schooldays to prompt his friend to help him die:

> Good Volumnius,
> Thou know'st that we two went to school together;
> Even for that our love of old, I prithee
> Hold thou my sword-hilts whilst I run on it.

Similarly, Rosencrantz and Guildenstern were Hamlet's 'schoolfellows', and in a play full of huggermugger and duplicity this is seen as a natural source of strength and camaraderie. It should have provided a bulwark against treachery, but it did not, and its failure to do so is yet another symptom of everything that is rotten in Denmark.

But it was not just boys who made lasting friends at school. Girls did too. The fact that girls were educated at all may come as a surprise, but that certainly was the case although they did not as a rule proceed to grammar school. Shakespeare is perfectly clear on the subject of girls at school. When in *A Midsummer Night's Dream* Hermia feels beset from all sides, she appeals to her tall friend Helena in the name of 'all the counsel' that they shared, their 'sisters' vows', the happy hours they spent together when they 'chid the hasty-footed time' for parting them, their 'school-days' friendship, childhood innocence', when they sat together at needlework on a single cushion creating flowers between them on their samplers. At ABC, or petty, school girls acquired domestic skills, and learnt the alphabet from a hornbook, just like the boys with whom they shared benches during class. That girls thought of themselves as having a shared past from having been 'at school' together, just like boys, is clear from Helena's exclamation about Hermia: 'O, when she is angry, she is keen and shrewd. / She was a vixen when she went to school, / And though she be but little, she is fierce.' These references do not in themselves prove that there was a girls' school in Stratford, but it is difficult to see how else Shakespeare would have known about girls at school. As the father of two daughters aged twelve and ten years old when he was writing *A Midsummer Night's Dream*, he would have had a parent's experience of the schooling of girls in Stratford. Anne Hathaway, Shakespeare's wife, came from a prosperous Shottery farm, and may have attended a Stratford ABC school. Were it not for the fact that it *seems* to be the case that she was several years his senior, it would be possible to wonder whether the two met at school.

As it happens, evidence of a girls' school in Stratford is to be found in the records of the dreaded Bridewell Prison in London concerning two Stratford women, Elizabeth Evans and Joyce Cowden, who eked out a living as prostitutes in the early seventeenth century. Elizabeth was the daughter of a Stratford cutler, William Evans, and, it was alleged, 'went to a house of ill report in Moore lane' and to another such house in Islington. Joyce Cowden testified that she had been 'to school together at Stratford-upon-Avon' with Elizabeth, and one George Pinder from Stratford identified Elizabeth's father as a cutler in Stratford.[1] The girls seemed to have been plying their trade together in London for at least three or four years before their arrest. According to Pinder, Elizabeth and her friends were 'very poor' and unable 'to maintain' themselves, implying that when they could not make an honest living they resorted to soliciting. It is not impossible that Pinder was their pimp. Stratfordians stuck together in London, it seems, even those who were consigned to the margins of society.

The story of the two girls is intriguing and pitiable, but primarily interesting for its indication that there was a primary school for girls in Stratford, though the corporation records do not specifically refer to one. Boys and girls probably attended the same petty school in Church Street and were only segregated later around the age of seven or so. If the premises of the girls' school were the same as the boys' it must have made both sexes' lives so much more bearable, turning the school into a place that may at least have held out the prospect of childhood romances rather than just being a place of austere learning and all-male bonding. Brutus and Cassius are fine, Tom Sawyer and Becky Thatcher are better, at least when at the ages of seven or ten.

In the absence of the missing parchment register, the size of the King's New School is a matter of guesswork, but it has been estimated that some forty or so pupils were taught by the master at any one time.[2] A likely figure can be arrived at if the average number of children per family is multiplied by the number of those – twenty-eight aldermen and chief burgesses – whose children were entitled to free education. If these each had three children at the school, with perhaps four years between the eldest and youngest, they alone would add up to eighty-four children. The school may have had as many as eighty or ninety children enrolled in any given year.

The King's New School's founding principles reflect the moral earnestness of this Tudor project. The Latin charter that re-established the existing school as the King's New School during the incorporation of Stratford states that the Crown was

> moved by the extraordinary love and affection to the end that we bring up the youths of our kingdom in the aforesaid county of Warwick so that the coming generations shall derive from a childhood more cultured and imbued of letters than was accustomed in our times, and that, when they will have come to a more advanced life, they shall go forth more learned, undoubtedly appreciating the English Church of Christ (whose changes in the land we are now carrying out), taught no less in literary affairs than in precedence for the benefit of all our kingdom, we do . . . establish a certain Free Grammar School with one Master . . .

Rarely can restructuring of a town have had such far-reaching consequences. The incorporation of the borough translated it from its mediaeval manorial and feudal status into a largely autonomous self-governing and semi-democratic oligarchy. From 1553 onwards the upper echelons of Stratford consisted of fourteen aldermen who chose the fourteen chief burgesses: together they formed the Common Council. Each September, before the feast of St Michael the Archangel, the aldermen and burgesses chose a mayor or 'bailiff' for one year, to be approved by the Earl of Warwick before he could be sworn in. Almshouses, like the school, had stood in Church Street since the fifteenth century; now they became the responsibility of the borough. The town set up a charity in favour of 'a certain alms House for twenty-four paupers', paying the poor four pence every seven days. Poor relief now became an integral part of the newly incorporated borough.

The schoolmaster's salary was fixed at £20 annually, to be paid in four equal instalments. Like the mayor, he too had to be approved by the Earl of Warwick. It was a good salary compared with others in the kingdom, and signalled to all how highly the borough valued education. The schoolmaster lived in rooms at the back of the school's premises in an annexe directly south of the Gild Chapel. The King's New School also had an usher, who combined teaching the lower forms with the duties of a janitor. The masters of the King's New School needed to be well qualified, with the stamina to deliver a complex and demanding syllabus, and they were. Those who taught William Shakespeare are of particular interest.

Of the seven masters who served the Stratford School between 1554 and 1582, six were Oxford graduates (Brasenose, St John's, and Corpus Christi) and one Cambridge (Christ's College). The preponderance of Oxford graduates may be significant, or simply a consequence of the fact that it is closer to Stratford. The link with Corpus Christi is interesting because the rumour that Shakespeare died 'a papist' originates with William Fulman (1632–88) and Richard Davies (d. 1708), who were both attached to this particular college in the seventeenth century. They are also at the root of another Stratford story about Shakespeare which may be true after all in spite of having long been dismissed as almost self-evidently apocryphal.

Walter Roche of Corpus Christi was the first master likely to have encountered Shakespeare. He taught at the King's New School from Christmas 1569 to Michaelmas 1571 and then resigned from the mastership, but the borough records for 1574 and 1582 show that he stayed put in Chapel Street. The written records show him witnessing deeds by John Shakespeare in 1573 and again in 1575, and between 1574 and 1578 he served as rector of Clifford Chambers, a few miles south of Stratford. Roche hailed from Lancashire, a fact of no particular importance except that he was succeeded by two more Lancashire men – and Lancashire was the heartlands of the Catholic resistance in England. It is tempting to see a pattern here, some kind of underground Catholic link. Roche may have just taught the infant Shakespeare.

The suspicion arises naturally that Roche perhaps formed part of a recusant network reporting back to its controllers through his old college or indeed through the Lancashire connection. It is probably – but not certainly – a coincidence that Roche, Fulman, and Davies were all at Corpus Christi, at different times and over a period spanning more than a hundred years. There are many different kinds of coincidence in this story. The fact that Roche settled into life in Stratford after retiring would seem to suggest that he was not tainted by recusancy, unless of course he was a 'sleeper', a long-term inactive spy patiently biding his time while embedding himself in the enemy's ranks. Was Roche induced to make way for the master who succeeded him? After all, at £20 a year the job of master was not to be taken lightly, and that three-year gap between his departure from the King's New School and his rectorship at Clifford Chambers further fuels suspicions.

Enter the new master Simon Hunt who almost certainly taught young William Shakespeare at the King's New School for four years, until he left in 1575. Hunt had been educated at St John's College, Oxford, Edmund Campion's college from 1558 until 1570. It is not absolutely certain, but it is likely that Hunt was a Jesuit or 'seminary priest' in the making, probably the same Hunt who in around July 1575 enrolled at the University of Douai, one of the high citadels of Northern European Catholicism. In other words, he left the school to enrol in the Jesuit seminary. The Jesuit Hunt died in 1585 in Rome, where he had succeeded Robert Parsons, leader of the English Jesuits abroad, as English Penitentiary at St Peter's.[3]

If this Jesuit was indeed the same person as the teacher at the King's New School, it begins to look as though the school was being targeted by recusants with a view to indoctrinating its young charges, since religious education formed part of the syllabus. But there was another Simon Hunt, who died at Stratford in 1598 with an estate valued at £100.[4] There is at least a possibility that he rather than the Jesuit was the former Stratford school teacher. The two Simon Hunts, the three masters with Lancashire connections, and three from the same Oxford college, all serve to muddy the waters concerning the prevailing faith at Shakespeare's school.

It was in the year of Hunt's departure that the world of London and the court descended upon Warwickshire, and the lavish entertainments laid on for the Queen by the Earl of Leicester at Kenilworth provided one of the grandest spectacles of Elizabethan England. The Queen stayed for nineteen days, but it was on the warm evening of Monday 18 July 1575 that she was treated to a pageant of the Lady in the Lake, featuring Arion riding on a dolphin's back. It may have been that midsummer night that the seed of one of the greatest comedies in the English language was first planted: in *A Midsummer Night's Dream*, written twenty years later, Oberon remarks to Puck that he once

heard 'a mermaid on a dolphin's back / Uttering such dulcet and harmonious breath / That the rude sea grew civil at her song'. Cupid that
night took aim at 'a fair vestal thronèd by the west', but his shaft was

> Quenched in the chaste beams of the wat'ry moon,
> And the imperial vot'ress passèd on,
> In maiden meditation, fancy-free.

It was safe by then to talk about Cupid's shaft missing its mark, for
Leicester was dead, and the maiden world of the Queen was a matter
of historical record. The local people flocked towards Leicester's country seat in droves that balmy night of 18 July. John Shakespeare, with
his eleven-year-old son William in tow, may well have been among
them, for it is not unlikely that Stratford's aldermen and chief
burgesses were invited guests at this most sumptuous of outdoor festivities. There is every reason to think that the high plot of *A
Midsummer Night's Dream*, with Puck, Oberon, and Titania, carries at
least the memory of the imprint of Leicester's Kenilworth extrava-
ganza, while the magical forest of the 'wood near Athens' is redolent
of a July night spent under a full moon in the rambling woodlands
and clearings of Warwickshire, perhaps in the '*les busshes*' area of
Snitterfield, a mile or so across the wold from Shakespeare's grandfather's home.

During his schooldays the young Shakespeare must have seen plays
at Stratford Gildhall. Various troupes of players passed through the
town from time to time, and one such performance in Gloucester
Town Hall in the same year as Kenilworth was recalled afterwards by
Shakespeare's contemporary Robert Willis. Such was the impact on
him of the play that 'when I came towards man's estate, it was as fresh
in my memory as if I had seen it newly acted.' Lest this be miscon-
strued as praise for drama, the Puritan Willis hastened to urge it as an
example of how impressionable children are, warning against allowing
them to see 'spectacles of ill examples and hearing of lascivious or
scurrilous words, for that their young memories are like fair writing-
tables'.

Luckily, Willis's excellent memory has left a fleeting glimpse of
what it must have been like to see just the kind of play that would
have been put on at Stratford's Gildhall. It was what they called 'the

Mayor's play' that the eleven-year-old Willis saw in Gloucester Town Hall. Attendance was free with the mayor paying the players according to their desert. 'My father took me with him, and made me stand between his legs, as he sat upon one of the benches, where we saw and heard very well.' The dramatic fare enjoyed by the good people of Gloucester that night in 1575 was *The Cradle of Security*, which reads like a cross between *The Magic Flute* and *A Midsummer Night's Dream*. Three ladies, having caused the king to desert 'graver councillors' and then

> joining in a sweet song, rocked him asleep that he snorted again, and in the meantime closely conveyed under the clothes wherewithal he was covered a vizard, like a swine's snout, upon his face with three wire chains fastened thereunto, the other end whereof being holden severally by those three ladies, who fell to singing again and then discovered his face that the spectators might see how they had transformed him, going on with their singing.

This was probably rather more thrilling than the subsequent entry of two armed Old Men, who break the spell in the names of 'the End of the World and the Last Judgement'. It is quite possible that the (unnamed) players who staged this play in Gloucester also took it to Stratford: like Willis, young William Shakespeare might well have stood transfixed by spectacles such as these while being held by his father. He did not require *The Cradle of Security* to write his later masterpiece about animal metamorphosis. Unlike most of the other plays, *A Midsummer Night's Dream* owes a debt to country pageantry and folklore though it lacks an obvious source. One of its many wonders is the unbounded relish with which Bottom is transported all the way into the bower of the fairies' queen. What in Spenser's epic poem *The Faerie Queene* was a stern and damned place, the Bower of Bliss, in Shakespeare metamorphoses into an innocent vision of sex and beauty granted to the irrepressible Bottom, who loves to play all parts at once. The play may be the purest fiction, fashioned from Shakespeare's memories of his salad days in the country.

It was in the same year 1575 that John Shakespeare bought the western two-bay wing of the house in Henley Street, the deed witnessed by the former schoolmaster Walter Roche. The Shakespeares' fortunes were in the ascendant and young William now walked home to one of the largest houses in the town, probably accompanied by his brother Gilbert. Hunt had gone too, and the King's New School appointed yet another master, Thomas Jenkins, like Hunt from St John's College, Oxford; he taught Shakespeare during the most impressionable period in his life, his years of puberty and early teens, from eleven to fifteen, between 1575 and 1579. Though born in London, Jenkins was Welsh[5] and in Stratford he found himself surrounded by Welshmen. There was John Welsh, whose real name was Edwards, and the ironmonger and prominent town councillor Lewis-ap-Williams, a Fluellen (that is, Llewellyn), a butcher by the name of Griffin-ap-Roberts, one Morris Evans, and others. The Welsh were a distinctive feature of Stratford. They had probably migrated to this particular market town in the south Midlands because of the opportunities it afforded for work and trading.

A scene in Shakespeare's *Merry Wives of Windsor* features an entertaining parody of Latin lessons with a Welsh parson, Sir Hugh Evans, who is probably modelled on Jenkins.[6] It is the first scene of Act IV, in which young William Page, pitted against the parson, provides a wonderful parody of a Latin class played out before the uncomprehending Mistress Quickly and William's mother Margaret Page. Mistress Quickly does not of course understand a word of Latin, but responds to what she thinks, from what they sound like, the phrases must mean – 'genitive case' becomes 'Jinny's case', and *hic, haec*, and *hoc* turn bawdy when she imagines that Sir Hugh is teaching the boy to 'hic' and to 'hack' and leading him to *horum*, or whoredom. Communication is further hampered when Sir Hugh comically Welshes the English language almost as much as Mistress Quickly misunderstands the Latin, making 'fritters of English', according to Falstaff. Evans displays a number of phonetic idiosyncrasies that Shakespeare presumably associated with Welsh speech from his time in Stratford – 'prain' for 'brain', 'prabble' for 'brabble', 'focative' for 'vocative'; 'woman' becomes 'oman', and later he uses 'Got' for 'God', 'pinse' for 'pinch', and the locution 'I pray you'. Some were deployed again in the affectionate parody of Shakespeare's most notable Welshman, Fluellen in *Henry V*.

Evans's pronunciation of Latin and English and his quirks of English syntax are as comic as the Latin bouncing off Mistress Quickly, but it is a benign and affectionate scene and Sir Hugh is portrayed with considerable indulgence. He calls the boy 'William' throughout, when he might rather have been expected to use his surname 'Page'. Shakespeare elsewhere enjoys playing on his own name, so he may be signalling that this boy is really *him*, and no one else; conversely, it may simply be that in the King's New School in Shakespeare's time the boys were called by their first names rather than their surnames. It is perhaps unwise to make assumptions about Elizabethan schools based on their later equivalent. Some masters may have enthusiastically 'breeched' (flogged) their charges, but perhaps not at the King's New School: flogging is threatened to William Page but immediately countermanded with 'Go your ways and play, go.'

Shakespeare's wordplay with the collision of Latin and English phonetics is impressively sophisticated: the rhetorical demands made by the Elizabethan theatre never cease to surprise, though in this particular case the cross-linguistic jokes may have been written in especially for the Queen, whose command of Latin was legendary. Even so, it represents but a small part of Shakespeare's education as reflected in his work. His school syllabus included a deep grounding in classical rhetoric and the pupils were trained in Latin versification and read Latin plays; those of Terence, Virgil, Ovid and Horace featured prominently. In Ovid, and particularly the *Metamorphoses*, Shakespeare discovered an imaginative world that profoundly affected him; the great Roman poet became his favourite classical author, even above Virgil. It has been said that Shakespeare would have left his grammar school with a command of Latin expected only of a university classical graduate in the twenty-first century. Indeed, in an intellectual climate that expected the older boys at school to communicate in Latin rather than in English, it might well have been greater. A letter written in fluent Latin to his father by the eleven-year-old Richard Quiney, Jr, future brother-in-law of Judith Shakespeare, is usually cited in this connection.

On the other hand, it would be wrong to overplay the achievement of writers from the past in mastering what is, after all, 'just' another language. It is worth remembering that throughout the Middle Ages and early Renaissance Latin was the *lingua franca* of educated people, the European language of international and diplomatic communication. Shakespeare also learnt English at his school, and drew on this in *Love's Labour's Lost*. This time he fields two pedants, a curate called Sir Nathaniel and a schoolmaster by the name of Holofernes, fresh from a dinner of 'sharp and sententious' conversation. But they are no match for the page Moth and the clown Costard who outwit them even at plain punning and language games. Holofernes is obsessed with the misfit between English spelling and English pronunciation:

> I abhor such fanatical phantasimes, such insociable and point-device companions, such rackers of orthography, as to speak 'dout', *sine* 'b', when he should say 'doubt'; 'det' when he should pronounce 'debt' – 'd, e, b, t' not 'd, e, t'. He clepeth a calf 'cauf', half 'hauf'; neighbour *vocatur* 'nebor' – 'neigh' abbreviated 'ne'. This is abhominable – which he would call 'abominable'.

Holofernes is on the losing side against the modernizers, as his use of the archaic form 'clepeth' for 'speaks' further suggests. Shakespeare, like Jonson, was forever excited by language and loved experimenting with it. Not that he did not avail himself of the great retro-chic poem of the period, Spenser's *The Faerie Queene*, when it suited him to do so, though like Jonson he may have had his doubts about Spenser's wisdom in reverting to Malory's fifteenth-century usages in search of a language for an English epic. Shakespeare's deep and dynamic love affair with English must have been fostered by the study of grammar and rhetoric at school. The sheer pleasure afforded by translating from Latin into English and back again into Latin, from *lapis* to 'stone' and from 'stone' back to *lapis* (and not 'pebble', as William does in *The Merry Wives of Windsor*) was the staple nourishment of his schooldays. By then the Bible had been available in English for at least forty years, and the English people heard God talk in their own language. Now everyone could talk to the Almighty without intermediary, and could listen to God's word in church and understand it.

From the gusto with which the adult Shakespeare recalled his schooldays, he had clearly enjoyed his time in Church Street, those many anxious early-morning walks to school notwithstanding. Latin tuition and classical literature, declining adjectives and conjugating verbs and role playing were some compensation. This was one of the most formative periods in his life for learning, for forming friendships, and above all for acquiring a set of intellectual perspectives that far transcended the horizons of Stratford. In his teachers young William first met people who had been educated at Oxford or Cambridge. He may himself have wanted to go on to university, but he probably left school not long before Thomas Jenkins did, almost certainly because of the collapse of his father's business. It must have been deeply humiliating if he was the only one among all the chief burgesses' and aldermen's sons at school whose father headed for some kind of bankruptcy. The children at the King's New School represented the new self-making bourgeois elite of Elizabethan England and to be the son of a failure perhaps marked the young Shakespeare for good, possibly accounting for the striving and endless investing in property and tithes that became such a characteristic feature of his life.

There was a further shadow over this period of Shakespeare's life: his sister Anne died. Under the date 4 April 1579 the Stratford parish register records the burial of 'Anne daughter to Mr. John Shakespeare'. Her grief-stricken parents laid out eightpence for the bell to be tolled for her, one penny for each year of her life. It must have been a tremendous shock for William, for his little sister was the only one of his siblings to die during his youth – unlike many of his contemporaries, he had at least been spared the too-common mortality of a succession of infant siblings. There is no way of knowing how Anne died or whether there was any connection between her death and the fact that her father John's erratic career on the Stratford council hit the shallows at around this time.

Later that same year, on 17 December 1579, another event left its mark on the adolescent Shakespeare: the death by drowning in the Avon of Katherine Hamlet. The river's treacherous currents claimed victims every year, and Katherine had drowned at Tiddington, a mile or so upriver towards Charlecote. The body of poor Katherine Hamlet was exhumed from the cemetery of Alveston and the inquest to establish whether she had drowned by accident or committed suicide was held at Warwick on 11 February 1580, presided over by the town clerk Henry Rogers, steward to Sir Thomas Lucy at Charlecote as well as the town's coroner. It may have been in Shakespeare's mind when he came to portray the death of Ophelia in *Hamlet*. The inquest report found that she had gone to draw water from the river at Tiddington and that, 'standing on the bank of the same river', she suddenly slipped and fell in. It was an accident. Why there was a suspicion that she had taken her own life cannot be known, but an unwanted pregnancy was a common reason for a young woman to drown herself. In *Hamlet*, the mad Ophelia wanders about singing of young men who insist on having sex when given the chance, leaving maids no longer maids when they depart from their bedrooms.

The river Avon defines the town of Stratford for the very good reason that it is an integral part of it. Quite how rough it could be is evident from the detailed account of the flash flood that struck the town in Armada year. No one had ever witnessed anything quite like the river's ferocity, not even 'old father Porter' of legendary longevity, the living chronicle of the area who died at the age of 109 in 1584. He had seen every flood since the reign of the Queen's grandfather but nothing, it seems, on this scale. It was around eight in the morning on Thursday 18 July 1588 when the Avon unleashed its power and

> brake up sundry houses in Warwick town and carried away their bread, beef, cheese, butter, pots, pans, and provisions; it took away ten carts out of one town and three wains with the furniture of Sir Thomas Lucy's; it broke both ends of Stratford Bridge . . . It did take away suddenly one Sale's daughter of Grafton out of Hilborow meadow removing of a hay cock that she had no shift but get up upon the top of the haycock and was carried thereupon by the water a quarter of a mile wellnigh, and till she came to the very last bank of the stream, and there was taken into a boat and so was saved, but both she and the two that rowed, boat and all, was like to be drowned but that another boat came and rescued them soon. Three men going over Stratford Bridge when they came to the middle of the Bridge they could not go forwards and then returned presently but they could not go back for the water was so risen it rose a yard every hour from eight to four.

The Avon has as many faces as Stevie Smith's River God, sly, treacherous, and triumphalist. But it has a benign and gentle side too.

As a child during the dog days of summer Shakespeare must surely have bathed in the river with his siblings. Many years later, in a play written, during his retirement, with his successor at the King's Men, John Fletcher, Shakespeare has Cardinal Wolsey reflect on his over-confident, hubristic behaviour:

> I have ventured,
> Like little wanton boys that swim on bladders,
> This many summers in a sea of glory,
> But far beyond my depth. My high-blown pride
> At length broke under me, and now has left me,
> Weary and old with service, to the mercy
> Of a rude stream that must for ever hide me.[7]

Young William, and later his son Hamnet, might well have been among those little boys using inflated pigs' bladders to support them in the water. A compulsive interest in water and drowning detectable in Shakespeare's plays might well date from his boyhood on the river, from the brilliant nightmare vision of Clarence sinking down to the 'slimy bottom of the deep' and its scattered 'dead bones' in *Richard III* to the drownings and resurrections in *Twelfth Night* and *The Tempest*. The idea that Shakespeare had no direct source for *The Tempest* might well be countered by the suggestion that this brilliant parable of redemption and the wishful triumph over death by water was after all based on the darkest imaginable source, real death by drowning as exemplified by Katherine Hamlet and by the consequences of a sporadic unleashing of the river's elemental powers.

The ten years which followed after 1579 were among the hardest in Shakespeare's life, among the most difficult and uncertain for the entire nation. In Stratford the decade was marked by the arrival of yet another new master at the King's New School. His name was John Cottom, and he too was from Lancashire. He had graduated from Oxford the same year as his predecessor Jenkins, and the presumption must be that the two knew one another. No recusant finger has ever been pointed at Jenkins, but there is no certainty that he and Cottom were not in league with each other, any more than there is about Roche and Hunt. Like Roche, Cottom served two years only at the King's New School. Jenkins was paid £6 by the Stratford chamberlains for surrendering his mastership to Cottom in July 1579, but the records do not say why.

Cottom's move to Shakespeare's school in 1579 coincided with the mission to England being planned by the Jesuit William Allen, who ran the English College at Douai, and by Robert Parsons, the English Penitentiary at Rome. Not much later Parsons secured a blessing for the mission from the General of the Society of Jesus, Claudio Acquaviva. Campion landed in England on 24 June 1580 and was put up at Sir William Catesby's house Bushwood in Lapworth, ten miles or so from Stratford; Robert Parsons was also living in the Midlands at this time. Thomas Cottom, younger brother of the newly appointed Stratford schoolmaster, was a Jesuit, and a companion of Edmund Campion. When he was arrested in June 1580 Thomas Cottom was carrying a secret letter addressed to John Debdale of Shottery. It seems inconceivable that he should not have been hoping to meet his brother John at the King's New School, since his mission to Shottery took him to within less than a mile of Church Street. Thus was the King's New School linked to the heart of the Catholic resistance. The record does not say so specifically, but probably the school's latest master was forced out of his job in 1581 by the national events that were then unfolding. Returning to his father's home in Lancashire, John Cottom became a prominent local recusant. He was in no mood to surrender his religion. Neither was the family whom his brother had intended to visit, the Debdales of Shottery.

3

Meeting the Neighbours in 1582

IN THE MEANTIME, John Shakespeare's business affairs were plunging ever more deeply into insolvency – that much is clear from his attempts to raise money by selling off property in Wilmcote and Snitterfield, the ancestral villages of the Ardens and Shakespeares, and his failure to attend council meetings between January 1577 and 6 September 1586, probably for fear of arrest for debt. During this period his fellow aldermen treated him with considerable forbearance when it came to fines and levies. On 19 November 1578, for example, when the council instructed all aldermen to pay fourpence weekly towards poor relief, John Shakespeare is one of only two out of the fourteen 'who shall not be taxed to pay anything'.[1] It has been suggested that he shunned the town as a recusant and that the family fortunes collapsed as the result of a string of (unrecorded) fines levied on the Shakespeares as obdurate Catholics, but this seems untenable. There is simply no evidence for it.

There is evidence that Shakespeare's father was deeply committed financially in wool-dealing, not all of it legal. Large sums of money changed hands in these unregulated transactions, and when the going was good fortunes could be made. The man from Henley Street, who had married well and invested wisely, was characterized by Nicholas Rowe as 'a considerable dealer in wool'. It was a notable first, long before anyone else commented on the fact that John Shakespeare had been trading in wool on a grand scale. Wool was so important in the local economy, second only to malting, that it is scarcely surprising if John Shakespeare was involved like almost everyone else. This probably included turning part of his premises in Henley Street into a woolshop. Indeed, it may be that he bought the western wing of the property with his wool-dealing operations in mind, hoping to expand the business. New legislation in the late 1570s restricting the wool trade may have cost this dealer dearly.[2]

By the time he joined his father's business in, probably, 1578 or 1579, William knew how his home town worked, economically and politically. Stratford was bustling, busy, and competitive. It was a microcosm of Elizabethan England and included just about every profession, art, craft, and trade imaginable, and this at a time when almost everybody also farmed, owned orchards, and kept livestock ranging from hens and cocks to pigs and sheep.[3] On Thursdays the population doubled or trebled as traders and farmers from the surrounding villages converged on the market, like a frenzied beehive as stalls radiated out from Market Cross into the adjacent streets, every inch of space tightly controlled by the council. The glovers constituted an elite fraternity among stallholders and occupied pride of place at the Market Cross. Stratford in the late sixteenth century must have felt like the centre of its own universe. Small fortunes could be made here, even if the town had its poor and was afflicted at least three times during Shakespeare's lifetime by severe fires as well as plague.

Away from the bustling town centre, Stratford was still very rural in places, full of orchards with apple, quince, pear and cherry trees, and there were ashes, chestnuts, crabs, limes, maples, oaks, and planes. Several different kinds of elm could be found in and around Stratford, grown for timber on plantations towards Tiddington on the east bank of the Avon; others, perhaps the large classic English elms, served as borough boundary markers. A council minute for 8 October 1617 records: 'At this hall it is agreed that 2 elms shall be set up at the place where the other two elms were cut down by Evesham way.' The reason for the immediate replanting was that these two felled elms marked the outer south-western boundary point of the borough, known at the time as 'Two Elms'.

Elms visually defined Elizabethan Stratford. It is not clear why they should have been so much more important than oaks, of which the abundant supply in the Forest of Arden had provided mediaeval Stratford with most of its building timber. As a rule, elms grew from earth mounds or boundary ridges between the houses, or else in the groves and orchards in the town and around it. It is known exactly where a number of them stood in 1582, the year of Shakespeare's marriage, because that year Stratford corporation published a survey of all its property, including an inventory of its trees.

Freeholders like John Shakespeare, George Whateley, the Quineys and many others in Henley Street were covered by a separate later manorial survey of 1590, but of course corporation tenants and free-holders lived side-by-side, and records of the disputes between them – sometimes including boundary elms – can be very informative. A case in point is the boundary quarrel between the freeholder George Whateley of Henley Street and his neighbour to the east, the corpo-ration tenant Richard Reeve, he of the 'inmake' fine. In the spring of 1557 Whateley and Reeve were in dispute about which of them owned the border elm that stood between them near Whateley's barn. The council found in favour of Whateley, and further instructed Reeve that he had to 'set and pitch his mounds between him and William Smith'.[4] It seems that Reeve posed problems for his neighbours on either side.

The 1582 survey includes about a thousand elms to which proba-bly another two or three hundred should be added to take account of the freeholders' elms. Borough tenants paid for elms as part of their rent: Humphrey Bracer assured the council that of the twenty-eight elms on his property, his 'predecessor' had already paid for four of them, and he was eager to be remitted at least those four. It is easy to see why: elms were expensive for their owners. In 1594 John Gibbes, a wealthy man, had to pay an impressive sum to the corporation 'for elms in his orchard in Henley Lane' (today's Windsor Street). A total of 26 elms and 12 ashes grew in his orchard, but only elms were taxed, it seems: from the levy on this orchard it appears that the 26 elms cost him 40 shillings, or roughly one and a half shillings per elm. This was serious money for the time, and again leaves it open to question why anyone would bother to grow elms when they attracted such heavy taxation.

The country end of Henley Street and the entire area stretching west of Henley Lane (or Hell Lane) consisted of orchards, elm groves, and fields. So did the backs of the houses on the south side of Henley Street, in the triangle formed by Mere Pool Lane, Henley Lane, and Henley Street. Four elms grew behind William Greenway's barn which stretched back south towards Wood Street.[5] Greenway lived as a freeholder in Bridge Street but rented premises and a barn opposite and east of the Shakespeares, not far from his in-laws the Cawdreys. The Shakespeares knew him well. He operated a mail shuttle service between Stratford and London, and had interesting and dangerous family connections. One of the material facts about Shakespeare's Stratford that the corporation survey of 1582 and the manorial survey of 1590 help to consolidate is that the town's streets were not terraced, as has been argued from time to time; rather, almost all the houses were separated by passages between them, marked off by boundary ridges and elm trees.

In the sixteenth century Henley Street was a heaving thoroughfare for traffic heading towards Coventry and Birmingham. It was cobbled or metalled and it had been so since before 1557 when the town council referred to 'the repairing of the paving of the streets in Stratford'. It seems that the streets of Stratford had proper 'pavements' and it was the responsibility of the house owners and tenants to maintain them, and to mend them if they were broken.[6] Almost everyone in this street was in business, and would have been keen to pick up passing trade as it trundled through the town. Indeed, such was their acumen and eagerness that the good burghers of Stratford even tried to trade when they were not supposed to. The majority of all the summonses to the so-called bawdy or consistory court were for trading outside licensed hours, usually after the bell that summoned the citizens to church had stopped ringing. The transgressors preferred business to prayer, and who can blame them.

Shakespeare, strolling down Henley Street, would have seen not trees and a rural, provincial idyll but a busy and competitive crowd of people selling their wares quite literally from out of their windows, used as improvised stalls. The scene would have resembled a daguerrotype of a bustling 1880s East London street such as Brick Lane, and similarly congested with carts and horses. And almost everyone would have been talking to everyone else. People did. The printed word was not yet the disseminator of news it later became; instead, a highly effective jungle telegraph or rumour mill kept everyone in the picture. In the second part of *Henry IV*, Shakespeare described it as 'Rumour painted full of tongues'. This was the world that he knew, and it is echoed in a fine moment in *King John* when

Hubert of Angers relates the rumour about young Arthur's death. In these lines a twentieth-century Stratford antiquarian, Edgar Innes Fripp, detected a specific memory of Henley Street:

> Old men and beldams in the streets
> Do prophesy upon it dangerously.
> Young Arthur's death is common in their mouths,
> And when they talk of him they shake their heads,
> And whisper one another in the ear;
> And he that speaks doth grip the hearer's wrist,
> Whilst he that hears makes fearful action,
> With wrinkled brows, with nods, with rolling eyes.
> I saw a smith stand with his hammer, thus,
> The whilst his iron did on the anvil cool,
> With open mouth swallowing a tailor's news,
> Who, with his shears and measure in his hand,
> Standing on slippers, which his nimble haste
> Had falsely thrust upon contrary feet,
> Told of a many thousand warlike French
> That were embattailèd and ranked in Kent.
> Another lean unwashed artificer
> Cuts off his tale, and talks of Arthur's death.[7]

This vivid scene, particularly the telling detail of the tailor who in his haste put his slippers on the wrong way round, sounds like something Shakespeare may well have witnessed for himself in Henley Street – the Shakespeares' neighbours to the east were indeed a tailor and a blacksmith. The tailor was a bigamist by the name of William Wedgewood and the blacksmith was Richard Hornby. The Hornbys stayed on for ever in this house and their home still stands today and is now linked umbilically to the Birthplace as its shop and official exit. Of all the many professions carried on in his home town, Shakespeare seems to have opted for those of his family's neighbours.

One of the distinctive features of this cameo is its comic, life-like detail. The young Shakespeare was not only a fast and avid learner, but also a keen observer. The gestures – the gripping by the wrist, the rolling eyes, the hurriedly put-on slippers – bespeak not only a man who watched carefully how people behaved but one who instinctively knew how to render his observations on the page in a few telling words, inviting his readers to think visually. He does this time and again, and it is there from the outset. The little boy who watched the tailor and blacksmith in Henley Street is still there in the adult writer who conjures up a street scene from memory. 'Always assimilate' seems to have been the motto of the young Shakespeare. It makes perfect sense that, as we shall see, the first, and very public, attack on him should charge him with over-assimilation, plagiarism.

Presumably Will Shakespeare occasionally spent an evening with some of his friends at one of the two grand local inns down at the bottom of Bridge Street, the Swan or the Bear – perhaps the Bear since its owners the Sadlers were friends of the Shakespeares. It was run for a generation by 'Barber of the Bear', and Shakespeare knew him all his life. It might be instructive to accompany Will homewards. The year is 1582, the year Shakespeare courted Anne Hathaway, made her pregnant, and married her. Perhaps he ran into some of his former schoolmates, those same young men who would eventually land him in trouble, and perhaps they were just like the young men in *Romeo and Juliet*, always spoiling for a fight and always talking about girls.

Just before entering Henley Street Shakespeare would have passed the Newalls' Angel tavern and then the home of his supposed god-father William Smith (the current number 1 on the right-hand side). In 1582 a large pile of logs belonging to Smith was leaning precariously against Newall's Angel, and damaging it; Smith was ordered by the town council to remove it. Newall's landlord was the Catholic Arthur Cawdrey, whose brother was a priest. Smith was not a freeholder but rented his property as a tenant of the corporation. Its rateable ground rent of 8 pence indicates that it was a substantial house, though the 1590 survey suggests it was less than half the size of the Shakespeares' home further down the street. Smith also owned a sizeable barn on the south side of Henley Street, nearly opposite the Shakespeares.

Next on his way homewards Will would pass the relatively modest abode of the Ainges, with a frontage of some thirty feet or so. John Ainge was a licensed baker. His house was one the Shakespeares must have known well since it was formerly the home of Roger Sadler, a friend of John Shakespeare's and appointed constable with him. The freehold belonged to the rich and powerful John Clopton, and the house must have possessed a special bread oven, for Roger Sadler had also been a baker. At some point Sadler had toyed with the idea of diversifying by keeping an ale-house as well, but the council sternly reprimanded him and forced him to choose between baking or running a tavern. If he preferred the latter, he would be expected to put up a proper ale-house sign: Sadler opted for baking. Eventually, long before this imagined walk of 1582, he moved out to a house on the corner of High Street and Sheep Street. On his death in 1578 he left his estate to his wife Margaret and to Hamnet Sadler, William Shakespeare's friend. His debtors included Richard Hathaway of Shottery, the future Mrs William Shakespeare's father, and there is mention in his will of 'sureties for John Shakespeare' – perhaps he wanted to help his old friend out even in death, since the Shakespeare fortunes were now in the decline which was to afflict them for the next twelve years or more.

The next house that Shakespeare passed was a grand one and, just possibly, the one in which he met his future bride. What are now numbers 4 and 5 Henley Street, then belonged to one of Stratford's most distinguished citizens and public servants, the glover George Whateley. It is not impossible that Shakespeare was apprenticed to him rather than to his father, but the custom locally seems to have been for sons to be apprenticed to their fathers; certainly the Shakespeares' neighbours' son, George Badger, Jr, was apprenticed to his father as a glover in 1596. Whateley was mayor in the year Shakespeare was born and his house, like John Shakespeare's, doubled up as home and woollendraper's shop. It boasted glass in the hall, the parlour, and the upstairs chamber, a sign of prosperity. Beehives ('stalls of bees') stood in the garden, and wax and honey were among the things to be found in its 'apple chamber', which may have formed part of the buttery. There was also a cellar, a granary for corn 'next to the garden', a 'stable', a gatehouse, and, at the back, a barn, garden, and yard. The frontage of the property was just under 80 feet, making it the second-largest in Henley Street after John Shakespeare's. George Whateley was decidedly rich, and in his will in 1593 he endowed a school in his native Henley-in-Arden.

From the Whateleys' house to his own was a two-minute walk for Shakespeare, past another seven or eight houses and barns, one formerly the property of Gilbert Bradley, his brother Gilbert's likely godfather.[8] Now it belonged to the whittawer William Wilson, who in 1579 had married an Anne Hathaway from Shottery, the daughter of one George Hathaway, probably the uncle of the future Mrs Shakespeare's father Richard Hathaway *alias* Gardner – so the two Anne Hathaways of Shottery and Henley Street were second cousins. As whittawers and glovers from the same street the Wilsons and Shakespeares would have known each other well. After a fire in 1596 the Wilsons had to rebuild their house, unlike the more fortunate Shakespeares who were spared that fate. Their dwelling was on the site of the present public library, directly east of a gutter that cut right across Henley Street on a north–south axis. Through this conduit, which at the time was called 'the cross gutter before Bradley's door', flowed the Mere. It was hardly a deep stream, but it was enough of a stream to be a striking feature of the town's landscape, not too wide to be covered – presumably – by large flagstones to allow carts to cross, but wide enough to stop the fire that devastated the eastern part of Henley Street in 1596 from spreading further west. Just to the south-west of Henley Street, at Rother Market, the Mere formed a pool which was known until recently as Mere Pool, hence the name Meer Pool Lane for Mere Street. It has been suggested that Shakespeare died from drinking Mere water, but the people of sixteenth-century Stratford would no more have dreamt of drinking from the Mere or any other brook than Londoners would from the Fleet river. The borough bye-laws of Stratford are full of threats and sanctions connected to hygiene.

The town was punctilious about regulating its sanitation, and rightly so. Some twelve years before Shakespeare's birth, his father John was fined for keeping an unlicensed muck heap outside his home in Henley Street – an offence the more reprehensible when the official rubbish tip for this area of the town was less than eighty yards away from the Shakespeare home, at the so-called 'country end' of Henley Street, across the road from Peter Smart, himself a former corporation chamberlain. Smart's house was the last one on the same north side of the street as John Shakespeare's. Opposite were the wheelwright William Chambers and his neighbour Thomas Patrick, and the rubbish tip sat between their houses. Years earlier the muck heap on Henley Street had been privately owned by Chambers;

Patrick must have protested about it, for the council had forced Chambers to screen his neighbour Patrick from it by means of a fence. The severity of the fine Chambers was threatened with underlined how seriously the town rated the nuisance caused by untended rubbish.

Originally these designated muckhills were contracted out, but eventually the town council took them back under its direct control and made a handsome profit from them. Around the time of Shakespeare's birth there were six municipal dunghills altogether, at the bottom or 'nether end' of Sheep and Bridge streets, in the gravel pits in Tinker Street (Scholars' Lane), in Greenhill Street 'by Nicholas Lane's hedge', in Church street by John Sadler's barn, and 'in Henley Street one other dunghill in the old place accustomed' – that is, the one near Chambers.[9] These dunghills were cleared away twice a year, at Whitsun and Michaelmas. Only certain kinds of refuse could be disposed of on the common muckhill, and fly-tipping was illegal. Butchers were required to deposit the waste from slaughter at certain designated points outside the town after 9 p.m. The bye-laws stipulated that offal had to be disposed of out of the town and into the country, on a daily basis probably, by borough sub-contractors like Chambers and his colleagues, who levied a small fee for their services. Some – like Rafe Cawdrey – chose to ignore this ruling, and their selfish disregard for basic hygiene incurred the wrath of the town fathers, as did butchers who poured the blood from slaughter into the common gutters.

The borough insisted that the gutters be kept free of offal and human waste. Such phrases as 'for not scouring their gutters they are amerced' and 'for not keeping clean his gutter' are common in the record of fines. On 14 April 1559 John Shakespeare is to be found again among those offenders who failed to keep their gutters clean. It is a tribute to the town's vigilance in these matters that there were comparatively few outbreaks of serious disease and food poisoning. It is often assumed that the Elizabethans' sense of smell must have been somewhat blunted, but their penchant for strewing sweet rushes in their houses and their obsession with sweet breath suggests otherwise. In *The Tempest* Caliban's fishy smell offends Trinculo's nostrils, as does his own odour later: 'Monster, I do smell all horse-piss, at which my nose is in great indignation.' It may well be that the Elizabethans were intensely aware of the necessity for hygiene precisely because they had so few opportunities to wash and keep clean. There were strict injunctions against dogs fouling the streets, pavements and gutters, and there were bye-laws against dogs roaming free in the streets, or going unmuzzled; bitches on heat were a recurrent source of concern. Ducks and geese were not supposed to go about unattended, nor were unringed pigs.

The first house beyond the Mere was the smithy of Richard Hornby. With the stream running past his house Hornby was well placed for his blacksmith's business, which required a plentiful supply of water – probably one reason why the Hornby family lived here for so long. The next building was two houses which had been joined and merged into a large home by the 1580s, owned by a cantankerous tailor from Warwick, William Wedgewood. A contemporary document describes him as 'contentious, proud and slanderous, oft busying himself with naughty matters and quarrelling with his honest neighbours', and the Earl of Warwick noted that he never wanted to see him again.[10] Richard Hornby was just the kind of 'honest' neighbour that Wedgewood routinely annoyed, and sure enough it was not long before they became embroiled in a boundary dispute. Hornby's house and the tailor's were separated by one of those earth mounds. Where the customary elm would have stood there was a 'post' on Wedgewood's side to mark off the boundary of his property. The two men were firmly ordered by the council each to maintain his half of the boundary mound, which ran the whole distance between Henley Street and Gildpits. Wedgewood had left Stratford by 1575. There is no record of him falling out with his neighbours to the west, the Shakespeares.

The home William Shakespeare reached on this imaginary journey in 1582 was still the biggest house in Henley Street. Things were not so good, but the family had not so far needed to sell up – though John Shakespeare was starting to shift his assets. This may have involved the sale of the house in Greenhill Street which he had acquired in 1556, since no trace of it survives among later Shakespeare transactions – unless of course it had been sold in 1575 to finance the purchase of the western two bays of the Henley Street house. They cannot have come

45

cheap, since Henley Street enjoyed a certain cachet among the Stratford elite. Though the house doubled as a working glover's premises and as a woolshop, there seemed to be plenty of room for the seven Shakespeares. Possibly by 1582 the death of their youngest daughter no longer dominated their lives and they were able to harness all their energies to weather the decline in their fortunes and hope that at some point things would look up again.

In the light of his extraordinary later achievements it is not easy to imagine the young Shakespeare as a glover, but there is no reason why he should not have been a good glover too. Gloving was one of the top crafts of the period, and presumably he would not have turned up his nose at his own father's profession – which had after all secured the family's initial prosperity. In Rowe's words, Shakespeare appeared 'to have given entirely into that way of living which his father proposed to him'. Someone had to take the Shakespeare gloves and other produce to the Market Cross on Thursdays, and if his father could not, it had to be someone else from the house.

The Shakespeares may have owned the biggest single frontage in Henley Street, but the Whateleys were wealthier now, and there was at least one other family who were also richer and more influential. The Quineys were the first family of Stratford after the Cloptons and Combes. If the phrase 'social mobility' did not exist at the time, the concept certainly did: Shakespeare himself and his entire family exemplify it, as do others who made good. The Quineys were yeoman merchants who had become a local dynasty through a propitious marriage alliance with another family of Henley Street grandees, that of Thomas Phillips who had served with Adrian Quiney in the first-ever group of aldermen in newly-incorporated Stratford. The Phillipses lived some way up west from the Shakespeares, between the Ichiver-Johnson house (later the White Lion Inn and eventually the site of the Birthplace archives) and Peter Smart's house. Theirs was a substantial property, consisting of a large barn and a three-bay house called the 'fursen' house.

Directly west of the Shakespeares lived a family named Badger, who enjoyed close links with the Quineys. The George Badger who occupied this house during Will Shakespeare's time in Henley Street may have been Richard Quiney's godfather.[11] The Badger house boasted an impressive frontage of about 50 feet or so and was probably separated from the Shakespeares' house by a narrow garden rather than the customary earth mound. Eventually Badger bought a narrow strip of land between John Shakespeare and himself for fifty shillings, a not inconsiderable sum. According to the deed of sale this strip or 'toft', which ran the entire length between Henley Street and Gildpits, measured half a yard in width and twenty-eight yards in length.

Why Badger wanted this land has never been satisfactorily explained; after all, there was probably an extant boundary which was the shared responsibility of both parties. It is just possible that Badger, an 'obstinate' Catholic, wanted to erect a wall or a fence, for privacy. It may be that he was preparing to set up a safe house for local Catholics. The truth of the matter cannot now be known, but it is a fact that Badger never reneged on the old faith of his forebears. The Jesuit mission of 1580 used the Midlands as a central plank, and Badger would have known about it as surely as the Catholics over in Shottery. There is no evidence of Campion and Parsons passing through the Badger house during this period, but none that they did not. Stratford was after all wide open, except for the toll gates down at the bridge. And then there were the Catholic Cloptons in their large mansion not far away in the nearby Welcombe Hills: from the Cloptons to the Badgers in Henley Street was a journey of about forty minutes across the fields in the sixteenth century. The hamlet of Shottery, almost equidistant from Stratford in the other direction, was traditionally a crucible of organized Catholic resistance. Young William Shakespeare married into a Shottery family with whom his father had had business dealings years earlier. He would have been aware of pretty well all the local allegiances. It is a tribute to the prevailing climate of tolerance in Stratford even in the troubled 1580s that most of its citizens just got on with their lives, keeping religion at arm's length when it came to business and much else.

There was another Catholic connection in Henley Street, through the carrier and 'postman' William Greenway, who ensured that people like Badger's son Richard, who joined a firm of London stationers, did not lose touch with their families in Stratford. The return journey to London took an experienced well-horsed traveller less than three days each way; it is not known whether Greenway made it once a month, or twice. As well as himself shuttling between London and Stratford, Greenway also seems to have provided the means for others to do so. It is not at all clear why Greenway operated this service, why he himself went off to London with a certain regularity – but, as so often in Stratford, where there is doubt it is worth explaining the Catholic angle.

Greenway lived in Middle Row, where he ran a draper's business. But he also rented a house and a barn on the south side of Henley Street, probably opposite Hornby.[12] There is no clear indication of why Greenway should have required these additional and rather expensive premises, corporation property featuring four elm trees. An informed guess might suggest that he used them for stabling horses, that in fact he ran a kind of livery stables, perhaps in partnership with the blacksmith Hornby to shoe his horses. With these substantial property holdings Greenway eventually allied himself through marriage with his Henley Street neighbour William Cawdrey, brother probably of the butcher Rafe Cawdrey from Bridge Street among whose children were a son named George and a daughter, Ursula. It is this Ursula Cawdrey whom Greenway married in 1569. His brother-in-law George was a zealous young Catholic who may well have met Jesuits during their stay in the Midlands, and was ordained a Catholic priest within three years of Campion's death on 1 December 1581.

Not long before this Greenway had had occasion to visit Robert Debdale of Shottery in London. Young Debdale had come over with Campion and was now interned in the Gatehouse prison at Westminster, usually the first port of call for Catholic prisoners before they were carted off to the Tower or one of the other major London prisons. It was on 3 November 1581 that Greenway, acting on behalf of the Debdale family, took Robert two cheeses, a loaf of bread and some money. It is inconceivable that Greenway should not have gossiped about this visit with his family and his friends and neighbours in Henley Street, or that the fate of young Debdale was not a major talking-point in Shottery and Stratford – the more so since these were the weeks immediately preceding the execution of Campion.

This time Debdale was released from the Tower, but his reprieve was only temporary and five years later, at the age of twenty-six, he was executed in London. Only two years earlier he had been received into the Society of Jesus in Rheims where he had overlapped with young George Cawdrey. These two Catholic Stratford boys obviously knew each other well, and both presumably also knew Will Shakespeare. Assuming Will harboured Catholic yearnings, he had no need to follow his former schoolmaster John Cottom to Lancashire – the Catholics were literally on his doorstep in Stratford, and he needed to look no further than Shottery to meet the die-hards. The role played in the Catholic insurgency by this small hamlet on a brook in a gentle dip a mile or so to the west of Stratford awaits a full investigation. Here was a community locked into recusancy where a few closely knit families lived cheek-by-jowl in mutual support.

Whether William Shakespeare did indeed feel attracted to one faith rather than the other is impossible to determine. His works provide little guidance. Unlike Spenser in *The Faerie Queene* or Milton in *Paradise Lost*, he never declares a preference. The glorious muddle over religion in *Hamlet*, whether that of the Catholic purgatory or the Wittenberg theses, echoes the divided allegiances of the nation – and perhaps of the Shakespeare family. When religion finally does emerge as an imaginative force in the last plays, and particularly *The Tempest*, it is blandly ecumenical, a general spiritual source of comfort.

The need for 'discretion' must have been easily apparent to young William Shakespeare. His Catholic schoolmasters presumably influenced their charges when they could, and must have found Stratford fertile ground. Declared Catholics like Robert Debdale and George Cawdrey were his near-contemporaries, and young William probably questioned Greenway about Debdale and his imprisonment as eagerly as anyone else in Henley Street. Of course he talked to the 'messenger' from across the street, just as the tailor and smith gossip with each other in *King John*. Of course he would have known that the Badgers were recusant Catholics, though perhaps not their involvement with the cause; his parents almost certainly would. One of the greatest riches of Shakespeare's imaginative works is his extraordinary ability to see everything from different points of view, as true of the plays as a whole as of his soliloquies. It is commonly interpreted as an intrinsic part of the sweep of his talent and range, and so it is. But it surely derives specifically from his response to life as he encountered it on the brink of adulthood, in a provincial town divided along sectarian lines but not radically against itself. The good people of Stratford were too engrossed in business, materially too competitive even, to be swayed totally by politics or religion. The world of national politics was best left to the local lords of the manor. They ran the show anyway, or so people assumed.

For that matter, throughout his life Shakespeare distrusted demagogues and particularly, perhaps, the so-called tribunes of the people. It is a theme that runs through the plays, from the very early second part of *Henry VI* and the rebellion spearheaded by Jack Cade to the rabble-rousers in the late tragedy *Coriolanus*. The businessman in Shakespeare ever erred on the side of conservatism and scepticism, but as the child of a half-century that had seen people die in the name of religion in a struggle between two faiths he could be both everything and nothing. Above all he was 'careful'. The fate of Debdale and the threat to Cawdrey, building on the stirrings of sedition at his school, may all have contributed to forging an identity that would always be hard to pin down. Shakespeare became elusive not as a response to the generic conventions of drama but because being elusive could be a matter of life and death in the country in which he grew up. No one can possibly know what John Shakespeare told his sons as, one after the other, they attended the King's New School. But it seems likely that, whether or not his own views leaned towards one creed rather than another, he instructed them to keep their noses clean where politics and religion were concerned.

By the time he had reached the age of eighteen Shakespeare had probably been working for his father for three or four years. That they were difficult years can hardly be doubted, for the council continued to treat the Shakespeares sympathetically in their straitened circumstances. Will had grown up as a rich boy, and now here he was struggling to keep the family afloat, or at least to save them from having to sell their home in Henley Street; to judge from other properties in the same street may have been worth anything upwards of £500. This period of his family's humiliation must have rankled deeply with Shakespeare, and may be the reason why he could never really leave Stratford behind, even when he was away from it.

4

Enter Wife and Daughter: 1582–3

T OWARDS THE END of the summer of 1582 Will Shakespeare made
Anne Hathaway pregnant. He was eighteen years and four
months old, she may have been twenty-six. She is thought to have
been his senior by eight years only because the inscription on her
tombstone declares that she was sixty-seven when she died in 1623.
She would have been baptized in 1556, but unfortunately the parish
records for Holy Trinity only start in 1558. Equally, the numbers 1 and
7 are easily confused in inscriptions, but if she was sixty-one rather
than sixty-seven when she died, a closer contemporary of Will's, she
would have been baptized about 1562, falling well inside the time
limits of the existing Holy Trinity register. Of course, she may have
been recorded not at Holy Trinity at all but rather at one of the
adjacent parishes; if so, nothing has yet come to light about her.

There was a connection between the Hathaways of Shottery and
the Shakespeares of Henley Street long before their children married:
John Shakespeare twice stood surety for Anne Hathaway's father
Richard Hathaway *alias* Gardner in 1566, and paid off substantial
debts for him. The Hathaways were major players in Shottery, and
Hewlands Farm there had been in their possession from at least 1543.
The higher house towards the gardens was probably added by Anne's
brother Richard in the early seventeenth century, but the hall, the
buttery, and the imposing old bake-oven belonging to the main building, the fifteenth-century farm, would all have been familiar to the
young Anne Hathaway, and perhaps to Will Shakespeare; perhaps,
because it may be that he did not do much of his courting here. The
location of the farm just beyond Shottery burn is a rural idyll, fitting
perfectly with Celia's directions in *As You Like It* to the 'sheep-cote'
in a dell 'down in the neighbour bottom', where a 'rank of osiers'

stretches past a 'murmuring stream'. In the eighteenth century the Stratford antiquarian John Jordan (1746–1809) called the prospect south from Anne Hathaway's ancestral home 'one of the finest meadows in England', and so it remains.

There is no way of knowing how Will and Anne met, or how they found the opportunity for what in *Measure for Measure* Shakespeare called the 'stealth of our most mutual entertainment'. It is clear, however, that they had sex during the summer of 1582, before they were married. 'Young men will do't if they come to't, / By Cock, they are to blame', the grieving Ophelia intones, and she continues with 'Quoth she, "Before you tumbled me, / You promised me to wed",' to which she imagines the young man replying, '"So would I 'a' done, by yonder sun, / An thou hadst not come to my bed."' Without a doubt this is Shakespeare recalling his own teenage sexual encounters, the difference being that as a young man he did honour his commitment to Anne, and married her. No wonder he is so sympathetic to young Claudio and Juliet in *Measure for Measure*, already lawfully married before sexual congress took place, even though their union had yet to be sanctioned by the church. Will and Anne consummated their relationship regardless of church and religion. When Anne told him that summer that she was missing her 'courses', the phrase commonly in use at the time, he must have known exactly what it meant.

On Tuesday 27 November 1582 William Shakespeare and Anne Hathaway were granted a special licence to marry. She was three months pregnant and they were in a hurry, so they required a licence from the Worcester diocesan consistory court to allow them to marry without the full three proclamations of the banns. Canon law forbade the asking of banns between Advent Sunday, which fell on 2 December 1582, and the Octave of Epiphany on 13 January 1583, leaving only 30 November for a single reading of the banns, which is indeed what the bond lodged the day after the grant of the licence stipulated. As a minor Will Shakespeare was not required to be present on that Tuesday in the south aisle of Worcester Cathedral where the consistory court convened.

The grant of the licence in the Bishop's Register at Worcester on 27 November 1582 reads, tersely, '*Item eodem die similis emanavit licen-*

cia inter Willelmum Shaxpere et Annam Whateley de Temple Grafton':
'On that same day was issued a similar licence between William
Shakespeare and Anne Whateley of Temple Grafton'. The following
day, Wednesday 28 November 1582, a bond of sureties was posted by
two farmers from Shottery, Fulke Sandells and John Richardson,
friends of the bride and her family. The purpose of this bond, which
at £40 was a significant sum, was to indemnify the Bishop and consistory court in case of legal action arising out of impediments to a
marriage which had not gone through the usual procedures. It seems
to have been a formality, but the penalties were certainly stiff. This
bond states that

> The condition of this obligation is such that if hereafter there shall not
> appear any lawful let or impediment by reason of any precontract,
> consanguinity, affinity or by any other lawful means whatsoever but
> that William Shakespeare on the one party and Anne Hathaway of
> Stratford in the diocese of Worcester, maiden, may lawfully solemnize
> matrimony together and in the same afterwards remain and continue
> like man and wife according unto the laws in that behalf provided, and
> moreover if there be not at this present time any action, suit, or quar-
> rel or demand moved or depending before any judge ecclesiastical or
> temporal for and concerning any such lawful let or impediment, and
> moreover if the said William Shakespeare do not proceed to solem-
> nization of marriage with the said Anne Hathaway without the consent
> of her friends, and also if the said William do upon his own proper
> costs and expenses defend and save harmless the right Reverend father
> in God Lord John [Whitgift] Bishop of Worcester and his officers for
> licensing them the said William and Anne to be married together
> with once asking of the banns of matrimony between them and for all
> other causes which may ensure by reason or occasion thereof, that then
> the said obligation to be void and of none effect or else to stand and
> abide in full force and virtue.[1]

According to the grant of the licence Shakespeare married Anne
Whateley of Temple Grafton, a hamlet four miles south-west of
Stratford, while the *bond* identified the bride as Anne Hathaway of
Stratford. The bonds and the entries granting licences in the
Worcester register generally agree, but not in this case. The entry for
the licence in the Bishop's Register was almost certainly copied from

the application for the licence (called the 'allegation'), which would have contained all the relevant details of the various parties involved.[2] It follows that the woman whom William Shakespeare married was called Anne Whateley of Temple Grafton in the allegation or application that no longer exists. She is the same as the Anne Hathaway of the bond – that is, Anne Whateley from Temple Grafton of the register and allegation and Anne Hathaway from Stratford of the bond are both Anne Hathaway from Shottery. For reasons that are not now fully understood, the church authorities in Worcester accepted a bond for a bride who had two different names and two different addresses.

How Anne Hathaway from Shottery became Anne Whateley from Temple Grafton on 27 November 1582 is one of the enduring mysteries of the Shakespeare story. The 1582 bond was only discovered in 1836 by the brilliant Stratford antiquarian Robert B. Wheler (1785–1857), so it follows that until the publication of Rowe's Life in 1709 no one in the wider world knew that Shakespeare had married Anne Hathaway. Rowe knew of neither the register nor the bond, but he did know the bride's true identity. Shakespeare, he wrote, 'thought fit to marry while he was yet very young' and 'his wife was the daughter of one Hathaway, said to have been a substantial yeoman in the neighbourhood of Stratford'; he says nothing about Anne's seniority to William. It is a mystery how he knew about Anne's parentage; the only written records from the period available to him in 1709 were the registers of Holy Trinity, and they are silent on the subject of Shakespeare's marriage, while Anne's maiden name does not feature on her gravestone, which merely describes her as 'Anne wife of William Shakespeare'. Rowe does not engage with Anne's pregnancy because he knew nothing about the Worcester entry and the strong indication it afforded of Shakespeare's impetuous sexual behaviour. But he did know, and without access to any of the sources now available, who she was. In 1709 the surname of Shakespeare's bride was revealed for the first time, and in a widely available text.

Rowe's authority was the oral tradition of Stratford and, ultimately, the playwright William Davenant, who lived long enough to know the acclaimed Restoration actor Betterton, Rowe's main source for his 'Life of Shakespeare'. In Rowe's words, Betterton's love of Shakespeare 'engaged him to make a journey into Warwickshire, on purpose to gather up what remains he could of a name for which he had so great a value.' Betterton was born in 1635 and became an important Shakespearian actor in the post-Restoration theatre; he may have travelled up to Stratford sometime between the 1660s and 1680s.[3] If Betterton did indeed go to Stratford, the earlier he went the more reliable the information he imparted to Rowe is likely to have been, since Shakespeare's daughter lived until 1662 and his granddaughter until 1670, while his sister's family continued to live in Henley Street for 180 years after his death.

Anne's father Richard Hathaway had died in September 1581, and shortly afterwards her brother left home for Tysoe, near Stratford; Anne too may have left Shottery after her father's death – perhaps neither she nor her brother got on with their stepmother Joan and their various younger step-siblings. Almost nothing is known about the mother of Anne Hathaway, her four brothers (Bartholomew and three Richards), and her sister Catherine, or where she came from, but she and Richard Hathaway must have married at some point in the 1550s. However, it is tempting to think that she was a Whateley of Temple Grafton, that Anne Hathaway returned to Temple Grafton after her father's death because it was her mother's home village, and that the people who drafted the application for the Worcester licence were Anne's mother's family from Temple Grafton, while the bond was posted on behalf of the Hathaways, who owed John Shakespeare for past favours.

In looking for the church where Will and Anne married it would be helpful to know where Anne's father wed his second wife Joan. Holy Trinity is the obvious place because in his will Richard Hathaway asked to be buried in the churchyard, but there is no record of such a union in the church's register. Similarly, it is not known where Anne's brother Bartholomew married. Later Hathaways were as happily affiliated to Holy Trinity as Richard seems to have been, so it is hard to argue that the family might have had some principled objection to using the Stratford parish church. Yet it has been suggested that ideological objections led Will and Anne to choose a church other than Holy Trinity – a church just like that at Temple Grafton, for example, where the minister was a notoriously stubborn Catholic.

On 2 November 1586, at the height of the trouble with Mary Queen of Scots and in the wake of Anthony Babington's trial for high treason in London, the church commissioners published a document entitled 'A survey of the state of the ministry in Warwickshire'. They had scrutinized the ministers of the various parishes with a view to stamping out or rolling back recusancy. Stratford-upon-Avon was given the all clear, but the vicar of Temple Grafton did not find favour. He was John Frith, 'an old priest and unsound in religion'. He could, it seems, 'neither preach nor read well', and his main interest was the curing of 'hawks that are hurt or diseased, for which purpose many do usually repair to him'. He was clearly a recusant, but to all appearances a harmless eccentric – or maybe he only seemed so.

It may be that Frith's interest in hawks was not quite as innocuous as the Protestant church commissioners thought, for the role of hawker was one of the preferred disguises adopted by fugitive Jesuits in England. This is clear from John Gerard's account of how he went to ground after landing near Mundesley in Norfolk in November 1588. He needed a plausible excuse for being where he was, and chose to pretend that he was a hawker looking for his stray falcon. According to Gerard, he had no sooner parted from his companion Edward Oldcorne than he saw people heading towards him. He went up to them and asked whether they had seen his hawk: 'perhaps they had heard its bell tinkling as it was flying around?' He intended to convey the impression that he was looking for his bird, as a falconer would, so they would not think it odd that he found himself in unfamiliar lanes, but instead 'would merely think that I had wandered here in my search.' He was credible enough on that occasion, and the good Norfolk people commiserated with him over his lost hawk.

Knowing this, it is permissible to look back at old John Frith of Temple Grafton's passion for hawks and wonder whether it was not a cover for Catholic activities, enabling both Jesuits and ordinary recusants to repair to this particular church and priest under the pretext of having their hawks seen to. If so, Frith was not found out, though the authorities clearly knew of his Catholic sympathies. He was vicar of Temple Grafton for many years, so would probably have known Anne Hathaway's mother and the Whateleys of Temple Grafton well. That John Frith married William Shakespeare and Anne Whateley-Hathaway cannot be ruled out, and might even be likely if there were some evidence that the couple wanted to marry in the old faith. But the records for Worcester suggest otherwise. In cases where the entry in the Worcester register is supported by documentary proof of where a couple subsequently married, the records demonstrate that the parish cited in the Worcester grants of licences tends to be that of the bride's residence rather than the groom's or the parish where the marriage took place. This lends weight to the idea that Anne was a Whateley from Temple Grafton.

Two further aspects relating to the marriage require consideration: the chapel at Billesley, and the odd business of Shakespeare's father dragging himself out of retirement from the town council to vote just at the time when his son was having sex with Anne Hathaway. The chapel at Billesley has long been high on the list of potential settings for the Shakespeare wedding, because Shakespeare's granddaughter Elizabeth was married there in 1649 to John Barnard of Abington Hall. What has never been established is why she should have chosen Billesley, of all places, now little more than a clump of farms less than a mile or so across the wold from Shakespeare's mother's home in Wilmcote. It may indeed be that its proximity to Mary Arden's home suggested it to Will and Anne for the wedding, and later to Elizabeth. Who is to say that the Shakespeare who loved the countryside so deeply had not played or roamed around here? The same survey that damned Temple Grafton sounds a mellow note about Billesley. The parish was serviced by one 'Robert Spenser, no preacher nor learned, a companion and goodfellow in all companies well liked and commended of his parishioners for an honest quiet fellow as ever came among them'. Perhaps Anne and Will were married not by a recusant priest, but by an approved servant – if similarly wanting in educational polish – of the Anglican church.

So there is a distinct possibility that towards the end of November or perhaps on Saturday 1 December 1582, William Shakespeare married Anne Whateley of Temple Grafton, daughter of the deceased Richard Hathaway of Shottery and his first wife. If the wedding did indeed take place on 1 December 1582, immediately after the reading of the banns on the previous day, then the Shakespeares were married on the first anniversary of Campion's martyrdom in London; if the marriage took place in a recusant church such as Temple Grafton it would be irresistibly tempting to make a connection between the timing of the wedding and some kind of deliberate act of commemoration of Campion – yet the biological imperatives that lay behind the expedition of this marriage must not be forgotten. It is possible that Anne's mother was a Whateley from Temple Grafton; it was certainly this side of the family who, if they did not give her away, at least completed the application for the licence to marry which lies behind the entry in the Bishop's register in Worcester. A separate bond for *both* parties (which remained undiscovered until the nineteenth century) was posted by friends of the Hathaways, and in it Anne is referred to as a Hathaway. Temple Grafton is possible as the setting for the marriage, but the wider evidence from Worcester regarding licences and places of marriage does not support the suggestion, leaving the way open for the claims of the chapel at Billesley.

Where did Will Shakespeare and Anne Hathaway meet? There was no particular reason for young Will Shakespeare to find his way to Shottery, where his family had no relatives; but the Shakespeares of Henley Street are on record as knowing the very same Richard Hathaway of Shottery who was Anne's father. If Anne lived in Temple Grafton, as seems to have been the case in 1581–2, it is most unlikely that Will would have met her there. It may be, however, that the answer lies rather closer to home, in Henley Street. There is no corroborative documentary evidence to support the idea, but it is not impossible that Anne Whateley was related to the Whateleys of Henley Street, perhaps a cousin or a second cousin of the family, and that in the months between her father's death in September 1581 and November 1582 she was in the habit of visiting her relatives in Henley Street. None of this can be proven, of course. The Henley Street Whateleys had strong Catholic connections, and George Whateley's brothers John and Robert were both recusant priests. Robert was reported by the Recusancy Commission of 1592 for Henley-in-Arden as 'an old priest called Sir Robert Whateley, who used to come to his friends, he being a man of four score year old', which seems to suggest he visited his friends' homes to say mass in secret, as did many another recusant priest. Of course in 1592 any eighty-year-old priest would almost inevitably be a Catholic. A second certificate by the recusancy commissioners of 25 September 1592 about Henley-in-Arden refers to 'one Sir Robert Whateley presented there for a recusant, an old massing priest, resorting often thither, but hardly to be found'. It is open to speculation whether either Robert or John Whateley married Will Shakespeare and Anne Hathaway (or Anne Whateley) in their parish church over at Henley-in-Arden – an intriguing thought that awaits further exploration. None of the Shakespeare wills or wills related to them seems to refer to the Whateleys, but nor is there any reference in Shakespeare's will to the Hathaways. Perhaps they opposed the marriage in 1582, or perhaps Anne wished to break off all contact with her father's new family.

The Whateleys of Henley Street were grand, and remained so throughout the period of the Shakespeares' misfortunes; if they underwrote Anne's marriage out of loyalty to her mother, the Shakespeares could be thought to have done well with this union. Unfortunately, the only documented connection between George Whateley and the Shakespeares is that they were both glovers and whittawers, and lived in the same street. Or is it?

As it happens there may be another connection, and it involves one of the minor mysteries of the Shakespeare story. There was a town council meeting on Wednesday 2 September 1582 – just about the time when Will and Anne's daughter Susanna was conceived. This Michaelmas meeting was the most important of the year, for its remit was to elect the new mayor for the following twelve months. What marks this meeting as particularly special is that John Shakespeare emerged from his house in Henley Street on this day and walked to the Gildhall to vote – something he had not done since January 1577 and did not do again before he was dismissed from the council in September 1586. However, there is no doubt that on this one day John returned to public office: he has been 'pricked', that is checked in by a dot against his name, and the clerk has indicated how he voted. The question is – why now?

On that Wednesday in September 1582 the council of fourteen aldermen and eleven burgesses were to choose their new mayor from three alderman candidates: Adrian Quiney, John Sadler, and George Whateley. Sadler won with eleven votes to Quiney's eight and Whateley's two. The only people to vote for Whateley were Quiney's own son (voting against his father) and William Smith. John Shakespeare voted for his old friend John Sadler, one of the wealthiest property owners in the town. It is a puzzle to know why so many votes were cast for John Sadler; he never served as mayor but excused himself, probably on the grounds of ill-health, and was probably infirm at the time of the election. The office of mayor was as expensive as it was prestigious, but Sadler was so rich that he was unlikely to balk at the cost. The runner-up Adrian Quiney (whose grandson one day married John Shakespeare's granddaughter) duly served as mayor of Stratford in 1582–3 in lieu of Sadler. However opaque the politics of this particular meeting may seem four hundred years on, it is fairly clear that something was up. Why else vote for an ailing man who was unlikely to serve and whose election was bound to cross Whateley, leaving him those paltry two votes.

The presence of John Shakespeare is surely significant. It can hardly be that Sadler needed his vote: there must have been a personal reason for John to come out of the house where he seems to have been living to all intents and purposes under house arrest. It is known that Will and Anne were lovers, but very little else is about the Shakespeare family during this month: the temptation must be to connect this one fact with John's behaviour. If they are linked, then John Shakespeare's vote against Whateley appears to have been a hostile act, confirming that Anne was indeed related to this family, and that the two Henley Street clans had come to grief over the love affair between her and Will. This early, it is unlikely to have been because Anne was pregnant, since this was probably not yet known. It may be that John Shakespeare rejoined the council briefly and voted as he did to remind Whateley of his status before all his assembled peers. His fellow councillors must have been stunned to see him there after so many absences.

Once they were married the young couple would have lived together, as was the custom, with Will's parents in Henley Street. By 1582 the house was pretty full, and with Edmund Shakespeare barely two years old it must have been noisy too, noise Will and Anne soon added to with their baby. As Anne's pregnancy progressed, they must all have been working out ways of getting along together under the same roof, as a series of complex negotiations. All is mere speculation, of course, but it is likely that the small change of domestic life absorbed much of the young couple's energies. During the day Will was probably working as a glover downstairs in the eastern part of the building and in the barn at the back of the garden with his father John and brother Gilbert while his mother and Anne shared the rearing of little Edmund (and later Susanna) and oversaw the wares displayed in and sold from the windows facing out into Henley Street, dealing with customers from the town or passing trade on its way up to Coventry and Birmingham or down to Oxford and Banbury. No doubt they also helped with preparing the skins and leather to be moulded and cut into gloves.

That the newly-wed couple needed a bedroom and some privacy is self-evident, and it is interesting to imagine it, based on the available evidence and clues. Their bed, like Kate's in *The Taming of the Shrew*, would have had pillows, bolsters, coverlets, and sheets. There was undoubtedly a chamber-pot. Eventually there will have been a cradle, later a truckle-bed for the children as they outgrew the cradle. If Shakespeare's parents occupied the room called 'the best chamber' or 'the great chamber' in two contemporary inventories of the Henley Street house, Will and Anne probably lodged across the stairs in the so-called 'stairhead chamber' or 'the chamber of the hall', the second-best bedroom.[4] In winter, warmth would have been provided by the main fireplace and chimney, diffused through the open-plan design of the house. Later, during her father's long months away in London, Susanna probably slept in her mother's bed while her siblings shared the truckle-bed.

At the back of the house there was undoubtedly a privy or jakes – a 'place of easement', as polite Londoners called it. The smell from the vats of urine used in the preparation of leather for glove-making probably did not overwhelm the home, as has been suggested, for acidic deposits discovered in the soil near the bottom of the former Henley Street garden suggest glovers' activities in this area; perhaps the vats sat in a barn there. There was presumably a well, and neither the Shakespeares' privy nor any of the glovers' vats would have been sited anywhere near it. The Shakespeares owned a big barn on Gildpits, at the far end of the bottom of the garden, very likely glovers' work premises and a storage space for wool, and perhaps built by John Shakespeare for this purpose in the first instance.

As homes went, the Henley Street house was as good as any – and indeed better than most, since it was the single largest three-bay house in the street. The way the ground rent was pegged to a proportion of burgage reveals that John Shakespeare's original purchase in Henley Street property in 1556 was of the eastern bay of the house, which to this day conveys the impression from the outside of being a self-contained dwelling. The 1590 list of Manorial Tenants (effectively freeholders) of Henley Street rates the eastern wing at 6 pence ground rent, exactly half a burgage, and the western part of the house, the two smaller bays, at 13 pence, just more than a complete burgage.[5] According to the best-informed current opinion on the house the whole three-bay structure, running to an impressive 90 feet of frontage, is really one rectangle. The western two bays must at some point have been partitioned off from the eastern one, for John Shakespeare's 1575 purchase records 'two messuages' with two gardens and two orchards. In other words, it seems that until 1575 the Henley Street house was divided into three discrete units consisting of the Shakespeares' eastern bay and a middle and western bay. It is just possible that some of the inner partitioning of the house was retained or restored by John Shakespeare as his family expanded after 1575, which could explain why the Hiccox inventory uses the plural 'houses'. Conversions were not uncommon at the time and the young couple would, one imagines, have been grateful for space to themselves.

On Sunday 26 May 1583 Anne and William Shakespeare took their first-born, a baby daughter, to be baptized. The little girl the young father held in his arms at the font of Holy Trinity was given the name Susanna, not to be found in his family or Anne's, and not at all common in Stratford. At this period, a name strange to the parents' families could be traced to a godparent, as was the case with the next two Shakespeare children, the twins Hamnet and Judith, to whom it is almost certain that the Shakespeares' friends Hamnet and Judith Sadler stood as godparents.

The name Susanna appears for the first time in Stratford in 1574, and Susanna Shakespeare was only the sixth girl in the town to be so named. It was favoured by Puritans and derives from the Apocrypha and Susanna, the virtuous wife of Joacim. If Susanna was named after anyone locally it is likely that she was Susanna Woodward, wife of the same Richard Tyler who was later taken out of William Shakespeare's will.

The fact that Susanna Woodward had a sister named Judith and two daughters called Susanna and Judith is surely not a coincidence. John Shakespeare and Tyler's father William had served together on the town council in the 1560s, and William Tyler may have been Shakespeare's godfather. There would be a family logic to William and Anne Shakespeare asking young Tyler's wife to stand as godparent to Susanna, a second generation godparenting by the Tylers of the Shakespeares: William Tyler to William Shakespeare, followed by Susanna Tyler (née Woodward) to Susanna Shakespeare – and perhaps even Susanna Tyler's sister Judith Woodward to Judith Shakespeare. The choice of a Puritan name for his daughter is another of those contradictory pointers to Shakespeare's religious inclinations. The ramifications have yet to be pursued, but if Anne and Will Shakespeare chose Susanna Woodward as their first-born's godmother it would be instructive to find out why they might have done so. The Woodwards lived in Shottery Manor alongside the Burmans and Paces, neighbours of Anne Hathaway's family, and of the devoutly Catholic Debdales.

Susanna Woodward was the granddaughter of Robert Perrott, the Puritan owner of Luscombe Manor in Snitterfield and a wealthy brewer, and lessee of a building that survives intact today in Rother Market as the White Swan but was in the sixteenth century a tavern called the King's Hall or the King's House. Its striking sixteenth-century mural of Tobias and Raphael was only rediscovered in 1927 and can again be enjoyed in the same spot where it has sat for centuries. It is so close to Henley Street that Shakespeare must have seen it and probably occasionally had a drink in front of it. The daughter of Master Richard Woodward, Susanna, was the only one of her siblings not to inherit anything from her wealthy Puritan grandfather. It seems that she married twenty-two-year-old Richard Tyler in the teeth of family opposition because Perrott's will stipulates that her siblings stood to inherit from him the 'residue of my stock and goods' provided that they 'be dutiful and obedient and match themselves in marriage with the consent of their parents'. Even her father Richard Woodward's will cut her out while leaving some money for her son's schooling. To be doubly disinherited must have been a bitter blow for Susanna and her husband Richard Tyler. But was it mere pique at work here, or is there a religious angle? Perhaps the Tylers were too Catholic for the Puritan Perrott, and marrying a Tyler Susanna Woodward crossed a sectarian divide the rest of her family could not bridge. Yet the names she and her husband chose for their children suggest otherwise, and the odds are that Susanna and Richard were Protestants. If so, Will and Anne Shakespeare may have chosen to ally themselves to one of the few committed Protestant families of Shottery.

If there is a Shottery connection, it may be because Anne Shakespeare had the final say over her daughters' names, and chose their godparents from her only Protestant friends in Shottery. Perhaps she left Shottery for this reason. Reconciling this with the recusant Whateleys, or for that matter with Shakespeare's mother Mary Arden and her surmised Catholic Arden links, is another problem. If Anne Hathaway was a committed Protestant, however, it would dispose of any suggestion that she and Will might have sought a Catholic priest to marry them, and makes Billesley with its conformist vicar an even more likely setting for their wedding.

Further evidence also suggests a distinctly Protestant slant to Anne and Will's choice of name for their first-born. Of the six Stratford Susannas from this period, three were so named in the space of six weeks: Susanna, daughter of William Perrott (Robert Perrott's cousin) on 9 April 1583, Susanna, daughter of Richard Baker on 29 April 1583, and Susanna Shakespeare on 26 May 1583 – three Susannas, two born into families of arch-Protestants. Strange company for William Shakespeare particularly when there is other evidence about his faith that seems to point in a diametrically opposite direction.

The Sunday before Susanna's baptism in Holy Trinity was Whit Sunday, 19 May 1583. For this Whitsun, Stratford Corporation had commissioned a pageant, laying out 13s. 4d. toward the expenses of 'Davy Jones and his company for his pastime at Whitsuntide's'.[6] This is the first such entry for home-grown talent in Stratford. In 1569 when John Shakespeare was mayor or high bailiff of Stratford the Queen's Players were paid 9s. and the Earl of Worcester's 12s. Davy's must have been an impressive show to warrant such lavishness. If Davy Jones had had to cajole the council into hiring him as impresario along with a supporting company, some of the credit for his success could presumably be put down to his connection to the powerful

Quineys, whose writ ran in Stratford: in June 1577 Jones had married Elizabeth Quiney, sister of the future mayor Richard Quiney. The corporation accounts do not record any further payments to him in the years that follow, but the name Davy occurs repeatedly in Shakespeare's *2 Henry IV*, a play with a number of autobiographical resonances harking back to the Midlands if not directly to Stratford. Perhaps Davy was also a kind of model for Bottom in *A Midsummer Night's Dream*, and his 'company' or troupe included callus-handed men who 'toiled their unbreathed memories' to entertain the good burghers of Stratford on that day. But it is just as possible that the 'company' consisted of the schoolchildren of the King's New School and perhaps Gilbert Shakespeare among them and even Will's fourteen-year-old sister Joan, assuming that the statutes against cross-dressing did not apply to amateur theatricals such as these.

That children from the grammar school may have taken part in this pageant is suggested by a reference to Whitsun festivities in an early play, *The Two Gentlemen of Verona*. When Sebastian (Julia in disguise) is quizzed by Silvia about 'his' height, 'he' replies that Julia was just as tall, for 'he' was clad in a gown of hers in the Whitsun play:

> . . . for at Pentecost,
> When all our pageants of delight were played,
> Our youth got me to play the woman's part,
> And I was trimmed in Madam Julia's gown,
> Which servèd me as fit, by all men's judgements,
> As if the garment had been made for me;
> Therefore I know she is about my height.
> And at that time I made her weep agood,
> For I did play a lamentable part.
> Madam, 'twas Ariadne passioning
> For Theseus' perjury and unjust flight,
> Which I so lively acted with my tears
> That my poor mistress, movèd therewithal,
> Wept bitterly; and would I might be dead
> If I in thought felt not her very sorrow.

So close to the baptism of his daughter, it seems likely that Will, if he went to the Whitsun pageant, went without Anne. The venue might have been the large ground floor room in the Gildhall or perhaps more probably, the grammar school's gardens. There is an air of carnival about these local pentecostal festivities, adaptations of Ovid or plays about Robin Hood and merry old England, far removed from the pusillanimous Puritanism that one day paid the most illustrious company in the country *not* to play. There is no reason why the pageants put on by Davy Jones should have been any different from those recalled by Julia, and Shakespeare clearly expects that his audience will have their own experience of these 'pageants of delight'. It is fairly certain that Davy & Co. did not always 'stand upon points', any more than Peter Quince does when speaking the prologue to the burlesque of Pyramus and Thisbe in *A Midsummer Night's Dream*. In *The Winter's Tale*, a much later play, and one deeply rooted in rural Warwickshire, a young princess dressed as a shepherdess recalls pentecostal fun and games: 'Methinks I play as I have seen them do / In Whitsun pastorals.' It may be that Davy Jones's was the first-ever Maying pageant in Stratford; certainly Shakespeare seems never to have forgotten these boisterous attempts at drama, returning to them time and again in his plays.

Shakespeare's work reveals nothing to indicate his personal reaction to parenthood, but the plays contain some wonderful portrayals of children – little Macduff, for example, or, more darkly, the adolescent Juliet, or Mamillius and Perdita in *The Winter's Tale*. In considering Shakespeare the poet and dramatist it must never be forgotten that he was a man grounded in the realities of everyday life in all their highlights and shadows, as part of an extended family in a world recognizably domestic, mutually supportive and demanding, in a house still standing today. Mary Arden and John Shakespeare will have expected there to be more grandchildren soon, and with John's fortunes at a low ebb may well have felt apprehensive about this. Even with John's elder sons helping out in the business, supporting an ever-increasing number of children must have been quite a tough prospect, but one that had to be faced at a time when there was no effective contraception.

In the late summer of 1584 Anne Shakespeare was pregnant again, and on 2 February 1585 she and Will took their twins Hamnet and Judith to be baptized. Anne was probably still only 29, and there was no reason why she should not have had several more children; her mother-in-law Mary Arden was after all around forty when she had her youngest, Edmund. It may be that these were comparatively happy times for the young couple even if business was no longer what it had been in the halcyon days before John Shakespeare's great crash. There is no reason to think that Shakespeare did not love Anne Hathaway at this time, that he and she did not have many intimate conversations, and partic-ularly about the rearing of their children. He obviously relished domestic scenes like the one in sonnet 143 in which a mother chases a runaway chicken while her baffled infant is trying to keep up with her. And he was clearly bewitched by his twins, a fascination incom-parably articulated in two of the greatest 'twin' plays ever written, *The Comedy of Errors* and *Twelfth Night*, the latter featuring boy–girl twins just like his own. For Will Shakespeare in the early 1580s, life in Henley Street may have been happier than has sometimes been assumed.

Just as well perhaps, because out in the world things were very bad, and 'the world' was not far away from Henley Street. Within a few months of Susanna's christening in May 1583 something happened, the effect of which was felt in some form or other by everyone locally: Edward Arden of Park Hall, head of the grand and ancient Catholic family of Arden was arrested. Many in Stratford must have been shocked when this venerable family was hauled down to London, indicted and destroyed on what were then, and are now, thought to have been trumped-up charges. Their fate must have brought home to the Shakespeares and others just how dangerous a place their country really was. Sir Thomas Lucy from Charlecote, of a rival, and ardently Protestant Warwickshire family and next to the Earl of Warwick one of the most powerful men in the region, was also involved. In brief, the fall of the house of Arden was triggered when Arden's son-in-law John Somervile was heard to boast in an inn near Banbury that he was heading down to London to kill the Queen. Only a seriously unbal-anced man would have voiced such a threat in a public place. He was arrested and put to the torture. In theory, torture was illegal under English law; in practice, as most people were well aware, it was a favoured device of those concerned with the security of the realm, though its use was denied and these denials went unchallenged in the courts. When the Jesuit poet Robert Southwell protested at his trial in

1595 that he had been tortured ten times, the Queen's tormenter-in-chief, Richard Topcliffe, interjected: 'If he were racked, let me die for it.' Southwell replied, 'No, but it was as evil a torture, of late device.' Topcliffe's scoffing retort was: 'I did but set him against a wall', a cynical euphemism for a torture that is described in detail by John Gerard who suffered and survived it.

Somervile implicated the Ardens, and the Queen's inquisitors arrived in Warwickshire shortly afterwards, setting up their headquarters with the Lucys of Charlecote. Relations between the Ardens and Lucys had long been strained, and the time for settling old scores had come: it was Sir Thomas Lucy who arranged for the Ardens to be escorted under armed guard to London. Lucy had been a Justice of the Peace since 1559, and Shakespeare's father John would have met him during his tours of duty as chamberlain and mayor in the 1560s. He was repeatedly entertained at the corporation's expense at the Bear and Swan inns. The grim story of Somervile and the Ardens left its mark indelibly on Warwickshire. While it may be wrong to judge the sixteenth-century judicial system from our modern perspective, or to underestimate the danger that the nation felt itself to be in from foreign Catholic powers at the time, it is impossible to ignore the extent to which the state wielded its power ruthlessly.

Everyone in Stratford knew about the nemesis visited on the Ardens. In his *Antiquities of Warwickshire* (1656), the country's first-ever historian, Sir William Dugdale, recorded the fact that people locally blamed the Earl of Leicester, brother of the Earl of Warwick, son of a traitor and darling of the Queen. Arden had publicly insulted Leicester, who never forgave him, while he bided his time in his neighbouring fee of Kenilworth and Warwick. The Lucys of Charlecote eagerly toed the Leicester line on religion. It must have earned them considerable hatred among the recusant community and from like-minded people in the county. Be that as it may, they were big and powerful by the standards of the ordinary people of the borough. Even so someone would dare to cross them before the end of the decade. That person was William Shakespeare.

How and why he found himself doing battle with powerful members of the local gentry remains so shrouded in mystery that alternative theories to account for the elusive so-called 'lost years' between 1585 and the first appearance of Shakespeare's name in London in 1592 have been put forward. There is an argument that Shakespeare returned to his family's alleged Catholic roots, following John Cottom to Lancashire to join the household of Sir Thomas Hesketh at Houghton Towers under the name of Shakeshaft. A carefully documented literature has grown up around this hypothesis of Shakespeare, resolutely Catholic, escaping to Houghton Towers, but to argue that he followed in the footsteps of his contemporaries Debdale and Cawdrey, for example, albeit in a less radical fashion, poses many questions and involves a series of assumptions about the Shakespeare family's allegiances.

Archdeacon Richard Davies of Gloucestershire noted late in the seventeenth century that Shakespeare 'died a papist'. This is not impossible – if John Gerard is to be believed, some of the very persecutors of the Catholics died in the old faith of their forefathers. Yet after all there is no hard evidence to connect Shakespeare to Lancashire, and of course there were Catholics aplenty on his very doorstep: his neighbours next door in Henley Street, the Badgers, were Catholic, as were the Whateleys, Cawdreys, Cloptons, Greenways, Ainges, Reeves, and others. Any one of them, no doubt, could have accomplished the spiriting away of an eager and intelligent young man. The fact remains that the so-called 'lost years' between 1585 and 1592 have assumed a mystique of their own, perhaps largely because it seems inconceivable that a man whose brilliance was so soon to be revealed should have left no more trace of his existence during this time than a casual reference in the context of a land dispute between his parents and Edmund Lambert.

5

Poaching from the Lucys: 1587

AN EXPLANATION FOR Shakespeare's disappearance from view after the birth of his twins in 1585 was given in 1709 by Nicholas Rowe:

> In this kind of settlement [that is, his marriage] he continued for some time, till an extravagance that he was guilty of, forced him both out of his country and that way of living which he had taken up; and though it seemed at first to be a blemish upon his good manners, and a misfortune to him, yet it afterwards happily proved the occasion of exerting one of the greatest geniuses that ever was known in dramatic poetry . . . He had, by a misfortune common enough to young fellows, fallen into ill company, and, among them, some, that made a frequent practice of deer-stealing, engaged him with them more than once in robbing a park that belonged to Sir Thomas Lucy of Charlecote near Stratford. For this he was prosecuted by that gentleman, as he thought, somewhat too severely; and, in order to revenge that ill usage, he made a ballad upon him. And though this, probably the first essay of his poetry, be lost, yet it is said to have been so very bitter that it redoubled the prosecution against him to that degree that he was obliged to leave his business and family in Warwickshire, for some time, and shelter himself in London.

Though its credibility has been repeatedly impugned, this is the only account with roots reaching back into the seventeenth century to offer any explanation for Shakespeare's abandonment of his wife and family. At the very least it has the authority of a written source with links as far back as Shakespeare's lifetime, and unless there is reason to think that Rowe, and with him Betterton and, possibly, Davenant, aimed to mislead posterity, there is no good reason to distrust Rowe. The poaching story, moreover, can be cross-referenced to other late seventeenth-century accounts which Rowe could not possibly have been aware of, accounts that bear independent corroborative witness to this same story.

There is no reason why someone as scrupulous and intelligent as Rowe should seek to perpetuate a fiction, one that is moreover damaging to the moral character of his subject. Rowe had no interest in making up a scabrous piece of gossip. It is worth remembering that the greatest Shakespeare scholar and antiquarian of the nineteenth century, James Orchard Halliwell-Phillipps, and Sidney Lee, the author a classic essay on Shakespeare in the original *DNB* (1897), both admired and trusted Rowe. Writing in 1887 Halliwell-Phillipps stressed 'Rowe's general accuracy' and the fact that, a few minor errors notwithstanding, his biographical sketch was drawn up 'mainly from reliable sources . . . every word of his essay deserving of respectful attention'.[1]

Of course information gets mangled in transmission, and one fact commonly cited against Rowe is that Charlecote did not possess a deer park in Shakespeare's time. That may be so, but this first great Elizabethan mansion in Warwickshire, built in the year of the Queen's coronation, surely sat in woodlands rich in chestnuts, elms, oaks, and sycamores. There was certainly a warren, with plenty of game in it for hunting, including hare, pheasants, and roe deer – the roes of Charlecote may have been in Shakespeare's mind when he wrote 'fleeter than the roe' in *The Taming of the Shrew*, and referred to 'the fleet-foot roe' in *Venus and Adonis*. Even if it were the case that *only* roe deer roamed at Charlecote, it is not entirely clear why this should matter so much. Other nearby landowners, including the Grevilles of Alcester, owned fallow dear, and Shakespeare refers to different kinds of deer in his plays. As a game reserve, the Lucys' warren was patrolled by several gamekeepers; they were there for a purpose, and perhaps one of them arrested the young Shakespeare. In *Titus Andronicus* one of the characters asks 'What, hast not thou full often struck a doe, / And borne her cleanly by the keeper's nose?' Perhaps Will Shakespeare tried it once too often.

Like many a country-bred youth before and since, it is likely that Shakespeare learned his hunting skills quite legally, beating up game for legitimate hunters. But, according to Rowe, he teamed up with others who 'made a frequent practice of deer-stealing' and with them robbed 'a park that belonged to Sir Thomas Lucy of Charlecote near Stratford' – a reference that serves to locate Lucy's residence for the benefit of a London audience, but does not incontrovertibly place Shakespeare's poaching in the park at Charlecote. Nevertheless, even if the park at Charlecote was a rabbit warren rather than a deer park, on purely logistical grounds the odds are that if Shakespeare poached from the Lucys it would have been at Charlecote, simply because the grounds lie fairly close to Stratford – but only 'fairly'. Anyone wanting to convey a poached deer from Charlecote to Stratford would have found it an arduous task. It might be taken by water, for the Avon skirts the western edge of the park on its way down to Clopton bridge. The alternative would be to transport the illegal cargo by cart or on horseback towards Ingon and from there to Stratford. The Warwick road into Stratford would have been too exposed for poachers to use and they would have had to cut through the Welcombe hills, carrying their booty on horseback. That this was the most practical way of doing it seems clear from an entry in the Chamberlain's Accounts of January 1595 which notes that for 'Master Greville's buck', eaten at the swearing-in of the new bailiff and town council of 4 October 1594, the council incurred a 'keeper's fee and horse hire', suggesting that the buck was brought by Greville's keeper 'on the back of a horse'.[2] The total outlay for the gift came to 30s. 6d., which gives some idea of the sums the Lucys might have lost from poaching.

In the hunt in *3 Henry VI* Shakespeare may have been recalling his nights as a poacher:

> Under this thick-grown brake we'll shroud ourselves,
> For through this laund anon the deer will come,
> And in this covert will we make our stand,
> Culling the principal of all the deer.

The use of the word 'laund' meaning 'glade' occurs in only one other place in Shakespeare's works, in *Venus and Adonis* ('and homeward through the dark laund runs apace'), published in 1593. Its presence there is significant because the poem was carefully proof-read before publication probably by Shakespeare himself, suggesting that the usage is therefore undoubtedly his.

Deer skins were used in gloving, and it is not impossible, given John Shakespeare's economic misfortunes, that young Will was looking for some free food and a useful hide. In the late sixteenth century poaching was a relatively light offence, punishable only by a fine. In the 1580s Lucy agitated in Parliament for tougher laws against poachers, a fact perhaps connected to a rash of nocturnal raids on his game: it is hard to think why else he should have been so exercised over this issue at just this time. According to Rowe, Shakespeare was caught by Lucy's men and punished – in his own estimation – rather 'too severely'. Perhaps Lucy, the chief local Justice of the Peace, acted as prosecutor, judge, and jury in this case.

It looks as though the glover Will Shakespeare was always, first and foremost, a writer. According to Rowe, he retaliated against the Lucys by writing a ballad – so Bottom hoped Peter Quince might write about his night with the fairy queen, the difference being, according to Rowe, that the Lucy 'ballad' was a scurrilous satire. It appears to survive in two quite different versions, which successive commentators have tried to discredit without producing any hard evidence against their authenticity. The ballads were recorded in the eighteenth century, giving rise to the suspicion that they are forgeries by local people increasingly conscious of the value of Shakespeare as a marketable commodity and seizing the opportunity afforded by Rowe's reference to the ballad as 'lost'. One version is said to have come to light in the late 1680s when Joshua Barnes, professor of Greek at Cambridge, presented his hostess at a Stratford inn with the gift of a gown in exchange for the following two stanzas:

> Sir Thomas was too covetous
>   To covet so much deer,
> When horns enough upon his head
>   Most plainly did appear.
>
> Had not his worship one deer left?
>   What then? He had a wife
> Took pains enough to find his horns
>   Should last him during life.

The phrase 'covetous' occurs frequently in Shakespeare, and the reference here is particularly to Sir Thomas's surplus of deer and horns, notably those cuckold's horns bequeathed to him by his dear/deer/doe, his wife. Edmond Malone, who recorded this mini-ballad in the eighteenth century, warned that the source from which it was taken was 'full of forgeries and falsehoods of various kinds'. Yet whoever wrote it knew about Lucy's marital problems in the 1580s, and Shakespeare's plays are full of 'horn' jokes.

The other ballad can be directly connected with passages in one of Shakespeare's plays. The text is preserved by one of Shakespeare's first great editors, Edward Capell (1713–81), who remarked that this ballad, or rather this single extant stanza from a larger whole, 'has the appearance of genuine'. Its pedigree is traced back through a Thomas Wilkes, grandfather of the person who gave the ballad to Capell, to one Master Thomas Jones of the village of Tardebigge near Stratford-upon-Avon. This Jones, who died in the year 1703,

> aged upwards of ninety, remembered to have heard from several old people at Stratford the story of Shakespeare's robbing Sir Thomas Lucy's park; and their account of it agreed with Master Rowe's, with this addition – that the ballad written against Sir Thomas by Shakespeare was stuck upon his park gate, which exasperated the knight to apply to a lawyer at Warwick to proceed against him. Master Jones had put down in writing the first stanza of this ballad, which was all he remembered of it, and Master Thomas Wilkes (my grandfather) transmitted it to my father by memory, who also took it in writing, and his copy is this:
>
> > A parliament member, a justice of peace,
> > At home a poor scare-crow, at London an ass,
> > If lousy is Lucy, as some volke miscall it,
> > Then Lucy is lousy whatever befall it:
> > > He thinks himself great,
> > > Yet an ass in his state,
> > We allow by his ears but with asses to mate.
> > > If Lucy is lousy, as some volke miscall it,
> > > Sing lousy Lucy, whatever befall it.[3]

Jones was a familiar Welsh surname in Stratford, and while there is no provable connection between the Jones who preserved the ballad and the Davy Jones of the Whitsun revels, it cannot be ruled out.

Davy Jones was married to a Quiney so would have known the Shakespeares' business rather well, as these two families were evidently close. There were Joneses at Stratford who married Hathaways in Shakespeare's lifetime, and according to Thomas Jones his sources were the old people of Stratford-upon-Avon. Lest his readers miss the pun in 'lousy/Lucy', Capell helpfully explains that people in Warwickshire pronounce 'lousy' like 'Lucy'. He then adds, intriguingly, that the same Jones who handed down the ballad is also the source for the story connecting Shakespeare to the part of Old Adam in *As You Like It*, so it may be that Thomas Jones was at some point a neighbour, in Stratford or somewhere else, of one of Shakespeare's relatives who once saw him act. No deceased Thomas Jones is to be found in the relevant Tardebigge parish registers, which may suggest that he lived, and indeed died, elsewhere – Stratford, perhaps, though there is no record of a Thomas Jones for the right period, either. If this Master Jones could be identified as having belonged to the wider Quiney-Jones family, he would be a significant witness to the Shakespeare story. It may or may not be a coincidence that Mary Hart, born in 1641 and the granddaughter of Shakespeare's nephew Thomas Hart from Henley Street, lived in Tardebigge at the same time as Master Thomas Jones.

The ballad is without doubt an insulting swipe, the more so if there were any way of knowing that Sir Thomas Lucy had large, sticking-out ears; but probably the ears are there above all to underpin the ass metaphor. Either way this is an offensive piece of writing, and to call Lucy a louse-ridden ass reckless. If Shakespeare did pen it, he must have known that serious consequences were likely if it were traced back to him. Through his father Will Shakespeare would have known about the long arm of the Lucys and their accommodation with Protestant power. No lesser person than the Queen had spent two nights at Charlecote in Shakespeare's lifetime. It was hardly the place of a yeoman glover to lampoon a Lucy. If Shakespeare took on the Lucys because they had helped destroy the Ardens, or because their gamekeepers had caught him and given him a good hiding, he took a tremendous chance. It is sometimes alleged that, unlike many of his fellow dramatists, Shakespeare never fell foul of the Establishment. Perhaps he had learnt a bitter lesson in his youth.

A clue to Shakespeare's authorship of the ballad may lie in its use of 'volke' for 'folk', which occurs in *King Lear* when Gloucester and Edgar are challenged by Oswald: Edgar is disguised as a poor peasant, and his language sounds rural and uncouth. In the quarto of 1608, behind which lies Shakespeare's own manuscript so that the phonetics are definitely his, is his version of rural speech:

> EDGAR: Good gentleman, go your gate. Let poor *volk* pass. An 'chud have been swaggered out of my life, it would not have been so long by a *vortnight*. Nay, come not near the old man. Keep out, 'che vor' ye, or I'll try whether your costard or my baton be the harder; I'll be plain with you.

As in the ballad, voiced fricatives are substituted for unvoiced in the two words in italic. And if indeed 'some volke miscall' 'lousy' and 'Lucy', the convenient confusion of the two in some people's pronunciation offered an obvious opening opportunity. If the ballad is genuine, it was written by an angry and fearless young man, who even in his anger played with words.

One of the most intriguing corroborators of the poaching story is Richard Davies, he who alleged that Shakespeare died a Catholic. He was the chaplain of Corpus Christi College in the 1670s, and also linked the poaching story to *Merry Wives of Windsor*. Davies's remarks are interleaved with some bland notes by William Fulman, a scholar at Corpus Christi, whose papers he somehow inherited, including Fulman's correspondence with Anthony Wood, who in turn knew John Aubrey and the Davenants. Wood and Davies also knew each other, Wood referring to Davies's 'red and jolly' complexion, of the kind induced, as he noted, by fish dinners at Corpus Christi. Fulman had merely jotted down the year and place of Shakespeare's birth, but Davies added to these that Shakespeare was

> much given to all unluckiness in stealing venison and rabbits particularly from Sr —— Lucy who had him oft whipped and sometimes imprisoned and at last made him fly his native country to his great advancement. But his revenge was so great that he is his Justice Clodpate and calls him a great man and that in allusion to his name bore three louses rampant for his arms.

This is the first ever written reference to Shakespeare's alleged poaching. Clearly Justice Clodpate is, if not a mistake, a joking reference to Justice Shallow, and just as clearly Davies corroborates Rowe as well as spotting, as Rowe did, the possibility of a link between the poaching at Charlecote and *The Merry Wives of Windsor*.

Finally, a striking few lines in a late play by Shakespeare merit some consideration. The idiom of the play, *The Winter's Tale*, is rural, pastoral, and Warwickshire, and its world consists of sheep-shearing fairs, travelling pedlars, shepherdesses and maying queens. It was probably written in Stratford during the spring of 1611. In the third act of the play a full-blown storm is raging when there enters a shepherd, searching for two lost sheep by the seaside and in reflective mood:

> SHEPHERD: I would there were no age between ten and three-and-twenty, or that youth would sleep out the rest; for there is nothing in the between but getting wenches with child, wronging the ancientry, stealing, fighting – [*Horns*] Hark you now! Would any but these boiled-brains of nineteen and two-and-twenty hunt this weather?

Thus Shakespeare perhaps looking back on his own turbulent teens and early twenties. He was twenty-three when last heard of in Stratford, cited alongside his parents in a lawsuit of 1587 against Edmund Lambert over his mother Mary Arden's estate in her native village of Wilmcote. He certainly got a woman with child when he was barely eighteen, and it very much looks as though he is also admitting to having committed the other misdeeds, 'wronging the ancientry, stealing, fighting'. 'Ancientry' at the time could mean both one's elders and also nobility and stately traditions, as in 'full of state and ancientry' in *Much Ado about Nothing*, so Shakespeare seems to be recalling his youth as a time of impulsive sexual behaviour and the price he paid for it, of being disrespectful to his parents, and of wronging the Lucys.

The picture that has emerged of the young Will Shakespeare is of someone who may have been closer in temperament to the notoriously louche Christopher Marlowe than is commonly supposed, and in the mellow glow of *The Winter's Tale*, a play with its share of suffering which somehow manages to end on a note of peace and stasis, he seems to look back at his own early years with some regret. Sir Thomas Lucy had died in 1600, and in this play written more than a decade later, Shakespeare seems to be blaming the folly of youth for his actions of the 1580s. Perhaps part of him never quite forgot how fortunate he had been to come through after such tough beginnings, and recognized that if the Lucys did persecute him unjustly, they also unwittingly launched him on a brilliant career in London. The join between the play and Shakespeare's memory of his own past life is very intimate. Reflecting, the shepherd hears the sound of hunting youths ('boiled-brains of nineteen and two-and-twenty') off-stage, and just then finds little Perdita (she grows up in his household, but is revealed to be a princess, and reconciles the warring houses of Sicily and Bohemia). This is the turning-point in the play, and the old shepherd tells his son, who saw Antigonus eaten by a bear, 'thou met'st with things dying, I with things new-born.' 'Perdita' means 'the lost one', but she it is who brings peace and plenitude to the feuding families in the play. Looking back in 1611 at the events of a quarter of a century earlier, perhaps Shakespeare saw the hunt at Charlecote as his own crossroads. He too had been lost but in retrospect he saw that his loss had turned into his greatest gain. It was fate indeed.

Until 1586 or 1587 Shakespeare seems to have managed to stay out of trouble. He had the responsibility of three small children, and was perhaps also the acting head of the family, for John Shakespeare's situation had become more precarious than ever: in September 1586 he finally lost his seat on the council, because 'he doth not come to the halls when . . . warned nor hath not done of long time.'[4] Perhaps this left the family even more exposed to debt collectors. But sometime in 1587 Shakespeare seems to have slipped up. Rowe characterized Shakespeare's companions as habitual deer poachers, and said that he fell in with them 'more than once'; perhaps they plotted their felonious expeditions in one of the great local inns, just as Falstaff and his crew do the Gadshill robbery in the opening scenes of *1 Henry IV*. If the riotous behaviour of London apprentices at the time is anything to go by, then Stratford will also have had its share of aggressive and restless young men. Though knives were everywhere, not just in butchers' shops, there were relatively few violent crimes in the Stratford of the time – but there were brawls, and one later cost Shakespeare's friend Richard Quiney his life, while another ended with a butcher stabbing the owner of the Swan to death.

Elizabethan Stratford boasted a small prison, a few doors south of the mediaeval 'Cage', on the corner of High and Bridge Street, which had become a private house and business premises. The borough's accounts from time to time note expenses incurred in running the 'jail', but there are no references to anyone actually being kept prisoner there – except, it seems, Shakespeare's uncle Harry. It was a similar story with other elements of penal correction, like the stocks and the ducking-stool. The stocks were outside the home of Shakespeare's friend Hamlet Sadler, at the corner of High and Sheep Streets. As a little boy at school in Church Street Shakespeare must have walked past the stocks at least four times a day during the week, so they were part of the furniture of his mental landscape, one perhaps hard to visualize today. It might seem probable that he and his friends should have been stocked for their activities at Charlecote, and it is tempting to see in the conversation between Kent in the stocks and the Fool in *King Lear* the re-enactment of a painful real-life memory, but the corporation is remarkably silent about their use, while referring freely to their upkeep; and the same is true of the cucking-stool, known locally as the 'gumstool', the seat into which scolds were strapped before being ducked in water. The town fathers showed due care for its good function, yet nowhere in the extensive borough documentation is there any reference to its actual use. Anna (also Agnes) Spurton was a prime candidate for the gumstool, declared by the borough court 'a common scold and an unquiet woman'; so was Elizabeth Wheeler, who appeared before the so-called Stratford Bawdy Court 'for continually brawling and abusing and not attending church'. On one occasion she notoriously railed against the court with the words 'God's wounds, a plague a God on you all, a fart of one's arse for you', for which she was excommunicated – a more severe punishment than ducking in the Avon or the Mere Pool, the bracken pond at Rother Market.

Most infringements of the law were small local affairs, almost invariably to do with the borough bye-laws. Offences such as fly-tipping were duly noted down, and survive in the corporation records, but there is nowhere a reference to Shakespeare and the Lucys – which is not to rule out the possibility that something may yet come to light. What is baffling is the recklessness of the young Shakespeare in seemingly compounding his theft with provocative ballads. In the late 1580s Shakespeare's life must have seemed to him to be unravelling as the Lucys rendered his existence in Stratford unbearable.

He also had a long memory. Shakespeare never quite forgave the Lucys and ten years after the events in Charlecote he would once more return to this fray, again through the written word and in the wake of his second major clash with the authorities. If life in the early and mid 1580s had been hard for the two households in Henley Street, it would become much tougher still now that the eldest son, presumably the main breadwinner of the house, had become a felon. His anger and frustration we can only imagine. As a mere yeoman he could not possibly hope to win against the Lucys, but he tried anyway. He showed courage and daring and a kind of wisdom in directing his attack at Lucy's private life rather than his politics, but he also let down his family badly, and not for the first time. There had clearly been problems over his marriage to Anne Hathaway and now to have inflicted this on his family when their fortunes were already at a low ebb showed scant regard for them. If he turned poacher to put food on the table in Henley Street that is one thing, but if it was sheer lawless camaraderie that is a different matter altogether.

Fortunately the Shakespeare family seems never quite to have hit rock bottom: they did not sell the house in Henley Street, nor the barn or garden at the back. So if Will went poaching it was probably because he enjoyed hunting and the challenge, because he and his friends felt as little bound by the law as Falstaff and his cronies in the *Henry IV* plays. Like them, he seems to have been a man who was earnest, far-sighted, even puritanical, yet simultaneously a reveller and adventurer, Hal and Falstaff in one. If he was indeed caught poaching at Charlecote, the ballads would not do, even for a joke.

6

Bound for London: 1587

A ND SO, IN around 1587, at the age of twenty-three, William Shakespeare embarked on the journey to London, perhaps to escape the threat of prison and persecution. There was no better place to seek refuge. It was becoming one of the biggest and fastest-growing cities in Europe, and the population had swollen to 170,000. Of course there were Stratfordians there, but schoolfriends like Richard Field were not likely to shop him to the Lucys. The Lucys' writ did not run in London. It must have been heart-breaking to leave behind his parents, his siblings, his wife, and particularly his children, Susanna barely five and the twins only two years old – and to part, too, from everything he had known up to that day, the childhood memories of those early years in the golden Stratford of the broad streets and the thousand elms, as Homer might have put it. If it was all his fault, he presumably felt very guilty, and must fervently have hoped that the future would bring salvation. Now he must rely on his father to look after his and Anne's children as well, but at least Gilbert was now twenty-one and doubtless could be trusted to do his bit and to call on the other grown-up children for assistance. If William had not valued his family before, he must have done so now. He never invested in London property during the twenty years that he worked there, and it may be that the reason lay in the pain of leaving Stratford; perhaps he vowed to himself that if he were ever granted a second chance at home he would never leave again.

The moment came when William Shakespeare stepped out of the house in Henley Street, turned left and walked towards Back Bridge Street knowing that he would not return that evening or for many evenings to come. The young glover can have had no notion of his future as he made his way out of Stratford towards Clopton Bridge and then headed south towards Banbury or Oxford. As he turned the corner of Henley Street he must have wondered when he would again see the faces of those most dear to him. *The Two Gentlemen of Verona*, one of Shakespeare's earliest plays, dating from the early 1590s, perhaps captures a memory of this first parting. The speaker is Lance, and he is recalling how, when he left home, his entire household was moved to tears – except his dog Crab:

> LANCE: Nay, 'twill be this hour ere I have done weeping; all the kind of the Launces have this very fault. I have received my proportion like the Prodigious Son, and am going with Sir Proteus to the Imperial's court. I think Crab my dog be the sourest-natured dog that lives: my mother weeping, my father wailing, my sister crying, our maid howling, our cat wringing her hands, and all our house in a great perplexity, yet did not this cruel-hearted cur shed one tear. He is a stone, a very pebble stone, and has no more pity in him than a dog. A Jew would have wept to have seen our parting; why, my grandam, having no eyes, look you, wept herself blind at my parting. Nay, I'll show you the manner of it: this shoe is my father; no, this left shoe is my father; no, no, this left shoe is my mother; nay, that cannot be so neither; yes, it is so, it is so, it hath the worser sole. This shoe with the hole in it is my mother, and this my father – a vengeance on't! There 'tis. Now, sir, this staff is my sister, for, look you, she is as white as a lily and as small as a wand. This hat is Nan, our maid. I am the dog, no, the dog is himself, and I am the dog – O, the dog is me and I am myself; ay, so, so. Now come I to my father: 'Father, your blessing.' Now should not the shoe speak a word for weeping; now should I kiss my father; well, he weeps on. Now come I to my mother. O that she could speak now like a wood woman! Well, I kiss her; why, there 'tis; here's my mother's breath up and down. Now come I to my sister; mark the moan she makes. Now the dog all this while sheds not a tear, nor speaks a word; but see how I lay the dust with my tears.

By the time he wrote this Shakespeare had been back and forth between London and Stratford repeatedly. The darkest night of his early life was over, and he had a sense that success was heading his way. Thus was he able to turn a scene of sorrow and parting to one of impeccable comedy.

Lance's reverie is peopled with suggestive figures: a mother and father, a blind grandmother, one willowy sister, and a maid called Nan, though no brothers are mentioned, nor any children. But there were pets, a cat and a Crab. Animals as pets, pure and simple, were probably a luxury, yet most households of the period probably had at least one cat, to keep down mice and rats. Dogs too were usually working animals, ratters, again, or guardians of a farmer's flocks against foxes and ferrets rather than thieves, though a man might have a favourite dog.

Did Shakespeare, on that long journey south, have it in mind even then to join a theatrical company? The year of his departure, 1587, had been a vintage year for drama in Stratford, with no fewer than five troupes performing in the ground floor of his old school, including the Queen's, Sussex's, Essex's, and Leicester's Men. It is hard to believe that what he saw of them should not have awoken his own gift for rhetoric and theatre supposing that it still lay dormant.

Around the time that Shakespeare left Stratford and disappeared from the records for five years, something happened in the village of Thame that has a possible bearing on the turn his future would take. In a close called the White Hound on the evening of 13 June 1587 a brawl developed between two actors from the touring Queen's Men theatrical company and in the ensuing fight John Town killed William Knell. The Queen's Men was then the première company in the land, with Richard Tarlton as its star until his death the next year, founded in 1583 as a propaganda tool by Sir Francis Walsingham, Secretary of the Privy Council and the Queen's spymaster-general, along with the Earl of Leicester.

Actors were always fighting, of course, but two aspects of this particular altercation may have been significant for Shakespeare. Most obviously, there was now a vacancy in this company, and it has been suggested that it provided Shakespeare with his first opening in the theatre. Certainly Shakespeare, if he was still in Stratford at this point, would have known of Knell's death almost at once because the company, now one man short, proceeded from Thame to play in Stratford. On the other hand, it seems most unlikely that an unknown young glover should have been taken on to replace Knell, not least because the Queen's Men were soon joined by the actor John Symons, probably hired in Knell's stead. This is not to say, of course, that Shakespeare did not fall into conversation with the players, and decide at once that this was what he really longed to do.

The second connection with Shakespeare is more plausible even in its uncertainties, and founded in fact. Nine months after Knell's death his sixteen-year-old widow Rebecca married one John Heminges, from Droitwich in Worcestershire – at the time an actor in the Queen's Company and the same Heminges who later led, with Henry Condell, the syndicate responsible for producing the First Folio of Shakespeare's works. Heminges and Rebecca Knell produced fourteen children after their marriage in 1588 and were apparently devoted to each other until her death in 1619. It would be nice to know how Heminges came to join the Queen's Men, and whether or not he encountered Shakespeare in Stratford. Droitwich is less than twenty miles from Stratford and Heminges is a Stratford name – the beadle of the town in 1601 was another John Heminges – so that links between the actor John Heminges and the Heminges of Stratford, Shottery, Snitterfield, and indeed Temple Grafton, where Anne Hathaway probably lived at the time of her marriage, cannot be ruled out. It seems very likely that the Shakespeares knew families called Heminges, but there is no way of knowing whether they were related to the player from Droitwich. Even if they were, Heminges had lived and worked in London since 1578, and was made free of the Grocers' Company in April 1587, so it is more likely that he and Shakespeare met in the capital in the late 1580s. Presumably the theatre was in his blood, as it was in Shakespeare's. Heminges and Shakespeare became partners when the Lord Chamberlain's Men was created in 1594, but they probably knew each other well before then, perhaps after Shakespeare started to make a name for himself as a playwright.

The journey from Stratford to London on which Shakespeare now embarked involved a well-trodden road which ran from Stratford to Banbury through Pillerton Priors, Edgehill, and Drayton on what is now the A422. From Banbury the road took the traveller into west London by way of Aylesbury, Amersham, and Uxbridge; and from here through Hayes and Hanwell to Shepherd's Bush, Paddington and Tyburn (Marble Arch); then down Tyburn Road (today's Oxford Street), and hence into the walled City of London proper. This seems to have been the preferred route at the time, but another route, slightly longer, ran from Stratford to Oxford and then bore down on London through Wycombe or High Wycombe and Beaconsfield to

Uxbridge. Private or privately rented carriages travelled the roads and tracks that linked the Midlands to London, but there was as yet no regular coach service: people travelled on foot or, if they could afford it, rode. The hundred-odd miles from Stratford to London was a less daunting walk at a time when people as a rule walked far more. Even Ben Jonson, forty-six years old with a huge gut, did not balk at the prospect of walking from London all the way up to Scotland and back on a visit to his friend Drummond of Hawthornden.

Will Shakespeare, probably on foot, would have carried with him money for staying at various inns on the road, a pouch with water, and perhaps a memento or two of those he left behind. The roads were busy in those days, and reasonably safe. Later, in his more prosperous days, Shakespeare would travel on horseback and stay in the kind of inn recorded by William Harrison in his section on 'Our Inns and Thoroughfares' in Raphael Holinshed's *Chronicles* (1587), Shakespeare's main source for the history plays. Harrison noted proudly that English inns were 'very well furnished with napery, bedding, and tapestry', that the table linen was 'commonly washed daily', and that each lodger lay in 'clean sheets, wherein no man hath been lodged since they came from the laundress or out of the water wherein they were last washed.' A guest received a key to his room, and 'if his chamber be once appointed he may carry the key with him, as of his own house, so long as he lodgeth there.' Travellers arriving on horseback paid not for their rooms, but for their horse or horses' livery, but those on foot were charged one penny for a bed. Harrison's inns were of considerable size, able to lodge 'two hundred or three hundred persons and their horses at ease'.[1] What with their grooming and stabling, the horses needed at least as much space as the human residents.

On that first trip young Will's roadside accommodation must have been rather different, much more like that 'enjoyed' by the two carriers in *1 Henry IV.* There are no clean sheets for the men, who even when they are already running late are up long before dawn. It is dark and they need lanterns to see. Their first concern is for the horses, which suffer from poor riding and shoddy saddling as well as the 'bots', an intestinal worm passed on in dank provender. The 'house', they claim, is not what it used to be, and if proof were needed they have been badly bitten by fleas. They were not even given 'jordans' or chamber-pots, and had therefore to relieve themselves into the fireplace which, they ruefully concede, only further lowers the standards of the hostelry. The fleapit comically portrayed here is a far cry from some of the sophisticated London hostelries which flanked Bishopsgate, Aldersgate, and particularly Borough High Street, or 'Long Southwark' as it was known at the time – or from the Bear and the Swan in Stratford, for that matter. The Swan is known to have boasted impressive quantities of linen along with a wide assortment of drinks, as well as outside privies and an ample supply of chamber-pots for its patrons' comfort.

In the same scene in *1 Henry IV* a rascal called Gadshill appears and asks Tom, the second carrier, when he means to be in London. Tom, who is heading from Rochester to Charing Cross, replies, 'Time enough to go to bed with a candle.' The meaning of this quip is not entirely clear, but it seems to suggest that Tom intends to be in London if not by nightfall, at least before the night is over, so that he can have a well-deserved rest. From this it appears that the distance from Rochester to central London, at least thirty-five miles as the crow flies and therefore considerably more on the road, could be covered in a long day's trek with a reasonably fit horse.

As it happens it is possible to form a fairly accurate idea of the journey from Stratford to London and back in the late sixteenth century because in 1590 a delegation from Stratford descended on the capital. Since they were there on corporation business an itemized record of their expenses or 'bill of charge' was kept so that these could be reclaimed from the borough. Among the delegates were the Stratford town steward Master John Jeffereyes and 'Barber of the Bear', a man of substance and an ally, probably, of the Shakespeares. At the time of this London visit Barber was Alderman of the Chamber and its treasurer, hence his inclusion.

Setting out on 15 May 1590 on their journey south to present a petition to the Privy Council and particularly Cecil, Lord Burghley, Barber and Jeffcreyes spent the first night in Oxford, where they laid out three shillings on their supper and 'horse-meate'. Their lodging is not itemized separately, presumably because it was included in the feed for the horses. The following day they proceeded to Wycombe where they lunched and fed their horses before pushing on to Uxbridge. Here they spent Saturday night and 22 pence on their own supper, and the same on provender. Lodging was again included in the three and a half shillings fee, rather more than they had paid in Oxford. Then as now, it seems, the closer one drew to the capital, the higher one's bill. The next day, Sunday 17 May, they were in London for both lunch and dinner, at a cost of only two shillings. They had probably left their horses somewhere in the Elizabethan equivalent of a hire-car dropping-off point. The total cost for keeping their horses in London over a fortnight came to a princely thirteen shillings and eight pence. Although we cannot be sure where they stayed, the Bell in Carter Lane south of St Paul's is a safe guess, since it was the preferred inn of Stratfordians.

Among the expenses reclaimed by the two councillors was the hire of a boat to Greenwich, where the court was in residence, and impressive honorariums of twenty shillings and five shillings respectively for the services of one Master Cowper. Barber and Jeffereyes did something else, too. One entry in their bill of charge reads 'Friday for Master Greene's dinner [lunch] and ours xxd supper iis.' Lunch (on this occasion at least) was cheap, and dinner or supper expensive. The possible significance of Greene is that he may be a relative of Shakespeare's cousin, Thomas Greene, who would eventually turn up in Shakespeare's grand home in Stratford. Did Barber and Jeffereyes call on this Master Greene for legal advice before meeting counsel and Cowper the following day; or was Greene the QC they had visited earlier? Thomas Greene, Sr, the father of Shakespeare's cousins Thomas and John, had been buried at Stratford only two months before this meeting, on 6 March 1590. He was called Thomas Greene *alias* Shakespeare, which may suggest that he was the brother of Master John Greene of Warwick and that these Greenes and John Shakespeare were kinsmen.[2] Certainly the younger Thomas Greene called the playwright 'my cousin Shakespeare'. He would one day become town clerk of Stratford and his brother John acted for Susanna Shakespeare over the Blackfriars gatehouse that her father had purchased earlier. This same John was training at Clement's Inn in the mid 1590s just when Shakespeare was living in London and writing a play featuring a lecherous old country Justice of the Peace named Shallow who loves to reminisce about his salacious past at Clement's Inn. Shakespeare reveals a considerable knowledge of the law which he may well have picked up from the two Greene boys. Clement's Inn (John Greene) and Middle Temple (Thomas Greene), inns of chancery and court respectively, are both places associated with Shakespeare, through 2 *Henry IV* and *Twelfth Night*.

We may never know for certain, but there is no real doubt about the closeness of the Greene family to Shakespeare, whatever the specific nature of their links. Taking a kinship between Shakespeare and the Greene family for granted, it is tempting to speculate that on this day of convivial hospitality the conversation might at some point have touched on the young glover whom at least two of those present knew well. Was he the ghost at the feast? By this time Shakespeare had been in London for more than two years; within a few short months of Barber and Jeffereyes' visit he was probably the acknowledged author of seventeen poems to one of the rising stars of the London aristocracy, and commanding the attention of just the kind of people whose help they were seeking to enlist.

The Stratford councillors stayed on until Saturday 30 May 1590, when they set out for home. They took a slightly different route back, bypassing Oxford and travelling by way of Uxbridge, Aylesbury, and Banbury. A few months later Jeffereyes was down in London again, his brief this time to petition the Privy Council and specifically Lord Burghley to allow the corporation to nominate their own vicar and schoolmaster, such nominations having been hitherto in the gift of the Earl of Warwick, albeit he usually nodded through the council's choices. Jeffereyes also sought permission 'for one fair and market more', to reflate the stagnant local economy. By the end of the first day, travelling by way of Banbury, Jeffereyes got as far as Stratton Audley, a hamlet well south of Banbury and near Bicester. The following morning he pushed on to Aylesbury where he lunched before making his way to lodgings in the small village of Chenies on the Amersham Road.

It is worth stopping, like Jeffereyes, at Stratton Audley. It is midway between Stratford and London, and not far from the ancient village called Grendon Underwood. Writing about Shakespeare in 1681, John Aubrey wrote that he began early to make essays at dramatic poetry, which at that time was very low, and his plays took well. He was a handsome, well-shaped man, very good company, and of a very ready and pleasant smooth wit. The humour of . . . the constable in *A Midsummer Night's Dream* he happened to take at Grendon in Bucks. which is the road from London to Stratford, and there was living that constable about 1642 when I first came to Oxon. Master Jos.[eph] Howe is of that parish and knew him. Ben Jonson and he [Shakespeare] did gather humours of men daily wherever they came.

In the margin to 'Grendon' Aubrey added, 'I think it was mid-summer night that he happened to lie there'. Aubrey has got it a little wrong, of course, as Dogberry is a character in *Much Ado about Nothing* and not in *A Midsummer Night's Dream*, but that is less signifi-cant than his claim that Shakespeare and Jonson based their characters on real people, and that the model for Dogberry was not only alive in 1642 but that one Master Howe had known him. The parish records reveal that a Master Howe did indeed live at Grendon in 1642: the Reverend Mr Thos [Thomas] Howe heads a list of village contribu-tors to the Irish campaign in 1642.[3] The collector received the sum of £4 3s. 6d. 'for Grendon Underwood by the hands of one Mr Howe the minister but whether the acquittance was given to him or the high constable I do not remember.'

Unfortunately, this Master Howe was a Thomas, while 'Jos'. for Joseph is the undoubted reading of Aubrey's manuscript; of the forty-three people on the list of contributors there are no fewer than fifteen Thomases, and not a single Joseph – Thomas seems to be one of the most common first names in Grendon, and a search of the Grendon parish records reveals not one Joseph Howe in the parish. There is, however, a Josias Howe, son of Thomas Howe, who was christened on 29 March 1612, and it is surely not past belief that in 1642 Aubrey should have met a minister called Thomas Howe, and in writing about him some forty years later misremembered his first name. If Aubrey had somehow got wind of a Shakespeare connection with the small village of Grendon, the logical thing would have been for him to consult the local minister. There is no 'Dogberry' to be found among the Ireland contributors, and this comic name would seem to be wholly Shakespeare's creation – except that in the Grendon records there is a name that might have inspired him: a William Soulberry is listed in 1642, perhaps the William, son of Humphrey Soulberry, who was christened on 7 December 1599. So there were Soulberrys living in Grendon in the late 1590s, and *Much Ado about Nothing* is commonly dated to 1598–9. Did a Soulberry of Grendon Underwood become Dogberry of Messina in the crucible of Shakespeare's imagination? There is no way of establishing who the constables of the parish were – still less whether they were given to egregious malapropisms – but there is enough to suggest that there might be more than a grain of truth lying behind Aubrey's account. Moreover, the words 'dog' and 'soul' may be more chosen than might at first appear. It was commonly rumoured at the time among the Catholics that one of the coteries frequented by Marlowe enjoyed word games which included spelling God's name backwards. To the Catholics this served to highlight the incompatibility of the language of revealed religion – the word of God – and that spoken by ordinary people in the street. If 'God' becomes 'dog', then 'soul' might too. Shakespeare was a master punner, and at a time when the language he handled with such wit and inventiveness was being played with for their own ends by people possessed of a fraction of his gifts, some such pun or allusion cannot be ruled out.

7

Early Days in Shoreditch: 1587–90

WHEN SHAKESPEARE FINALLY arrived in London, perhaps by way of Stratton Audley and Grendon, the obvious thing would have been to seek work as a glover; instead, as Rowe reports, he seems to have made more or less straight for the theatres. He will have seen the authoritarian and repressive face of the city long before any of its glories revealed themselves. As he strode up from Shepherd's Bush through what are now Holland Park Avenue, Notting Hill, and Bayswater Road the first landmark he will have glimpsed from afar was the towering triangular, cross-beamed gallows at Tyburn (the middle of today's Edgeware Road at Marble Arch, now commemorated by a memorial stone). The high gallows' triangularity is mentioned in *Love's Labour's Lost*, where Berowne refers to the three-cornered shape of those high gallows: 'Thou makest the triumviry, the corner-cap of society, / The shape of love's Tyburn that hangs up simplicity.'

The multiple gallows had been erected as recently as 1571, but the site had been the main place of execution in London since Chaucer's time, the late fourteenth century. If young Will was conscious of having fallen foul of the law at home in Stratford, the site of Tyburn possibly gave him pause for grim reflection. He had almost certainly never seen an execution for Stratford was clear of such horrors, though Warwick was not, and the English countryside was dotted with gibbets. The gibbet was a fact of life in Shakespeare's England that should not be ignored, because to do so is to short-change Shakespeare and his contemporaries. Only in appreciating the horror of the ultimate penalties exacted by the state in the name of policy or justice can the depth of conviction that led hundreds of young Catholic Englishmen to embrace an unimaginable death for the sake of their faith and their salvation as they saw it be equally appreciated.

In London, public executions took place in whichever part of the city seemed symbolically most fitting to the government. Thus, for example, on 20 September 1586 Anthony Babington and his fellow conspirators were executed in Holborn outside the church of St Giles-in-the-Fields, close to where they had plotted their alleged coup to supplant Queen Elizabeth with Mary Queen of Scots (near today's Centrepoint). Five years after Babington, the priest Edmond Gennings was quite literally slaughtered alive outside Gray's Inn Fields. His suffering horrified onlookers – except, it seems, the sadistic Richard Topcliffe, who relished such spectacles and preferred to enjoy them hovering on the scaffold. At Gennings's death the hangman carelessly flung one of his upper quarters into the basket, and an arm dangled over the edge. Catholic martyrologists say that when a recusant woman eagerly clutched the dead man's hand his fingers came off miraculously in her grip, leaving her in possession of a precious relic.

John Rigby died a similar death on the Old Kent Road in June 1600, found guilty of recusant recidivism. His fate haunted the Jesuit John Gerard who was responsible for Rigby's conversion. In his autobiography Gerard recalled that, as Rigby was dragged on a hurdle to the scaffold, he passed the Earl of Rutland. Seeing 'what a well-built and handsome man he was', Rutland exclaimed, 'You were made for a wife and children, not to die for your faith.' Rigby replied, 'As for a wife, I ask God to bear me out that never in my life have I had intercourse with a woman.'[1] Rigby's death is the stuff of nightmares:

> After he had been cut down by the hangman he stood upright on his feet like a man a little amazed, till the butchers threw him down. Then coming perfectly to himself he said aloud and distinctly, 'God forgive you. Jesus, receive my soul.' And immediately another cruel fellow standing by, who was no officer, but a common porter, set his foot upon Mr Rigby's throat, and so held him that he could speak no more. Others held his arms and legs while the executioner dismembered and bowelled him, and when he felt them pulling out his heart, he was yet so strong that he thrust the men from him who held his arms. At last they cut off his head and quartered him . . . The people going away complained very much of the barbarity of the execution; and generally all sorts bewailed his death.[2]

The facts of Elizabethan life cannot be sanitized. The same people who one day watched men being disembowelled for their religion might the next be found enjoying *As You Like It* or *Twelfth Night*, almost exactly contemporary with the death of John Rigby. The executions were intended to terrify and to deter, but while some – Ben Jonson, for example – were intimidated, almost all the Catholic priests and Jesuits remained steadfast when confronted with such deaths. Shakespeare displays a robust sense of humour about gallows in his plays; for him they were an everyday fact of life, as presumably they were for most of his contemporaries. Yet in his only major dramatic meditation on capital punishment, *Measure for Measure*, he pulls away from this moral brink at the last minute. In this play Shakespeare also recalls the penalty of pressing to death, passed on a prominent Catholic noblewoman a few years earlier. It seems that Shakespeare's humanity, his own private and imaginative morality, prevented him from exploiting to the full the cruelty of his times. The author of the greatest emotional roller-coaster in the English language, *King Lear*, apparently could not condone such acts inflicted by man upon fellow human beings. With regard to the taking of human life, sanctioned though it is by the Bible, Shakespeare refuses to be cowed by his time.

When he arrived in London, drama had recently burst into life, just as Sir Philip Sidney had predicted in his *A Defence of Poetry* (*c.*1582–3). According to Rowe, Shakespeare 'was received into the company then in being, at first in a very mean rank; but his admirable wit, and the natural turn of it to the stage, soon distinguished him, if not as an extraordinary actor, yet as an excellent writer.' It cannot now be known how the theatre and Shakespeare met, but when they did there must have been a *coup de foudre*, and that was that. Quite what Rowe means by 'a very mean rank' is not clear, although common sense suggests that Shakespeare must have begun as a proverbial dogsbody. A story reported by Samuel Johnson in the preface to his 1765 edition of Shakespeare's works may cast light on this; as the story is said to have originated with Rowe, Johnson appends it to his reprint of Rowe's *Life*:

> *To the foregoing accounts of Shakespeare's life I have only one passage to add, which Master Pope related, as communicated to him by Master Rowe.*

In the time of *Elizabeth*, coaches being yet uncommon, and hired coaches not at all in use, those who were too proud, too tender, or too idle to walk, went on horseback to any distant business or diversion. Many came on horse-back to the play, and when *Shakespeare* fled to *London* from the terror of a criminal prosecution, his first expedient was to wait at the door of the playhouse and hold the horses of those that had no servants that they might be ready again after the performance. In this office he became so conspicuous for his care and readiness that in a short time every man as he alighted called for *Will. Shakespeare*, and scarcely any other waiter was trusted with a horse while *Will. Shakespeare* could be had. This was the first dawn of better fortune. *Shakespeare* finding more horses put into his hand than he could hold hired boys under his inspection who when *Will. Shakespeare* was summoned were immediately to present themselves, *I am Shakespeare's boy, Sir.* In time *Shakespeare* found higher employment, but as long as the practice of riding to the play-house continued the waiters that held the horses retained the appellation of *Shakespeare's Boys.*

There is no reason for Pope to have fabricated this story, and it has the ring of authenticity, not least because it reveals a competitive and entrepreneurial Shakespeare, every inch his father's son. The record suggests that throughout his life he was always competitive, ever the astute businessman and investor. The reference to 'the practice of riding to the play-house' consolidates the credibility of the passage. It is not clear how familiar with the early history of the Elizabethan professional theatre Rowe, Pope, and Johnson were, but the fact is that riding to the theatre belongs to the days before the Rose and the Globe, when London's two play-houses were set in open fields in Shoreditch and Moorfields at some distance to the north of the city gates.

That Shakespeare fetched up in Shoreditch is confirmed by John Aubrey, who remarked that 'he was not a company keeper, lived in Shoreditch'. Here, in this north London 'liberty' – that is, a parish outside the jurisdiction of the City of London – stood the Theatre, built by the Burbage family. It opened its doors in 1576, and was followed the next year by another playhouse not far down the road, the Curtain, near the site of today's Hewett Street. These Burbages were in all likelihood a Kentish family, but Stratford too was familiar with the name, which was that of the mayor of the town in 1558. That Will Shakespeare knew, or knew of, the Burbages of Stratford cannot be doubted, since one of his father's most protracted lawsuits involved one William Burbage of the town.[3] In Shoreditch the Burbages lived inside the old inner cloister yard of what had been, before the Reformation, the priory of St John the Baptist, Holywell. In the 1580s the old priory was still surrounded by fields on all sides, green spaces across which large crowds of people trampled on most afternoons, before and after performances.

When Shakespeare first laid eyes on the Theatre it sat within an eight-acre square. Curtain Road and Shoreditch High Street marked its western and eastern borders while Bateman's Row and Holywell Lane hemmed it in from the north and south respectively. These streets survive today and under these same names, but additional ones have since been driven into the plot. The Theatre sat almost exactly north of New Inn Yard, which cuts through the middle of the square on an east–west axis. Since 1920 a plaque on numbers 86 and 88 Curtain Road has commemorated the building credited with helping to launch the most illustrious career in English drama. Not only was this playhouse the first professional English theatre, but a direct line of descent links it physically to both the first and second Globe theatres. The reign of the Theatre could therefore be said to stretch from 1576 to the closure of all London playing spaces by the Puritans in 1642. The Theatre did not quite verge on New Inn Yard, but a crumbling edifice known at the time as Great Barn did. This the Burbages had converted into tenements or flats, to generate additional income; Shakespeare may have lived there during the early years of his career.

The playing spaces were of course never entirely respectable, whether in Shoreditch or on Bankside. In Elizabethan London, theatres and brothels or 'stews' existed cheek-by-jowl. Nevertheless the area around Holywell and the two playhouses remained relatively uncontaminated by brothels and pimps, probably because many wealthy Londoners were investing in Finsbury and Moorfields around the time when the playhouses sprang into being. The entire area to the north and west of Bishopsgate and Bedlam, straddling the site of what is now Liverpool Street railway station, prospered from its development into a sort of garden suburb, with formal parklands and second homes for wealthy Londoners, a kind of *rus in urbe*, country-side in the city. As London's population swelled towards 200,000 in around 1600 the northern green spaces of the Tudor city were being rapidly eroded. The district west of Bedlam became a patchwork quilt of gardens verging on the common sewer and the tenters in Moorfield. Further up were the archery butts and the windmills in what was then called Finsbury Fields. Today the same area is bordered by London Wall to the south, Bunhill Row to the west, Old Street to the north, and of course Bishopsgate and Shoreditch High Street to the east. By the end of the sixteenth century it was effectively a haven of isolated holiday homes. In his famous *Survey* of 1603 Stow noted disapprovingly that it had become an *enclosed* garden district for the rich and foolish. He rued the fact that they were building 'many fair summer houses . . . some of them like midsummer pageants, with towers, turrets, and chimney tops, not so much for use or profit as for shew and pleasure.' These second-home owners were a far cry, he wrote, from the 'ancient citizens' of London who used their wealth to provide hospitals and alms houses for the less fortunate.[4]

Not all the houses were grand. Some were just cottages, discreetly screened off from the two lanes (today's Appold Street and Primrose Street) which at the time cut through the area directly east of what is now Finsbury Square. It was here, and within less than a hundred yards or so of the Curtain and the Theatre, that the Jesuits pitched the headquarters of the spiritual insurgency they planned to conduct. Henry Garnett, leader of the English Jesuits in the late 1580s, writing on 17 March 1593 to his superior in Rome, Cardinal Claudio Acquaviva, remarked that many London citizens 'own small gardens beyond the city walls, and a number of them have built in these gardens cottages to which they resort from time to time to enjoy the cleaner air.'[5] Such a 'holiday home' would provide the Jesuits with perfect cover, since they were outside the city walls, comparatively inaccessible to nosy neighbours and therefore safer, but at the same time were more accessible to recusants than anywhere inside the City gates.

By the time the great 'copperplate' map of Tudor London was drafted in *c.*1557 there were at least three houses in the garden patchwork that became Finsbury Fields. Many of these small properties lay empty much of the time and were therefore of no obvious interest to the security services who were busy patrolling suspect districts and even houses. For several years Garnett ran the Jesuits from here, and pro-vided shelter for visiting fathers. The cottage he rented was permanently shuttered up. The lane or path that gave access to it seemed secure enough. No fires were lit except after dark, even in deepest winter, and all the cooking was done at night, so that there should be no tell-tale smoke billowing from the chimneys. The cot-tage was a safe if harsh place. When it was finally raided in 1591, almost nothing was found and no one was arrested; what was confis-cated was not enough to incriminate the Jesuit sympathizer who was present. This was because the cellar of this cottage boasted a substan-tial priesthole, built by the master mason of the Catholics, that fervent supporter of the Jesuits' cause, Nicholas Owen. An aspiring Jesuit himself, he was known as 'Little John', as distinct from his friend and companion 'Long John of the little beard', John Gerard. Government agents searched everywhere for the hide-out they knew probably existed, and stumbled across it in the end – pure Dogberry, displaying none of the fearsome acuity that usually characterized the procedures of the intelligence network operated by the Cecils and Walsingham. Or perhaps Garnett had the presence of mind of the cottage's caretaker to thank for the fact that his papers and many other things were not discovered.

It is probable that Garnett's cottage had been betrayed, but the events that triggered the raid were haphazard enough, involving *inter alia*, a youth who claimed to have spotted a Jesuit he had previously seen in Spain – a case of mistaken identity. It is tempting to see all this as a diversion, perhaps to protect an agent from being exposed, but the particulars of the search and the fact that it involved Richard Young, the chief justice of Middlesex and a close collaborator of Topcliffe, make it unlikely. Young would have taken as much care to pounce at just the right moment as the intelligence services had five years earlier in the summer of 1586, when they destroyed the Babington plot, leading inevitably to the execution of Mary Queen of Scots, and the attempted Armada invasion of 1588.

Garnett's story intersects indirectly with the story of Shakespeare, Marlowe, and the wider Catholic nation's relationship with this area and the theatres. It was in Hog Lane (Worship Street) that Father William Weston was captured on 3 August 1586. He had just returned to London and was knocking at the door of one of the few houses here when he was arrested by someone who seemed to be a private individual but was in fact the keeper of the Clink prison in Southwark. Weston tried to resist the arrest until a passing butcher threatened to knock him out. Weston had had the extreme bad fortune to walk into a surveillance operation involving Babington, at that moment holed up in Robert Poley's house in Hog Lane – unaware to the end that Poley was working for the government, though just before his capture he sent his treacherous friend a short note that begins 'My beloved Robin, as I hope you are, otherwise of all two-footed beings the most wicked'. It is possibly the most poignant of all the documents in the Babington tragedy. Intriguingly, 'the most wicked' Poley was one of the three men who were present when Christopher Marlowe died in Greenwich.

Weston had been recognized, and the team watching Babington may have assumed that he was part of the conspiracy. The government clearly suspected the area to be a hotbed of Catholics, and acted accordingly. While wealthy men invested in summer cottages, the authorities erected a gallows on Curtain road. On 28 August 1588 the priest William Gunter was executed at 'the new pair of gallows set up at the Theatre', and on 5 October 1588 William Hartley suffered the same fate here, 'his mother looking on'.[6] Shakespeare was by then probably well dug in at Burbage's playhouse. If so these two deaths may have been his first sight of man's inhumanity to man. But such punishment neither deterred the Catholics nor instilled in the likes of Marlowe a respect for the law: not far from the new gallows, in the very same Hog Lane where Weston was arrested, Marlowe and the poet Thomas Watson killed William Bradley in a brawl in 1589. Watson and Bradley had been involved in a feud, but it seems to have been just the kind of thing that happened to Marlowe or that he caused to happen. Evidently the area was in effect Marlowe's backyard, for the court records indicate that at the time of the killing he lodged in Norton Folgate, obviously to be close to the theatres where his plays were being performed.

Probably the actors more or less stayed put here. It seems there were several taverns or inns where they could gather to drink, or of course to meet women. When the Swiss traveller and student of medicine Thomas Platter visited London he stayed at an inn outside Bishopsgate, perhaps the Dolphin near St Botolph's, or a hostelry further up towards Spitalfields and Hog Lane. In his diary he conjures up a vivid picture of Shoreditch tavern life, noting in particular the fact that men and women mingled freely, just as they did in the audience at a playhouse. Women dropped in at these taverns both on their own and in small groups, to drink and laugh together, perhaps even to get to know the players. Will Shakespeare may well have been among these rumbustious pub-crawling players – the raucous tavern scenes at the Boar's Head in the two *Henry IV* plays certainly spring straight from the heart of this world of inns and taverns.

8

Likely Lads: Kit Marlowe and Will Shakespeare

L IKE THE YOUNG provincial who probably lodged in one of Burbage's 'rents' while tending to customers' horses, established actors and writers similarly lived close to the Theatre. These included the daredevil Marlowe, the poet Thomas Watson, and the playwright Robert Greene. Marlowe had overlapped at Cambridge with Greene for three years. Greene had been at St John's, earlier the college of Elizabeth's chief minister Cecil, later the college of the young Earl of Southampton. In 1588, just when Shakespeare was first pitching his tent in Holywell Lane, the legendary comedian and actor Richard Tarlton died. He was 'lying at that time in the house of one Em Ball in Shoreditch in the county of Middlesex', allegedly 'a woman of very bad reputation'; if this 'Em Ball' was not Robert Greene's mistress, she was probably closely related or 'in all likelihood her daughter'.[1]

It was the obvious thing for the men who were involved in professional drama in the 1580s to settle near the theatres. Marlowe lived either here or a stone's throw away to the south in Norton Folgate (the area included the current Norton Folgate and Folgate streets as well as what was to become Spitalfields Market) because he needed to be close to the playhouses. He also wrote parts with particular actors in mind, first and foremost Edward Alleyn, one of the great stars of the age alongside Richard ('Dick') Tarlton, Richard Burbage, Will Kemp, and Robert Armin. Alleyn was not a comic specialist like Tarlton but excelled in the rolling epic and tragic scripts Marlowe penned for him. Through acting and marriage alliances he became wealthy and eventually bought the manor of Dulwich, where in 1619 he founded the College of God's Gift, now known as Dulwich College.

Christopher 'Kit' Marlowe's symbiotic relationship with Alleyn perhaps served him ill in the long run, for his plays, whatever their brilliant poetic verve, suffer from a sense of having been written primarily as brilliant declamatory rhetoric, a vehicle for a single voice. Shakespeare, on the other hand, wrote dialogue in which characters communicate dramatically. He seems always to write instinctively for an ensemble cast. One, perhaps two, of Marlowe's plays were written when he was still up at Cambridge, suggesting that unlike Shakespeare he was less aware of the theatre as a profession involving a group of people – his plays never quite sound the note of 'total theatre' that is so characteristic of Shakespeare's. Ever more a great dramatic poet than a poetic dramatist, he was pilloried by one of Shakespeare's Puritan contemporaries, Edward Rudyerd, as 'a Cambridge scholar, who was a poet and a filthy play-maker'. By 'filthy' he meant atheistical and Machiavellian.

That Marlowe was a poet first and a dramatist only second is not surprising, for the records show that he was simply not present enough in London to become immersed in the theatre as an actor and writer, for all that he and another playwright, Thomas Kyd, shared lodgings and wrote in the same chamber – perhaps even inside the Rose – at some point in 1591. Marlowe never seems to have acted or owned shares in the various companies to which he belonged at different times. The extant documentation for his life seems to indicate that he was busy above all on behalf of Her Majesty's government; or else he was perhaps just behaving badly for his own selfish purposes.

The theatres had been active in Shoreditch for ten years when in 1587–8, the likely year of Shakespeare's arrival, they struck gold with the brilliant and revolutionary Tamburlaine.[2] In celebrating the fourteenth-century Tartar warrior king who proudly proclaims 'I am a lord, for so my deeds shall prove, / And yet a shepherd by my parentage' the play was blasphemous and atheistical as well as dangerously subversive – nothing could have been more antagonistic to the so-called Great Chain of Being, that Tudor fiction about an organic society in which everyone occupied an ordained, allotted place with the king or queen, by divine right, at the top of the heap. Moreover, the maverick and self-created royalty, even divinity, of Tamburlaine seems to enjoy the full blessing of its youthful author. The very first words spoken on stage belong not to Tamburlaine but to Marlowe as Prologue, and they warn off the political and moral faint-hearts:

> From jigging veins of rhyming mother wits,
> And such conceits as clownage keeps in pay,
> We'll lead you to the stately tent of War,
> Where you shall hear the Scythian Tamburlaine,
> Threat'ning the world with high astounding terms
> And scourging kingdoms with his conquering sword;
> View but his picture in this tragic glass,
> And then applaud his fortunes as you please.

This is a self-advertising, defiant, and fearless new voice. That the play was passed by the censor reflects the relative tolerance extended by the state towards the new art-form of theatre. Shakespeare's arrival in London could hardly have been more propitious. It was the year of Marlowe, and the play to see was *Tamburlaine* – or the two *Tamburlaines*, since it is possible that Marlowe wrote the sequel almost immediately, to capitalize on the commercial success of the original. The two works mark a turning-point in English drama, and the likely venue for *Tamburlaine* was the Theatre in Shoreditch, where *Dr Faustus* (1588–9) played the following year.[3]

In 1587 Marlowe became the unchallenged king of the theatre, as contemporary dramatists knew immediately. No one else could write like him. This was the most finely tuned poetic ear in the country. The magic of Marlowe's blank verse stems from its sonorous grand-iloquence and epic reach, his instinctive and apparently effortless ability to sound the right notes and, through his poetry, to conjure up entrancing vistas and thus explore foreign lands of the mind in his audience's imaginations. A highly accomplished classicist, he had translated Ovid's *Amores* while still at Cambridge and there too, prob-ably in partnership with his friend Thomas Nashe, had written *Dido Queen of Carthage*, a play based on Virgil's great epic poem, the *Aeneid*. The Cambridge angle to Marlowe's life is of enormous importance to understanding who he was and, perhaps, how he became so strangely free-thinking. And of course it bears on his allegiances, since it is above all through his run-in with the authorities in Cambridge and the subsequent intervention of the Privy Council in London that we know that Marlowe was indeed involved in the murky world of intel-ligence.

This is not the place to discuss at length Marlowe's record in espionage. Suffice it to note that the Privy Council instructed Cambridge in 1587 to award Marlowe his MA. The minutes of the meeting record that far from being a suspect papist, as Cambridge feared, he was doing sterling work on the Crown's behalf. In other words, if he was sniffing around Rheims which harboured a notorious Jesuit college run by Cardinal William Allen, it was at the behest of Her Majesty's secret service. More than any other in Europe it was probably this school which trained young Englishmen for martyrdom. As far as the Privy Council knew, Marlowe was a loyal servant. Marlowe's seven Cambridge years, from 1580 to 1587, matter notably because of the people he met while he was there. These included the same Robert Greene who attacked him repeatedly alongside Shakespeare and Thomas Nashe. Both Greene and Nashe were Marlowe's contemporaries at Cambridge. Also overlapping with Marlowe, if only for a period of two years or less, was Henry Wriothesley, the young third Earl of Southampton and protégé of the most powerful man in the land, Elizabeth's chief minister, Burghley.

There is little doubt about Marlowe's homosexuality, proclaimed after his death in a string of scandalous allegations by a government agent named Richard Baines. Baines had himself several years earlier infiltrated the same Rheims seminary that Marlowe may have targeted and which had aroused Cambridge's suspicions. Baines had got much further than Marlowe and enrolled in the college. When his cover was blown he was arrested and tortured by Allen before being released. It seems that he did not crack or, if he did, that he might have agreed to become a double agent. Whatever the truth of the matter, Baines was certainly closely enough connected with Marlowe (they had worked together as counterfeiters and were both hauled before Sir Robert Sidney in Flushing) to lend credibility to the charges in his 'Note containing the opinion of one Christopher Marly concerning his damnable judgement of religion and scorn of God's word.'

The statements attributed to Marlowe in this document were outrageous at the time, but are strangely prescient of modern free-thinking and Marxist views about power and the abuses of religion, particularly the way religion is used by its acolytes to repress the people. The note implies that Marlowe had a leaning towards Catholicism, notwithstanding his scorn for religion, but the most hard-hitting allegations charge that Marlowe's contempt for religion went together with a love of his own sex. According to Baines, Marlowe claimed that 'the woman of Samaria and her sister were whores and that Christ knew them dishonestly', that 'St John the Evangelist was bedfellow to Christ and leaned always in his bosom, that he used him as the sinners of Sodoma, that all they that love not tobacco and boys were fools.' And so the note continues, referring also to Marlowe's interest in money-forging, something which he had already done while in Flushing although he was apprehended before he and a goldsmith by the name of Gifford Gilbert could do any damage. At the time Marlowe and Gilbert had been betrayed by this same Richard Baines who had been their 'chamber-fellow'. When Baines alleged that Marlowe had asserted that 'he had as good a right to coin as the Queen of England and that he was acquainted with one Poole a prisoner in Newgate who hath great skill in mixing of metals', he knew exactly what he was talking about.

However malicious the specific phrasing of the note, which seems designed to inflict maximum damage on Marlowe's reputation, the fact remains that most of the assertions are probably true, being independently corroborated by other witnesses like Marlowe's one-time room-mate Thomas Kyd. The character portrayed is also consonant with the one that comes across in both the plays and the historical record, of a wild tearaway always up to mischief and repeatedly involved in fights. At least three of these, two in London and one in Canterbury, ended in court.

But if the glowing tribute he paid Marlowe seven years after his death can be trusted, Shakespeare, his junior by two months, came to admire and perhaps even love this same homosexual, brilliant, and dangerous Kit Marlowe. Circumstantial evidence suggests that it would have been odd indeed had they not been close as friends and rivals. Their backgrounds were similar, Shakespeare the son of a glover, Marlowe of a cobbler. Both were born in 1564, one in Stratford, the other in Canterbury. Marlowe went to the great cathedral school in Canterbury, Shakespeare to a modest local grammar school – modest only by comparison with the great schools of the land like Eton, however, and it is a noteworthy fact that the headmaster of Eton was paid only £10 a year, Stratford's schoolmaster

£20. After their schooldays, their paths diverged: Marlowe proceeded on an Archbishop Matthew Parker scholarship to Cambridge where he was a 'sizar', a student supported financially by his college, while Shakespeare possibly did not complete his grammar school education. But the two men also responded very differently to their environment.

Marlowe and Shakespeare were surely aware of each other, since they both wrote for the playing companies known as Strange's Men and then Pembroke's Men, they lived in the same part of town, and one was probably homosexual (Marlowe) the other bisexual. That there was a rivalry between Marlowe and Shakespeare and that it expressed itself in specific works is argued by Stephen Greenblatt, who writes that the contest between these two gifted young poets progressed 'from the momentous early works, *Tamburlaine* and *Henry VI*, to a brilliant pair of strikingly similar history plays, Shakespeare's *Richard II* and Marlowe's *Edward II*, and an equally brilliant pair of long erotic poems, Shakespeare's *Venus and Adonis* and Marlowe's *Hero and Leander*.'[4] There is little to gainsay in this. It makes and reinforces the important point that there are just too many parallels between the two dramatists' literary endeavours for them to be a coincidence.

Shakespeare and Marlowe may have emerged as a double act at the Theatre in Shoreditch in the late 1580s when both men were in their mid twenties. What is known of Marlowe's short life is on the face of it incompatible with his being a friend of the kind of person Shakespeare seems to have been. But there is that suggestion of delinquency in Shakespeare's escapades in Charlecote Park, and although the two men were clearly different temperamentally, that is in itself no bar to friendship. And there was another side to the tearaway Marlowe. In Canterbury in November 1585, at the house of Katherine Benchkin, mother of one of his Cambridge friends, Marlowe and various relatives including his father witnessed the Benchkin will; Marlowe read it out 'plainly and distinctly' before signing it. Initially there is incongruity in the idea of the future author of *Tamburlaine* mundanely discharging his duties as an educated young man, reading aloud from a will as the most literate person present in a room in a house in Canterbury – yet human beings are infinitely complex. The author of *Tamburlaine* could brawl, spy, translate Ovid, be friends with the gentler, brilliant young Shakespeare, and yet be himself. Shakespeare knew all this, none more so.

Shakespeare's first response was no doubt to Marlowe's poetic talent, and they also had Ovid in common. Marlowe had translated Ovid at Cambridge, as Shakespeare undoubtedly had at school, and Ovid was plainly a perceptible influence, for in a remarkable survey of the English literature of the day published in 1598 one of Shakespeare's contemporaries, Francis Meres, described him as the English Ovid. But there was one side to Marlowe's life that Shakespeare never touched, at least not as far as is known. This was Marlowe's links to the intelligence services. They would have set alarm bells ringing with anyone like Shakespeare who was eager to grasp the opportunity the theatre afforded him to earn money to support a family at home. After all, unlike the maverick from Canterbury, Will was a father of three children, and the cost of dissidence was horrendous as Shakespeare knew well from the human heads that adorned several of London's gates and notably London Bridge.

If Shakespeare lived a double life, as a secret Catholic and outwardly conformist Anglican, Marlowe would undoubtedly have been an irresistible magnet. But while Shakespeare's drama is no more a drama of faith than Marlowe's, lines like those spoken by Machiavelli as Prologue to *The Jew of Malta* sound a note completely alien to anything Shakespeare wrote. When Machiavelli proclaims that religion is cant, 'but a childish toy', and that 'there is no sin but ignorance', he takes the audience into a febrile political world that Shakespeare never touches. Neither Iago in *Othello* nor Edmund in *King Lear*, both characters divorced from conventional Christian morality, would ever articulate anything like this, even if it is possible to imagine their characters secretly embracing such views. A still stronger contrast is provided by Shakespeare's *Richard III* from the first cycle of histories. When Richard first comes to prominence in the third part of *Henry VI* he taunts that he 'can add colours to the chameleon, / Change shapes with Proteus for advantages, / And set the murderous Machevil to school.' And he does, but never in the way Marlowe would have written him. For Richard III, to be Machiavellian is to be devious, ruthless, and practical, and to kill – and to have fun on the way. Marlowe's Barabas also enjoys his wickedness to the full, but the

Prologue articulates something quite different from the play, reflecting views on religion that are remarkably similar to those attributed (rightly or wrongly) to Marlowe himself. The fact that in *The Jew of Malta* they are spoken by that bogeyman of the Elizabethans, the Florentine political philosopher Nicolò Machiavelli, who was sometimes known as McEvil as well as 'Old Nick' (the Devil), makes no difference. Such 'safe' distancing fooled no one, particularly when the villain of the piece was, for good measure, also its endlessly resourceful comic protagonist.

There can be little doubt that both Marlowe and Shakespeare were fascinated by politics and political philosophy. Marlowe engaged with it directly, practically, personally – he was in the thick of it – but for Shakespeare it was a much more internalized affair, a deep and relentless search for a national identity through a series of English history plays, from *King John* through the Plantagenets and finally all the way to the reign of *Henry VIII* and the prophecy of peace and prosperity under Elizabeth I. Shakespeare's fascination with history, and English history in particular, is evident everywhere, and the ten plays dealing with the nation's destiny probe and question loyalty, morality, even the divine right of kings if it finds itself divorced from moral foundations or legitimacy. It is possible that it was Marlowe who inspired or fostered Shakespeare's lively interest in history. He has in the past been credited with writing parts of the *Henry VI* plays, and there is certainly proof of his having borrowed from the third part of *Henry VI*, suggesting that Marlowe was perhaps as relaxed about borrowing from Shakespeare as Shakespeare was about echoing others when it suited him to do so.

As it happens, there is a play that reads like a collaboration between Shakespeare and Marlowe. The distinct Marlovian strain in *The Taming of a Shrew*, about 1589, points either at Marlowe as collaborator, or emphatically at Shakespeare trying to write like Marlowe, that is the tyro modelling himself on the star.[5] Shakespeare's hand is evident at the levels of phrase and metaphor, and in some striking broader similarities between this play and *A Midsummer Night's Dream*, particularly the characters called Sly and Bottom. In *A Shrew* Sly wakes up from a vision of himself transformed into a lord watching a play and tells the tapster who wakes him, 'I have had / The bravest dream tonight that ever thou / Heardest in all thy life.' This seems to anticipate Bottom's awakening from sharing the bower of Titania: 'I have had a most rare vision. I have had a dream past the wit of man to say what dream it was. Man is but an ass, if he go about t'expound this dream.'

By themselves these two comparable passages might be no more than a coincidence, the chosen motif in both notwithstanding. But the verse of *A Shrew* sounds a sub-Marlovian Shakespearian note, for example, when women's eyes are said to be 'fairer than rocks of pearl and precious stone' and lovelier ultimately than 'the morning sun, / When first she opes her oriental gates.' This reads like a dry-run for some of the key metaphors of *Romeo and Juliet*, and there is yet another analogous passage in *A Midsummer Night's Dream*. When Oberon tells Puck that they are privileged spirits, he notes that he 'like a forester the groves may tread / Even till the eastern gate, all fiery red, / Opening on Neptune with fair blessèd beams, / Turns into yellow gold his salt green streams.' The language of *A Shrew* carries a Marlovian charge in its luminosity and in the hard-edged precious stones which adorn its texture.[6] There is a straining throughout the play towards some form of Marlovian sublimity, but it always just misses. In the end Shakespeare is simply not Marlowe, whose lofty style soars on the tailwind of his poetic Midas touch. No one else, except possibly Shakespeare or Jonson at the limit of their rhetorical powers, could pull off Marlowe's sweeping and resonant classical style. By the time Shakespeare wrote *A Midsummer Night's Dream* six years later he had assimilated his Marlovian lessons. From static metaphors about suits 'spotted with liquid gold, thick set with pearle' (*A Shrew*) Shakespeare was now fashioning lines in which the full moon is 'decking with liquid pearl the bladed grass' (*Dream*). The one is descriptive, the other a dynamic metaphor painting in words the magic of a midsummer night under a full moon in a Warwickshire wood near Athens, and that during a daylight performance in the London theatre of the time. As for the melting pearls, they are very much a Shakespearian theme. Shakespeare loved pearls and they figure throughout his works, from Silvia's 'sea of melting pearl which some call tears' (*The Two Gentlemen of Verona*) to Cordelia's tears in *King Lear*, 'as pearls from diamonds dropped', and finally to the 'pearls that were his eyes' in the marine metamorphosis in *The Tempest*.

If *A Shrew* was written in 1589 it would have started life as an Admiral's or a Strange's property before migrating to the Pembroke's Men whose figurehead sat on the Privy Council. Through the Pembroke's Men Shakespeare and Marlowe sailed into the orbit of Sir Philip Sidney's family, for the Earl of Pembroke was the husband of Sidney's sister Mary Herbert. When Marlowe evoked Ferdinand Lord Strange (for whose company he had written plays) to Sir Robert Sidney in January 1592, did he also tell Sidney that he was at that very moment working for his brother-in-law?[7] The main plot of *A Shrew* features the 'taming' of a young woman by a young man to the point where, at the end, she casts herself as a penitent daughter of Eve who urges all women to obey, love, keep and nourish their husbands. The stage direction reads: '*She lays her hands under her husband's feet.*' The Petruchio character in *A Shrew*, Ferando, has won his wager in causing this self-abasement of a woman, called Kate just as she is in the better-known play *The Taming of the Shrew*.

A Shrew has an induction which features one Sly, but this induction truly frames the play and at the end Sly wakes up as if from a dream. He also wakes in the course of the play itself, and during one such intervention protests that he will definitely have no sending to prison: after all, 'am not I *Don Christo Vary*?' He is hardly Don Anything, he the 'whoreson drunken slave' of the opening line of the play, who has sunk into an intoxicated stupor by line 19. The point is that Sly's '*Don Christo Vary*' is a play on the name 'Christopher', Marlowe's first name, meaning 'carrier of Christ', from the Latin *Christus* and *ferre*. This may be Shakespeare's 'sly' feeding into the play of clues through the use of real names from his circle of acquaintances, a thing Marlowe never does, so that this is a further indication of Shakespeare's authorship. *A Shrew* is perhaps his breaking-away work, the play in which he worked free from the influence and idiom of his friend and mentor Marlowe, what Bullough called his 'first shot at the theme'.[8] Not only does it use rare words such as 'chud', which Shakespeare used again in *King Lear* and may have used earlier against Sir Thomas Lucy, but other usages also point to Shakespeare, among them the words 'lief' and 'liefest', meaning 'dear' and 'dearest'. Shakespeare uses 'liefest' once elsewhere, in *2 Henry VI*, a play from the early 1590s and thus closer in date of composition to *A Shrew* than most.

Then in May 1591 Marlowe, the Admiral's Edward Alleyn and his brother John, with Augustine Phillips, George Bryan, Thomas Pope, and perhaps John Heminges, all defected from the Theatre, the culmination of a fierce row the previous November between the Alleyns and the Burbages. Heading south, the breakaway group teamed up with the tycoon Philip Henslowe, Southwark entrepreneur, brothel-keeper, and owner of the Rose. They joined Lord Strange's Men, which is how Marlowe came to boast to the governor of Flushing in January 1592 that he knew Ferdinando Strange. The split must have been a traumatic event for the Theatre and its owners the Burbages, even though the playhouses were not as a rule, it seems, linked to any specific, permanent companies, so that the loss of players did not entail the closure of the house. The system of one company/one house came in later with the creation in 1594 of the London-based Lord Chamberlain's Company, which after 1599 played at the Globe theatre and eventually at both the Globe and the Blackfriars. The first records of one particular company associated with a single house for an extended period of time are found in Henslowe's account book (the so-called *Diary*) for 1592, which records a five-month-long association between the Rose theatre and Lord Strange's company. Nevertheless, in 1591 the Theatre at one stroke lost its star writer and its chief actor, as well as several other important players. Marlowe probably moved to live south of the river in Southwark, near the Old Kent Road – he was after all Kentish, and a frequent visitor at Thomas Walsingham's house at Scadbury in Chislehurst in Kent. His absence from the Theatre and probably from Shoreditch too may have been keenly felt by his friend Shakespeare, but it also provided him with an opportunity. Those who remained of the Lord Admiral's Men at the Theatre now needed someone to fill Marlowe's shoes, and Shakespeare delivered the goods. There were just two, possibly three, other dramatists in the frame – Kyd, Greene, and perhaps Peele. Kyd however soon teamed up with Marlowe, as indicated by the records of their room-sharing in 1591, leaving Greene and Peele as senior dramatists; it is not known whether Peele was involved with the Theatre and the Admiral's Men at the time of the split.

Graduating from horse-holding Shakespeare probably worked for the Burbages as a jack-of-all-trades – jobbing actor, reviser of plays, junior collaborator, prompter, bookkeeper, and generally useful person about the house. His exceptional facility with language must soon have revealed itself and the company, probably Lord Strange's or Pembroke's, seems to have had the good sense to recognize it. Perhaps he breathed new life into old plays, as when in Peter Shaffer's play *Amadeus* Mozart takes a promising but wooden piece of music by Salieri, sits down at the keyboard and, improvising on Salieri's basic musical line, causes the piece to soar on angels' wings. Having been merely well-crafted before, it has now become magic. This might account for some of the jealousy and frustration Shakespeare provoked in his fellow dramatist Robert Greene and why he was eventually accused of plagiarism and arrogance. Marlowe, with a voice as distinctive as his own, was immune to such treatment, of course – and Marlowe had hit the ground running, as it were, writing successfully for the theatre before he worked in it professionally. It was only with the three *Henry VI* plays in about 1590–1 that Shakespeare similarly struck gold, drawing fulsome tributes from Marlowe's friend and fellow Cambridge man Thomas Nashe and enjoying a run of shows unprecedented in the theatre of the period. No wonder that from time to time it has been suspected that Marlowe had a hand in this first cycle of history plays.[9]

9

Living the Sonnets: 1590–onwards

Marlowe's departure from Shoreditch set Shakespeare free. In the two and a half years between 1590 and the closure of the London theatres in 1592 he wrote the second and third parts of *Henry VI*, a blood-curdling tragedy with flashes of brilliance, *Titus Andronicus*, *The Two Gentlemen of Verona* and *The Comedy of Errors*, the last, possibly one of the greatest comedies ever written, revolving (not entirely surprising, perhaps, for this father of twins) around two sets of same-sex twins.[1] Shakespeare was a fast developer, as the sure-footedness of *The Comedy of Errors* amply testifies. No one else in the period achieved anything like it, and if *The Comedy of Errors* were the only play of Shakespeare's to survive he would still be considered to have possessed the most instinctive dramatic flair for the timing of comic scenes of anyone writing at the time.

It seems safe to suppose that the friendship between Shakespeare and Marlowe now became a friendly rivalry, with their plays in Shoreditch and at Bankside competing for the same audiences. It may be that Shakespeare missed the company of the excitingly lawless Kit Marlowe, yet fate, good fortune, or a mutual friend had put the young Earl of Southampton in his way the year before. Young Henry Wriothesley, third Earl of Southampton, had grown up in the London household of the powerful Cecils. Its head was the most adroit politician in the land, William Cecil, Lord Burghley, a relic from the age of Henry VIII and Queen Mary and the present Queen's chief minister and most trusted adviser. The Cecils occupied a grand brick-and-timber mansion in the Strand, opposite the Savoy, backing up towards Covent Garden and wedged between what are now the Lyceum and the London Transport Museum; Burghley Street now recalls the Cecils' presence here. At this palace in the Strand Southampton lived as Burghley's ward, as did Burghley's son Robert Cecil, Southampton's senior by more than ten years, who was being groomed to succeed his father. Among the private tutors to be found in this intellectual pow erhouse was the provost of St John's College (Burghley was Chancellor of Cambridge, and an alumnus of St John's).

At a time when a person's physical appearance was commonly thought to reflect his or her inner self, when physical blemishes were all too often laid at the door of a judgemental Superior Being, Robert Cecil, heir to his father's gifts, deviousness, and addiction to hard work, was a cripple, a hunchback with splayed legs and a deformed spine. He was a year older than Shakespeare, and it seems likely that the two men must have come to know each other, because from 1591 Cecil sat on the Privy Council alongside the powerful Hunsdons, cousins of the Queen, who were patrons of the arts, and closely connected to Shakespeare's company. At a time when England was ostensibly struggling to survive and to face down the Catholics, it seems odd that the Privy Council should have involved itself as in- timately as it did with monitoring the burgeoning activities of the theatres – yet as well as Edmund Campion and Henry Garnett, head of the English Jesuits, they also interviewed Ben Jonson about sus- pected papist material in *Sejanus*.

Though certainty is not possible, it seems likely that Robert Cecil and young Southampton were close. When Southampton was later found guilty of treason, Cecil's intervention saved him from certain death. Southampton's mother was a die-hard Catholic, while the Cecils' Protestant credentials were unimpeachable, and Robert Cecil was married to Elizabeth Brooke, daughter of Sir William Brooke, Lord Cobham, who during his brief tenure of the office of Lord Chamberlain subjected Shakespeare and his company to the most notorious act of Protestant censorship of the age.

That Shakespeare knew Southampton well is a matter of record, and he seems to have made his acquaintance in the summer of 1590. Southampton had returned to London from Cambridge the previous year and enrolled at Gray's Inn. At the university (which he had entered at the tender age of twelve) he had been a younger contemporary of Marlowe, Nashe and Greene, the last two of whom were at St John's during his early years there. One of them may well have introduced the young aristocrat to Shakespeare. His narrative poems *Venus and Adonis* and *The Rape of Lucrece*, published in 1593 and 1594 respectively, are both dedicated to Southampton. Though the dedications are cast in the formal language of Elizabethan court literature, there is little doubting the intimacy of tone, particularly of that to *The Rape of Lucrece*:

> To the Right Honourable Henry Wriothesley, Earl of Southampton, and Baron of Titchfield.
>
> The love I dedicate to your Lordship is without end: whereof this pamphlet without beginning is but a superfluous moiety. The warrant I have of your honourable disposition, not the worth of my untutored lines, makes it assured of acceptance. What I have done is yours, what I have to do is yours, being part in all I have, devoted yours. Were my worth greater, my duty would show greater, meantime, as it is, it is bound to your Lordship; to whom I wish long life still lengthened with all happiness.
>
> Your Lordship's in all duty, William Shakespeare.

Whereas in his dedication of *Venus and Adonis* Shakespeare had been somewhat reticent about the propriety of choosing a prominent member of the aristocracy for a patron – 'so strong a prop to support so weak a burden' and only 'the first heir' of the poet's invention – in *The Rape of Lucrece* he writes without the slightest inhibition. He feels free to express his 'love' and enjoys, so he states, a reciprocal affection. What is much more remarkable than any professed 'love' affair between a glover from Stratford and a leading young aristocrat is the fact that it was openly advertised in both publications. *Venus and Adonis* went through nine editions in Shakespeare's lifetime and was more frequently alluded to in the period than any other among his works. Of the nine editions *The Rape of Lucrece* had gone through by 1655, no fewer than five or six in Shakespeare's lifetime, one of them in the year of his death. 'Everyone' knew about the relationship, and in the seventeenth century it was rumoured that Southampton had been munificently generous to Shakespeare, to the tune of £1,000. According to Rowe, Shakespeare

> had the honour to meet with many great and uncommon marks of favour and friendship from the Earl of Southampton . . . There is one

instance so singular in the magnificence of this patron of Shakespeare's that if I had not been assured that the story was handed down by Sir William Davenant, who was probably very well acquainted with his affairs, I should not have ventured to have inserted that my lord Southampton at one time gave him a thousand pounds, to enable him to go through with a purchase which he heard he had a mind to. A bounty very great, and very rare at any time.

This gift of a thousand pounds perhaps helped to redeem both Shakespeare's father's debts and his own fines, as well as funding the acquisition of property. It seems a huge sum, but it is the very figure that was current in Stratford-upon-Avon gossip in the middle of the seventeenth century. Thus the Reverend John Ward noted in his diary in 1662 that 'Shakespeare supplied the stage with two plays every year, and for it had an allowance so large that he spent at the rate of £1,000 a year, as I have heard.'[2] Ward carefully, and twice, stresses the fact that he has 'heard' this reported in Stratford. Possibly the £1,000 to which he refers results from a conflation of rumours about Shakespeare's large earnings and the gift to him from Southampton, but the reference cannot be dismissed any more than a further testimony can be ignored. According to the Reverend Joseph Greene (1712–90), scholar, master of Shakespeare's school, antiquary, and almost casual discoverer of Shakespeare's last will, writing in *The Gentleman's Magazine* in 1759, the 'unanimous tradition of the neighbourhood where he lived is that by the uncommon bounty of the then Earl of Southampton he was enabled to purchase houses and land at Stratford, the place of his nativity'. Greene's reference to a 'unanimous tradition' in the 'neighbourhood' is important. It is unlikely that Rowe, Ward, and Greene were all wrong. A thousand pounds was the equivalent of two-thirds of the building costs of the magnificent Second Globe Theatre of 1614. If he spent it all on property, rather than paying off fines and debts, Shakespeare could have bought as many as ten houses in Stratford and still have cash in hand.

Perhaps this lavish gift was Southampton's practical 'thank-you' for *Venus and Adonis* and *The Rape of Lucrece*. Both poems were printed by Shakespeare's Stratford friend Richard Field, and if it was not through Shakespeare himself it may have been through Field that the story of Southampton's spectacular gift found its way back to Stratford. Field was one of Shakespeare's closest friends throughout his life, and in a very late play, *Cymbeline*, Shakespeare paid him one of his most cryptically wrought tributes. When its heroine Innogen is asked her master's name, she replies 'Richard du Champ. (*Aside*) If I do lie and do / No harm by it, though the gods hear, I hope / They'll pardon it.' 'Du Champ' means 'of the field', of course, and in his Spanish language publications Field usually signed himself 'Ricardo del Campo',[3] but only those closest to him were aware of Richard Field's marriage to a French Huguenot, the widow of his former employer, and capable of appreciating the arch aptness of the Gallic allusion.

And there is more. When Innogen dons male attire she assumes the name 'Fidele', 'the loyal one' (French, *fidèle*). In the play it serves to underline her faithful, selfless character as an innocent wronged wife, but it is also very close to an anagram of 'Field'. These two punning references leave little room to doubt that Shakespeare is conducting some kind of private dialogue with Field beyond the fiction of the play. By doubling as Field's fictional *alter ego* in the guise of Fidele, the unshakeably loyal Innogen pays a stirring tribute to the printer from Bridge Street in Stratford-upon-Avon – Richard Field, Richard Fidele or Faithful. At the height of Shakespeare's friendship with Southampton, Field may have been batting for Shakespeare. It seems that he was always there for him which is probably why Shakespeare finally put him in *Cymbeline*.

Perhaps no relationship in his life left as deep a mark on Shakespeare as that with Southampton. At its most innocuous it was a friendship of homage and patronage, at its most daring a full-blown homoerotic affair which stopped just short of physical consummation. The question is whether the authorities and particularly the Cecils and the powerful Earl of Essex would have tolerated the young earl ever being drawn into the ambit of homosexual players and theatre entrepreneurs. The young man's dazzling looks must have invited sexual advances from both genders – that he was androgynously beautiful is evident from the various surviving portraits of him, particularly from the striking miniature by Nicholas Hilliard dating from 1594 which shows Southampton at twenty-one, sultry and effeminate-looking, with long flowing hair. This was almost certainly the face that launched the 154 most famous sonnets in the English language; small wonder that the poet warns his friend of the dangers of narcissism and self-destruction. In sonnet 93, a strikingly intimate and erotic poem about the young man's beauty, this same face is said to have been decreed by Heaven to be the place where 'sweet love should ever dwell'. But, the poet warns, this outward beauty must be a true mirror of the soul, or else the young man's looks will one day catch him out: 'How like Eve's apple doth thy beauty grow, / If thy sweet virtue answer not thy show.' The youth's appearance might prove to be a brittle and cruel sham waiting to be exposed, a hostage to time – Oscar Wilde made the same point in his parable about Dorian Gray. Where hair was concerned Southampton certainly had the edge, for Shakespeare's baldness is all too evident in the two authenticated representations of him that survive. He possibly lost his hair quite young, but he remarks wistfully in the early play *The Comedy of Errors* that 'There's no time for a man to recover his hair that grows bald by nature.' To the question why time 'is such a niggard of hair, being as it is so plentiful an excrement', the reply comes, 'because it is a blessing that he bestows on beasts, and what he hath scanted men in hair he hath given them in wit.'[4]

There is no consensus on whether the *Sonnets* are pure fiction, or an imaginative documentary record of real events. Some of their best readers and editors have always conceded that they appear to reflect episodes from a real-life story, and that they can legitimately be seen as a partly subjective record of a particular time in Shakespeare's life. At once an exhilarating rhetorical exercise and a profound reflection on the human condition in general, the poems are yet to some extent conventional and generic. Their topics include the promise of youth and the ravages of age, the inevitable passage of time, man's natural desire to evade death and to reproduce himself through procreation, the poet's ability to confer a superior kind of immortality through commemorating the object of his affection in verse, sexual betrayal, and the conflicting loyalties of friendship and romantic love. But there are also quite clearly moments in them that convey the impression of a poetic diary, a record of a real-life turbulent relationship involving a number of different people, both male and female.

Literary criticism has been reluctant to assign the poems a firm date, and chronological elasticity has become entrenched as a cardinal virtue. The history of the poems from the surmised writing of the initial verses in 1590 to the publication of the entire cycle in 1609 encompasses almost twenty years. But to accept a time-span of 1590–1609 is to so broaden the scope of any search for real-life parallels as to render the search all but useless. And in fact there is no hard evidence for dating the writing of the poems to any time after 1599, when sonnets 138 and 144 appeared in a collection called *The Passionate Pilgrim*. Since some general chronological diary-style principles clearly underlie the story revealed by the cycle, and since 144, which is only ten poems off the conclusion of the entire cycle, can demonstrably be dated to no later than 1599, it stands to reason that all the poems were almost certainly around by then. If so, some of the few poems which have traditionally been dated late and which scholars have matched with some confidence to outside events after 1599 may need to be reassessed.

One such poem with an apparently identifiable reference to the outside world is sonnet 107. It starts with 'Not mine own fears, nor the prophetic soul / Of the wide world, dreaming on things to come' and contains the lines 'The mortal moon hath her eclipse endured, / And the sad augurs mock their own presage.' The phrases 'mortal moon' and 'her eclipse' have been widely read as references to the death of the Virgin (and hence lunar) Queen on 24 March 1603, while the smooth transition to the Stuarts which followed could be said to have given the lie to the prophets of doom: they themselves join in the rejoicing at this political triumph and, relieved, laugh at their own false 'presage'. Such interpretations may be valid in the abstract, but there are equally good reasons for dating 107 to the mid 1590s instead – when Shakespeare wrote *A Midsummer Night's Dream*, a play in which he quite plainly compares the queen to the moon, and plays with lunar images. The inspiration for his moonlit play and poem could be found in one or both the full lunar eclipses of 24 April and 18 October 1595.

It could be argued that Shakespeare inserted 107 much later, as a freshly composed poem, into Thomas Thorpe's 1609 collection. But there was no reason in 1609 for him to write a poem about the death of the queen in 1603. Further 'facts' or documentary records, moreover, favour dating all the poems to before the autumn of 1598. In that year Francis Meres wrote in *Palladis Tamia, Wit's Treasury* that 'the sweet witty soul of Ovid lives in mellifluous and honey-tongued Shakespeare, witness his *Venus and Adonis*, his *Lucrece*, his sugared sonnets among his private friends.' Meres's lengthy tome was entered in the Stationers' Register on 7 September 1598. His reference to Shakespeare's sonnets as circulating among the poet's 'private friends' seems to imply that there were several copies of them around at the time, and that Meres and others outside the inner Court loop had either read them or got to hear of them, so that they were being read in London for a while before *Palladis Tamia*. It is not possible to prove this, yet there may be a particular reason for bringing forward the latest likely date of composition to August 1596 – for it was then that Shakespeare's son Hamnet died in Stratford. It is hard to imagine a grieving father and husband writing deeply involved love poetry to a youth who, whatever spell he cast over the poet, seems to have been self-absorbed, shiftless, and untrustworthy.

That the relationship dramatized in the *Sonnets* took place in the early to mid 1590s may perhaps be borne out by sonnet 94, one of the most frequently anthologized of all the poems. It opens with 'They that have power to hurt, and will do none . . .' reaching the conclusion in the final couplet that 'For sweetest things turn sourest by their deeds: / Lilies that fester smell far worse than weeds.' The line about festering lilies is quoted verbatim in *Edward III*, and the line which follows it in the play, 'And every glory that inclines to sin / The shame is treble by the opposite', paraphrases the thirteenth line of the same sonnet 94. The thought process is the same; the play and the sonnet are demonstrably closely related. There is now almost universal agreement that Shakespeare had a major hand in *Edward III* and some scholars think that his main collaborator was Marlowe: the play must therefore date from before May 1593 when Marlowe died, and sonnet 94 likewise. *Edward III* dates from the early 1590s and thus contemporary with the *Sonnets*. The commonly voiced assertion that some of the poems in the cycle lie beyond the expressive rhetorical power of the younger Shakespeare seems misplaced, since even the early solo works are strikingly mature. *Titus Andronicus* may be a violent orgy, but it is also a brilliant piece of theatre and its linguistic texture is rich and complex, as are the early comedies and the second and third parts of *Henry VI* and *Richard III*. Shakespeare was obviously a fast learner, already possessed of a muscular dramatic syntax and an exceptional gift for images through which he illuminated perception, adding imaginative depth to everything that his similes or metaphors touched.

The argument here is for all the sonnets having been written between 1590 and 1596. The first seventeen poems encourage the young man to marry in order to replicate himself; in thus appealing to the youth's pride and vanity, the poet seems to want to trick him into marriage. At the time Southampton was being urged by Burghley to marry Elizabeth de Vere – daughter, as it happens, of the same Edward de Vere, Earl of Oxford, who was subsequently championed by some as the author of Shakespeare's plays. The irascible Oxford, pederast, patron of boy-actors and enemy of Sidney, the only Elizabethan nobleman ever to be charged with sodomy, was also Burghley's son-in-law. For young Southampton thus to defy Burghley took some courage. It may be that Burghley, as Master of the Wards, was not quite as determined and ruthless with his charges as he reputedly was in politics – but here he was being thwarted and snubbed, and probably fairly publicly, by a young man who had spent nearly five years in his own household. However, he did not, it seems, exact punishment, at least not yet.

Shakespeare's first seventeen sonnets were perhaps written as a gift for Southampton on his seventeenth birthday, 6 October 1590. They demonstrate that chronology was one of the structural principles behind the cycle. But mere poetry was not enough to change Southampton's mind, and Shakespeare abandoned the attempt. Sonnet 18, one of the best-known, begins 'Shall I compare thee to a summer's day?' and ends confidently with a promise of eternity conferred by the poet's art on the fair youth. Sounding a very different note from what has gone before, it signals a significant shift in the relationship between the poet and the young man, between Will Shakespeare and Henry Wriothesley. Shakespeare was presumably commissioned to write those first poems to the young earl, and by someone acting in the Cecils' interest, if not by Burghley or Robert Cecil themselves. But how had they come to know of his existence? It is hard to imagine two such busy men wending their way to the playhouse in Shoreditch. Even had they done so, in the late 1580s Shakespeare's star had hardly yet ascended high enough to attract their attention. That he was making an impact in London was however undeniable, and it may be that *The Taming of a Shrew* gave him the kind of exposure that would have led them somehow to notice him – it is after all a play about persuasion to marriage.

Oddly enough, Cecil House did in fact procure the help of a 'resident writer' to hold a mirror up to Southampton's recalcitrant nature. He was John Clapham, one of Burghley's secretaries, and he wrote a Latin verse poem titled *Narcissus* and dedicated to Southampton, the young man's first such gift. This poetic pamphlet translates the Narcissus story into an English setting, but retains the basic moral of the Ovidian tale, that self-love is ultimately futile and destructive. If Clapham was co-opted to coax the young man into seeing the error of his ways, why not Shakespeare? But if the Cecils did indeed bring Shakespeare into the fray, they got more than they bargained for. From 18 onwards, the sonnets record a dramatically changing relationship with the young man.

In sonnet 20, written almost immediately after 18, Shakespeare calls the youth of the poems 'the master-mistress of my passion', a phrase that fully confronts the androgynous nature of the relationship that is developing. What follows from sonnet 20 until the last poem in the sequence is nothing less than a kind of highly wrought imaginative diary of the poet's relationships with his friend and lovers. In 20 the youth is said to be possessed of all aspects of womanhood, such as gentleness and physical beauty, while being superior to the so-called fair sex by virtue of his constancy and truthfulness. But just in case, and as a strategic caveat, Shakespeare notes that Nature had equipped the young man with a penis, and thereby set him off-limits:

> A woman's face with nature's own hand painted
> Hast thou, the master-mistress of my passion;
> A woman's gentle heart, but not acquainted
> With shifting change as is false women's fashion;
> An eye more bright than theirs, less false in rolling,
> Gilding the object whereupon it gazeth;
> A man in hue, all hues in his controlling,
> Which steals men's eyes and women's souls amazeth.
> And for a woman wert thou first created,

Till nature as she wrought thee fell a-doting,
And by addition me of thee defeated,
By adding one thing to my purpose nothing.
    But since she pricked thee out for women's pleasure,
    Mine be thy love and thy love's use their treasure.

As yet the poet is careful and diplomatic, but this *is* a love poem from one man to another, from a married yeoman father of three to one of the great nobles of the land. Now, far from writing to persuade the earl to marry, the poet writes as his adoring lover. Quite how intense the relationship had become can be gleaned from sonnet 27. 'Weary with toil I haste me to my bed', the poet proclaims, but then finds that he is too lovesick to sleep. As he lies gazing on the dark, the way blind people do, his 'soul's imaginary sight' shows up the youth's 'shadow to my sightless view, / Which, like a jewel hung in ghastly night, / Makes black night beauteous and her old face new.' Shakespeare used this conceit again in one of the most celebrated love scenes ever written. When Romeo first catches a glimpse of Juliet, he exclaims that she 'doth teach the torches to burn bright. / It seems she hangs upon the cheek of night / As a rich jewel in an Ethiop's ear, / Beauty too rich for use, for earth too dear.'

That Shakespeare should echo his own desperate love for Southampton in the lyric language of Romeo and Juliet should neither surprise nor shock. This was clearly how he imagined ideal love, even if his for Southampton lacked any chance of the consummation so readily granted to his teenage lovers. It had begun with a fatherless young nobleman whom he had set out to rhyme into marriage, probably at the behest of the Cecils, and developed into a spiritual love affair. His relationship with Southampton, while not of a physical nature, was a kind of infidelity, according ill with his troth-plight to Anne Hathaway ten years earlier, when he had sworn to forsake all others. Even so, the absence of sex from the relationship may explain why he never once refers to his own status as a married man.

Nine years separated the poet and youth. In sonnet 22 the poet rues this fact, but defiantly asserts:

My glass shall not persuade me I am old
So long as youth and thou are of one date;
But when in thee time's furrows I behold,
Then look I death my days should expiate.

The transience of time and the decay of beauty, particularly the fading bloom of young women, is of course a traditional motif of love poetry and sonnets, nowhere more poignantly conveyed than in a sonnet addressed by Pierre de Ronsard (1524–85) to his unobtainable beloved, 'Quand vous serez bien vieille, au soir, à la chandelle, / Assise près du feu, dévidant et filant (When in the future you are old, at night, and spinning by the light of a taper, sitting by the fire)'. Ronsard had been Mary Stuart's poetry teacher and a founding member of the Pléiade, an influential school of lyric poetry which left its mark on Shakespeare's *Sonnets*. Here the young woman is reminded that one day in the future all that will be left of her beauty will be a collective memory that once, long ago, it inspired Ronsard's poetry.

This conflict between eternity and the inevitable biological decay of all humankind is present in the *Sonnets* from the outset, and particularly in the first seventeen. In the later poems the friend is promised eternity through the poet's art instead, but at the same time the poet's own age and mortality start to become an obsession. If only he and the youth were more perfectly matched, if only there were not these years between them. He writes of being 'old', but this carried a different implication at the end of the sixteenth century, as sonnet 138 demonstrates by yielding an upper age limit. 'And wherefore say not I that I am old?' Shakespeare asks: it is 1599, and he is thirty-five years old at most, probably less. In late Elizabethan England life expectancy was about forty-five, so a man might well think himself 'old' at thirty-five. In the *Sonnets* age is moreover a dialectical concept, defined with reference to the relationship of a younger with an older man.

A powerful statement about the poet's age and readiness for death occurs in sonnet 73. It is one of the supreme lyrics in the cycle and conjures up a sunset view of the poet, of someone who is close to the end of his life and at peace with it. The rhetorical texture and felicitous density of the poem show Shakespeare at his most assured. Sonnet 73 is one of a quartet of poems (71–74) which seem to have been written in the wake of a serious illness; it is calm and seductive, if not death-embracing:

> That time of year thou mayst in me behold
> When yellow leaves, or none, or few, do hang
> Upon those boughs which shake against the cold,
> Bare ruined choirs where late the sweet birds sang.
> In me thou seest the twilight of such day
> As after sunset fadeth in the west,
> Which by and by black night doth take away,
> Death's second self that seals up all in rest.
> In me thou seest the glowing of such fire
> That on the ashes of his youth doth lie
> As the death-bed whereon it must expire,
> Consumed with that which it was nourished by.
>> This thou perceiv'st, which makes thy love more strong,
>> To love that well which thou must leave ere long.

The poet's sickness culminates in these lines; in the two preceding poems Shakespeare urges his friend not to mourn him after he has become the fare of 'vilest worms'. Such is his love for the youth that he does not wish his death to cause him the slightest grief. He would prefer it if his friend forgot him at once, 'for I love you so / That I in your sweet thoughts would be forgot, / If thinking on me then should make you woe.' If sonnets 71–74 record a time when Shakespeare was dangerously ill, 75 manifests a distinct change of tone or mood, away from death towards convalescence, sustenance, and life: 'So are you to my thoughts as food to life, / Or as sweet seasoned showers to the ground.' The sickness may have been connected with the plague that struck London in the summer of 1592. Perhaps he caught and survived it. His incapacity may have left an opening for the rival poet, who enters the fray at just this point.

10

The Rival Poet: 1592–3

I T IS MORE than halfway through the cycle that the rival poet enters: in sonnet 78 Shakespeare refers to 'alien' pens now seeking the young man's patronage. By the next poem their number has contracted to one, the poet conceding that his 'sick muse' must yield to 'another'. Almost immediately afterwards, in sonnet 80, the other poet has become the rival poet. The verse of this poem, its similes and metaphors, contain important clues to his identity.

> O how I faint when I of you do write,
> Knowing a better spirit doth use your name
> And in the praise thereof spends all his might,
> To make me tongue-tied, speaking of your fame!
> But since your worth, wide as the ocean is,
> The humble as the proudest sail doth bear,
> My saucy bark, inferior far to his,
> On your broad main doth wilfully appear,
> Your shallowest help will hold me up afloat,
> Whilst he upon your soundless deep doth ride,
> Or, being wracked, I am a worthless boat,
> He of tall building and of goodly pride.

The marine imagery launched in 'ocean', 'proudest sail', 'broad main', and 'soundless deep' anticipates the other poem referring significantly to Shakespeare's rival, which begins 'Was it the proud full sail of his great verse, / Bound for the prize of all-too-precious you?' (sonnet 86). Why the poet chooses to convey the competing relationship between himself and the rival in terms of barks, shallow drafts and stately ships negotiating the deep ocean of the fair friend's generosity is one question; to the other, the identity of the rival, one word in this sonnet may contain a clue, *the* clue perhaps: *'might'*.

Shakespeare's use of the word 'might' to render the distinct tenor of the rival poet's verse points to Marlowe more than to any other writer of the period. Many years later Ben Jonson, comparing his dead friend Shakespeare to his peers in an elegy written in 1623, concluded that Shakespeare did 'our Lyly outshine, / Or sporting Kid, or Marlowe's mighty line.' So Jonson, searching for an epithet to typify Marlowe's verse, like Shakespeare hit on 'mighty'. Preferring Shakespeare's verse even to Marlowe's 'mighty line' was the supreme literary tribute Jonson could pay his friend, the last salvo in the literary rivalry between the two greatest dramatists of the age, delivered by the third greatest. It may well be that 'mighty' was a coterie word applied by the poets and dramatists, the *cognoscenti* of the period, to Marlowe's verse.

Shakespeare rarely refers to his contemporary rivals among the dramatists, but in *As You Like It*, written seven years after Marlowe's death, Phoebe, on falling in love with Rosalind, exclaims: 'Dead shepherd, now I find thy saw of might, / "Who ever loved that loved not at first sight?"' – she has, it seems, read Marlowe's *Hero and Leander*, and here quotes line 176 from the first sestiad. Contemporary writers and players would instantly have recognized the quotation. Nor, in this strikingly discursive literary play, is this the only reference to the poem. In the scene which follows Rosalind laughingly dismisses the idea that men might die 'in a love-cause'. Leander, she notes, 'would have lived many a fair year though Hero had turned nun, if it had not been for a hot midsummer night for, good youth, he went but forth to wash him in the Hellespont, and being taken with the cramp was drowned', her spoof of *Hero and Leander* a further suggestion that Shakespeare is commemorating Marlowe in this play. His use, like Jonson's, of the word 'might' to identify Marlowe connects with the idiom of the sonnets about the rival poet. When Shakespeare thought of Marlowe's verse the word 'mighty', meaning 'above a mortal pitch', came to mind by instant association.

There are two further significant links between Marlowe and *As You Like It*, a play set in Shakespeare's own back yard in the Forest of Arden and featuring a country yokel called William. The first is a cryptic reference to Marlowe's violent death in Deptford in 1593. Apropos of almost nothing Touchstone, the play's clown, remarks that 'When a man's verses cannot be understood, nor a man's good wit seconded with the forward child, understanding, it strikes a man more dead than a great reckoning in a little room.' The phrase 'strikes a man more dead' is oddly anticipated in the second (86) of the 'rival poet' sonnets, when the poet wonders whether it was the rival's supernatural gifts that so intimidated him: 'Was it his spirit, by spirits taught to write / Above a mortal pitch, that struck me dead?' The line from the play is now commonly read as an allusion to the events of May 1593 and specifically to the very wording of the coroner's report, which noted that Marlowe and his fellow diners 'could not agree about the sum of pence, that is, le recknynge'. A row ensued which, according to the inquest, resulted in Marlowe's death at Ingram Frizer's hands.

In alluding to Marlowe's death Shakespeare is alone among his contemporaries in using the word *reckoning* brought to prominence in the coroner's inquest, which would seem to point to some kind of inside knowledge. It would have been easy enough for him to ask Southampton about Marlowe; the Cecils must have known what happened, and what the Cecils knew Southampton might find out. And that may very well be how Shakespeare discovered this detail, even if he was only given the official version, that it was a senseless brawl over money that had robbed him of a close friend and the country of one of its greatest and most promising writers. And the official version may conceivably be true, notwithstanding the elaborate and overly convoluted statements about where the parties sat, and the way the killing of Marlowe could be twisted and turned until it became a legitimate act of self-defence. After all, a fight over traded insults was just another instance of the impulsive behaviour that Marlowe had exhibited throughout his short life.

There may well be another bow in the direction of Marlowe in *As You Like It*, in Rosalind's transvestite alter ego, Ganymede. When she and Celia set out on their quest into Arden, Celia asks what she should call her friend, now that she will be a woman disguised as a man. Rosalind replies: 'I'll have no worse a name than Jove's own page, / And therefore look you call me Ganymede.' The homosexual connotations of the name 'Ganymede' were common currency in a classically educated society, and Shakespeare was taking a chance in having his resourceful tomboy heroine label herself in effect an effeminate homosexual, the equivalent of the modern word 'queen'. But for all that the play toys in this way with homoerotic situations – as, for example, Phoebe falling in love with Rosalind – it never transgresses into open homosexuality. At the very end of the play Rosalind steps out of the fiction as the Epilogue, and teases the audience about her androgynous status. The play boldly explores homosexual attraction, but hardly deals with homosexuality proper, like Marlowe's *Edward II*.

There are cogent reasons for considering Marlowe seriously as the rival poet. If the Cecils still thought to woo their theatrically obsessed ward through poetry, what finer or more famous exponent than the cobbler's son from Canterbury? Since the late 1580s he and such friends as Edward Alleyn, the star of his company and the player of all his major roles, had been the unchallenged masters of the English stage, first at the Curtain and latterly down at the Rose on Bankside. Marlowe had been known to the Cecils at least since the intervention of the Privy Council that secured him his Cambridge degree – as Chancellor of the University, Lord Treasurer, and Privy Councillor, Burghley must have been partly responsible for the decision in Marlowe's favour. The Council's confidence in the good service Marlowe had done the state may have come from a briefing by Sir Francis Walsingham, the head of the Elizabethan intelligence service and the father-in-law of Sir Philip Sidney. It is a moot point whether Marlowe had been enlisted, or whether he volunteered his services.

Among his exemplary tales of lovers in *Narcissus*, Clapham includes that of Hero and Leander. Marlowe's *Hero and Leander* is an inventive and scintillating poem about first sexual love between a boy and a girl separated by the sea. It features a brilliant scene of Neptune as an old lecher who in a moment of erotic abandon fondles the perfect contours of Leander as the boy swims across the Hellespont. The homosexual encounter is portrayed with just as much gusto as the love affair between the girl and boy, if not more. Marlowe almost certainly did not know Clapham's poem, but probably chose Hero and Leander because the bisexual story provided a perfect paradigm for an erotic pitch to the androgynous Southampton. *Hero and Leander* may constitute an attempt by Marlowe to woo Southampton away from Shakespeare, throwing down a literary gauntlet to his friend and rival, daring him to match it, with himself as Neptune and Southampton as Leander, with the same flowing locks.

Hero and Leander first crop up in Shakespeare's early solo play *The Two Gentlemen of Verona*, but feature also in three plays in which Shakespeare was probably involved as collaborator, *A Shrew*, *King Leir*, and *Edward III*. The reference to their story in *King Leir* is the most immediately intriguing as far as Marlowe is concerned, because Gonorill receives Cornwall with 'As welcome as Leander was to Hero, / Or brave Aeneas to the Carthage queen.' Two lines, two mythic allusions, and two literary works by Marlowe, who had written *Dido, Queen of Carthage* while still at Cambridge. In *Edward III* the sex-crazed king woos the countess by telling her that she is fairer

> by far than Hero was,
> Beardless Leander not so strong as I;
> He swom an easy current for his love,
> But I will through a Hellespont of blood
> To arrive at Sestos where my Hero lies.

The tale of Hero and Leander with its aura of risqué sexuality may have been one with which both Shakespeare and Marlowe toyed in the years preceding the plague closure. If Shakespeare was indeed bisexual, at least in temperament if not in practice, he must have found Marlowe liberating, if not downright exhilarating. Marlowe knew no taboo. He was unconventional and brilliant and Will Shakespeare may have become his 'bosom lover', to borrow Portia's phrase about Antonio and Bassanio.

If anyone could bring out Shakespeare, it was Marlowe. The real-life plot here seems barely submerged in the poetry. In Shoreditch Shakespeare and Marlowe quite probably became close friends and dramatic collaborators before Shakespeare was drawn into the Southampton circle. It may even have been Marlowe who introduced them to each other when the sixteen-year-old Southampton joined Gray's Inn. He may have watched from the sidelines as the relationship between Shakespeare and the young earl deepened into something rather more than friendship, before himself joining the band of Southampton's declared suitors alongside, perhaps, his Cambridge contemporary Thomas Nashe.

The first edition of Nashe's picaresque novel *The Unfortunate Traveller*, completed on 27 June 1593, was addressed to Southampton. The dedication takes the shape of a convoluted epistle which does not survive in later versions of the text, probably because it was no longer wanted. Nashe and Marlowe undoubtedly knew each other at Cambridge where they overlapped for six or seven years, Nashe graduating from St John's in 1586 and Marlowe from Corpus Christi in 1587. The young Southampton turned up at St John's in 1585 at the age of twelve and stayed there until 1589. It is inconceivable that at St John's Burghley's ward should not have known Nashe, who was then in his late teens. It is not unlikely that Southampton also knew Marlowe, a few minutes' walk down the road at Corpus Christi, who was twenty-one in 1585. He may already have enjoyed a reputation among the *literati* as a poet and classical translator, though it is not recorded in the university annals. Some scholars believe that his first play, *Dido Queen of Carthage*, may have been written in collaboration with Nashe while they were both at Cambridge, that is around 1586 (both their names appear on the 1594 publication of *Dido*), on the grounds that the diamantine rhetoric and verbal pyrotechnics of *Tamburlaine* did not spring fully formed from Marlowe's head, but that to forge such a distinctive voice he must have been writing and experimenting steadily during his last years in Cambridge. The question is whether this Cambridge literary coterie consisted of ganymedes or catamites (the Latin name for the Greek boy Ganymede or Catamitus). If Marlowe knew Southampton in Cambridge (the earl was still barely fourteen when Marlowe left), he may have been attracted to the young aristocrat just as everybody else seems to have been. Perhaps Southampton was a willing catamite and thus served as a model for the 'female wanton boy' Ganymede who partners Jove in the opening scene of *Dido*; or perhaps he was a 'bedfellow', to use another phrase attributed to Marlowe in describing, not without blasphemy, the relationship between Christ and St John the Evangelist.

In the summer of 1592 Marlowe must have been looking for new lifelines. The plague and Privy Council between them had cut the players and writers off from their lucrative livelihood, the London theatres. It is true that they were able to make some kind of living by touring. That Marlowe's company certainly did is known from the survival of some of his friend Edward Alleyn's correspondence with his wife and his father-in-law Henslowe during the period when he was touring in the country after being forced out of London. All the main London playing venues were closed from the summer of 1592 until roughly the same time in 1594.

Thus it seems likely that circumstances – the closure of the play-houses, the opportunity offered by what looks like a serious illness of Shakespeare's, and a growing attraction to Southampton – prompted Marlowe to make his first bid, with *Hero and Leander*, for the young earl's patronage. Shakespeare's *Venus and Adonis* was entered on the Stationers' Register on 18 April 1593, suggesting that it must have been written earlier that spring or during Lent; if *Hero and Leander* was composed in competition with Shakespeare's poem, as seems likely, it would date from around the spring of 1593. It is almost certainly Marlowe's last work.

The poem itself, Shakespeare's repeated tributes to Marlowe, and the use of the word 'mighty' are not quite enough to identify Marlowe as the rival poet. But there is another clue that consolidates the argument. In sonnet 86, the rival is said to be mentored by 'spir-its', and thus enabled to strike the poor poet dumb:

> Was it the proud full sail of his great verse
> Bound for the prize of all-too-precious you
> That did my ripe thoughts in my brain inhearse,
> Making their tomb the womb wherein they grew?
> Was it his spirit, by spirits taught to write
> Above a mortal pitch, that struck me dead?
> No, neither he, nor his compeers by night
> Giving him aid my verse astonishèd.
> He, nor that affable familiar ghost
> Which nightly gulls him with intelligence,
> As victors of my silence cannot boast;
> I was not sick of any fear from thence.
> > But when your countenance filled up his line,
> > Then lacked I matter; that enfeebled mine.

The implication is that the rival poet moves in mysterious, perhaps even dangerous, circles – but that this should not be thought to cow the poet. Shakespeare asserts that the reason for his 'silence' is that the fair friend has willingly lent himself to becoming the subject of the rival's verse, thus robbing Shakespeare of any reason for writing. Circumstantial information about the rival's set of friends, 'his compeers by night', can be deduced: it has long been suspected that Shakespeare is here having a dig at what was then called the 'school of atheism' or 'school of night', perhaps in response to a pamphlet by the leading Jesuit Robert Parsons.[1] In 1592 Parsons had written of 'Sir Walter Ralegh's school of atheism' and accused Ralegh of presiding over a 'school wherein both Moses and our Saviour, the Old and New Testaments are jested at, and the scholars taught among other things to spell God backward.' While the Jesuit Parsons is clearly partisan, the notion of a school of atheism sorts well with the wild and iconoclastic views attributed to Marlowe by both Baines and Marlowe's former room-mate and fellow playwright Thomas Kyd.

The 'school' was headed by Henry Percy, the ninth Earl of Northumberland and Marlowe's exact contemporary, and Sir Walter Ralegh. It comprised writers, scholars, poets and dramatists like Marlowe, George Peele, Thomas Watson, George Chapman, John Florio, the poet Matthew Roydon, and two '*magi*', the mathematician Thomas Harriot and the scientist Walter Warner. Even Giordano Bruno, the famous Italian oculist, may have been associated with it during his stay in England. In 1595 Northumberland married the sister of the Earl of Essex which suggests that Southampton may also have been close to members of this club. The fact that one of the best-known lyrics of Elizabethan England, Marlowe's 'Come live with me and be my love', was countered by Ralegh with a lyric of his own on the same topic suggests that this club was probably intimate as well as exclusive. It may also have been distinctly Catholic in its orientation, through the Earl of Northumberland, whose family, like Southampton's, traditionally aligned themselves with the old faith. Among its adherents was Ferdinando Lord Strange, the very patron of players whom Marlowe claimed to know when he was summoned before the governor of Flushing.

What renders it probable that the reference to 'compeers by night' alludes to the 'school of night' is that Shakespeare uses just that phrase in Act IV of *Love's Labour's Lost* and in a context that at once brings to mind the *Sonnets*. *Love's Labour's Lost* was probably written in late

1594 or early 1595. In the passage in question the king tells the young nobleman Berowne that his love Rosaline 'is black as ebony', provoking from Berowne a paean to blackness, notwithstanding the king's protest that 'Black is the badge of hell, / The hue of dungeons, and the *school of night.*' (Arden Shakespeare). The similarity to the *Sonnets* is immediately apparent, the rhetorical texture is very similar – further encouragement to anchor the 'rival poet' sonnets in the time-span 1592–4.

Having made this briefest of appearances in the cycle, the rival poet mysteriously vanishes. He is there one moment and gone the next. No reason is given for his disappearance, and Shakespeare barely has a chance to engage with him. It seems almost that he surrenders at once to the rival's superior talent, as if he could not possibly compete. Then, nothing. It is as if the rival had never existed. There is no indication whether the youth returned to the poet, or the rival found another object of adulation. Nothing in the sequence gives the slightest hint of any further plot line regarding the other poet. This again suggests Marlowe, who was killed at Deptford in May 1593. The case is further reinforced by the fact that in the late summer of 1592 both he and Shakespeare were the targets of a savage invective penned by Robert Greene, one of Marlowe's Cambridge contemporaries, whose posthumously published pamphlet is one of the most notorious documents of Elizabethan theatre history. It is the first undoubted London notice of Shakespeare and it is not flattering, accusing him of plagiarism. *Greene's Groatsworth of Wit bought with a million of repentance* was entered on the Stationers' Register on 20 September 1592 and the passage involving Shakespeare reads:

> there is an upstart crow, beautified with our feathers, that with his tiger's heart wrapt in a player's hide, supposes he is as well able to bombast out a blank verse as the best of you: and being an absolute Johannes *factotum*, is in his own conceit the only Shake-scene in a country.

The general meaning is clear – Shakespeare is a devious, importunate and bumptious literary thief. Greene's use of metaphor and simile is quite specific, the crow having since antiquity been as closely associated with mimicry as the magpie is with thieving. In Aesop's fable the crow is tricked by the fox who appeals to her vanity, and this sense may be submerged in Greene's broadside; perhaps more to the point is the story of Roscius and the cobbler's crow, from Macrobius. Greene had earlier used this very fable in *Francesco's Fortune*, an attack on Edward Alleyn whom he mockingly called Roscius, after the legendary Roman actor of that name. Greene challenged 'Roscius' to admit that, like Aesop's crow, he was decked in someone else's feathers, that he had nothing to offer other than what the cobbler taught him: 'and if the cobbler hath taught thee to say *Ave Caesar*, disdain not thy tutor because thou pratest in a king's chamber.'[2]

Greene's attack on Shakespeare may be more barbed and specific than is commonly assumed. The clue is to be found in inside knowledge that happens to have survived. Like Roscius *alias* Alleyn, Greene suggests that Shakespeare has beautified himself with others' feathers, but may be making a more specific comparison to the cobbler's crow, who cannot sing anything by himself. Alleyn depended wholly for his great parts on Marlowe, the son of the cobbler from Canterbury, and was therefore a cobbler's son's crow. Greene might have cast Shakespeare similarly as a cobbler's crow, a versifying imitator who owes everything to the much more accomplished Marlowe. 'Shakespeare-the-crow' is plagiarizing 'Marlowe-the-cobbler', Greene implies. In so doing he provides further circumstantial evidence about the rivalry between the two chief playwrights of the age or, as he saw it, the mercurial flawed genius of the theatre and a pushy literary thief who had not gone to university. As if this were not bad enough, it may be that the phrasing of Greene's charge of plagiarism and theft hides a glancing blow at the one thing in Shakespeare's past that he must have been particularly troubled about, his run-in with the Lucys. Shakespeare later referred to Greene's sniping as a 'vulgar scandal', but he must have smarted from the attack, and been apprehensive about the damage to his reputation. Shakespeare was keen to preserve his good name in a society that valued 'honour' above life. To the Shakespeares of Stratford, to be able to enjoy the esteem of their peers may have meant more than to most, in the light of their history of debt and (probably) small-scale felony.

Greene had a point. One of the more disconcerting features of Shakespeare's works is his tendency to 'borrow' his plots from other writers, sometimes following them very closely indeed. In accusing

Shakespeare of plagiarism, predatory ambition, and arrogance, Greene quite intentionally lifted a phrase from Shakespeare's third play about Henry VI, one of the early masterpieces of the fledgling Elizabethan theatre. As the Duke of York, father of the future Richard III, stands captive on a mole hill, Queen Margaret taunts him with the blood-soaked handkerchief of his young son Rutland. The grief-stricken and doomed father responds to this perversion of feminine nature by apostrophizing the queen as a 'tiger's heart wrapped in a woman's hide', the very line Greene borrowed and adapted to insult its author.

If Greene was clearly not happy with Shakespeare, nor was he with Marlowe. It is sometimes overlooked that in *Groatsworth* he tore into Marlowe for the second time in four years, this time directly accusing him of atheism and political cynicism, asking 'Why should thy excellent wit, His gift, be so blinded that thou shouldst give no glory to the giver? Is it pestilent Machiavellian policy that thou hast studied?' Machiavelli speaks the Prologue to Marlowe's *The Jew of Malta*, and in shifting his focus from the play to the poet's life Greene is levelling serious charges. He was then on his death-bed, to which he also alludes, and died before the pamphlet appeared. It was left to his publisher Henry Chettle to face the repercussions of Greene's attack, and he soon apologised.

> About three months since died M. Robert Greene, leaving many papers in sundry booksellers' hands, among other his Groatsworth of wit in which a letter written to divers playmakers is offensively by one or two [Marlowe and Shakespeare] of them taken; and because on the dead [Greene] they cannot be avenged, they wilfully forge in their conceits a living author [Chettle]; and after tossing it to and fro, no remedy but it must light on me. How I have all the time of my conversing in printing hindered the bitter inveighing against scholars it hath been very well known; and how in that I dealt, I can sufficiently prove. With neither of them that take offence was I acquainted, and with one of them [Marlowe] I care not if I never be; the other [Shakespeare], whom at that time I did not so much spare as since I wish I had, for that as I have moderated the heat of living writers and might have used my own discretion (especially in such a case) the author being dead, that I did not, I am as sorry as if the original fault had been my fault, because myself have seen his demeanour no less

civil than he excellent in the quality he professes. Beside, divers of worship [people of high rank] have reported his uprightness of dealing,
which argues his honesty and his facetious grace of writing that
approves his art.

Marlowe was alive when this was written, and though Chettle professed not to care about being acquainted with him, he did point out
in his own defence that in fact he had edited out other parts of the
attack on Marlowe – probably charges of homosexuality. Chettle
can have had little or no inkling of Marlowe's political double life.
Even Cambridge did not until the Privy Council and the university's
Chancellor enlightened it. But bisexuality or homosexuality would
have been much harder to conceal, to hide from cliquish gossip. If the
actors knew, as they surely must, then publishers like Chettle could
also find out. The 'divers of worship' were probably from either the
Privy Council or Cecil House – effectively one and the same at the
time – or from Southampton himself.

A striking allusion in one of the sonnets may indicate that it was
indeed Southampton and his friends who caused Chettle to think
again and publish a retraction. In sonnet 111, one of a triad of poems
in which Shakespeare laments the iniquity of his lot as an actor
(110–112), he identifies Fortune as the guilty goddess who 'did not
better for my life provide / Than public means which public man-
ners breeds'. His name, he claims, 'receives a brand' from acting and
'almost thence my nature is subdued / To what it works in, like the
dyer's hand.' The 'brand' seems disproportionately strong, until the
lowly social status of players is recalled: they were little more than
vagabonds unless they wore the livery of a particular lord. 'Brand' is
usually read in just such terms, the poet rueing the fact that he
is little more than a licensed vagrant. But the sonnet which follows
suggests that 'brand' may refer quite specifically to the attack on
Shakespeare by Robert Greene. In 112 the poet acknowledges his
friend's support when the poet was the subject of a 'vulgar scandal'
and slander which in the end failed to touch him because of the
young man's loyal support. The poet only cares, he affirms, about his
friend's opinions, be they good or bad; those of others are of no
consequence:

Your love and pity doth th'impression fill
Which vulgar scandal stamped upon my brow;
For what care I who calls me well or ill,
So you o'er-green my bad, my good allow?
You are my all the world, and I must strive
To know my shames and praises from your tongue –
None else to me, nor I to none alive,
That my steeled sense or changes, right or wrong.
In so profound abysm I throw all care
Of others' voices that my adder's sense
To critic and to flatterer stoppèd are.
Mark how with my neglect I do dispense:
   You are so strongly in my purpose bred
   That all the world besides methinks are dead.

At the end of the sixteenth century the word 'vulgar' remained close to its Latin root *vulgus*, meaning public or 'published', in the public domain. As for 'scandal', the phrase variously meant moral lapse, damage to reputation, injurious rumour, slander, or malicious gossip. The gist of sonnet 112 is that in response to a public attack on the poet the aristocratic youth rose to his rescue and, by 'o'er-green-ing' the poet's 'bad', championed his innocence, or 'good'. This is Shakespeare's one and only use of 'o'er-green', or anything similar. Ostensibly the meaning of this coinage must be something on the lines of mitigating, rendering harmless, excusing. If however this only usage is a specific allusion to Robert Greene, the 'scandal' must be nothing less than his diatribe against Shakespeare.

This is the only reference in all 154 sonnets to a public scandal and to the bad-mouthing of the poet ('calls me well or ill'). Its occurrence in conjunction with an unusual coinage which happens to contain the name of Shakespeare's chief detractor at this period can hardly be a coincidence. A strong case could be made for reading 'so you o'er-green my bad, my good allow' on the lines of 'so long as you, unlike my detractor Greene, focus on my good parts' (where the 'over' of 'o'er-green' is interpreted as 'over and against, in the teeth of'); or else 'o'er-green' could mean turning Greene's slander into praise. The possibly punning allusion to Greene's name should cause no surprise, for it may be Shakespeare simply returning a compliment, Greene having taken Shakespeare's surname in vain with 'Shake-scene' in *Groatsworth*. Sonnet 112 is nothing less than an act of homage and gratitude to Southampton for his role in *l'affaire* Greene.[3]

That Shakespeare had been upset by Greene's attack can surely not be in doubt – why else would people in authority have dressed Chettle down? The fact that Chettle was put in his place with regard to Shakespeare but not necessarily Marlowe gives food for thought. The attack on Shakespeare was literary above all; on Marlowe it was personal, political, and theological, a much more inflammatory cocktail. The fact that the maverick spy and crypto-Catholic atheist died in the house of one Eleanor Bull, who was herself a cousin of one of the Queen's confidantes and related to Burghley may have a sinister logic of its own. There were many reasons why Marlowe might get into serious trouble, including a fiery temper and too many quarrels, and any or all may have been in play at the so-called reckoning in Deptford in May 1593. It is unlikely that what really happened and why will ever be known, but the fact that he died in a house with tentacles back to the Cecils at a time when they were promoting Southampton's marriage suggests the possibility that Marlowe and Southampton may have enjoyed ganymedic relations, neither of them for the first time and in Southampton's case probably not for the last.[4] Perhaps the Cecils felt that having a paedophiliac homo-sexual son-in-law in the Earl of Oxford was bad enough, and he moreover the father of the young woman whom they were trying to marry off to Southampton. It is unlikely that Marlowe was killed because of his sexuality, but if he was wooing the young earl and threatened to compromise him, it would only have compounded the risks he took.

11

A Twenty-first Birthday Poem: 6 October 1594

IN A NUMBER of sonnets the poet mentions absenting himself from
the fair youth – presumably Shakespeare taking off for Stratford-
upon-Avon periodically to see his family, or touring for prolonged
spells with the company during prohibition periods. It is clear that by
the time he was writing the *Sonnets* Shakespeare made his journeys on
horseback rather than on foot. The opening line of sonnet 50 conveys
the poet's sadness with which he leaves:

> How heavy do I journey on the way
> When what I seek, my weary travel's end,
> Doth teach that ease and that repose to say
> 'Thus far the miles are measured from thy friend'.

Presumably these were sometimes Shakespeare's thoughts as he sat in
Henley Street thinking of Southampton in London, and perhaps he felt
guilty about having them. His young children were growing up and he
must have seen great changes in them every time he crossed the thresh-
old of that house in Henley Street after a spell in the capital. Doubtless
he was excited at the thought of seeing them, so that the hired jade
carrying him occasionally felt the spur that 'sometimes anger thrusts
into his hide, / Which heavily he answers with a groan.' Perhaps he felt
that no doubt he should have been settled in Stratford, making a local
name for himself as a glover and being a good father to his children –
yet there he was, spending long periods of time in London, undoubtedly sowing many wild oats. These divided feelings may be the reason
why he never put down roots in the capital. It had all been so different when he set out from Stratford six years earlier. A poem about
leaving Stratford, which has been acclaimed as his first sonnet, begins
'How careful was I when I took my way / Each trifle under truest

bars to thrust / That to my use it might unusèd stay / From hands of falsehood, in sure wards of trust.'[1] The cadence of the verse is remarkably similar to the opening lines of 50 ('How heavy do I journey on the way'), and perhaps the later lyric, when the poet is travelling in the opposite direction, intentionally echoes the first.

The three main poems of separation, 97, 98, and 99, all post-date Marlowe's death in May 1593. All three sonnets are artfully structured around the seasons. The poet remarks that his absence from his friend has been 'like a winter' with 'old December's bareness everywhere' around him, despite the fact that he has been away during summer and autumn. The use of a standard conceit whereby the missing lover turns the very seasons into their opposite by his absence need not automatically detract from its evidential value. If the chronology of the cycle is valid and it is accepted that Marlowe was the rival poet (who has been out of the frame for the span of ten sonnets), the separation to which Shakespeare refers in the three sonnets occurred some time in the summer and autumn of 1593. He was probably at home in Stratford-upon-Avon, to sit out the closure of the theatres and to work on *The Rape of Lucrece*. As far as it can be determined he was not on the road, unlike some other players.

The great Edward Alleyn was among those touring, and during this period of late summer 1593 he and his father-in-law Philip Henslowe conducted a vivid correspondence about what it was like in the city and for those who were left behind. Henslowe sent the actor greetings, particularly from Alleyn's wife, his 'mouse', whose 'commendations comes by itself which, as she says, comes from her heart and her soul praying to God day and night for your good health'. After reassuring Alleyn that their house 'on the Bankside right over against the Clink' was spared by the plague, he relates how severe it had been, killing one Robert Brown's wife, children, and entire household over in Shoreditch – presumably friends of Alleyn from his days at the Theatre before 1591. He then moves seamlessly, without apparent change of register, from the horrors of the plague to domestic matters such as furniture (notably Alleyn's 'bedstead') and spinach beds. These and the garden are thriving, but he rues the fact that while his 'orange-coloured stockings' were dyed there was 'no market at Smithfield neither to buy your cloth nor yet to sell your horse for no man would

The house in Henley Street in which Shakespeare was born and where he lived from 1564 until he left Stratford in the late 1580s

An animated street scene from the period, showing a central gutter, a tavern, a waste collector with horse and cart, and a woman publicly fouling the pavement, to the delight of a pig and the amazement of all the other onlookers

The recently identified house of Shakespeare's mother Mary Arden in the Warwickshire village of Wilmcote

Anne Hathaway, Shakespeare's future wife, spent her childhood in this large farm house in Shottery near Stratford

Right: The revered Jesuit Edmund Campion, shown here in a contemporary sketch. Above his head can be glimpsed an angel with a martyr's crown

P EDMVNDVS CAMPIANVS Q PR E SOC IESV LONDINI
PRO CAT FIDE MARTYR CONSVMAVIT P DEC 1581

Below: An original Tudor mural still to be found in The White Swan in Stratford-upon-Avon. It shows Tobias with the archangel Raphael to his left, parting from his parents to redeem his father's bond in a far-off city

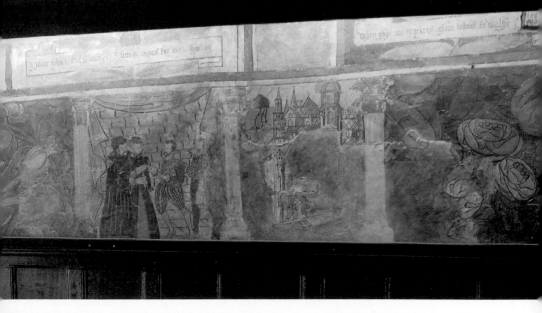

Above: In this chapel at Billesley near Wilmcote Shakespeare's granddaughter Elizabeth Hall-Nash married John Barnard in 1649, perhaps as a tribute to her grandfather who may have married Anne Hathaway here in 1582

Left: The old entrance to Billesley chapel through which William and Anne Shakespeare may have left as husband and wife in 1582.

Clopton Bridge was called 'great and sumptuous' in Shakespeare's time; trade and traffic between Stratford and London have passed across it since the Middle Ages and still do so today

Richard Burbage acted in the same company as Shakespeare and played many of his most important tragic roles

A putative portrait of Christopher Marlowe from c.1585; he may have been the rival poet of the *Sonnets*

The Lucys' manor on the Avon at Charlecote, from inside the same grounds in which Shakespeare may have been caught poaching in the late 1580s

The 1588 'Armada' portrait of Queen Elizabeth I, painted in the year of the naval battle from which England emerged victorious

St Paul's cathedral still boasts its spire in this detail from a famous Tudor map of London (the so-called 'Copperplate'). Blackfriars, the Fleet river, Bridewell prison, and Baynard ('Benams') Castle are clearly visible

Claes Jan Visscher's view of London as it was around 1600. In the foreground to the west of London Bridge are St Mary Overy, the palace of the Bishop of Winchester with the Clink prison, and the first Globe Theatre and Bear Garden

In this miniature by Nicholas Hilliard of Henry Wriothesley, third earl of Southampton, the young earl's mane and androgynous good looks are evident

Robert Devereux, the second earl of Essex, from a 1596 portrait at just the time when Shakespeare was clashing with the licensing authorities over using the name Oldcastle

The 1596 Shakespeare coat-of-arms from a draft copy surviving in the College of Arms, displaying the motto '*non sanz droict*' and showing the transversal spear that runs across the escutcheon offer me above four pound for him therefore I would not sell him but have sent him into the country till you return back again'. Henslowe and Alleyn's use of 'mouse' and 'good sweetheart and loving mouse' as terms of endearment for daughters and wives anticipates Shakespeare's similar usage in *Hamlet*. The prince, urging his mother to refrain from sex with Claudius in the future, orders her no longer to 'let the bloat king tempt you again to bed, / Pinch wanton on your cheek, call you his mouse.' It may well be that Will called Anne his loving mouse. Clearly the phrase was current at the time, like the affectionate use of 'Jug' by Alleyn for his wife who, like Shakespeare's sister, was called Joan.

On 1 August 1593 Alleyn urged his family at home in London to take special precautions against the plague by keeping the house 'fair and clean'. His mouse should throw water before her door at night both at the front and back of the house and 'have in your windows good store of rue and herb of grace'. He was obviously a keen gardener, because he finds time to remind her that 'all that bed which was parsley, in the month of September you sow it with spinach for then is the time'. He would do it himself, he writes, but cannot because he will not be home until All Hallows. On 14 August Henslowe and Joan reply, addressing their letter 'To my well-beloved husband Master Edward Alleyn one of my Lord Strange's players this be delivered with speed.' In this letter Henslowe reproves his son-in-law for not writing, and thus leaving his wife desperately worried:

> for we heard that you were very sick at Bath and that one of your fellows were fain to play your part for you which was no little grief unto us to hear . . . we feared it much because we had no letter from you when the other wives had letters sent which made your mouse not to weep a little but took it very grievously thinking that you had conceived some unkindness of her because you were ever wont to write with the first and I pray you do so still for we would all be sorry but to hear as often from you as others do from their friends for we would write oftener to you than we do but we know not whither to send to you . . . your garden and all your things doth prosper very well thanks be to God for your beans are grown to high hedge and well codded . . .

It is evident that a lively correspondence was carried on between touring actors and their spouses in London. Joan, moreover, knew

141

what the other players were doing because she kept in touch with their wives. The actors' spouses formed coteries in London while their men were out of town. It is likely that Shakespeare and his family exchanged letters very similar to the Alleyn–Henslowe correspondence. Alleyn or Henslowe might perhaps have shed light on Marlowe's fate, but did not. It almost looks as though everyone who knew Marlowe also appreciated that this business was best left alone. The written record is not helpful here, but the fact that the eventual publication of Marlowe's *Hero and Leander* coincided with the death of Burghley should perhaps point to a link: it is not impossible that Marlowe had towards the end of his life made an enemy of the most powerful man in the land.

As for Shakespeare, there is no certainty about what he did in the summer and early autumn of 1593. If he was in Stratford it is most likely that he helped out his father in his glover's shop in Henley Street, and took a hand with farming and the rearing of his children. As it happens there is an intriguing trace in the documentary record that may add substance to this hypothesis, the gloves of Alexander Aspinall who succeeded John Cottom as headmaster of the King's New School. He served the longest term of any of its masters and was successful over the years in sending boys up to Oxford from Stratford. Two, George Quiney and Henry Sturley, both sons of parents whom Shakespeare knew well, eventually returned to teach at their old school. Aspinall became Holofernes in *Love's Labour's Lost*, and Shakespeare alluded to him in *Henry V*.

In 1594, the year of *Lucrece*, Aspinall married Ann Shaw, the widow of a wool driver by the name of Rafe Shaw whose son July was a friend of Shakespeare's from their days together in Henley Street when the Shaws had lived at the country end of the street near Henley Lane; many years later, July Shaw witnessed Shakespeare's will. Not long after Shakespeare's death a rumour started in Stratford that when Aspinall gave his new wife a pair of gloves as a betrothal present the verses that went with them were written by Shakespeare. Certainly there may be a pun on the word 'will', since this is one of Shakespeare's favourite subjective signature tunes in the *Sonnets*: 'The gift is small, / The will is all: / Alexander Aspinall'. Shakespeare may not only have written the verses, but made the gloves as well. Aspinall and

Will Shakespeare must have been friends by 1594 and probably before then since he was teaching Shakespeare's children. At the time of Aspinall's wedding Shakespeare was almost certainly in Stratford because of the prolonged closure of the London theatres. The dates line up. If Shakespeare was to give anyone a betrothal present in his home town it had to be then, and the fact that it was a present of *gloves* only adds to the plausibility of the gift. Gloves and verses were what the Shakespeares of Henley Street had to offer above all else during this period. Aspinall gave a book to the school (which bought a chain specially to secure it), which suggests that the master may have been a bit of a bibliophile, something which he and Master Shakespeare at New Place probably had in common. After their marriage in 1594 Alexander and Ann Aspinall moved to 21 Chapel Street, next-door but one eventually to the Shakespeares, where they shared a house with Aspinall's new step-son July. The Shaw–Aspinall back garden bordered on those of Nash and New Place, and their house survives to this day. Aspinall now joined his new wife's lucrative business of malting and trading in wool. No more teaching and living in the master's house above the council chamber where he had spent so many years that long after his departure it was still known as 'the Chambers over our Council Chamber wheare Mr Aspinall dwelled'.

While making gloves and penning pithy epigrams for wedding gifts Shakespeare was also writing *Lucrece* and his separation sonnets which he may have posted to Southampton in London, through William Greenway and perhaps through Field when the latter visited the Midlands. During the summer and early autumn of 1593 Shakespeare was apparently rediscovering nature. In sonnet 98 he records 'From you have I been absent in the spring, / When proud pied April, dressed in all his trim' has brought everything to life. A glorious, almost Romantic evocation of spring follows only to be dashed by the wintry effect of the friend's absence. But not even winter can restrain the sheer pleasure that flows from the poet's pen at the sights and scents of rolling carpets of spring flowers and the next poem, 99, continues with flowers such as lilies and York and Lancaster roses and, perhaps, the occasional apothecary rose, 'a third, nor red, nor white, had stol'n of both'.

It is tempting to see this as pure Warwickshire, to suppose that

Shakespeare drew strongly on the countryside in these poems precisely because he was back it when he was writing them. He is the most lyrical rural dramatist of his age, perhaps truer to his country roots by some distance than any other writer of the period. Who but the author of *A Midsummer Night's Dream* could start a sonnet with 'The forward violet thus did I chide: / Sweet thief, whence didst thou steal thy sweet that smells, / If not from my love's breath?' and conclude, 'More flowers I noted, yet I none could see / But sweet, or colour, it had stol'n from thee?' Not until Keats was there such another as he who compared poetry to the 'mournful hymns' of a nightingale which 'hush' the summer nights (102) but, unlike the cockney poet who avidly attuned himself to nature, Shakespeare knew nature from growing up in it. As far as the inherent magic of nature as a subject matter is concerned, he presages Wordsworth. From 102 it appears that the poet's ardour has cooled a little – or so it might seem to the youth, the poet notes apologetically.

If nothing else Shakespeare's enforced plague break from the London stage granted him extra time with the children. It may not have seemed so precious there and then, but it would surely become so in retrospect. That time would tragically not lie too far in the future, although he had of course no way of knowing this. It is easy to see why Southampton should have become so very dear to Shakespeare. The young aristocrat was not only one of the most dazzling stars in the Elizabethan firmament, but also appears to have been exceptionally generous. If he did indeed give Shakespeare a thousand pounds it is likely that he was thereby instrumental in rescuing Shakespeare from the threat of indigence and of persecution by the Lucys, and raising his stock immeasurably in the eyes of his contemporaries both in Warwickshire and London. He had given Shakespeare back his life and elevated him above his dreams, and all this in recognition of his talent for poetry. It seems, to adapt a phrase from Falstaff, that Southampton was not only brilliant in himself but the cause of brilliance in other men. Shakespeare's talent was not just making waves in the London theatre now – it was attracting the best people in the land.

In poems 102, 103, and 104 Shakespeare and Southampton are reunited. Shakespeare was now back in London, so that these poems date from after the summer of 1594, when the theatres reopened. It appears that the youth was worried about his looks, though he can hardly have aged much during the separation. Another reason for this anxiety that suggests itself is his twenty-first birthday, on 6 October 1594. It is quite possible that sonnet 104 was written as a birthday gift to the earl, who was now officially of age.

> To me, fair friend, you never can be old.
> For as you were when first your eye I eyed,
> Such seems your beauty still. Three winters cold
> Have from the forests shook three summers' pride;
> Three beauteous springs to yellow autumn turned
> In process of the seasons have I seen,
> Three April perfumes in three hot Junes burned
> Since first I saw you fresh, which yet are green.
> Ah, yet doth beauty, like a dial hand,
> Steal from his figure and no pace perceived;
> So your sweet hue, which methinks still doth stand,
> Hath motion, and mine eye may be deceived.
>   For fear of which, hear this, thou age unbred:
>   Ere you were born was beauty's summer dead.

That the young man's eyes feature so prominently in the poet's reminiscence may reflect the fact that Southampton's luminous blue eyes were as distinctive a feature and as commonly remarked upon at the time as his flowing hair. If the chronology sketched in the poems is generally correct, then 104 would fall around Southampton's twenty-first birthday, assuming that he and Shakespeare had indeed first met in 1590, and that the first seventeen sonnets were written for the earl's seventeenth birthday. That the poems refer to the seasons in the way they do may be no more than convention – but then again it may not, since it was just about this time that England experienced three of the wettest summers yet known. The weather in 1594 was spectacularly bad, and not just during the summer months. Rain storms in March were followed by hail showers and more rain in May, and throughout June and July 'it commonly rained every day or night'. After a lull in August the wet weather returned in September, in time to rot the crops, so that the prices for rye and wheat rocketed. This is presumably the natural catastrophe behind Titania's speech in

A Midsummer Night's Dream, on 'the green corn rotting, the drowned fields, and the mud filling up the nine men's morris'. It depends, in part at least on the audience recognizing the allusions to bad weather.

Paradoxically, it was in this water-logged spring of 1594 that Stratford-upon-Avon suffered the worst fire in its history. Starting at nine in the morning on 13 May, it burnt down more than a hundred houses and barns. It destroyed £2,000-worth of the town's most precious commodities, barley, corn, and malt. For one of the chief malting centres in the Midlands, this was a disaster. According to the record, the conflagration 'came by the negligence of an old woman put in trust to tend the fire of a brew house and fell asleep'. The wind played its part, as did the lack of a fire brigade. Instead of trying to contain the fire by fetching water and detaching houses from one another with the firehooks kept at the Market Cross for just this purpose, the men of Stratford were 'occupied for the most part in carrying out their stuff out of their houses into the fields and into the midst of the street'. Only towards nightfall was the fire overcome. If Shakespeare was in Stratford on this day, he would have been in the thick of it. The fire raged right opposite the Shakespeares' house, and destroyed the Cox and Cawdrey homes.

There is no reference in the *Sonnets* to this local calamity, nor does it feature as prominently in the minutes of the borough council as might be expected. It is mentioned in a petition from the borough to the Chancellor of the Exchequer at Michaelmas 1594 ('we which by the late casualties of fire are so greatly impoverished'), but it is cited there primarily to support the case for repairing the chancel and south aisle of Holy Trinity church. Indeed, the fire seems to have triggered a minor building boom which produced at least two very fine town houses, Harvard House and the Shrieve's, both near the epicentre of the fire. Neither house can be said to be representative of a borough which by now included a substantial underclass of poor and vagrants, but their building indicates that the town carried on business almost as usual. Which may be why Shakespeare did so too.

If the 'three hot Junes' mentioned by the poet in sonnet 104 are not a mere stylistic convention, they probably refer to the more recent 'proper' summers including that of 1593.[2] One corollary of dating sonnet 104 to shortly before Southampton's birthday on 6 October

1594 is that 112, the Greene poem with its allusion to the 'vulgar scandal', must be later than October 1594. This makes good sense in the context of a chronological sequence, since 112 is preceded by two theatre poems. It is the autumn of 1594, the plague had abated, the theatres had reopened, and Chettle's apology had not only safeguarded and consolidated Shakespeare's theatrical career but also cleared his name. Shakespeare now found himself joining a new company, the Lord Chamberlain's, headed by Lord Hunsdon. The company drew into it some of the best talent in the London theatre – Shakespeare, Burbage, Condell, Heminges, and Kemp are among those listed in the 'cast' of the First Folio. Most of the stars of the time were there, except for those in the Admiral's who stayed with Alleyn and Henslowe at the Rose on Bankside and further south of the river at Newington Butts near Elephant and Castle. The Lord Chamberlain's chief writer was an asset and a star – there was none better, now that Marlowe was dead. Shakespeare would do for the Lord Chamberlain's what Marlowe had done for Alleyn, and then some.

12

Taming the Dark Lady: 1594–onwards

THE DARK LADY enters the scene in sonnet 127, some time after October 1594 – exactly where she should, since she probably became Shakespeare's mistress in the autumn of 1594, during the first playing season after the two-year closure period. 'Dark Lady' makes her sound exotic and *dangereuse*, a Queen of the Night or Cleopatra figure, but refers rather to her complexion. She was probably a dark-skinned woman. In marshalling this kind of detail, the poet appears to point to a woman of flesh and blood rather than a generic one. She plays the virginals, and there are repeated references to her 'raven black' eyes and her dark skin tone; there are indications that she may be foreign, with an accent that the poet finds both alluring and irritating: 'Nor are mine ears with thy tongue's tune delighted,' he writes, echoing and contradicting his earlier 'I love to hear her speak'. Or perhaps this is a comment on her singing to the accompaniment of the virginals. He has watched her play, and the poem starting 'How oft when thou, my music, music play'st / Upon that blessèd wood . . . Do I envy those jacks that nimble leap / To kiss the tender inward of thy hand' carries an erotic charge evocative of the poetry of John Donne.

The most plausible candidate for the Dark Lady has long been Emilia Bassano, daughter of Baptista Bassano, a renowned court musician from a Venetian Jewish musical dynasty. Her skin colour would probably have been olive rather than English 'white'. She was five years younger than Shakespeare and four years older than Southampton. In October 1592 she married a French musician by the name of Alfonso Lanier, so that her baby was born legitimate in 1593.[1] If she was the Dark Lady, her affair with the poet appears to have begun after her marriage, for in Sonnet 152, one of the last poems, the poet accuses her of breaking her marriage vows and also, by having an affair with the fair youth, her more recent troth-plight to the poet:

> In loving thee thou knòw'st I am forsworn,
> But thou art twice forsworn to me love swearing,
> In act thy bed-vow broke and new faith torn . . .

The poet confesses that he is himself guilty of breaking the faith he had pledged years earlier – which can only refer to his vows of fidelity to Anne Hathaway. This particular poem about breaking faith must have been written sometime after the affair started. It is likely that Shakespeare first laid eyes on Emilia Bassano in the company of the man who had kept her as his mistress, Lord Hunsdon. A superb portrait of Hunsdon, dated 1591 and signed 'by Mark Gerards', survives. Hunsdon was sixty-six years old, and his face is that of a handsome, grand patrician. He was first cousin to the Queen, the son of Anne Boleyn's sister, and the founder of Shakespeare's new company, the Lord Chamberlain's. Although Emilia had undoubtedly been Hunsdon's paramour before the birth of her son Henry in 1593, the relationship ceased after her marriage to Lanier. It is now that she met Will Shakespeare, whose sonnets to young Henry Wriothesley may have already have been circulating in London. The occasion of the fateful meeting between Shakespeare and Emilia may have been a performance of the greatest play ever to be put on at the Theatre, *Richard III*.

Shakespeare had written the audacious history play *3 Henry VI* by the summer of 1592, because a phrase from it was quoted disparagingly against him shortly afterwards by Robert Greene. Perhaps too, he had already written *Richard III* when the playhouses closed. This monumental play, Shakespeare's second-longest after *Hamlet*, can have left no one in any doubt about who would be king of the London stage should Marlowe ever cease to write. More alarmingly perhaps, even if he continued Shakespeare would overtake him. In Tennyson's words, Marlowe was only ever the 'morning star' to Shakespeare's 'dazzling sun'. Those in the know, that is fellow playwrights and discerning audiences, would have guessed as much after *Richard III*. Had Shakespeare suffered the same fate as Marlowe in 1593 that play alone would have secured his fame. If Shakespeare had not finished *Richard*

III with its brilliantly funny and resourceful crook-backed hero before the closure of the theatres, he was probably at work on it during the first few months of prohibition. Over the two years of the interdiction he had plenty of time to write and fine-tune the play. Its length may indeed be a consequence of it having been written in large part away from the playhouse, so that it could not be rehearsed or revised on the stage as the writing went on. But when the houses reopened in 1594 *Richard III* was ready. It was probably the first play that the newly constituted Lord Chamberlain's company put on to celebrate their launch in the late summer of 1594. Shakespeare knew it was brilliant, and so did they. And London audiences seem to have concurred.

The character of Richard of Gloucester emerges as early as *2 Henry VI* and then bears down inexorably like a 'usurping boar' as the Wars of the Roses plays draw to an end. His very deformity is repeatedly and unsentimentally apostrophized as a 'foul stigmatic', 'heap of wrath', and 'foul indigested lump'. He of course joins in with gusto in joking about his crippled spine. He is the biggest single character Shakespeare created before Hamlet, and perhaps shared something more than just a love of theatricality with his creator. Apart from killing and the pursuit of power, Richard's chief pleasure is women. He revels in his ability to seduce them despite his 'foul indigested lump'. In Richard III Shakespeare has created a radical character whose moral shortcomings are simply swept before it by his huge dramatic presence.

Like the women whom he chooses to woo, audiences have always been entranced by Richard, and particularly, it seems, women. One notable story about the play dates from around the time that *Richard III* was first playing in London:

> Upon a time when Burbage played Richard III there was a citizen grew so far in liking with him that before she went from the play she appointed him to come that night unto her by the name of Richard III. Shakespeare, overhearing their conclusion, went before, was entertained and at his game ere Burbage came. Then message being brought that Richard III was at the door, Shakespeare caused return to be made that William the Conqueror was before Richard III, Shakespeare's name William.

This is what John Manningham, a barrister at Middle Temple, recorded in his diary on 13 March 1602, some eight years after

Burbage first played Richard III. Burbage was Shakespeare's junior by four years and the only actor in London who could compete with Alleyn. His Shakespearian roles included Richard III, and eventually Hamlet, Lear, and Othello. It is not clear where or when this early performance took place, but the odds are that it would have been at the Shoreditch Theatre in 1594 when playing resumed. The presence of women in the playhouse audiences was common, and one foreign resident noted how freely English women comported themselves at public shows: 'The plump and buxom display their bosoms very liberally, and those who are lean go muffled up to the throat,' remarked the chaplain to the Venetian embassy, Orazio Busino, after attending a court entertainment in January 1618. The Manningham story would seem to confirm English women's relative sexual freedoms. Here after all is a citizen's wife making herself freely available to a player, something which the twenty-first century may well accept but which sits perhaps rather more doubtfully with the society of the 1590s.

None of the participants in this miniature sexual comedy seems to be unduly troubled by it, any more than the narrator. Manningham's phrase 'at his game' is the equivalent of 'having sex', and about as neutral if not a shade more indulgent and jocular. Burbage was a bachelor at the time (he married his wife Winifred around 1600), but Shakespeare had been a married father for at least ten years before *Richard III*. The 'citizen' in question might have been a widow of independent means who had the run of her house at night, or the wife of a husband in the country, or a wealthy prostitute. Whoever she was, she clearly loved the theatre and probably had independent means of some sort. The tale of Shakespeare, Burbage, and the citizen's wife also exists independently of the diary entry by Manningham, in a pamphlet by Thomas Wilkes entitled *A General View of the Stage* (1759):

> One evening when *Richard III* was to be performed, Shakespeare observed a young woman delivering a message to Burbage in so cautious a manner as excited his curiosity to listen to. It imported that her master was gone out of town that morning, and her mistress would be glad of his company after play; and to know what signal he would appoint for admittance. Burbage replied 'three taps at the door' and 'It is I, Richard the Third'. She immediately withdrew and Shakespeare

followed 'till he observed her to go into a house in the city; and enquiring in the neighbourhood he was informed that a young lady lived there, the favourite of an old rich merchant. Near the appointed time of meeting, Shakespeare thought proper to anticipate Master Burbage and was introduced by the concerted signal. The lady was very much surprised at Shakespeare's presuming to act Master Burbage's part, but as he, who had wrote *Romeo and Juliet*, we may be certain did not want wit or eloquence to apologize for the intrusion, she was soon pacified, and they were mutually happy till Burbage came to the door and repeated the same signal. But Shakespeare popping his head out of the window, bid him be gone, for that William the Conqueror had reigned before Richard III.

According to this version Shakespeare followed her 'into a house in the city' – from, presumably, Curtain Road in Shoreditch. A 'young lady' who was the 'favourite', that is mistress, of a rich old man would fit Emilia Bassano and Lord Hunsdon well enough, and the address in the city may have been Blackfriars, where Hunsdon lived. By the autumn of 1594 Emilia was married and the mother of a baby boy – called Henry after his father, Henry Carey Hunsdon. The bond between her and Hunsdon was clearly such that she made sure her son carried his blue-blooded father's name. She might still have been based in Blackfriars after her marriage.

It would be curiously fitting if Shakespeare's first sexual encounter with his mistress took place, after an afternoon's showing of *Richard III*, inside the precincts of the former Dominican abbey – coincidentally where his printer friend Richard Field lived and worked at the time – for it is sandwiched between Ely Place to the north (where Richard spotted the strawberries) and Baynard Castle directly to the south (Richard's family home). Wilkes's account has been dubbed 'embellished', but this would only hold if he could be proved to have based his account on Manningham, and as it happens Manningham's diary only came to light in the nineteenth century. It is unlikely to be a forgery, since the major Shakespeare forgeries only started with William Henry Ireland (1777–1835) and John Payne Collier (1789–1883). Manningham may have heard the story about Shakespeare and Burbage from his roommate Curle and jotted it down later that night; or else he had it from a senior member of the

Inner Temple by the name of Touse, who later held the highest office at Inner Temple; if it was Touse, the story's credibility is enhanced. As for Wilkes, he seems to have gleaned his version from a printed or perhaps a handwritten source which is now lost.

The jaunty reference in both versions of the story to William the Conqueror is a reminder that Will Shakespeare was demonstrably fond of toying with names, including his own. A passage in one of the plays may be connected with this story of Will Shakespeare the conqueror and Richard Burbage. If the link could be proven – and the date of the play, 1594, certainly fits – then it could be assumed with fair confidence that the story of Burbage and Shakespeare was current in London by the mid 1590s, and a source of fun for actor and writer alike. The play is the one known from its title in the First Folio as *The Taming of the Shrew*. In the mid 1590s it may have been known by another title altogether, one perhaps tantalizingly suggestive of this very story of adulterous love and sexual triangles. The opening lines of the Induction of the play feature the following exchange between Sly and the hostess Marian Hacket:

SLY: I'll feeze you, in faith.
HOSTESS: A pair of stocks, you rogue.
SLY: You're a baggage. The Slys are no rogues. Look in the Chronicles – we came in with Richard Conqueror, therefore *paucas palabras*, let the world slide. Sessa!

This is the only direct reference to the Norman conqueror in all of Shakespeare's works. The joke depends on the audience instantly recognizing that the conqueror was William, not Richard. It may represent a piece of private banter between the playwright and Richard Burbage, who probably played both Petruchio and Sly. 'Richard Conqueror' would have added piquancy if spoken by an actor whose name was Richard, particularly since he was hardly related to the conqueror of 1066 but was undoubtedly the 'conqueror' of the Theatre now, the new emerging star of the London stage. It may even be that he enjoyed the stage sobriquet 'Richard Conqueror' during just this period of *Richard III* when his rocketing fame started to compete with Alleyn's and perhaps threatened to eclipse it. It seems obvious that his success in *Richard III*, in which a Richard played a

Richard, made Richard Burbage 'Richard Conqueror'. And yet this very Richard Conqueror had been pipped to the lady, as it were, by William Shakespeare, who shared a name with the Norman conqueror. If as seems likely the story became the stuff of London gossip almost at once, Shakespeare may well have alluded to it in a play written a few months after it happened. This then would strongly suggest that *The Shrew* was written in late 1594, shortly after *Richard III*, that it alludes to the real-life seduction of one of Burbage's fans by Shakespeare, and that at the time Shakespeare relished his libertarian reputation. This need not come as a surprise: exhibitionism and spectacle were his business, after all, and if that included self-exhibition, then so be it. As regards the story line of the *Sonnets*, *The Shrew* corresponds roughly to the Dark Lady poems which succeed 126.

What may well have galvanized Shakespeare into writing *The Shrew* was the publication in 1594 of *A Shrew*. Perhaps he felt indignant at the thought of one of 'his' plays being thus printed without even the slightest acknowledgment of him, and by a rival company, or perhaps he saw an opportunity: he would rewrite the play and make it indisputably his own, show them what he could do – hence the utter Warwickshireness of the Induction: few things could be more personal than that. When *A Shrew* was first published in 1594 it was advertised as 'A pleasant conceited history called The Taming of a Shrew As it was sundry times acted by the Right honourable the Earl of Pembroke his servants'. Both Shakespeare and Marlowe were associated with Pembroke's company at some point. They put on Shakespeare's *Titus Andronicus* and *3 Henry VI* at just the time around 1592 when Marlowe was giving them *Edward II*, further suggesting that Marlowe and Shakespeare were still very much in touch, if not actively collaborating, as late as 1592. *The Shrew* was Shakespeare's first nod in the direction of Marlowe since his death eighteen months earlier. If Shakespeare was keen to flag up his independence from Marlowe, it seems he was also ready to pay him homage. Grumio's 'Beloved of me, and that my deeds shall prove' contains an arch echo of one of Marlowe's most famous lines, Tamburlaine's 'I am a lord, for so my deeds shall prove', and his pitch for Bianca is similarly an elegy to the rhetorical glory that was Marlowe's. His house, he claims, is 'richly furnished with plate and gold', the walls covered with 'Tyrian tapestry', and his 'cypress chests' full of 'fine linen, Turkey cushions bossed with pearl, / Valens of Venice gold in needle-work'. As in the earlier play, one Christopher Sly starts off the action: 'I am Christophero Sly; call not me "honour" nor "lordship". I ne'er drank sack in my life, and if you give me any conserves, give me conserves of beef' – a plea for solid English fare that fails to deter the Lord from wilfully mistaking Sly for one of his betters as part of an elaborate farcical joke. So Sly resorts to the big guns and sheds all pretence, starting with the aristocratic-sounding 'o' at the end of his name. 'Christophero' now becomes plain English Christopher:

> SLY: What, would you make me mad? Am not I Christopher Sly – old Sly's son of Burton-heath, by birth a pedlar, by education a card-maker, by transmutation a bear-herd, and now by present profession a tinker? Ask Marian Hacket, the fat ale-wife of Wincot, if she know me not. If she say I am not fourteen pence on the score for sheer ale, score me up for the lying'st knave in Christendom.

While *The Shrew* dovetails with the main plot line of *A Shrew*, retaining the name Christopher and also calling the shrew 'Kate', almost everything else is different. The setting shifts from Greek Athens to Italian Padua, and there is that Induction set in Warwickshire: *this* play could only have been written by someone from Warwickshire, someone who knew about Wilmcote and Barton-on-the-heath. English dogs called Merriman, Clowder, Silver, Belman and Echo run in and out of the play, which is informed by what seems a countryman's knowledge of hunting, for example, in the reference to 'the hedge-corner, in the coldest fault'. The multiple afflictions of Petruchio's ride display an intimate knowledge of horses, and what he did not know of his own experience Shakespeare could discover by popping out of his parents' home in Stratford to call on the Hornbys, or on Greenway across the street.

By framing his revised version of the play with two Warwickshire scenes, Shakespeare – the butt of a virulent charge of plagiarism two years earlier – signals his ownership of *The Shrew*. Perhaps after the plague-break, which must have seemed interminable, he felt that he had to put his stamp on his new (but not quite new) play. Later, when he wrote *King Lear* (1605–6) in the immediate wake of the publication of the 1590s *King Leir*, he seems no longer to have felt so assertive and defensive: after all, from 1598 on his published works proudly advertised themselves through his name on their title-pages. Shakespeare's recasting of the Induction of *The Shrew* reveals someone eager to prove himself. He was clearly a proud man, one determined, in the days before his writings for the stage were printed and published, to show the world that these were *his* works, and nobody else's. How better than to frame *The Shrew* with Midlands locations, and names that only he knew?

Many of the names are anglicized – Nathaniel, Joseph, Nicholas, Philip, Walter, Sugarson – but three in particular are not, and they contain important clues to Shakespeare's intellectual development and life during this period. Grumio and Tranio are straight from the Roman dramatist Plautus's play *The Ghost* (*Mostellaria*), a comedy Shakespeare clearly knew but does not seem otherwise to have used. To the extent that the sex scandal of Shakespeare, Burbage, and the sexy citizen may have found its way into *The Shrew*, the Dark Lady was there indirectly from the very start. A much more revealing detail that helps identify her with Emilia Bassano-Lanier is the name of Kate's father in *The Shrew*. In *A Shrew* (written in 1589) he was Alfonso, like Emilia's husband, but in *The Shrew* in 1594 he has become Baptista, like Emilia's father. The choice of 'Alfonso' may have been an accident of Italian literary convention; 'Baptista' appears to be grounded in an imaginative reality which conflates the worlds of fiction and fact, affording presumptive evidence that the Dark Lady was Emilia Bassano-Lanier. By implication, it further suggests that Kate Minola of Padua, daughter of Baptista, is based on Emilia Bassano of Venice, daughter of another Baptista.

The Induction to *The Shrew* opens with a clash over broken glasses between Christopher Sly of Barton-heath and his un-named Hostess. The location of the scene is not clear in the stage directions, but there are enough clues in the text to make identification possible. The hostess is one 'Marian Hacket, the fat ale-wife of Wincot'. With 'Cicely Hacket', who is called the 'woman's maid of the house' (she is really her daughter) she runs an ale-house in Wincot. That Wincot was Wilmcote, the home village of Shakespeare's mother Mary Arden, was forcefully advocated by Halliwell-Phillipps, who also noted that

'Marian Hacket, the fat ale-wife, was probably a real character, as well as Stephen Sly, Old John Naps, Peter Turf, and Henry Pimpernell'. All these are named in the Induction and would have been as familiar to Shakespeare as the rest of his Stratford contemporaries. They have not as yet been discovered in any parish records, but in itself this does not definitively rule out the notion that there were Hackets who ran an inn at Wilmcote.

While there is no absolute consensus on Wincot/Wilmcote, the majority opinion favours Wilmcote. A Stratford corporation minute of 11 November 1584 about Wilmcote refers to 'the tythes of wyncote', the very name used in the play ten years later. There may be a further reference to Wincot in *2 Henry IV*, when Davy asks Shallow to adjudicate a dispute between 'William Visor of Woncot against Clement Perkes o'th' Hill'. Woncot is probably Wilmcote; certainly Perkses were thick on the ground in the neighbouring village of Snitterfield, the home of Shakespeare's grandfather.[2] Not only that, but Shakespeare was aware of Snitterfield Perkeses by September 1581 at the latest, when his 'cousin' Robert Webbe married Mary Perks of Snitterfield; the couple took over Shakespeare's grandfather's leasehold farm on the corner of Bell Lane after Richard Shakespeare's death. The details of the Webbe–Perkes–Snitterfield links are set out with great lucidity in the minutes and accounts of the borough, as is information on one William Cook from the same hamlet.[3] Cook was closely involved in various transactions with Shakespeare's father and uncle as well as his Webbe cousins and Edmund Lambert, Mary Arden's brother-in-law. Moreover, he stood as godfather in 1586 to Robert Webbe's son William. He is significant because the same scene in *2 Henry IV* that features Perkes also makes much of a certain William Cook.

If Woncot is Wilmcote and the Perkeses and Cooke are from Snitterfield, then 'o'th' Hill' could also refer to a location in Snitterfield, which sits on two different levels, 'up' by the church and 'down' the hill near Bell brook. The Aston Cantlow parish registers, which cover Wilmcote, include the name Perkes, but no Hackets or Visors are listed; yet this is not conclusive proof that Shakespeare made up the names as he went along. Accepting that Wincot, Woncot, and Wilmcote are variations on the same village name, it seems as though Shakespeare was setting the Induction of *The Shrew* on the edge of the forest of Arden and in front of his maternal grandparents' house, Glebe Farm. Any ale-houses, taverns, or inns would have stood on or near the green then as now, with the Arden house either next door to a tavern or opposite it; or both, as is the case today.

It is possible that the title given this play in the First Folio, *The Taming of the Shrew*, is the original. Yet it would have been rather confusing and perhaps commercially foolhardy if all that differentiated the new Lord Chamberlain's play from the old Pembroke's on the play bills was a definite rather than an indefinite article, '*The Shrew*' rather than '*A Shrew*'. *The Shrew* may have been known by an altogether different title at first, one that fitted Shakespeare's personal circumstances at the time peculiarly well. Was *The Shrew* in fact the elusive and allegedly lost play, *Love's Labour's Won?*' That a play with this title once existed is suggested by its attribution to Shakespeare in a list made in 1598 in which all the other titles of his plays are given accurately.[4] The author of the list was the same Francis Meres who also knew Shakespeare's sonnets long before they were published, and the text in which it appears is again his *Palladis Tamia*. Meres lists twelve plays by Shakespeare although only four of them, possibly five, had been published in quarto when he compiled his survey in 1598; he could not however have known from the published four or five who had written them, since it was only in 1598 that the quartos of his plays were attributed to Shakespeare. Meres must have been on the inside, as is also suggested by the fact that he knew Shakespeare's 'sugared' and Ovidian sonnets eleven years before Thorpe published them in 1609.

Apart from the inclusion of *Love's Labour's Won* alongside *Love's Labour's Lost*, the most striking feature of Meres's list is the absence from it of *The Taming of the Shrew*. There is no conceivable reason why Meres should have omitted a play written only four years before he made his list, and of course he did no such thing. Rather, he included *The Shrew* by the title under which it was performed in 1594 and in a now lost quarto version – *Love's Labour's Won*. That *Love's Labour's Won* existed in the 1590s as a play by Shakespeare is not in doubt, since Meres is supported by the listing of a quarto with just that name in a stationer's book catalogue of 1603, discovered in 1953. As well as *Love's Labour's Won* the 1603 catalogue also features *The Taming of a Shrew* (but not *The Taming of the Shrew*) as a separate entry. The logical conclusion to be drawn from the joint evidence of Meres's 1598 survey and the 1603 sales list is that *Love's Labour's Won* and *The Shrew* are one and the same – that in the 1590s there existed a quarto of *The Shrew* bearing the title *Love's Labour's Won*. The play now known as *The Shrew* was being performed under the title *Love's Labour's Won* at least up to 1598, when Meres saw it, and the quarto still existed in 1603, when it was listed for sale. Further support is to be found indirectly in the entry on the Stationers' Register of 8 November 1623 for the First Folio. Had *The Shrew* never been published before the Folio, the expectation is that it would be listed there among the plays 'not formerly entered to other men' – but there is no trace of it. The reason must surely be that it had already appeared in quarto, just like all the other plays that are not listed in this entry. If a quarto of *The Shrew* under the title *Love's Labour's Won* were ever to turn up, it might contain that part of the Induction that seems to be so oddly missing at the end of the comedy in its present state in Folio.

Shakespeare probably wrote *Love's Labour's Won* on his return from Warwickshire in 1594, perhaps as his first contribution to the newly formed Lord Chamberlain's company and following hard on the heels of the publication of the Pembrokes' play *The Taming of a Shrew*, which was in all probability also mostly his. Soon afterwards, and perhaps because of the success of *Love's Labour's Won*, he launched into another play written as its twin, *Love's Labour's Lost*. The period of the two *Love's Labour's* plays, 1594–5, coincides with the height of Shakespeare's involvement with the young man of the *Sonnets* and the Dark Lady.

Love's Labour's Lost is one of Shakespeare's rhetorically most scintillating and opaque plays. In the teeth of the accepted idiom of romantic comedy it ends famously on a note of irresolution when the various pairs of lovers are instructed that their unions are to be postponed for a year. In Berowne's words, 'Our wooing doth not end like an old play: / Jack hath not Jill.' Here 'an old play' could possibly refer to the venerable genre of romantic comedy itself, but is more likely to allude to *Love's Labour's Won*, which concludes with the subjugation of Kate and her triumph over her sister Bianca. The very title of *Love's Labour's Lost* of course refers to 'an old play'. As in the Induction to *The Shrew*, so Shakespeare here provides a recognizable slice of English countryside. Even two of the seasons, Spring and Winter, are represented in the play's final song. As the cuckoo and owl swap roles, spring-time meadows are decked with daisies, violets, lady-smocks and cuckoo-buds, while in winter icicles hang from the wall, 'Dick the shepherd blows his nail, / And Tom bears logs into the hall, /And milk comes frozen home in pail'. In the meantime roasted crab apples hiss in the bowl 'while greasy Joan doth keel the pot', details echoing the domesticity of an Elizabethan home such as Shakespeare's own. Again, while the name 'Joan' is conventional and generic for wench, as in 'groan for Joan' or 'some men must love my lady, and some Joan', it also happened to be a favourite of the Henley Street Shakespeares – the name of two of Shakespeare's sisters, of the first-born who died in 1558 and of the one who at the time of *Love's Labour's Lost* was a twenty-six-year-old woman in Henley Street.

Like *The Shrew*, *Love's Labour's Lost* exhibits a raw sexuality, for example in its barely coded talk of young women making their boyfriends come by hand – and perhaps just as well, in view of the dire consequences, of full sexual intercourse, as when Costard informs Armado that Jacquenetta is pregnant by him: 'she is gone; she is two months on her way . . . unless you play the honest Troyan, the poor wench is cast away. She's quick, the child brags in her belly already, 'tis yours.' It was nearly thirteen years since Will Shakespeare had had to play the 'honest Troyan' to Anne Hathaway when she told him that she was 'quick' and that the child was his. Another distinctive shared feature of the two *Love's Labour's* plays is a smattering of Italian: Shakespeare's grasp of Italian was rudimentary but sufficient for him not only to quote but to pun in the language. Thus when Bianca's father in *The Shrew* asks 'is not this my Cambio?' she wittily replies 'Cambio is changed into Lucentio.' The joke lies knowing that 'Cambio' derives from the Italian *cambiare* (to change) and *cambio*, which can mean both transformation and exchange of currency.

It is a pleasant fantasy to think that Shakespeare might have picked up Italian from travelling to Italy, probably during the closure of the theatres after 1592. After all, the so-called 'Italy' of *The Two Gentlemen of Verona* (*c.*1591) could hardly be a more different country than that of the great Italian plays, *Romeo and Juliet* (1596–7), *The Merchant of Venice* (1598), and *Othello* (1604). There is no documentary evidence that Shakespeare travelled abroad in the early 1590s, although that does not mean that he never did, and there are indications that his travels were not confined to the road between Stratford and London. Thus in *King Lear* his powerful evocation of the drop of the cliffs at Dover suggest that he must have seen them at some point from out at sea — perhaps while touring with his company, as they did, for example, in the summer of 1596 when they played at Rye in August and at Dover in September. Queen Margaret's lines from the early play *2 Henry VI* seem to recall just such a sight, when she bids the winds blow 'towards England's blessed shore', noting that 'As far as I could ken thy chalky cliffs, / When from thy shore the tempest beat us back, / I stood upon the hatches in the storm . . .' This play emphatically belongs to the pre-1592 era, and perhaps at the very least Shakespeare popped across to France at some point just as Marlowe did to Flushing. His handling of the Dover cliffs is persuasive and the marine imagery in his plays suggests that he knew about sailing. Perhaps like Marlowe he was at some point issued with a passport by the Privy Council to go abroad. He knew enough French to write an entire scene in *Henry V* in French — and not just French, but French pressed into the service of cross-cultural French–English puns — and in *The Merry Wives of Windsor* he affectionately parodied French accents and mistakes in English. Other reasons for Shakespeare's knowledge of French have already been touched on, notably his friendship with Richard Field and his French family and his lodging in London with Huguenots.

The notion of Shakespeare making the Grand Tour through Europe and Italy is not one that stands up to scrutiny: it was not something people of his class and background did in the sixteenth century. The only way he could have travelled to Florence, Padua, Venice, Verona, or Rome — just a few of the Italian cities English travellers visited — would have been in the retinue of a great lord, someone like Southampton or the Cecils, but they were not on the Continent at that time. But rather than Shakespeare going to Italy, perhaps Italy came to him, in the shape of Emilia Bassano and John Florio. Giovanni Florio (*c.*1553–*c.*1625) was born in England, the son of an Italian Protestant refugee. He is best known for his translation of Montaigne's *Essays*, used by Shakespeare in *The Tempest*. Florio became Southampton's tutor in 1591, and turned the young earl into a keen and accomplished speaker of Italian. He had already produced two Italian grammars, *Florio's First Fruits* and *Florio's Second Fruits*. It is from the first of these that Shakespeare is quoting when in *Love's Labour's Lost* Holofernes intones: 'I may speak of thee as the traveller doth of Venice, '*Venezia, Venezia, Chi non ti vede, chi non ti prezia*'', which translates as 'Venice, Venice, he who has not seen you does not value you'. Florio could have taught Shakespeare about Italy, Italian customs, and the topography of the peninsula. He was, according to Ben Jonson, a keen lover of the theatre, and it is quite possible that he accompanied his play-addicted pupil Southampton to see Shakespeare's plays in Shoreditch. Perhaps after a performance of *The Two Gentlemen of Verona* Florio took Shakespeare aside to explain that Milan and Verona are *not* in fact separated by water. It may have been Florio who first told Shakespeare that Italy was inhabited by hot-headed young men spoiling for fights in the midday sun, and that Italy was above all the country of *amore*, of sonnets, and of *dolce stil nuovo*.

However Florio and Shakespeare met, Shakespeare's Italy had been radically transformed before he wrote *The Shrew* and *Love's Labour's Lost* and in good time for *Romeo and Juliet*, *The Merchant of Venice*, and *Othello*, the two last of course set in Emilia Bassano's native city. And from *The Shrew* onwards all things Italian in Shakespeare may have been inspired by his relationship with an Italian lover who also happened to be Jewish. Emilia seems to have been a talented, beautiful, dark-eyed, and mysterious woman – if occasionally, it seems, less than sweet of breath. The poet refers ungallantly to 'the breath that from my mistress reeks' – doubtless from the garlic that formed part of her diet. In *A Midsummer Night's Dream* Bottom warns his 'most dear actors' to 'eat no onions nor garlic, for we are to utter sweet breath', and the phrase 'the breath of garlic-eaters' is the greatest insult that Menenius can hurl at the plebeian mob whom he blames for exiling Coriolanus. But Emilia, mistress until recently of one of the most powerful men in the land, was not one to be content with a mere player, particularly one close to the gorgeous-looking Earl of Southampton. She knew her mind and was not afraid to take the initiative, something she did repeatedly in her busy seventy-six years of life, proceeding from Hunsdon to marrying Alfonso Lanier, becoming a mother, then starting an affair with Shakespeare and, eventually and at first behind Shakespeare's back, with Southampton, before returning to her husband sometime before 1597, when she called on Simon Forman.

13

A Will 'Made Lame by Fortune's Blows'

As well as the identity of the Dark Lady, Shakespeare's sonnets may hide clues to another secret, one unnecessarily shrouded in mystery largely because some of the most influential commentators on the poems decided long ago that what was apparently concealed simply could not be true. In a remarkable consensus of opinion, literary scholars have insisted that words such as 'limp', 'lame', 'disabled', and 'halting', all of them applied by the poet to himself, must be read metaphorically. It seems that the idea of a halting or even club-footed Shakespeare is too much to contemplate, and these scholars have consequently tended to play down the subjective quality of the poems in which these references appear. The 'lame' sonnets, taken literally, have even less popular appeal than the allegedly 'hydrocephalic' Droeshout portrait in the 1623 Folio or the balding bust in Holy Trinity. It is easy to assume that if Shakespeare had suffered from a disability, his contemporaries would surely have mentioned it – after all, they poked fun unblinkingly at lunacy and bedlam in plays like Thomas Middleton's *The Changeling*. They were far from squeamish about that kind of thing – yet even Ben Jonson, who was fairly voluble about the Stratford playwright after his death, has next to nothing to say about his appearance other than that he approved of the portrait in the First Folio. Since the *Sonnets* are the most personal and immediate lyrics and testimonials Shakespeare ever wrote, perhaps the evidence they afford should be viewed more positively.

Sonnets 37, 66, 89, and 90 all allude to disability. The poet was 'made lame by Fortune's dearest spite' (37), he despairs of having his 'strength by limping sway disabled' (66), he instructs his friend to speak 'of my lameness, and I straight will halt' (89), and he challenges the friend to 'join with the spite of fortune, make me bow' (90).

Almost always these references are read figuratively: verse after all often 'halts', and 'lame' retains this secondary meaning to this day. But quite apart from their ring of authenticity, there is no reason why the lame references should not be literally true. At the very least the possibility that Shakespeare, like Byron, may have had a limp in consequence of a childhood affliction like polio or *spina bifida*, or an accident like a fall from a horse, should be considered. In the *Sonnets* Shakespeare is addressing someone who knows him well, and the rhetorical framing of his condition suggests that the speaker and his addressee both *know* that this is something that troubles the poet. The first intimation comes in sonnet 37:

> As a decrepit father takes delight
> To see his active child do deeds of youth,
> So I, made lame by Fortune's dearest spite,
> Take all my comfort of thy worth and truth;
> For whether beauty, birth, or wealth, or wit,
> Or any of these all, or all, or more,
> Entitled in thy parts do crownèd sit,
> I make my love engrafted to this store.
> So then I am not lame, poor, nor despised,
> Whilst that this shadow doth such substance give
> That I in thy abundance am sufficed
> And by a part of all thy glory live.
> > Look what is best, that best I wish in thee:
> > This wish I have, then ten times happy me!

When the poet refers to having been 'made lame by Fortune's dearest spite' he means that he was crippled by Fortune at her most cruel and injurious: no one is to blame for his lameness, it is congenital, no guilt attaches to it. It is his disability which causes him to equate himself and the fair youth with an arthritic ('decrepit') father who miraculously recovers the use of his limbs through the sheer delight he takes in watching his animated child play and run about. The young man's plenitude fills the poet's sad lack. As an isolated instance in the *Sonnets* and the works generally this might be understood as a purely verbal artefact, to be read in the first instance without external reference. But other references in the *Sonnets* and in the plays point in the opposite direction, to the fact that Shakespeare was keenly interested in lameness, limping, and even in malformation of the spine. This last of course powers the dynamic of plays like *3 Henry VI* and *Richard III* whose crippled hero, the 'valiant crook-back prodigy / Dicky', loves being nature's freak; or so he claims when jibing about how dogs bark at his misshapen appearance as he passes by. A crook-back he may be, but he successfully woos a woman in front of her dead husband's coffin, a husband of whose murder he is guilty. The woman's name is Anne, the same as Shakespeare's wife. Was Shakespeare equally jubilant when he overcame his Anne's resistance to his advances?

Several years later Shakespeare reverted to the subject of congenital 'defect' in *Hamlet*, when he tells Horatio that the native custom of drunken revels damages the reputation of the Danes:

> So oft it chances in particular men
> That for some vicious mole of nature in them,
> As in their birth, wherein they are not guilty,
> Since nature cannot choose his origin,
> By the o'ergrowth of some complexion
> Oft breaking down the pales and forts of reason,
> Or by some habit that too much o'erleavens
> The form of plausive manners – that these men,
> Carrying, I say, the stamp of one defect,
> Being nature's livery or fortune's star,
> His virtues else be they as pure as grace,
> As infinite as man may undergo,
> Shall in the general censure take corruption
> From that particular fault. The dram of evil
> Doth all the noble substance of a doubt
> To his own scandal.
>   *Enter Ghost.*

There is a note here of special pleading, of heartfelt frustration about the fact that a small blemish should have the power to ruin the beauty of the whole body, destroying a person's entire physical and moral being by a single prominent flaw such as a birthmark. Never mind a person's many other virtues, 'be they as pure as grace' or otherwise infinite, the mole will override them like a black mark on an otherwise pure white canvas. Shakespeare is making a general moral point, using the 'mole of nature' speech as a hugely elaborate simile. What Hamlet says is demonstrably true, and it was ever thus. Few children are heroes in the school-yard for their wholesomeness; many are taunted for small physical blemishes. The author of the play (Shakespeare) and his hero (Hamlet) may converge in speaking these lines which occur just before the entry of Old Hamlet's ghost. In fact, the ghost enters on the cue 'scandal'. Shakespeare may himself have played the ghost. Rowe is again instructive here, noting that Shakespeare's

> name is printed, as the custom was in those times, amongst those of the other players, before some old plays, but without any particular account of what sort of parts he used to play; and though I have inquired, I could never meet with any further account of him this way than that the top of his performance was the ghost in his own *Hamlet* . . .

If this is true it means that in the play *Hamlet*, in which a son cannot come to terms with the death of his father and the remarriage of his mother, the ghost of the dead father was originally played by the father of a real-life schoolboy called Hamlet or Hamnet. But does the appearance of the ghost just happen to coincide with Hamlet's protest about the mole of nature, or is the timing more deliberate, artful, and local? In other words as Shakespeare wrote this scene did he know that he would be playing the role of the ghost, was he visualizing his entry, and was it perhaps this that triggered the lines about the mole of nature? It may be that one of the most celebrated passages of this iconic work of English literature is autobiographical, with Shakespeare again reverting to the predicament that had exercised him so profoundly in his sonnets. The ghost may limp, and the 'mole of nature' may be just that, a club-foot or spinal condition.

There is no way of being sure, of course, but further support derives from yet another role that Shakespeare played. The eighteenth-century editor Edward Capell reports that Shakespeare played Old Adam in *As You Like It*:

> A traditional story was current some years ago about Stratford that a very old man of that place, of weak intellect but yet related to Shakespeare, being asked by some of his neighbours what he remembered about him, answered that he saw him once brought on the stage

upon another man's back; which answer was applied by the hearers to his having seen him perform in this scene the part of Adam. That he should have done so is made not unlikely by another constant tradition, that he was no extraordinary actor and therefore took no parts upon him but such as this; for which he might also be peculiarly fitted by an accidental lameness, which, as he himself tells us twice in his Sonnets, v. 37 and 89, befell him in some part of life; without saying how, or when, of what sort, or in what degree; but his expressions seem to indicate – latterly.[1]

In the play Old Adam reveals that his 'old limbs lie lame' and Orlando describes him to the exiled court in the Forest of Arden as 'an old poor man, / Who after me hath many a weary step / Limped in pure love.' It is impossible to determine who might have been the seventeenth-century Stratford relative of Shakespeare who is referred to by Capell, though it is highly likely to have been one of the Harts of Henley Street. Descendants of Shakespeare's sister Joan Hart continued to live in Stratford until the end of the eighteenth century, and that they would have seen a performance of *As You Like It* is unlikely but not impossible. Capell is tapping here into a line of information independent from Rowe, since he goes on to mention '*another* constant tradition' which is indeed Rowe, as the phrase 'no extraordinary actor', which is borrowed from Rowe's 1709 *Life*, demonstrates. As in the case of sonnet 37 the language here does not have to mean anything as particular as the poet's own state of health – after all, old men do become lame and slow, and limp or halt along – but there is more lameness in the plays, notably in *King Lear*, and this may clinch it.

The already quoted part-line 'made lame by Fortune's dearest spite' from sonnet 37 is closely echoed in *King Lear* when Edgar replies to Gloucester's question about who he is with:

> A most poor man made lame by fortune's blows,
> Who, by the art of known and feeling sorrows,
> Am pregnant to good pity.

The quotation derives from the sixth scene of Act IV of the play. One of the most moving scenes in Shakespeare features Edgar as Poor Tom and two old men, one of them the octogenarian king, the other the adulterous Gloucester, here met on a heath above the cliffs of Dover. In the immediate context of the quotation Edgar claims to be a person who readily embraces compassion because he has known and felt sorrows through being made *lame* by Fortune – or that at least is the reading in the first published version of the play, the quarto of 1608 which was printed and published some two years or so after the play was first written and performed. It is widely accepted that the printed text of the quarto is based on Shakespeare's own autograph manuscript for the play, the longhand text that he produced during the spring of 1606. In his own papers Shakespeare therefore wrote 'lame', or something looking very much like it.

It is however a very odd train of thought, because it seems so specific; that is, 'lame' is precise in a way that 'humble' or 'sad' or any other adjective that fits naturally with a melancholy state of mind induced by Fortune's blows is not. It is therefore not at all surprising that the second version of the play to be published in the period, the Folio *King Lear* of 1623, should offer an altered reading, replacing 'lame' with 'tame' and, incidentally, also changing the preposition before 'Fortune'. In the Folio the line reads 'A most poor man made tame to fortune's blows'. The change to the meaning is not inconsiderable: the Folio's 'tame' offers a wider, more generally moralized and indeed flatter reading than the peculiar physicality of 'lame'. It is not known how the differences between the quarto and the Folio *King Lear* came about, although there are those who argue that Shakespeare himself revised the play after the publication of the quarto. If he did, then the change from 'lame' to 'tame' would appear to be proof that he felt uncomfortable with the somewhat unnatural cadence of his train of thought here. But others, notably the eminent bibliographer and librarian of Trinity College, Cambridge, W. W. Greg, have argued instead that a number of the most striking discrepant readings indicate different compositors and proof correctors – that is, the people setting the printed text from Shakespeare's own papers – guessing at the same manuscript and coming up with different answers.

This may in some ways be a more promising line of approach, at least as far as this particular local textual difficulty is concerned. Shakespeare wrote a widely used Elizabethan longhand called secretary, found in many Elizabethan documents and not easy to read. It was only gradually superseded by what was then called 'italic', more or less the hand in use today; the two gradually blended together. In

Elizabethan secretary, 'lame' and 'tame' look almost indistinguishable –
just as they can, of course, if written with less than scrupulous care
in modern italic. The two different readings in the quarto and the
Folio of *King Lear* would seem to have arisen from a transcription
error of the same longhand line which could be either 'lame' or
'tame'. But the fact that the phrasing in sonnet 37 is virtually identical to that in the quarto of *King Lear* – 'made lame by fortune's
dearest spite/blows' – is a strong indication that Shakespeare wrote
'lame' and not 'tame', and the 'tame' of the Folio is in all probability
a type-setter's or proof-reader's error. The 'lame' sonnet and the 'lame'
quarto of *King Lear* seem to consolidate the reading of the phrase
'lame'. It appears that Shakespeare instinctively identified the most
senseless blows of fortune with congenital lameness, and the most
likely reason for this is that he himself suffered from it: lameness is an
obsession with Shakespeare because of his own personal and private
experience of life.

A further example from the *Sonnets*, this time from 89, also contains
a pun on the poet's first name:

> Say that thou didst forsake me for some fault,
> And I will comment upon that offence;
> Speak of my lameness, and I straight will halt,
> Against thy reasons making no defence.
> Thou canst not, love, disgrace me half so ill,
> To set a form upon desirèd change,
> As I'll myself disgrace, knowing thy will.
> . . . For thee against myself I'll vow debate,
> For I must ne'er love him whom thou dost hate.

The poet imagines his 'lameness' to be at the top of the list of
things that give offence to the glamorous youth and offers, tongue-in-
cheek and punningly, to suspend or 'halt' it forthwith – 'halt' meaning
both 'to stop' and 'to limp'. Of course he cannot do that in real life,
he is saying: only at the level of language can he cease to halt, to stam-
mer, to sound pedestrian. If necessary he will take sides against himself
with the youth for, as the last line has it, 'I must ne'er love him whom
thou dost hate'. The poet knows the youth's wishes, or perhaps that
should be his 'will', which is also the poet's will, and the poet is Will

Shakespeare who is himself. The next sonnet, 90, takes up the 'hate' from the preceding poem and almost immediately reverts to the subject of disability:

> Then hate me when thou wilt, if ever, now,
> Now, while the world is bent my deeds to cross,
> Join with the spite of fortune, make me bow . . .

Once more the particular phrase works at the literal and the metaphorical level simultaneously. The poet may be bending from congenital damage to his spine, or he may be bowed by misfortune – such as, perhaps, the closure of the theatres because of the plague. Or the use of 'bow' may be triggered by the 'bent' and 'cross' in the preceding line, so that 'bent' and 'cross' between them generate 'bow' as in 'cross-bow'. This kind of instinctive, associative rhetoric is a striking feature of Shakespeare's verse generally and there may be nothing here beyond the inner abandon of Shakespeare's language, a free play of random sound-patterns and resonant phrases.

Yet all in all there is cumulative evidence for thinking that in his plays and his poems Shakespeare was deeply preoccupied by having a limp. He was as frank and open about the anguish this caused him as he was self-advertising about his first name in sonnets 135 and 136, which both stand out for their obsessive play on 'will' as wish or desire and 'Will', the name of the poet. The two poems are intimately linked in a number of ways and not least by being equally salacious when accusing the woman of having a will that is 'large and spacious' and yet not allowing the poet 'to hide my will in thine'. In the sixteenth century 'will' was a euphemism for both the male and female sex organs, so that the poet is here berating the woman for refusing him sex in spite of being equipped with a promiscuously over-used and larger than usual vagina. The word 'will' is used no fewer than thirteen times in sonnet 135, and one 'wilt'. Shakespeare concludes 135 with:

> So thou, being rich in Will, add to thy Will
> One will of mine to make thy large Will more.
> Let no unkind no fair beseechers kill;
> Think all but one, and me in that one Will.

The next poem continues on these same lines with its obscene salvo

'Will will fulfil the treasure of thy love, / Ay, fill it full with wills, and my will one'. Shakespeare concludes the sonnet with barbed magnanimity: 'Make but my name thy love, and love that still; / And then thou lov'st me, for my name is Will.' He is urging her to engage in auto-eroticism because by doing so she will love him too since, after all, his name and her vagina's are the same. The rhetorical tricksiness of these two poems in their play on will/Will is impressive if rather heartless and seemingly pointless. Later, in sonnet 143, the poet in a much gentler mode reverts once more to an explicit reminder of the fact that his name is indeed Will. The sonnet is brilliantly structured around the conceit of a busy housewife and mother setting down her baby to catch a runaway chicken while in the meantime 'her neglected child holds her in chase'. While the mother in the poem is chasing the chicken, her baby is running after her. This time the poet likens himself not to a sexual predator but to a bewildered toddler. Once his lover has caught the fluttering object of her quest she will return to the poet

> And play the mother's part: kiss me, be kind.
> So will I pray that thou mayst have thy Will,
> If thou turn back and my loud crying still.

The question that cries out for an answer is why the poet should be so free with his name. Most certainly the people to whom he was addressing these lines knew who he was. It is true that it gives him scope to joke as much as he pleases about men's and women's 'wills', but since he is not here writing for the theatre, where crowd-pleasing is of the essence, there is no need for him to be so forthcoming or to try to score points; presumably the poems were meant for private ears only. Or perhaps not, entirely – Shakespeare may have suspected all along that his poems would be distributed, and perhaps it was even something he hoped for. Whatever his reasons, he clearly loved playing with his name in this way, and it seems clear from the nature of the puns that such play was nothing short of self-induced sexual pleasure. Both the poet and his mistress are somehow at it together, he implies, and the world of the youth is left ever further behind, until she finally gets hold of the young man and buries him inside her own will: 'I guess one angel in another's hell' – the poet is forced to admit when he realizes that they are involved in their turn.

The Will poems explicitly collapse the artificial barriers that have been carefully set up to keep Shakespeare and the poet apart. While a measure of artistic decorum is maintained in the 'fair youth' poems, the poet now makes it clear that the speaker is himself, Will Shakespeare. It is possible that another name, one very close to Shakespeare's life, features too, and in ways which significantly illuminate the story behind the cycle and its likely publication history. The name is that of Anne Hathaway, who has been found in the penultimate line of sonnet 145:

> Those lips that love's own hand did make
> Breathed forth the sound that said 'I hate'
> To me that languished for her sake;
> But when she saw my woeful state,
> Straight in her heart did mercy come,
> Chiding that tongue that ever sweet
> Was used in giving gentle doom,
> And taught it thus anew to greet:
> 'I hate' she altered with an end
> That followed it as gentle day
> Doth follow night, who like a fiend,
> From heaven to hell is flown away.
>   'I hate' from hate away she threw,
>   And saved my life, saying 'not you'.

The Hathaway identification lies in the homophony of the name 'Hathaway' and 'hate away' in line 13 and Shakespeare, playful with language as he was, must have been more aware of it than anyone else.[2] If this is indeed an early love poem addressed to Anne Hathaway, it must date from the 1580s. The poem certainly feels very different from any other in the post-126 series, not only because of its unique use of octosyllabic lines. Written in an altogether gentler mode and idiom, it lacks the aggression of the Dark Mistress poems. Even if there were no Hathaway connection in this lightly wrought, conventional love lyric, it is out of place among the other sonnets, yet unmistakably by Shakespeare. Shakespeare himself is the only possible source for the manuscript from whence the poem was presumably taken for the sonnet series, since only he or his wife Anne would have had a copy. The likelihood that Shakespeare kept a copy of the poem is in itself interesting, suggesting that even as a seven-teen-year-old he took his writing seriously enough to want to preserve it.

Of all the sonnets, number 144, immediately preceding the Hath-away sonnet, is the most scandalous. It was published in *The Passionate Pilgrim* in 1599 and openly contrasts the poet's two illicit lovers and their gender:

> Two loves I have, of comfort and despair,
> Which like two spirits do suggest me still:
> The better angel is a man right fair,
> The worser spirit a woman coloured ill.

The counterpoint between the most nakedly adulterous of all Shakespeare's poems and one addressed to Anne Hathaway by a youthful Will Shakespeare years earlier is almost startling in its insensi-tivity; on the other hand, between them the twenty-eight lines of sonnets 144 and 145 may well represent a distribution of Shakespeare's love life up to August 1596 – his courtship with Anne, his love affairs with Southampton and Emilia Bassano. Like Will's and Anne's, Emilia Bassano's name too may have been written into the poems, notably in sonnet 151, which ends with a tribute to his mistress 'for whose dear love I rise and fall'. This deeply erotic poem about the Dark Lady is constructed around the dichotomy of body and soul. Inevitably it is the body which wins out: the moment the soul gives it the green light to love, the poet has an erection merely at the mention of the woman's name:

> My soul doth tell my body that he may
> Triumph in love; flesh stays no farther reason,
> But rising at thy name doth point out thee
> As his triumphant prize. Proud of this pride,
> He is contented thy poor drudge to be,
> To stand in thy affairs, fall by thy side.

This may be no more than the coded language of sexual intercourse and the rising and falling may be just that – but the fact that the poet's flesh rises specifically '*at thy name*' may have significance, since he has already made such play with his own name. The sonnet may merely be expressing a generic train of thought, but there may be rather more to it than that: the poet's rising at the woman's name and then falling by her side after standing in her affairs may suggest that there is something specifically 'rising' or 'falling' about her name. In Italian the poet goes from *alto* to *basso*, from high to low, and *basso* and 'Bassano' are of course cognates. It is tenuous, but the apparent evocation of her name combined with the particular local phrasing perhaps helps to consolidate the case for Emilia Bassano.

The early 1590s must have been among the most exciting in Shakespeare's life so far. His deepening friendship with Southampton could hardly fail to be exhilarating and inspiring. The story runs from 1590 to, probably, August 1596, when Hamnet Shakespeare died. By 1598 members of a London clique of *literati* had access to the bulk of the sonnets, and a year later two poems from near the end of the cycle were published in *The Passionate Pilgrim*. At no point is there a major misfit between the chronicle outlined in the *Sonnets* and what is knowable about the real-life characters whose story it is presumed to tell – Shakespeare, Southampton, Marlowe, and Emilia Bassano-Lanier. Their story seems to be this: for some unknown reason Shakespeare was roped in sometime before 6 October 1590 to persuade the glamorous young aristocrat Southampton, nine years his junior, to marry. As a result a strong bond of friendship grew up between the two men, and when Shakespeare was attacked by Greene Southampton seems to have called on Greene's publisher, perhaps accompanied by that large retinue of followers for which he was known. In his retraction the publisher Chettle acknowledged that important people had remonstrated with him. Two years later, when playing resumed in London after the plague, Shakespeare thanked Southampton for this intervention in one of his sonnets. During the 1592–4 closure of the theatres there is no record to show that Shakespeare was touring, so he probably went back to gloving part-time in Stratford during those two long years. He was now safe from the Lucys, thanks to the protection of Southampton.

During this period Shakespeare wrote two brilliant long poems, *Venus and Adonis* and *The Rape of Lucrece*. If he was in Stratford between late 1592 and the summer of 1594, he could easily have sent them to his London printers and publishers through the offices of his neighbour, the Stratford carrier Greenway: correspondence between Shakespeare's friends Quiney and Sturley established that a 'pony express' delivered mail between London and the Midlands in under 72 hours. But there was an even easier and more obvious way of conveying his precious poems to London, and perhaps even some of his sonnets to Southampton, and that was by passing them directly to his friend Richard Field in Stratford: they must surely have met then.

Shakespeare and Marlowe were probably friends as well as collaborators and competitors at the Theatre, the Curtain, and perhaps even at the Rose. During the spring of 1593 their literary rivalry broadened to include Southampton. Marlowe wrote *Hero and Leander*, and by so doing provoked Shakespeare to write *Venus and Adonis*. Marlowe had probably known Southampton as a boy at Cambridge, and could not now resist the ganymedic attractions of the young earl. He may have homed in on his target at a time when Shakespeare was quite ill. The brilliant '*mighty*' rival does not last very long in the cycle for the simple reason that he was killed in May 1593, presumably sometime soon after Shakespeare had written sonnet 86, in which he evokes 'the proud full sail' of Marlowe's verse.

The poet's repeated references to 'three years' convey a sense of the time-span of the Shakespeare–Southampton relationship. While 'three' is probably the most symbolic of all numbers, three years may here mean exactly that, time in the real world – as might be expected. By the time the last sonnets were written Shakespeare was at most thirty-five. This latest cut-off date can be established with reference to sonnets 138 and 144. Both were published in 1599, but Meres's reference to them in *Palladis Tamia* brings the date when they were written forward by another year at least, to 1598. Sonnet 138 was quite probably written at least two years before 1599, so that when Shakespeare calls himself 'old' in it he may have been thirty-three, significant as the age of Christ when he died.

The timing of the *Sonnets* and the accounts by Manningham and Wilkes of Shakespeare, Burbage, and the loose young woman converge to the point where it can fairly reasonably be assumed that the Dark Lady and the young mistress of an old merchant are one and the same. Shakespeare became involved with her in the autumn of 1594 while the newly constituted Lord Chamberlain's company were performing *Richard III* and before he wrote *The Shrew*. The Dark Lady was twenty-five, married and a mother at the time; she had been the mistress of the man who established the company for which Shakespeare was acting. She appears on the scene in late 1594 or early 1595 – sonnet 127 in the chronology of the poems – and is depicted as dark-skinned, musical, and sensuous. Then, although Shakespeare and Emilia Bassano are sexually involved, she makes a play for the young Southampton. She and the earl start an affair. The poet knows about it but, torn between sex with his hedonistic mistress and his deep Platonic love for the young man, rationalizes the situation in terms of his lovers loving each other because they both love him.

14

The Catholics and Oldcastle: 1594–6

I N 1594, THE year in which Shakespeare returned to the London
stage, the country was in an uneasy state of truce. It was six years
since the Armada and it would be another eleven before the Gunpowder Plot once more convulsed the nation. But throughout this
phoney peace the Catholic opposition was in ferment. The presence
at the death of Marlowe of Robert Poley suggests that the same
agents still policed the country who several years earlier had worked
to bring Mary Queen of Scots to perdition. After the death of Babington
and the arrest of Southwell, most Protestant Englishmen might have
thought that the snake had been both scotched and killed, to borrow
phrases from *Macbeth* in which Shakespeare directly alludes to the
Catholic struggle. But the authorities knew better, and were relentless
in their search for Henry Garnett, John Gerard, Edward Oldcorne,
Nicholas Owen, Robert Parsons, William Weston, Henry Walpole,
and others. By the mid 1590s Burghley was becoming a spent
force, both Leicester and Walsingham were already dead, and
Robert Cecil was not yet fully anointed as his father's successor. The
Privy Council, the country's chief executive organ of government,
was now wide open to the influence of a strong will, but though
Essex tried throughout the decade to achieve ascendancy over the
Cecils, he was never able to match the political skills of Robert
Cecil. Quite possibly the Jesuits were hoping to exploit these emerg-
ing fault lines. They certainly had good intelligence about the inner
workings of the Privy Council, for there are no better guides to
what divided the nation at the time than Gerard, Weston, and
Garnett.

Gerard, Garnett, and the others shadow Shakespeare's life. Despite
their activities, all seemed to be deeply patriotic. In all the severity of

their persecution, none of the missionaries voices the slightest animosity against any of their jailers except Topcliffe. There is no evidence that those loyal to the crown thought any more warmly of him than the Catholics, and indeed jailed him for corruption. He was a sadist and a 'butcher', according to the Catholics. Under warrant from the Privy Council, he had equipped his own torture chamber in a room in his house in Westminster churchyard with blacked-out windows. Unlike the Tower this dwelling lay outside the official control of the organs of state. This cruel, corrupt minor nobleman, the chief persecutor of the Elizabethan age, took the trouble to buy and gleefully annotate a published record of the Catholic martyrs. Among his marginalia and graffiti is a little figure dangling from the gallows.[1] Topcliffe was the 'swamp thing' of sectarianism, and his authentic voice rings forth from a macabre note written from the Marshalsea where, in 1595, he himself was briefly the victim, on a charge of libelling Privy Councillors. Petitioning the Queen, he warned her that in response to his misfortune 'the fresh, dead bones of Father Southwell at Tyburn and Father Walpole at York, executed both since Shrovetide, will dance for joy'. For all this, he failed to intimidate many of his victims, notably Gerard.

In the middle of the night of 23 April in 1594, near enough to Shakespeare's thirtieth birthday, a raiding posse rudely woke Gerard and Owen in their room in Golden Lane in Holborn. A few days later Gerard was interrogated for the first time by Richard Young and Topcliffe, who was wearing his court dress with a sword at his side. 'He was old and hoary and a veteran in evil,' Gerard wrote later. Topcliffe glared at him and identified himself – undoubtedly Gerard had heard of him. To emphasize his point he flung his sword on the table as if to suggest that he might use it. Gerard did not flinch, and refused to be cowed.

Gerard was twenty-nine at the time of interview. For six years he had repeatedly given various search parties the slip, most recently on Easter Monday 1594 at a place called Braddocks, a Catholic manor in Essex situated between Thaxted and Saffron Walden. The owner was a family by the name of Wiseman and their near neighbours included Penelope Rich, sister of the Earl of Essex. Gerard was trying to convert her, and eventually succeeded in doing so. While the raiders were swarming all over Braddocks, Gerard disappeared into one of Nicholas Owen's most ingenious priest holes, beneath the grate of a top-floor fireplace: the grate was floored in wood over which bricks were loosely laid, and its flue extended down into the room below. Though the existence of the chapel where he was hiding was betrayed halfway through a four-day search, Gerard was not found. At one point, two guards involved in the search party sat so close to the grate that he could overhear everything they said. When they decided to light a fire it burnt through the wooden floor of the grate: 'If they had entered', Gerard wrote, 'they would have seen me, for the fire had burned a hole in my hiding-place, and I had to move a little to one side to avoid the hot embers falling on my head.' As late as the 1930s Gerard's hiding-place at Braddocks was examined and its brickwork then 'looked as fresh as if Nicholas Owen had quarried it out only the week before'.[2]

Gerard was sent to the Clink in the summer of 1594. The Clink, long since become synonymous with 'prison', was small, and built on to the western side of the Palace of the Bishop of Winchester. The regime varied in severity, from prison to prison, and by all accounts the Clink was surprisingly liberal. The Catholics seem largely to have had the run of it. Mass was said regularly and on important feast days, and some prisoners managed to get keys to their cells and visit other internees with remarkable freedom. And there is at least one record of a Catholic priest, Father Thomas Leak, frequenting the Bankside theatres while serving a prison sentence in the Clink. Perhaps he also availed himself of the other pastimes on offer on Bankside – the taverns and stews, the bear- and bull-baiting. All lay within a few minutes' walk of Clink Street, which was fringed by a number of brothels including one called the 'Little Rose', at the top end of Rose Alley on Bankside, which belonged to Alleyn's entrepreneurial father-in-law Henslowe. South of the Clink a passage cut across between Dead Man's Place and New Rents. It formed the southern boundary of gardens that belonged to the Bishop of Winchester. During the three years which followed John Gerard would endure the rigours of the Elizabethan prison system in London.

Life could hardly have been more different for Shakespeare on his return to London in 1594. Initially he probably lodged in Shoreditch again, where the newly constituted Lord Chamberlain's Men were marooned at the Theatre and Curtain for the time being. After writing *The Shrew* and *Love's Labour's Lost* for the company Shakespeare gave them *Richard II* and *A Midsummer Night's Dream*, respectively a dazzling history play which is also a tribute to Marlowe's *Edward II*, and one of the greatest comedies ever written. At the time he was being pulled in three different directions all at once with the Dark Lady, Southampton, and Anne Hathaway all playing their part. That is probably why he followed the key poem about his sexual and spiritual infidelities, sonnet 144, with the so-called Hathaway lyric. These are the poles of his private life. His extraordinary candour in writing about them, with at times barely a hint of screening out of the self, reveals Shakespeare to be as defiant now as he had been seven years earlier when he crossed swords with the Lucys. Shakespeare's subjective 'I' is everywhere. His voice demands to be heard, he wants us to know that he is from Warwickshire and that it was he, the friend of the brightest young things in the country, who wrote *The Taming of the Shrew*, peeved perhaps by the fact that a rival company dared lay claim to ownership of his earlier play. He showed the Pembroke's Men by 'out-shrewing' them with the revised version of the farce, just as many years later he would return to *King Lear* in the wake of the publication of *King Leir*. There is a pattern here of a writer who, far from not caring about the status or authorship of his plays, may instead be deeply territorial about his intellectual property. It may be for just that same reason that he would later rush the 'good' quarto of *Hamlet* into print after the egregious first quarto hit the book stalls.

The scope of the imagination is severely tested in Shakespeare's *Richard II*, the most lyrical, poetically self-conscious, and bisexual of all his English histories, a world of spoilt young men. The play was written at the height of Shakespeare's affair with Emilia Bassano and it may be that he was as high on the elixir of love and success as Richard II is intoxicated by poetic language in one of the few plays in the canon to be entirely in verse. When all is lost Richard yearns to engender an imaginative kingdom through having his female brain mate with his male soul. He could almost be Shakespeare's double since this is after all exactly what Shakespeare did – create a world from airy nothings. Always he is present in his work, whether as poet-king Richard II or crookback–clown–king Richard III. Perhaps the sensation of being close to the centre of power derived from his association with Southampton went to the yeoman glover-poet's head, making him feel that he could take on these mighty roles. How cheerfully and readily he impersonated kings was revealed in the Manningham story about his fling at Burbage's expense. What he also did in *Richard II* was to trespass on forbidden territory in writing the deposition scene. Yet somehow he escaped censure when the prompt-book of the play was submitted, as statute demanded it should be, to the Lord Chamberlain's office for vetting. The play was duly performed.

A tax levy for the parish of St Helen's Bishopsgate from 1597 listing Shakespeare as a defaulter implies that he had lived there at some point between 1594 and 1596. The parish of St Helen's was close to Houndsditch, and the bulk of London's small Jewish community lived in the surrounding area. The burial of Emilia Bassano's father, that same Baptista Bassano who perhaps lent his name to Kate's father in *The Shrew*, is recorded in 1576 in St Botolph's, the church immediately south of Bedlam at the western end of Houndsditch, though he had lived near Charterhouse.

A Midsummer Night's Dream may, it has sometimes been suggested, have been written for the marriage on 19 February 1596 of Lord Hunsdon's daughter Elizabeth. Nuptial plays as such were rare in the period, but plays were certainly sometimes put on for wedding entertainments. If this play is indeed connected with this particular wedding, it must have been commissioned well in advance, and Shakespeare must have written it in late autumn of 1595 or over the Christmas period 1595–6. In the play's magicked wood near Athens, Bottom is allowed to join the queen of the fairy kingdom in her bower for a night of oblivion and sheer bliss. Anything goes in the lunar forest. The seeds of Bottom's dream were sown in the two *Shrew* plays, where male desire and fantasies were exploited to brilliant dramatic effect; how much more freely they can be exploited now that the mischievous lords of the earlier inductions have become Oberon and Puck. *A Midsummer Night's Dream* is a benign fantasy about love written at a time when Shakespeare's own love life was singularly complicated. Nevertheless, Shakespeare is supremely confident of his imaginative reach, revealing an almost naked pride in the power of his art. Oberon controls the unconscious dark, and his power over the irrational forces that are unleashed in the 'wood' (which at the time could mean 'mad') in the end usurps the authority of reason and paternalism symbolized by Athens. Here is the same confidence that looks to confer immortality on the young man of the poems through the act of writing.

It was probably during Lent of 1596 that Shakespeare started work on *King John*, in which various connections with his life and domestic circumstances in Stratford may be detected. There is the animated street scene with a tailor and a blacksmith trading gossip, and another that seems to touch him even more nearly. At the parley before Angiers the Bastard, exuberant illegitimate son of Richard the Lionheart and Lady Faulconbridge, protests that the city's defender Hubert has 'a large mouth indeed' and that he 'talks as familiarly of roaring lions / As maids of thirteen do of puppy-dogs'. There is something irresistibly vivid in the picture of thirteen-year-old girls talking 'familiarly' of puppies. In the context of the play the Bastard is poking fun at Hubert and, as the Lionheart's true heir, takes umbrage at Hubert's leonine similes and inflated Marlovian rhetoric – but there is more to it. The image is characteristically Shakespearian, warm, affectionate, and possessed of a poetic life that transcends its function in the dramatic context, a simile or metaphor that enriches literary experience well beyond its immediate context. Time and again it is in his similes that Shakespeare is at his most revealing and autobiographical. Shakespeare might well be thinking of thirteen-year-old girls because in the spring of 1596 his own daughter Susanna turned thirteen – and possibly there were puppies in the house in Henley Street, a new generation of Crabs, perhaps, offspring of that unsentimental Crab who so offended his master by not mourning their parting.

The portrayal of childhood in *King John* ranks among Shakespeare's most powerful, and must surely reflect his experience of watching his own children grow up. There is a mocking of baby-talk in the play when young Arthur is caught in the middle between his mother Constance and his grandmother Queen Eleanor. She beckons the little boy to her, coaxing him with 'Come to thy grandam, child.' Constance replies in a mocking parody of infant prattle with 'Do, child, go to it grandam, child, / Give grandam kingdom, and it grandam will / Give it a plum, a cherry, and a fig. / There's a good grandam!' In tears Arthur bids his mother stop with 'I would that I were low laid in my grave' – he is not, he protests, 'worth this coil that's made for me.' To be prematurely 'low laid' in his grave is precisely the fate that awaits poor Arthur, among Shakespeare's most poignant children, along with little Macduff, and Mamillius in *The Winter's Tale*.

When the boy is taken prisoner by his uncle and his mother Constance believes she may have lost him forever, she launches into the most heart-rending lament of a mother grieving over her son. Turning to the Pope's envoy, Cardinal Pandolf, and clutching at the Catholic promise of a resurrection in the flesh, she wails: 'I have heard you say / That we shall see and know our friends in heaven: / If that be true, I shall see my boy again.' But he will not be the same: instead his 'native beauty' will have vanished from his looks and the person she will meet in heaven will be marked and scarred by life and 'therefore never never / Must I behold my pretty Arthur more.' When the French king admonishes her to rein in her grief, Constance replies in language that may well reflect what was perhaps the greatest tragedy of Shakespeare's own life, the death or terminal illness of his son Hamnet:

> Grief fills the room up of my absent child,
> Lies in his bed, walks up and down with me,
> Puts on his pretty looks, repeats his words,
> Remembers me of all his gracious parts,
> Stuffs out his vacant garments with his form . . .
> O Lord, my boy, my Arthur, my fair son,
> My life, my joy, my food, my all the world,
> My widow-comfort, and my sorrows' cure!

It may be these lines are grimly premonitory – perhaps the Shakespeares were told in the spring of 1596 that their little boy was incurably sick, so that Constance's inconsolable lines may reflect his parents' reaction to the anticipated loss of Hamnet. As in life, so in the play: Constance mourns for her son *before* he leaps to his death, just as the Shakespeares may have been grieving for Hamnet even before he died. Constance's laments for her son cut so close to the bone that it is almost impossible not to relate them to Anne Shakespeare's sorrow over the loss of her only boy.

King John dramatizes conflicts from the reign of John Lackland, the brother of Richard Coeur-de-Lion, that same John who was forced into a showdown with Rome and eventually with his own barons over Magna Carta. No dramatist of the time could touch on the historical infallibility of Rome and the papacy without being acutely aware of the momentous implications of the 1534 Act of Supremacy, by which the sovereign was declared the supreme head of the Church of England. In *King John* Shakespeare's partisan portrayal of England's gallant defiance of the Pope's unctuous envoy, Cardinal Pandolf, reveals the poet as soundly Protestant. In 1596 he was keenly interested in Reformation politics and their presence has been detected by some in the two plays with which he follows *King John* in the summer of 1596, the *Henry IV*s. Here he gives us the ultimate lord of misrule, an oversized old reprobate by the name of Sir John Falstaff who shares his boozy kingdom with a red-nosed dypsomaniac called Bardolph, a bombastic, Marlowe-spouting Pistol, mine hostess Quickly, and a tart with a heart, Doll Tearsheet. Though the dramatic action is set in the early fifteenth century, in these two plays Shakespeare conjures up an image of what it was like to be in just such a tavern as the Boar's Head in the 1590s. Here are the waiters, the named rooms of the bigger inns and taverns, the itemized cost of sack and food, Falstaff passing out in a drunken stupor behind an arras tapestry overnight, and a general atmosphere of crapulous brawling and playing. They are plays of London life and politics, bursting at the seams with vitality and lin-guistic inventiveness.

It is easy to forget that the *Henry IV* plays were written probably between May 1596 and 8 August 1596, for the Holywell Theatre and would have been put on there, or perhaps at the Curtain – the Globe did not yet exist. Because the fact that there was a tavern called the Boar's Head in Southwark, and one moreover that was well known to players such as Edward Alleyn, has often caused the *Henry IV*s to be thought of as Bankside saturnalia above all, as have Sir John Fastolfe's associations with the Surrey side of the Thames. Fastolfe, of which Falstaff is one transliterated version, was an iconic figure in fifteenth-century Southwark where he owned considerable property, vying with the Bishop of Winchester for supremacy. He owned moated beer-houses opposite the Tower of London in Horsleydown Lane (they are clearly visible on the so-called 'Agas' map), and also the Boar's Head brewhouse in Borough High Street, or 'Long Southwark' as it was known in Shakespeare's time. Whatever else he was, Fastolfe was a brewer of some standing, while Falstaff excelled at consuming – perhaps the transliterative relationship between their names led Shakespeare to an arch active–passive, art–life pun.

At first Shakespeare did not call this mountain of language, wit, subterfuge, and corruption Falstaff at all, but Oldcastle. That is as much a matter of record as the fact that Shakespeare was forced to change the name to Falstaff because of outrage in the highest circles. The epilogue to the second part of *Henry IV* acknowledges the mistake and apologizes for it, stressing that the real Oldcastle was a (Protestant) martyr while the character in the play is only a cheerfully outrageous mischief maker: 'For Oldcastle died a martyr, and this is not the man' are the words that carefully distance Shakespeare's creation from the dangerous world of sectarian politics. Despite vigorous efforts over the years to prove otherwise, the dramatic role of Oldcastle–Falstaff remains resolutely apolitical. It is inconceivable that Shakespeare would have named his character Oldcastle at all had he been writing after 8 August 1596, because on that day Sir William Brooke, aged 69, the tenth Lord Cobham and father-in-law of Robert Cecil, assumed the office of Lord Chamberlain, and thus became the Queen's chief licensor of plays through the Office of the Revels; he held the post until his death seven months later, on 5 March 1597. The Cobhams were directly descended from Oldcastle, the proto-Protestant Lollard (or Christian fundamentalist) companion of the real Henry V, whom the king in the end had publicly burnt in Smithfield. In Foxe's *Book of Martyrs*, the chief Protestant primer and very well known to Shakespeare, Oldcastle's story is covered at length under the title 'The Trouble and Persecution of the most valiant and worthy Martyr of Christ, Sir John Oldcastle, Knight, Lord Cobham.'

Shakespeare had also undoubtedly read the long section on Oldcastle in Holinshed, one of his favourite sources: he knew what he was doing when he wrote Oldcastle. What he could not have anticipated was that the old Lord Cobham of his own day would become Lord Chamberlain. It is hard not to detect Cecil's hand in this. Like his father, Robert understood power and the need to control the arts. For him they may have been *panis et circenses*, as the Romans put it, bread and circus games to distract the people and keep their minds off rebellion. With his father-in-law pliantly orchestrating the revels Cecil must have hoped to enhance his power base at court. And he succeeded, at least in the short term.

Shakespeare was clearly fascinated by his own national history in a way that Marlowe, despite having written *Edward II* and *The Massacre at Paris*, and perhaps collaborated with Shakespeare on *Edward III*, was not: Marlowe was too deeply engaged in actively helping to shape his country's history to be able to look at the past like a historian. But his road was not Shakespeare's, who wrote no fewer than ten English histories. It is difficult to judge where Shakespeare stood with regard to the Reformation. His apparent lampoon on Oldcastle is balanced by an unmistakably patriotic stance in the conflict of authority between Rome and England in *King John*. The plays admit of no ruling either way, as far as his allegiances are concerned. In *Henry IV*, his choice of names that had the potential to cause offence remains baffling, but does seem to demonstrate that his was a restless and not easily subjugated nature. He hit upon 'Falstaff' through 'Fastolfe' in the first instance, transliteration yielding a non-historical character who may in the end owe his name as much to the fact that 'Fall-staff' evokes 'Shake-spear' as to the historical paradigm from Southwark. At the same time, the fact that the name of the character has some roots in reality seems a clear indication that, imaginatively, Shakespeare was committed to some version of historical truth in the *Henry IV*s, certainly where its major players were concerned.

The relationship between Hal (youth) and Falstaff (age) in the *Henry IV* plays echoes Shakespeare's life at this time, reflecting the similar discrepancy in age between the poet and the fair youth and coinciding with the latter stages of the *Sonnets*. The Gloucestershire settings of the second part of *Henry IV* convey a strong sense of Shakespeare drawing on his own experiences of life. In *2 Henry IV* Shakespeare takes us into his own backyard in the neighbouring county of Gloucestershire. He might have chosen Warwickshire just as he could have set one of his scenes, the one involving Shallow, Silence, and the hapless ragamuffins Mouldy, Shadow, Wart, Feeble, and Bullcalf, in a rural town called Stratford. Why not, since there were drill parades in Stratford in the sixteenth century and archery practice on the Bancroft on the river? This Shakespeare never did, and the absence of Stratford or Warwickshire by name is a surprising facet of his works when certainly his home county's flora is everywhere in them.

There may be a specific connection between Gloucestershire and Shakespeare. The discovery of names in the cemetery at Dursley in Gloucestershire that seem to correspond to some of the names in the play, may offer strong presumptive evidence that Shakespeare knew parts of Gloucestershire and, since one at least is known to have been a wool dealer, that he may have got to know them through his father's extensive wool dealings in the 1570s. In *Brief Lives* (1681) John Aubrey – born three years after the publication of the First Folio in 1623 and a mere ten after Shakespeare's death – remarked that Shakespeare 'understood Latin pretty well, for he had been in his younger years a schoolmaster in the country.' The source of this information was William Beeston, whose father Christopher Beeston had acted with Shakespeare and the Lord Chamberlain's Men at the Curtain in Shoreditch in Jonson's *Every Man in his Humour* in 1598, but such a promising pedigree may not be enough. It does seem intrinsically more likely that if Shakespeare did indeed know this part of the country, it was in connection with his father's business – perhaps he accompanied him on journeys to do with wool-dealings. Aubrey himself appears to contradict the schoolmaster hypothesis, for he goes on to note, Beeston's remark about teaching notwithstanding, that 'This William being inclined naturally to poetry and acting came to London I guess [at] about 18 and was an actor at one of the playhouses and did act exceedingly well.'

Such is the flavour of Aubrey's tantalizing account of Shakespeare, fascinating because of its closeness in time to the poet, yet clearly prone to error. Aubrey's claim that Shakespeare only returned home to Stratford once a year is not now widely believed, and his statement that Shakespeare's father was a butcher (rather than a glover and trader in wool) is demonstrably wrong, although – disconcertingly – Aubrey claims to have retrieved his information from some of Shakespeare's neighbours, who told him 'that when he was a boy he exercised his father's trade, but when he killed a calf he would do it in a high style and make a speech.' Since Aubrey was a younger contemporary of Shakespeare's family and their neighbours it is a puzzle that his sketch should be so patchy and flawed. Take into account his interviews with both William and Robert Davenant, and his mistakes become little less than perplexing.

Shakespeare's use of names offers perhaps a more promising line of enquiry. There are no fewer than four different Williams in 2 *Henry IV*: 'Will Squeal, a Cotsole [Cotswolds] man', Shallow's 'cousin William' who is a good scholar and at Oxford before heading for the Inns of Court, William Cook the cook, and William Visor of Woncot. The last two Williams appear towards the end of the play, in a scene in which Shakespeare again clearly draws on his own experience of life in the country. Here it is the petty and venal justices of the peace who rule the roost, reminiscing fantastically about their sexual exploits as students in London, old Shallow foremost among them. Shallow, like Shakespeare's 'cousin' John Greene, 'was once of Clement's Inn, where I think they will talk of mad Shallow yet . . . we knew where the bona-robas ["best tarts"] were, and had the best of them all at commandment.' Shallow is often played indulgently in the theatre, but Shakespeare's view of him was contemptuous. Shallow may not be as culpable as Falstaff, but he is complicit with the latter's abuse of the king's levy of troops, and the audience cannot help but side with Falstaff as he prepares to fleece Shallow. Clearly, Shakespeare's sympathies did not instinctively lie with the country at the expense of the city.

As well as Shallow and a William, this scene boasts a Davy – not the Davy Jones of the Stratford Whitsuntide festivities, but a country Davy nevertheless. The scene is rural, domestic and local, but it is not an idyll. It affords instead an inside view of country life, its administration, the sowing of headland with certain kinds of wheat, the lay of the fields, the settling of a blacksmith's bill for shoeing the horses and for his coulters, the docking of the cook's wages for losing sack (an expensive sweet Spanish wine bought at Hinckley Fair some thirty miles north-east from Stratford), and the impromptu and unprincipled settling of a lawsuit between two litigants. It brings to life the country reality that lies behind the matter-of-fact entries in the minutes and accounts of the Stratford corporation, providing the kind of detail that might be found in diaries or letters of the period written by farmers, if there were any.

If this scene has obvious links with Shakespeare's country roots, another passage in 2 *Henry IV* may be connected with one particular event in Shakespeare's life, the purchase of New Place, in the spring of 1597. The lines in question use an extensive and elaborate architectural analogy to underline the amount of planning that must go into any attempt to bring down a king and government. It refers to surveys, foundations, architects' models, costings, and the danger of running out of cash halfway through the project and being forced to abandon the house to the elements:

> When we mean to build,
> We first survey the plot, then draw the model;
> And when we see the figure of the house,
> Then must we rate the cost of the erection,
> Which if we find outweighs ability,
> What do we then but draw anew the model
> In fewer offices, or, at least, desist
> To build at all?

It seems from his intimacy with the processes of architecture and planning that homes and the building of them were on Shakespeare's mind in the summer of 1596. At the same time, he may also have been aware that the Underhills of Stratford, who then owned New Place, were in straitened circumstances.[3] Perhaps he already had his eye on their property in Chapel Street. It was in need of considerable repairs, it seems, but nevertheless remained a local status symbol. Equally, it is not impossible that rumours about its availability triggered his interest in houses.

It was a timely moment for Shakespeare to be thinking about houses, because in July 1596 Stratford was once again devastated by fire. Not quite as bad as the huge blaze that had raged in 1594, the 1596 fire hit the south side of Henley Street – the Shakespeares were spared yet again. The scorched ruins and wasteland opposite were a sight the Shakespeares had to endure for some while, as reconstruction on the south side of Henley Street was slow and pro-tracted.

If Shakespeare had been thinking of building, the fire and its impact may have caused him to reconsider his plans. Perhaps the plot on which he wanted to build was burnt, or the foundations had been incinerated. Certainly the fire meant that Stratford was set to launch into yet another rebuilding programme, and very likely everything began to seem too complicated, especially since he could not be there to supervise the new works. Perhaps this was a determining factor in his decision to buy rather than to build. The more so since New Place had probably come up for sale. Another aspect to the building simile in the play is that it looks as though Shakespeare may well have writ-ten the architectural passages in *2 Henry IV* after the Stratford fire. The elaborate house analogy occurs only in the Folio text of 1623, and not in the quarto of 1600 set from Shakespeare's own manuscript. In other words, the reconstruction of Stratford after July 1596 is echoed only in the second version of the play; this, though not printed until 1623 is very nearly contemporary at source with the text in quarto, suggest-ing that Shakespeare wrote the conflagration of July 1596 into the play shortly after the event. He had only recently completed the play, of course, but it had in any case to be revised because of the Oldcastle fiasco. Shakespeare, as so often finding the temptation to insert real life into his plays irresistible, took the opportunity to reflect on the after-math of the fire.

It might be expected that the most poignant correlation between real life and *2 Henry IV* would be found in the scene in which Bolingbroke lies on his death-bed in the Jerusalem chamber in Westminster, Hal at his bedside. There is a point at which Bolingbroke seems to have died and Hal, alone in the chamber with him, removes the crown from his head and leaves. But his father is not dead: he wakes one last time, sees that the crown is gone, panics, and calls for help. Yet Hal has not snatched the crown out of naked ambition; rather, he has taken it as his due as Prince of Wales, and in the full knowledge of its tremendous duties and responsibilities. The reunion of father and son on the king's death-bed is unique in Shakespeare. In Holinshed it is short and perfunctory; Shakespeare expands the scene, infusing it with sorrow and solemnity. He is not interested primarily in death, separation, and loss; the emergence of the self-redeemed heroic king seems to be the issue here. For this particular succession to be legitimate and untainted it has to be seen to be so; therefore Shakespeare takes his audience right into the royal bedroom to witness it, and to hear the dying king's repentance and expiation of his usurpation of Richard II. The overriding imaginative and political logic of the scene is against its value as documentary evidence about Shakespeare's life. It would surely be full of loss and pain if it reflected the father Shakespeare sitting at the bedside of his dying little boy, but there is not much domestic sentiment here; instead, the politics of succession and past usurpation loom large.

With no fewer than three plays, *King John* and the two *Henry IV*s, written in the spring and summer of 1596, it rather looks as though Shakespeare was trying to keep busy, perhaps because his son was dying. Perhaps his way of seeking solace was to immerse himself in writing and work: he wrote more during the period between Lent 1596 and Lent 1597 than at any other time of his life. On the other hand, it was also the case that in what may have been Shakespeare's darkest hour, his company could not afford to stand still, and it was now that the Burbages made a move that had far-reaching repercussions for the players, the audiences, and the particular shape that drama eventually assumed.

15

From Blackfriars to Bankside: 1596–9

IT STARTED PROSAICALLY enough with the lease of the Theatre coming up for renewal. Though the Burbages did not own the site on which their precious building stood, their investment in the building itself and in the entire Holywell plot of land had been extensive; by 1596 they were major landowners and rent collectors here. However, perhaps anticipating that the freeholder of the plot, one Giles Allen, might refuse to discuss terms and try to force them into surrendering the land, and with it the Theatre, the resourceful Burbages had their sights on another so-called liberty, the liberty of the Blackfriars in the middle of the City of London. The former Dominican monastery – Dominicans were known as Blackfriars, from their black and white habit – had become Crown property after the Dissolution of 1536, and as such constituted a 'liberty' in the heart of the City of London, which is to say that the City had no jurisdiction over it. This was the point, of course, since the City fathers harboured Puritan leanings, unlike the court, keen patrons of the players, who were also represented on the Privy Council by Lord Hunsdon. Provident as ever, the builder-patriach James Burbage set about the acquisition of the refectory or frater of the old monastery.

The old Blackfriars had grown and evolved into a privileged part of London over nearly 250 years, and after the Dissolution it was greedily vandalized by a new breed of Protestant carpetbaggers who developed it by destroying the former ecclesiastical buildings. By the time Shakespeare purchased the eastern gatehouse it had become a desirable residential area. Burbage paid £600 for the old refectory. All of it vanished in the Great Fire of London in 1666, but luckily an impression of the Blackfriars as it was in Shakespeare's time has suvived on the 'Agas' map and, in a bit more detail, on a recently discovered and very clear third sheet of copperplate. The Prior's garden or cloister is the convex bulge on the north-eastern edge with a fly-over gallery crossing over into the King's Wardrobe, while the inner cloister is the square marked as a colonnaded cloister walk on the map. The buildings which run north to south on the west side of the inner cloister constitute the Blackfriars theatre. The exact dimensions of the theatre were 66 feet by 46 feet. The entire Blackfriars precinct was on a slope, with a drop of 30 feet between the top at Carter Lane, and Shoemaker Row at the bottom. The upper part of the theatre was therefore on two floors and the southern side, which verged on Lord Hunsdon's property, on three (in 1629 Hunsdon's residence became The King's Printing House). Some hundred feet higher above the frater sat Lord Cobham's house. Its location corresponds to the northern side of today's Apothecaries' Hall, which has occupied this same site since the incorporation of its society in 1617. Cobham was thus not as close to the projected theatre as Hunsdon – but he was not far off, above another gallery crossing west from Blackfriars to Bridewell, and separating Cobham's garden from the frater. As the crow flies the distance from the old frater to St Andrew's-by-the-Wardrobe and the gatehouse Shakespeare bought measures 72 yards.

The Burbages acquired the frater early in 1596, but in November of that same year local residents successfully petitioned the Privy Council against granting permission for them to stage performances. They drew attention to the amount of noise a theatre would generate, its unbecoming proximity to St Andrew-by-the-Wardrobe, and the fact that Lord Cobham and Lord Hunsdon would have their peace shattered by such an enterprise in their backyard: 'near adjoining unto the dwelling houses of the right honourable the Lord Chamberlain and the Lord of Hunsdon . . . and besides that the same playhouse is so near the church that the noise of the drums and trumpets will greatly disturb and hinder both the ministers and parishioners in time of divine service and sermons . . .'[1] The frater was perhaps not quite as near St Andrew's as the petitioners suggested – but who wanted players in their back yard? Cobham, who had initiated the Oldcastle–Falstaff dispute, did not sign the petition against the opening of a theatre which would have operated within, literally, yards of his London home; but George Carey, second Lord Hunsdon, a future Lord Chamberlain, on the other hand did. Keen patron of the performing arts he may have been, but not when they were performing in his own back yard. His house would of course be directly underneath or downhill from the noise generated by the players above.

What is perhaps more surprising is that Shakespeare's lifelong friend Richard Field also put his signature to the document. It was scarcely two years since he had published Shakespeare's two long poems, *Venus and Adonis* and *The Rape of Lucrece*. The Vautrollier family into which Field had married at St Anne's Blackfriars in January 1589 had of course long lived in the precinct, and the poems were probably printed in Blackfriars. Possibly the Fields came under pressure from their Huguenot neighbours and Calvinist friends to sign the petition against the players; but did Shakespeare know that Field had signed, or did this betrayal, if that is indeed what it was, remain a secret? For the Blackfriars theatre project to come to nothing, even if it proved only temporary, must have been a blow to the company, although the losses could be mitigated by subletting the premises.

The Burbages had hired Peter Street to convert the frater, and old Burbage himself had moved into the Blackfriars precinct in anticipation, presumably, of the conversion work. The sense of urgency about all this suggests just how big a business the theatre was, the various prohibitions notwithstanding. Further proof was all too visible to the Burbages directly across the river from Blackfriars where a beautiful and ambitious playhouse had just risen. The Swan had cost an estimated £1,000 to build and must have been a taunting presence to the Burbages as they watched audiences boarding water taxis at Puddle Wharf for the five-minute hop to Paris Garden or Falcon stairs on the Surrey side of the river. It stood right there in the northeastern corner of Paris Garden Manor and can be seen on a 1627 map of the area where it is called 'Old Play house', presumably because by then it was thirty-one years old. The street grid here remains the same today as in Elizabethan times so that the Swan sat at the northwestern end of Hopton Street, slightly recessed towards the railway track which crosses here to Blackfriars.

The ghosts of the three main Bankside theatres hug the local bridges: the Rose (1587) and the Globe (1599) the west and east ends of Southwark Bridge respectively, and the Swan (1596) the eastern end of Blackfriars Bridge. Of the four London theatres that a Dutch traveller by the name of Johannes de Witt saw in 1596 – the Theatre, Curtain, Rose, and Swan – he found that the two on Bankside were the most impressive, particularly the newest: 'Of all the theatres, however, the most magnificent and the largest is the one whose sign is a swan . . . for the reason that it can accommodate 3,000 people.'[2] An audience of 3,000 is an awesome thought. De Witt dutifully sketched this rare and, for him, exotic playhouse; his drawing was copied by his friend Arendt van Buchel, and this copy survives in the University library of Utrecht. For once it is possible to see almost the theatre Shakespeare saw. It was clear that his company needed a new venue of some kind if it was to compete at all with the two Bankside theatres.

Their success was due in no small measure to the proliferation of river-taxis. The two worked hand–in–glove: by the time the Globe opened in 1599, full houses on the Surrey side of the river of a Saturday afternoon might mean up to 10,000 people, most of whom would have been ferried across by boat. Inevitably, any interdictions on playing impacted on the river economy. On one occasion, when Henslowe's Rose was closed, the watermen petitioned the Privy Council pointing out the intimate interdependent relationship between them and the playgoers and pleading that it may 'therefore please your good Lordships for God's sake and in the way of charity to respect us your poor watermen, and to give leave unto the said Philip Henslowe to have playing in his said house during such time as others have according as it hath been accustomed.'[3] The watermen hustled for business at their many mooring points. There were no queues, and passengers could pick whichever boat they fancied. Many of the wherries had comfortable and cushioned seats, usually for two, and a number boasted canopies to protect their customers from rain or hot sunshine. The arrogance and bumptiousness of the watermen were legendary, fuelled by the bonanza of the emergent playhouses on Bankside.

The Swan was built by an entrepreneur and loan-shark by the name of Francis Langley, whose moated manor stood nearby in a park. Shakespeare and Langley seem to have known each other, for both are mentioned in the same accusation of an offence ('writ of attainder') in the year following the abortive Blackfriars venture. It seems that Langley allowed the Lord Chamberlain's Men to perform at his theatre during 1596 – perhaps they wanted to try their luck on Bankside before launching into another potentially bruising venture. It seems likely that the experience of playing in a new and well appointed theatre was the spur that set them thinking about building for themselves.

If Shakespeare's company did indeed play at the Swan in 1596, why should the scene portrayed in the de Witt drawing not come from one of this plays? The question is – which one? It is the sparsest of scenes, in which two female characters are engaged together while a man holding a spear seems to bow in the foreground looking on. One of the two women is standing and seems to be talking rather insistently to the other one, who is sitting on a bench. The standing woman is holding what appears to be a bonnet perhaps removed out of deference to the seated lady, who has kept on her hat. Of Shakespeare's plays *The Two Gentlemen of Verona* regularly features scenes of two characters alone on the stage. It cannot be a Silvia–Julia scene, since Julia is disguised as a boy during her encounter with Silvia, whose attendant Ursula is present anyway, so if it is a scene from *The Two Gentlemen* it must represent one of the encounters between Julia and her waiting-woman Lucetta. The most likely is the first encounter between the two women; they are alone, and Lucetta offers her mistress a letter passed to her by Proteus with the words 'Peruse this paper, madam.' Julia pretends maidenly modesty and, though sorely tempted, refuses to accept it. 'What fool is she, that knows I am a maid, / And would not force the letter to my view,' she remarks to herself. Lucetta knows full well, of course, what is going on, and as she leaves she archly lets fall the paper; Julia recalls her, Lucetta picks up the paper, and the following exchange takes place:

JULIA: What is't it that you took up so gingerly?
LUCETTA: Nothing.
JULIA: Why didst thou stoop then?
LUCETTA: To take a paper up that I let fall.

JULIA: And is that paper nothing?
LUCETTA: Nothing concerning me.
JULIA: Then let it lie for those that it concerns.

After a few further quips Julia snatches the letter from Lucetta. This could be the very scene that de Witt sketched, with the standing woman, Lucetta, flaunting not a bonnet but Proteus's letter in her hand. The spear-carrier, who sports a beard just 'like a glover's paring-knife', might be Proteus's servant Speed who had passed his master's letter to Lucetta in the first place and left the main stage a mere three lines before the women's entrance, but has remained looking on while the two women argue over the letter. Two scenes later Speed eavesdrops on the encounter between Silvia and Valentine, commenting on it in a series of asides. Probably de Witt made his drawing from memory rather than on the spot, and perhaps conflated the two scenes in his mind.

It is possible that in 1596 Shakespeare's company was playing part-time south of the river at the Swan while the Theatre in Shoreditch played out its 'swan-song' season. He may still have been living in St Helen's Bishopsgate, and perhaps not far from his brother Gilbert Shakespeare, who by 1597 was listed as a haberdasher in St Bride's in Fleet Street in the City of London.[4] Gilbert remained loyal to his roots, standing bail for a considerable sum in Queen's Bench that same year for a Stratford clock-maker, William Sampson. The brothers had presumably been close since for a while John and Mary Shakespeare's only two children; certainly Will trusted his brother with his financial affairs in Stratford. It is not known exactly when Gilbert arrived in London, but his presence there in 1596–7, or perhaps earlier, presumably means that Will's secrets at this time, and notably his affair with Emilia Bassano, were known to Gilbert. And if he knew about his brother's behaviour, was the bond between them strong enough for him to keep quiet about it, if it was indeed reprehensible? Sibling relationships in Shakespeare's plays are notoriously complex and his portrayal of brothers, in *Hamlet*, *King Lear*, and *The Tempest*, is disturbing. Having left little trace in the official records, Shakespeare's London life remains largely a shut book today, but the presence in London of Stratfordians who were close to him – his brother, the Greene brothers, Richard Field, eventually Richard Quiney – makes it highly likely that his public life, the stage, was very public news in Stratford. How could his Warwickshire family and friends resist reporting at home just how big Shakespeare had become in the metropolis – the talk of the town no less, the main reason why thousands of people flocked to the playhouses.

A document 'which formerly belonged to Edward Alleyn', and was once in the possession of the great eighteenth-century Shakespearian Edmond Malone, suggests that Shakespeare had already moved to Bankside by 1596, presumably in order to be nearer to the Swan theatre. This document has since vanished, but it may surface again at some point in the future. That Malone would have made this up is inconceivable. He did not commit forgeries, he exposed them. The lost document places Shakespeare in Southwark near the Bear-Garden, in the liberty of the Clink, and somewhere in the vicinity of the Bishop of Winchester's palace and jurisdiction.[5]

When the Swan opened in Paris Gardens the area did not have a good reputation – although, surprisingly, the royal barge was moored here at Barge House stairs or Old Barge stairs. To judge from con-temporary accounts of this particular part of Bankside, the Queen's watchmen on duty at night on the royal barge must be imagined peering anxiously into the fog-bound banks of Paris Gardens: accord-ing to Burghley's intelligence gatherers, it was sparsely inhabited and densely wooded, a resort for furtive assignations between spies and the foreign ambassadors who controlled them, the riverside so thickly overgrown with trees and willows that even on moonlit nights one man could not see another. This wooded character stands out clearly on the Hollar and Wyngaerde drawings of the area, one of the marked differences between this and the northern part of the town. For Elizabethan villains, the stretch of Bankside area from the Clink to Narrow Wall, the path that skirted the arch of the river on its west-ward bend, was a hole-in-the-wall haven. Refuge from prosecution and punishment lay a bare five minutes' water-ride away on the Surrey shore – a fact known throughout London, and a bone of contention between the City and the Bishop of Winchester.

During much of July 1596 Shakespeare's fortunes seem to have been in the ascendant. His plays and poems were popular, and his company was planning a new theatre. He was making enough money to be contemplating building or buying a house in Stratford, to judge from the architectural references in *2 Henry IV*. Then the bottom fell out of his world. In London on 22 July 1596 the theatres were temporarily closed by a decree of the Privy Council following a plague scare; on 8 August 1596 Cobham took over as Lord Chamberlain; and in Stratford-upon-Avon on 11 August Hamnet Shakespeare was buried.

16

Wednesday 11 August 1596:
'Alack, my Child is Dead'

O N 11 AUGUST 1596 Shakespeare almost certainly stood at his son's graveside, either in the churchyard of Holy Trinity or in the church itself. The day of the funeral suggests that Hamnet had died on the weekend of 7–8 August. Among those mourning were his twin sister Judith, who had lost the brother with whom she had shared her entire life thus far, and his older sister Susanna, aged thirteen. It was the first funeral in the family for the Shakespeares had of late years been spared this particular sorrow. Others mourning with William and Anne and their two remaining children were presumably Shakespeare's parents, Hamnet's godparents, and other family and friends. It can never be known precisely where Hamnet Shakespeare's remains were committed to the earth, for eventually his bones will have been disinterred and placed in the charnel house which connected with the northern end of the chancel through a small door almost directly under where the bust of William Shakespeare is fixed today. According to Robert B. Wheler, who was fifteen when the ancient charnel house was demolished in 1799–1800, the building was by then severely dilapidated and contained an 'immense quantity' of bones. These were carefully covered over, and may still rest deep beneath the lawn to the north of the chancel, among them probably the bones of Shakespeare's son.

That the thought of the charnel house exercised Shakespeare considerably is clear from the curse on his grave which defies anyone to transfer his bones to the 'house of shanks'. The charnel house features prominently in only one of Shakespeare's plays (the phrase itself occurs twice), *Romeo and Juliet*, and that is also the play which may be most intimately connected to the death of Hamnet. It is inconceivable that the death of his son would not leave a mark on Shakespeare's work. *Romeo and Juliet* is his most anomalous tragedy, a play about two teenagers who are victims of fate and of the rash behaviour of their elders and friends. If it was inspired by the death of Hamnet it must have been written after August 1596, and there are a number of significant clues pointing firmly in just that direction. One is the publication of the first quarto of the play in 1597. The title-page notes that the play 'hath been often (with great applause) played publicly by the right Honourable the Lord of Hunsdon his Servants'. This establishes that a version of the play was in existence by 1597, being played by a company whose patron was the younger Hunsdon. The Lord Chamberlain's Men were known as 'Hunsdon's Servants' for a brief spell only, from 22 July 1596 to 5 March 1597; they were renamed the 'Lord Chamberlain's' on 17 March 1597, roughly a fortnight after old Cobham's death and in time for the younger Hunsdon to take over as Lord Chamberlain on 14 April 1597. *Romeo and Juliet* was therefore written after 22 July 1596, and by 17 April 1597 it had been performed 'often' by the players under Hunsdon. The seizure of the printing press used for the first quarto of *Romeo and Juliet* further narrows the field. This machinery was confiscated between 9 February and 27 March 1597, and among the printed work found at the time of the raid were the first four sheets of the first quarto of *Romeo and Juliet*.[1] The reference to 'Hunsdon's servants' and the seizure of the press make it possible to conclude that the play was in existence in some form or other at the latest by 17 March, perhaps even 9 February, 1597.

As to an earlier possible date, the play may contain an allusion to Essex's Cadiz expedition of March–June 1596, which resulted in the fall and looting of the city in June 1596, when Mercutio claims that Queen Mab sometimes 'driveth o'er a soldier's neck, / And then dreams he of cutting foreign throats, / Of breaches, ambuscadoes, Spanish blades, / Of healths five fadom deep.' News of the English success in battle had reached London by the end of July 1596 and shortly afterwards, according to Stow, on Sunday 8 August, 'great triumph was made at London'. A reference to Cadiz in *Romeo and Juliet* becomes more plausible in the light of an apparent allusion to the same expedition in *The Merchant of Venice*, when Shakespeare mentions the 'wealthy *Andrew*'. The captured Spanish galleon the *San Andreas* and the saga of the 'great diamond' looted from the fabulously wealthy *Madre de Dios* ensnared both Robert Cecil and the owner of the Swan theatre Francis Langley in a web of lies and deceptions.[2] It is likely that Cadiz and the Azores adventure of the following year were much on Shakespeare's mind, because Southampton took part in them. He was close to Essex, who led them, so it seems likely that Shakespeare knew a great deal about what was going on.

Romeo and Juliet was probably finished in the early spring of 1597, before John Danter's printing press was impounded. There is no way of knowing when Shakespeare started work on it, but it was presumably sometime after his son's death. The play is one of several in which Shakespeare follows a source text so closely that it seems he must have worked with a copy open on his desk. The action of the play, over less than a week, is set towards the middle of July, hence the references to the ancient English harvest festivals Lammas Eve and Lammas Tide, 31 July and 1 August respectively. 31 July is also Juliet's birthday. Some of the play's irrational violence, and particularly that of the bravos who open the play, is attributed to the heat of high summer, and in choosing to set his play at this time of year Shakespeare departs significantly from his main source. He also lowers his heroine's age, from sixteen in the source to a mere thirteen in his play. Juliet is the youngest of Shakespeare's heroines and her youth is repeatedly alluded to in the play. Since she is to marry, one way or another, she will not only have sex but may become a very young mother. When Juliet's intended, Count Paris, remarks to her father Capulet that 'Younger than she are happy mothers made', Capulet replies, 'And too soon marred are those so early made. / Earth has swallowed all my hopes but she; / She's the hopeful lady of my earth.' Shakespeare underlines the pathos of his young lovers' predicament by making them, Juliet in particular, almost children.

There may have been more to this business of extreme youth and the setting of the play in late July. Not only did Shakespeare's son Hamnet die during Lammas, but when her father was writing *Romeo and Juliet* Susanna Shakespeare was the same age in real life as Juliet is in the play. The line separating the worlds of fiction and reality becomes very faint indeed when it comes to Juliet's ghost–twin, Susan.

As a baby Juliet was suckled by Nurse, who had given birth to a daughter at the same time as Lady Capulet. But Nurse's daughter had died. Wistfully remembering her lost baby, for whom Juliet has long since become a substitute, Nurse muses that at 'Lammas-eve at night' Juliet will turn fourteen:

> Susan and she – God rest all Christian souls! –
> Were of an age. Well, Susan is with God;
> She was too good for me.

It is tempting to wonder whether Shakespeare did not comfort his wife and surviving children, and perhaps himself, with just these words, that Hamnet had been too good for them and was therefore taken to be with God.

The name Susan or Susanna occurs *nowhere* in Shakespeare's works outside this play: the only other Susan is one of the servant girls in the Capulet household, one Susan Grindstone. Furthermore, if Nurse in the play and Shakespeare in real life both have daughters called Susan of exactly the same age, then perhaps Shakespeare and Nurse are one and the same. Significantly, early on in the play Juliet is impatiently awaiting Nurse's return from her embassy of love to Romeo, and is late coming back. Hardly able to contain herself, Juliet exclaims 'O, she is lame!' – why else would she be so slow? Lameness and limping seem to be more than just metaphors in Shakespeare's *Sonnets*, so perhaps they are here, too; maybe Shakespeare played Nurse – a limping real-life playwright with a thirteen-year-old daughter called Susanna playing the part of a lame Nurse who is the mother of a daughter called Susan who would have been thirteen had she lived. It is Nurse who embarrasses Juliet by reminiscing about her infancy and minor childhood accidents. Nurse recalling Juliet's tumble and her husband's ribald teasing of the little girl about one day falling backwards (having sex) rather than forwards is the innocent domestic and affectionate stuff of comedy.

It is Nurse again who leads the lament for the dead Juliet after trying to wake her with 'lady', 'slug-a-bed', 'love', and 'sweet heart', phrases belonging to any loving parental figure that might come straight from the Henley Street household. The grief expressed by Nurse, Capulet, and Lady Capulet over the dead child is raw and heart-rending. The bereaved mother wailing 'O me, o me, my child, my only life! / Revive, look up, or I will die with thee!' could well be the language, or Shakespeare's memory of the kind of language, that was used over Hamnet, as may Capulet's 'O child, O child, my soul and not my child!/ Dead art thou! Alack, my child is dead,/ And with my child my joys are buried.'

The last scenes of *Romeo and Juliet* take place in a graveyard and in the charnel house or family vault of the Capulets where Juliet's kinsman Tybalt now rests. In the third scene of Act IV Juliet's vision before she swallows the draught that sends her into a death-like stupor is Shakespeare's most powerful articulation of what elsewhere he called the 'secret house of death'. It is surely an echo of his own thoughts about the ossuary at Holy Trinity where the bones of generations of Stratfordians were stacked, awaiting those of his eleven-year-old son Hamnet, newly resting in his premature winding sheet, the first of his generation to lie there. Juliet trembles at the thought of waking in the Capulets' tomb on her own; she dreads being 'stifled in the vault / To whose foul mouth no healthsome air breathes in'. In this place haunted by night spirits her ancestors' bones have been 'packed' for hundreds of years, lately joined by her cousin Tybalt, 'but green in earth' and 'festering in his shroud':

> Alack, alack, is it not like that I,
> So early waking – what with loathsome smells,
> And shrieks like mandrakes torn out of the earth,
> That living mortals, hearing them, run mad –
> O, if I wake, shall I not be distraught,
> Environèd with all these hideous fears,
> And madly play with my forefathers' joints,
> And pluck the mangled Tybalt from his shroud,
> And, in this rage, with some great kinsman's bone
> As with a club dash out my desp'rate brains?

What renders the play so poignant is the contrast between the defiant vitality and daring of its young lovers, their passionate innocence and physical desires, and the starkness of death. In no other tragedy with the exception of *King Lear* is there, ultimately, such an appalling sense of waste. And yet Shakespeare managed to conjure up a lively, funny maverick like Mercutio, at a time when he was presumably overwhelmed by grief, testimony perhaps to an iron resolve. Perhaps *Romeo and Juliet* was an act of solace and atonement, a determined creation of children in the teeth of adversity and death, children who, unlike his son, would be resurrected every time the Chorus stepped out to launch another performance. There was still a family to support: whatever grief Shakespeare felt, he had to push on and, if necessary, submerge it in his plays. The resulting work was a triumph and the company loved it, hence its many performances for Hunsdon.

Shakespeare probably stayed on in Stratford for a while after the death of his son, to comfort his family, to pursue his business interests, and to see through his father's imminent gentrification. John Shakespeare had applied as long ago as 1568 for a coat-of-arms, but had not then been successful; now he was. The grant of arms to the Shakespeares by Sir William Dethick, Garter King-of-Arms of the College of Arms survives in two paper drafts in a drawer at the College to this day. Letters patent on parchment issued to the family will have become their most cherished possessions, proof positive that the glover, magistrate, and mayor, John Shakespeare, was a man who could hold his head high again, as could his son and his grandchildren. Yet however precious, this document has vanished like so much else from the Shakespeare story. It must surely have accompanied Elizabeth Hall-Nash, the future Lady Barnard, when she finally left Stratford, and it may yet come to light, revealing perhaps something of the movements of the Shakespeare family in the seventeenth century, but little else is contained in the extant draft of the grant. Despite providing information offered by John Shakespeare in support of his claim, the grant is disappointingly reticent about the family.

What is plain from the grant of the coat-of-arms of 1596 and its 1599 confirmation is that the Shakespeares proudly stressed their association with the Ardens of Wilmcote, emphasizing as much as they could the suggestion that Mary Arden was related to the Ardens of Park Hall. Although it appears from the text of the 1599 issue that he initially considered letting the Shakespeares quarter the grand Arden arms, in the end Dethick was not convinced, and decided against it. The Shakespeares' claim to arms was grounded in their family's distinguished service under Henry VII and also the fact that John Shakespeare had served his town as magistrate and justice of the peace, but that is really all. There is little about the more distant origins of the Shakespeare family in Warwickshire other than that they had been resident there at least since the reign of Henry Richmond, that same king whose emergence at Bosworth Field in 1485 Shakespeare dramatized in *Richard III*.

The wording of the 1599 grant application enlarges importantly on the Warwickshireness of the Shakespeares in noting that John Shakespeare's great-grandfather was rewarded by Henry VIII 'with lands and tenements given to him in those parts of Warwickshire where they have continued by some descents in good reputation and credit.' The 'continued' is a little thought-provoking if, as is usually assumed, John Shakespeare was indeed hiding away from debtors in his fortress in Henley Street in the 1580s. But the 1596 award confirmed that John Shakespeare 'hath lands and tenements of good wealth and substance: £500' – that is, he was worth at least £500. Clearly by then Shakespeare had not only redeemed his father's debts, but had secured the family stock. Perhaps this was known outside Stratford and was what caused York Herald, who queried the Shakespeare arms during an unusual audit of Dethick's work, to scoff at the grant of arms to a player rather than an alderman. Southampton's rumoured loan of £1,000 may well have played a part in all of this.

Ten weeks or so after the death of his only son, plain 'Will' metamorphosed into 'Master Shakespeare', a title that became the butt of several jokes from his peers in due course, particularly Ben Jonson. They might joke, but no one could take it from him now. Shakespeare had probably already returned to London when notification of the grant came through in October 1596, and it is likely that it was he who collected the grant itself from Derby Place, site of the College today as it was then. In his complaint against Dethick's grant of arms to John Shakespeare York Herald noted on his drawing of the Shakespeare escutcheon 'Shakespeare the player by garter'. Nowhere else in the extant documents about the grant of arms is there a reference to William Shakespeare the player, so either this information was contained in one of the lost ones, or else Rafe Brooke – York Herald – had heard of the connection between John Shakespeare and Will Shakespeare the player elsewhere, and took it as further proof of the defective nature of this grant. Clearly John Shakespeare could hardly apply for arms on the grounds that his son had earned the right to them, but it seems almost certain that it was his son who conducted the negotiations.

The grant of arms would have provided Shakespeare with a sound pretext for heading back to the Midlands that autumn, should he have felt in need of one, something that he may have been particularly anxious to do now that one of his children had died. Perhaps the grant had something to do with his decision to buy New Place, a house that required a fair amount of restoration and tender care, but which would fully befit the new 'Master' and his family. Henceforth the Shakespeares were, like the Quineys and John Sadler, local meritocracy – big fish in a small pond. Whatever Will may or may not have done at Charlecote, there was no gainsaying his standing now in the community. Alone among the self-made burghers of Stratford – the Aspinalls, Badgers, Bakers, Barbers, Cawdreys, Fields, Greenways, Perrotts, Phillipses, Quineys, Rogerses, Sadlers, Shaws, Smiths, Sturleys, Tylers, Whateleys, and others – Will Shakespeare moved in the top London circles.

Not that the gently-born were always the safest of allies, as Shakespeare must have discovered just then. In the same month that his family was reaping the social rewards of claiming kinship with the famous Ardens of Park Hall, the name 'Arden' was once more the talk of London, indeed of England. One Edmund Neville, nephew of Edward Arden of Park Hall, had been held in the Tower since 1584 on charges relating to the so-called Parry plot, another murky conspiracy that may not have been anything of the kind. And he kept trying to escape. Shakespeare would have heard about these attempts as a matter of course, since every escape was cried out all over town to enlist the population's assistance in the chase.

In any case Will Shakespeare, writer of English literature, and Master Shakespeare, newly gentrified scion of the Ardens, would probably have been acutely conscious of Neville's presence in the Tower. In October 1596 Neville made a most daring bid for freedom, his third after two earlier failures. Neville had started to ignore his warders altogether, not greeting them or looking at them, just staring out of the window with his back turned. Secretly he was fabricating a mock-up of himself to take his place at the window at the right moment. The day of his flight he placed the dummy in the window, the head covered with a hat, hoping his warder would mistake it for the figure he had so often seen sitting just like that. In the meantime he had disguised himself as a blacksmith complete with tools dangling from his belt. When the warder came to leave his dinner as he usually did, Neville slipped out from behind the door where he had been hiding.

He did not get very far: he was spotted by a woman who knew that at that time prisoners' cells were strictly off-limits even to workmen, and that was that. The warder remarked almost comically to Neville, 'Will you never stop trying your tricks? Now get back with me.' This does not sound entirely true-to-life – perhaps the warder was in on it all along. Another warder came under immediate suspicion during a further break out the following year, and went into hiding with his family, fully funded by the Catholics. Coincidentally, this escape also involved an Arden, though not it seems a relative of the Warwickshire Ardens, but a Catholic by the name of John Arden. Oddly, however, there was in fact a tenuous thread connecting him with Shakespeare: Arden's confiscated lands had been surrendered to John Lanier, one of the Queen's musicians and the father-in-law of the Dark Lady of Shakespeare's *Sonnets*.

Not long after the grant of arms was confirmed to Shakespeare's father, the family suffered another setback. In December 1596 John Shakespeare's brother Henry died, followed in February 1597 by Henry's widow Margaret. Unlike his enterprising brother John, Henry Shakespeare had not covered himself in glory, but had spent most of his life farming in and around the ancestral Shakespeare village of Snitterfield and in Ingon, a few miles north of Stratford on the way to Warwick. He enjoyed the sad distinction of having been jailed for trespass in Stratford's prison in 1591 at the suit of the baker Richard Ainge from Bridge Street, a relative of the Henley Street Ainges. Whatever Henry did or did not do, however, his brother John was presumably not entirely indifferent to his death, or that of his sister-in-law. It is perhaps too easy to assume that death was a matter-of-fact reality at the end of the sixteenth century, one with which people learned to live. But that the pain was not necessarily any the less is clear from the language of loss in *King John*, *Romeo and Juliet*, and *King Lear*.

17

'Merry Wives' and New Place: 1597

IN THE SPRING of 1597 something caused Shakespeare to spar one
more time with his old nemesis, the Lucys. It became clear that his
rancour against the people who had humiliated him so many years
earlier had been simmering inside him all this time: now he chose to
revisit the scene of his crime, and in the highest literary court of the
land. It seems likely that the incoming Lord Chamberlain, George
Carey, second Lord Hunsdon, patron of Shakespeare's company while
Cobham was Chancellor, asked Shakespeare to write a play for him,
that he could offer as a homage to the Queen. Hunsdon had been
appointed to the prestigious Order of the Garter, as well as, after 17
March 1597, the office of Lord Chamberlain. He was thus especially
eager to please the Queen, and it was said that the Queen adored
Falstaff. The play Shakespeare delivered to the new Lord Chamberlain
was *The Merry Wives of Windsor*, a knockabout comedy in which
Falstaff chases a couple of willing 'ladies'. This was a turn of events
Shakespeare had clearly not anticipated for Falstaff, who is last heard
of in *2 Henry IV* on the point of accompanying Henry V to France.
The persistent rumour that the play was prompted by the Queen's
yearning to see Falstaff in love is as likely to be true as not, and that it
is set in Windsor, where on St George's Day, 23 April 1597, Hunsdon
was to receive the Garter in the Queen's presence, may be significant.

If the play was indeed written to order and at short notice in the
three or four weeks between 17 March 1597 and 23 April 1597, this
perhaps explains why it is largely in prose. Its comic timing is flawless.
Scenic and dramatic thinking came instinctively to Shakespeare —
but it may be that verse was a different matter: its sparseness in
Merry Wives seems to suggest that when Shakespeare wrote fast he did
not instinctively slip into metre. On the other hand, his facility in

verse was legendary, and conveyed the impression of being effortless. In a poem addressed to Jonson, Francis Beaumont offered to relinquish any 'scholarship' in order to keep his lines 'from all learning . . . as clear / As Shakespeare's best are'. Jonson himself made much of Shakespeare's 'nature' in his famous elegy to his dead friend in 1623, while conceding that Shakespeare had plenty of art. The very same volume which carries Jonson's tribute also includes a preface by Shakespeare's fellows and friends, John Heminges and Henry Condell. In their address 'To the Great Variety of Readers' they note that Shakespeare's fluency was such that 'His mind and hand went together, and what he thought he uttered with that easiness that we have scarce received from him a blot in his papers'. This harmonizes remarkably with one of Ben Jonson's later statements about Shakespeare, in his note-book *Timber, or Discoveries Made upon Men and Matter*, which postdates the Folio:

> I remember the players have often mentioned it as an honour to Shakespeare that in his writing, whatsoever he penned, he never blotted out line. My answer hath been would he had blotted a thousand, which they thought a malevolent speech. I had not told posterity this but for their ignorance, who chose that circumstance to commend their friend by wherein he most faulted.

Jonson's clear echo here of the word 'blot' in the First Folio, and in an almost identical context, suggests that by the 'players' who so praise Shakespeare's facility he means Heminges and Condell and the rest of the King's Men. Jonson was notoriously defensive about his own slow pace of writing and resented the charge of pedantry. That Shakespeare was said never to blot a line implies that his scripts were generally clean; any work in Shakespeare's hand might therefore legitimately be expected to be 'unblotted', clean, easy to read, fair and 'natural'. Now, the 164 lines in 'Hand D' of *Sir Thomas More* show a fluid, cursive and attractive secretary long-hand, and there is a very wide, though not universal, consensus that the hand is Shakespeare's. Yet what more than anything renders the *More* lines odd as Shakespearian autograph is that they contain a number of long-hand corrections and false starts, and entire lines that are crossed out. As only a tiny fragment from a huge body of nearly forty plays, the *More* lines are perhaps doubtfully representative of the whole, and at the same time the absence of corrections may be a fictive memory spawned by Shakespeare's obvious fluency. As so often with Shakespeare, the evidence provided by a manuscript seems to point in opposite directions at one and the same time.

Merry Wives came at the end of a particularly turbulent and traumatic period for Shakespeare, and as Rowe noticed long ago, in it he returned to Charlecote to settle old scores, scores already touched on in the portrayal of Shallow in the play which immediately precedes it, the second part of *Henry IV*. He now took the opportunity to relaunch his fight with the Lucys from a position of strength, in front of the highest power in the land, the Queen and court. His grudge against the Lucys was unrelenting, it seems: perhaps facing them down was a way of confronting his own past demons.

At the very start of *Merry Wives* Justice Shallow, Slender, and Sir Hugh Evans are gathered in Windsor. Shallow is determined to bring a Star Chamber case against Falstaff: 'Knight, you have beaten my men, killed my deer, and broke open my lodge,' Shallow charges, to which Falstaff mischievously replies, 'But not kissed your keeper's daughter?' (It is permissible to wonder whether the keeper at Charlecote had a daughter.) The action against Falstaff hinges on a business similar to the one that may have pitted Shakespeare against the Lucys, but with striking differences. Shallow and Thomas Lucy of Charlecote seem to have been very different characters. In *2 Henry IV* Shallow was shown up as an ineffectual, venal, weak, and bragging sexual fool, and none of the glimpses Shakespeare offers of Shallow's biography, as for example his training for the bar at Clement's Inn, fits with Lucy's life. The reason for thinking that Lucy and Shallow are connected lies not in their characters but in the opening lines of the play. Shallow and Slender are in full flow about Shallow's ancestry and coat-of-arms. According to Slender, for the last three hundred years all the Shallows have been armigerous: 'They may give the dozen white luces in their coat.' Shallow and the Welsh parson Evans now engage with this, playing on the double meaning of 'coat', a garment as well as a coat-of-arms, and punning on 'louse' and 'luce', just as Shakespeare had a decade earlier in his 'lousy Lucy' ballad:

SHALLOW: It is an old coat.

EVANS: The dozen white louses do become an old coad well: It agrees well, passant: it is a familiar beast to man, and signifies love.

SHALLOW: The luce is the fresh fish; the salt fish is an old cod.

A luce is a pike, a fresh-water fish, the most aggressive predator in the pond. To this day the visitor to Charlecote is greeted by a village sign with the ancient arms of the Lucy family on it, three luces or pike. By contrast, Shallow's coat-of-arms features a dozen luces – not like the real Lucys, except that one of the Lucy tombs in Warwick features the three luces quartered, making up Slender's 'dozen'.[1]

Shakespeare clearly felt that he was beyond the Lucys' reach now that he was close to some of the most powerful people in the land, and perhaps it was this that enabled him to reopen old wounds. And although the run of his career suggests otherwise, something of Shakespeare was always Falstaff – anarchic, relentless, perhaps even self-destructive. Not that he was in a position to play Falstaff to Shallow's Lucy, but there is clearly a private dimension lurking just beneath the surface of the play: Slender swears, intriguingly by his 'gloves', and Mistress Quickly enquires, of Slender, 'Does he not wear a great round beard, like a glover's paring-knife?' There is nothing much to these clues in isolation, but taken together they conjure up a rural community replete with the irate country justices of the peace, stolen deer, park lodges, game keepers or warreners familiar from the accounts of Shakespeare's own supposed youthful indiscretions. Rowe was the first to draw attention to the overlap of play and life and the parallels between Shallow and Sir Thomas Lucy, suggesting that Shakespeare's

> Falstaff is allowed by everybody to be a masterpiece . . . amongst other extravagances, in *The Merry Wives of Windsor* he has made him a deer-stealer that he might at the same time remember his Warwickshire prosecutor under the name of Justice Shallow; he has given him very near the same coat-of-arms which Dugdale, in his antiquities of that county, describes for a family there . . .

Rowe's reiteration of the word 'extravagance', which he had earlier applied to Shakespeare's poaching, suggests that he thought this apparent return to battle with the Lucys was on a par with that other 'extravagance' that first triggered the young man's flight from Stratford to London.

It rather looks as though, as well as the Lucys, Shakespeare used *Merry Wives* to satirize another of his well-placed tormentors, Lord Cobham, by conferring the name 'Brooke' on the needlessly jealous and ridiculous Ford; it is worth noting that in the Folio text of the comedy 'Brooke' is changed to 'Broome'. Cobham was dead, and his daughter Elizabeth, Robert Cecil's wife, had succumbed during a miscarriage in January 1597. Although the immediate Cobham links were therefore gone, it is intriguing that Shakespeare thought he could take on the authorities with impunity within six months of his gaffe over Oldcastle. The Cecils were always in evidence on royal occasions like the Garter ceremony, and he cannot have imagined that Robert Cecil would take kindly to further lampooning of his now-dead wife's ancestry. But Cecil knew Shakespeare, and conceivably rather approved of him in general; perhaps he was swayed by the sheer comedy of *Merry Wives*, one of the funniest and perhaps the most ingenuous plays Shakespeare ever wrote. Whatever political barbs it included, they are subordinate to its comic genius, and this presumably is why it passed muster, with the change of 'Brooke' to 'Broome'.

The first performance of *Merry Wives* was probably given in Windsor on 23 April 1597, and of course Shakespeare would have played in it himself. A month later he signed the contract that made New Place his. Officially, he was living in Stratford again.

There is no record of Shakespeare's brothers being involved in the transactions that culminated in this purchase, but it seems reasonable to assume that Gilbert, and perhaps also Richard, kept a watching brief for their brother. Otherwise, it seems unlikely that he could have secured that coveted house when others such as the Cawdreys, Quineys, Smiths, and Sadlers, some of whom held land and barns in the adjacent orchards and gardens off Chapel Lane, must surely have been circling around it too. Its sale to a London-based playwright with no apparent presence or allies on the town council would have been impossible without the support of his family. In 1596–7 Gilbert Shakespeare was living near his brother in London, and may have doubled as his agent and business partner. There is no record of Gilbert, Richard, or Edmund Shakespeare owning their own property in Stratford, and in this respect the Shakespeares are most unusual. Logically, they either moved into New Place with their brother in 1597, or else stayed put in Henley Street.

The ownership of New Place made a public statement. The house had been singled out in the survey of the kingdom by John Leland in the 1530s. The town, he wrote, boasted 'two or three very large streets' as well as 'back lanes', and it was 'reasonably well built of timber.' There was moreover 'a right goodly chapel in a fair street toward the south end of the town, newly re-edified by Hugh Clopton', and the same Clopton had 'built also by the north side of this chapel a pretty house of brick and timber, wherein he lay in his latter days and died.' After Clopton's death the house passed through several owners and finally to the family of the name of Underhill who sold it to Shakespeare in May 1597 for a paltry £60, although that may be the recorded figure rather than the actual sum of money that changed hands.[2]

The Underhills were a tormented, troubled clan but rich enough to be among only the few Stratford families required to provide arms for the defence of the realm in 1588. William Underhill was an Inner Temple lawyer, a clerk of assizes at Warwick, and an important local landowner. The large house may have become too much of a financial strain, however, for there is some evidence to suggest that Shakespeare had to spend money restoring it. The year after the sale, for example, the Stratford chamberlains record that the corporation paid Shakespeare 10 pence 'for one load of stone': this is usually taken to refer to stone left over from the renovations at New Place, and was used for work on Clopton Bridge.[3] Shortly after selling New Place to Shakespeare, old William Underhill died in suspicious circumstances; his eldest son Fulke was held to have poisoned his father, for which he was hanged at Warwick in 1599. The domestic tragedy of the Underhills could almost be a real-life paradigm for *Hamlet*. Perhaps Shakespeare thought so too when, like old Hamlet, he rested after lunch in his orchard or gardens in New Place. The property included barns, a cottage, and eventually two gardens and two orchards. It ran a goodly length down past 'dead lane', the name usually given at the time to Chapel Lane, which was also known as Walker Street or Dead Man's Lane. It was one of the most rural parts of town and rolled down in a gentle sweep to the Bancroft and the Avon.

The purchase of New Place marked a milestone in Shakespeare's life. If he had ever harboured thoughts about leaving his wife, these were probably shelved with the death of his son, though the fact that he seems to have been looking to build in Stratford the year before suggests that he was already planning to centre his domestic life there. Whatever sexual freedom he had enjoyed in London would be much more difficult to accommodate in Stratford – but had he enjoyed it? In London he had hardly lived in the kind of accommodation in which it was easy to conduct a sexual liaison. The evidence suggests that he tended to lodge with people.

New Place included ten hearths, and the main bedroom was probably at the back, overlooking the garden and orchards. The renowned engraver George Vertue has left a fairly good idea of the external appearance of the house in Shakespeare's time in two sketches he made during his visit to Stratford in October 1737. Vertue had the advice of someone – whose name he did not give – who remembered what New Place had looked like before it underwent radical rebuilding late in the seventeenth century. This information is corroborated by an oral reminiscence written down and published by Joseph Greene; it is possible this source was the same as Vertue's, although a descendant of the Harts, Shakespeare's only surviving family in Stratford in the eighteenth century, has also been suggested. By 1737 New Place had long since reverted to the Cloptons, who were responsible for the rebuilding: they had effectively pulled down the mansion that Shakespeare knew and replaced it with a brick house. By the time Sir John Clopton settled New Place on Hugh Clopton and his intended wife in September 1702 it was known as 'new house'. It survived for more than sixty years and was drawn by John Jordan in 1793. Jordan was a reasonably accomplished draftsman and lived locally; he was thirteen years old when the brick-clad New Place was demolished in 1759, so it is probable that he had known it, and remembered what it looked like. In other words, the 1737 Vertue and 1793 Jordan drawings, though in each case made some decades after the building they depict had disappeared, nevertheless very likely afford fairly accurate views of New Place as it was during Shakespeare's tenure, and again after the Clopton rebuilding.

The New Place that Shakespeare acquired in 1597 boasted a five-gabled, three-floor frontage, with a fine porch. Local ground rent records establish that its frontage measured about 58 feet (a single burgage), and a Stratford Rent Roll of 1561 calls it '*domum vocatam* the newe place' – a *domus* being a mansion house; all other houses in the town, including John Shakespeare's in Henley Street, are described in the same document by the usual phrase '*tenementum*'. New Place was grander than any mere *tenementum*. It was much larger than two of the best-preserved 1590s houses in the town, the so-called Harvard House on High Street and the Shrieve House in Sheep Street. With its remarkable carvings, the former is a perfect example of the town's new architecture after the fire of 1594; Shakespeare undoubtedly knew it, as he did its owner, Thomas Rogers, grandfather of the founder of Harvard University. As for the Shrieve's House, it belonged to William Rogers and then his widow Elizabeth Walker-Rogers at a time when Shakespeare was living not far away in New Place. The house doubled as a tavern and was well stocked with the large casks known as hogsheads, used for storing beer and wine; its inventory also included fourteen pounds of liquorice and six pounds of aniseed, neither one a common commodity in sixteenth-century rural England. It also must have enjoyed a certain reputation by virtue of the amount of glass in its hall and stairwell. Shakespeare's New Place, considerably bigger than either of these two, similarly had leaded glass panes. It had acquired the name of 'New Place' sixty-five years before the Shakespeares bought it. One of the most intriguing features of the Vertue drawing is the courtyard in front of the house. Even the best Stratford houses of the time were not usually recessed in this way, as the Harvard and Shrieve houses demonstrate, nor are other ancient houses in Stratford of the same vintage – the Falcon Hotel, or Mason's Court, or the White Swan in Rother Street. The New Place courtyard on Chapel Street contained, as Vertue notes, 'a long gallery' intended 'for servants'. This detail, a courtyard with servants' quarters before a recessed house, suggests that New Place was designed as a small manor, as befitted its privileged position so close to the Cloptons' chapel.

Vertue's informant may have been the Richard Grimmitt, born in January 1683, who in October 1767, then in his eighties, reported to the Reverend Joseph Greene that in his youth he had been a playfellow of Edward Clopton, and 'had been often with him in the Great House near the Chapel in Stratford called New Place'. Grimmitt recalled that 'there was a brick wall next the street, with a kind of porch at that end of it near the Chapel, when they crossed a small kind of green court before they entered the house, which was bearing to the left and fronted with brick, with plain windows consisting of common panes of glass set in lead, as at this time'.[4] Another source provided Greene with the most tantalizing and poignant detail of all about New Place in Shakespeare's time: Greene learnt from Sir Hugh Clopton, who was born in 1672, that when the Cloptons acquired New Place towards the end of the seventeenth century

> several little epigrams on familiar subjects were found upon the glass of the house windows, some of which were written by Shakespeare, and many of them the product of his own children's brain: the tradition being, that he often in his times of pleasantry thus exercised his and their talents, and took great pleasure when he could trace in them some pretty display of that genius which God and Nature had blessed him with.[5]

If only it could be proved that at home in Stratford Shakespeare engaged affectionately with his two daughters in educational word and spelling games. There is a hint here that they perhaps inherited some of his great talent. That he appears to have grieved for his lost son by writing his daughter into *Romeo and Juliet* suggests a father who passionately loved his daughters, never more so than when they were all he had left; that the bond between the poet and his two surviving children was deep seems undeniable in the light of the almost obsessive father–daughter relationships in the last plays.

A clue in a later document tends to ground and consolidate Sir Hugh Clopton's story while at the same time casting light on Susanna Shakespeare's literacy. Two of her signatures survive on documents from 1639 and 1647. She was fifty-six when she signed and put her seal to the first, and sixty-four when she signed the second, which may be why the 1639 signature seems a little more forceful. It is accompanied by the well-preserved imprint of her signet, quartering the Hall and Shakespeare arms. Exquisitely etched, the Shakespeare spear is clearly visible in the wax, tracing a slender transverse line across the miniature escutcheon. Susanna wrote a secretary hand, almost certainly like her father but unlike her daughter Elizabeth, whose distinct, attractive and predominantly italic signature, '*Eliza: Nash*', features alongside her mother's on the 1647 document. The story that may be behind this difference strongly suggests fathers teaching their daughters to write or, if they had been to petty school, continuing to coach them beyond school, lending credibility to Clopton's assertion. Susanna's husband John Hall wrote a principally italic hand at a time when the usual English hand was almost invariably secretary, and his daughter Elizabeth Nash wrote an italic hand because she had learnt it from her father, just as her mother used secretary because she had learnt it from her father William. One particular detail of Susanna's writing may, just possibly, point directly at her father.

It hinges on the single letter 'a' which appears three times in the first of Susanna Hall's two extant signatures. The first 'a' could easily be misread as a 'u', and the third is not quite closed at the top either; the middle 'a', ending the first name, is entirely common and unmistakable. This is significant because the printed versions of his plays set from his own longhand drafts suggest that Shakespeare's 'a's were unusually open, and easily mistaken for 'u's. A good example of 'a' and 'u' at odds occurs in the opening line of Hamlet's first great soliloquy, 'O that this too too sallied flesh would melt'. 'Sallied', meaning assailed, is the reading of the second quarto, used by most editors of the play as copy text. The Folio has 'solid', however, and Shakespeare may well have written 'sullied'. If as it appears both father and daughter occasionally left their letter 'a's open, it is surely because Shakespeare taught his daughter to write, thus passing on his idiosyncrasies, or she copied him, or both. (It is worth noting that in the 1647 signature Susanna's 'a's are perfectly formed.)

The purchase of New Place brought with it another very public status symbol for the Shakespeares, in the pews they were now expected to occupy in Holy Trinity. As a little boy and the son of the mayor, William would have enjoyed pride of place alongside his father and mother in the corporation's front pews in the Gild Chapel and Holy Trinity. Now here he was again, nearly thirty years on, this time under

his own steam and as the son of a gentrified father. Legal tenure of New
Place entitled its owner to a pew on the south side of the nave, 'near
the point where the present pulpit now stands', that is, two-thirds of the
way down the south aisle – and this is where Shakespeare sat with
his family from 1597 on.[6] By 1633, when Shakespeare's son-in-law
John Hall lived at New Place with his wife Susanna and their daughter,
the pew had migrated to the first arch of the north aisle, next to the
Clopton chapel. The Halls worshipped henceforth 'adjoining unto
the seat of William Combes, esq., and unto an arch in the said church
on the north side'. This was evidently regarded as a particularly prestigious pew, for the corporation objected to Hall's tenure of it, pointing
out that 'from time immemorial' the use of it had belonged to the aldermen's wives. That the occupants of the former Clopton mansion in
Chapel Street should be sitting close to the ancestral Clopton chapel
would appear to make perfect sense, but the borough council obviously
did not see it that way. During Shakespeare's residence if not earlier the
owners of New Place were probably moved from the northern aisle
precisely because they were no longer Cloptons.

By the time the Shakespeares moved into New Place, some ten
months or so had elapsed since the death of Hamnet; Shakespeare was
thirty-three. It is possible to imagine him here, writing more plays,
including all the great tragedies, perhaps in a study of his own, with a
window looking out over his orchard of apples, quinces, pears, and
cherries, and particularly vines. That vines grew in the great garden of
New Place is a fact, because some fifteen years after Shakespeare's
death a baronet by the name of Sir Thomas Temple requested some:
his sister-in-law, who had lived opposite the Shakespeares in what is
now the Falcon, had highly commended them. Susanna and John Hall
lived there with their twenty-three-year-old daughter at the time,
and it is likely that the house and gardens were much as Shakespeare
left them.

The scale of New Place was such that it could accommodate
Shakespeare's own immediate family several times over. His parents
and his sister Joan are known to have stayed put in Henley Street, but
nothing is recorded about the whereabouts of his brothers Gilbert,
Richard, and Edmund. In 1597 his youngest brother Edmund was in
his late teens and probably working in his father's business in Henley

Street and living in the house. At some point he would make his way
to London in his elder brother's footsteps and become a player. Very
little is known about Richard Shakespeare, who was twenty-three in
1597, except that he probably stayed in Stratford because in 1608 he
turns up in a 'Bawdy Court' summons, though it is not known what
this was about. As for Gilbert the bachelor, he was thirty-one now and
probably living in New Place.

Shakespeare seems to have been a busy man during 1596–7. If
A Midsummer Night's Dream was written for the second Lord
Hunsdon's wedding in February 1596, then in the fifteen months
between that and Hunsdon's elevation to the Garter on 23 April
1597 Shakespeare wrote *King John*, the two parts of *Henry IV*, *Romeo
and Juliet*, and *The Merry Wives of Windsor*, the last probably in a
mere three weeks or so. In August 1596 he buried his son, that same
October he oversaw the granting to his father of a coat-of-arms, in
December 1596 and February 1597 his uncle and aunt were buried,
and in the spring 1597, while writing *The Merry Wives of Windsor*
to order, he also concluded the purchase of New Place. He was
obviously a man of exceptional energy and incomparable talent,
but there is something compulsive about the giddy scale of his
activities during this period. It suggests yet again that the theatre
provided some sort of release – perhaps he wrote *Romeo and Juliet*
because he *had* to, and returned to the material in *King John*, a
Queen's Men's play from the late 1580s or early 1590s, for the same
reason: his child's sickness and death.

In the eighteen months from May 1597 to the start of 1599, however, Shakespeare seems to have written only two plays, *The Merchant
of Venice* and *Much Ado about Nothing*. Perhaps he was exhausted, or
perhaps he and the company were kept busy in other ways, searching
for a new permanent house now that the Theatre had fallen silent and
their original plans for Blackfriars had been thwarted – by, among
others, the very person who was now its patron. He also took to the
stage himself, appearing in Ben Jonson's *Every Man in his Humour* at
the Curtain in 1598. In the 1616 Jonson Folio he is listed among the
play's principal actors with top billing, ahead of recognized stars like
Burbage and Kemp – a point worth bearing in mind when considering
his surmised roles in plays like *Othello* and *King Lear*.

Shakespeare's value to the company as writer-in-chief was hence-forth unchallenged. He probably could afford to write whatever he wanted, above all to write plays which originated to some extent directly in his own experience. On his birthday in April 1597 he was probably at Windsor for the Garter celebrations with *The Merry Wives of Windsor*, along with other members of his company. A month later, on 17 May 1597, a few days after his purchase of New Place, Emilia Lanier called on Simon Forman. It is clear Emilia was back with her husband at this point and when she saw Forman it was to enquire about Lanier's prospects for advancement – a solicitous concern that included letting Forman touch her intimately. Most of what is known about Emilia Bassano-Lanier comes from Forman, who promptly put her visits in his notorious 'diary'. Forman was the king of shysters and charlatans in Shakespeare's London, a quack, an astrologer, and per-haps an abortionist, the real man behind the fiction of Jonson's conman Subtle in *The Alchemist*. Jonson cheerfully turned Forman's reputation to his advantage: once, according to his friend Drummond of Hawthornden, Jonson used the disguise of a soothsayer as a ruse to seduce a woman. Passing himself off as an old astrologer, he waited for her in a house in the suburbs 'disguised in a long gown and a white beard at the light of dim-burning candles, up in a little cabinet reached unto by a ladder.' The incident brings to mind Shakespeare's encounter with Burbage's admirer.

When Emilia Lanier visited Forman on 17 May 1597 it was specif-ically to enquire about her husband's prospects for a knighthood. Was it coincidence or emulation that set her on this quest so soon after John Shakespeare was finally granted his coat-of-arms? Having been the lover, in turn, of the Queen's first cousin, the darling of the London theatre, and latterly, and simultaneously, of both him and the glamorous Earl of Southampton, perhaps life with her husband seemed dull by comparison. If Forman's diary can be believed she was ambitious, keen to improve her standing in society, and suggestible, as indicated not only by her apparent faith in horoscopes but by her readiness to be seduced by him. With his habitual devil-may-care candour Forman records that when he visited Emilia Lanier at her house in Longditch in Westminster on 20 September 1597 he felt 'all parts of her body willingly and kissed her often'.[7] But she refused him intercourse. Earlier in this relationship he had helped her to miscarry a three-month-old foetus. The baby was already dead, his statement about its not kicking seems to suggest, so that this was not technically an abortion so much as an attempt to ease Emilia Lanier's pain. She had already complained to him of her inability to carry other pregnancies through to full term. His notable popularity with women was possibly not entirely unconnected with his ability to provide certain services such as terminations. As far as Emilia Lanier is concerned, his information about her establishes that by the spring of 1597 she was in a marriage which was physically still alive or else the baby was someone else's. She spoke to Forman with remarkable frankness about her affair with Hunsdon, who had died the year before, and he duly set down what she said in his diary. If she also mentioned her affair with a player and his best friend the Earl of Southampton, this Forman did *not* record it; but possibly she did not wish to advertise her licentiousness. Her affair with Hunsdon pre-dated her marriage and was thus not adulterous, and the Lord Chamberlain was beyond being brought down by a mistress. Perhaps she wanted to impress Forman; her several visits in the space of a mere five months suggest she enjoyed his company.

It was probably during the period between spring 1597 and Emilia's final visit to Forman in September of that year that she and Shakespeare finally parted. It seems that she must after all have talked to Forman about her affair with the king of London playwrights – and yet he recorded nothing. Curiously, however, in 1611, the year of his death, Forman saw no fewer than three of Shakespeare's plays at the Globe, *Macbeth*, *The Winter's Tale*, and *Cymbeline*; the last two were new plays. His only other reference to play-going was to a visit to the Curtain many years earlier, in the course of an amorous pursuit. Why is not known, but he now proceeded to record the most detailed contemporary accounts of theatrical performances to survive from that period. Perhaps his interest in the theatre was piqued when Burbage played him on the London stage in *The Alchemist* (1610), to the plaudits of the London audiences.

Forman knew the world of the London players through their wives, and in his den in Philpot Lane off Eastcheap, near where the Great Fire started, he gathered around him a motley clientele drawn from different parts of the city, including its rising middle class. Among them was a Marie Mountjoy, a French Protestant woman whose Huguenot husband Christopher had fled to London as a refugee from the St Bartholomew's Day massacre on 24 August 1572. The Mountjoys were 'denizens', or naturalized aliens. Mrs Mountjoy thought she was pregnant, but her baby seems to have been dead in her womb already, unless Forman lent a helping hand. Marie Mountjoy first called on Forman on 16 September 1597, just when Emilia Bassano-Lanier stopped seeing him. She too was conducting an illicit amorous liaison, details of which Forman duly noted, but does not assume her importance in the greater scheme of things until about 1602, when Shakespeare became a lodger in the Mountjoys' home. There may, however, be an independent link between Marie Mountjoy and Jane Davenant, the mother of the future playwright William Davenant and the woman long rumoured to have been Shakespeare's mistress. The Mountjoys and the Davenants probably knew one another, since Jane's brother Thomas Sheppard was a royal glover and Marie's husband Christopher made headgear for the court and they appear together on the same payroll. Jane had sought out Forman in January 1598, not long after Emilia Lanier and Marie Mountjoy. Her reason for doing so seems to have been malfunctions of her reproductive system since she repeatedly failed to bring babies into the world safely.[8]

18

Flight from the Fortress

WHILE SHAKESPEARE SETTLED into New Place, his contemporary John Gerard did the same in the Tower of London. After his arrest in Holborn Gerard was subjected to a three-year tour of London's prisons, which at that time contained large numbers of people guilty only of heeding their conscience and sticking loyally to their Catholic faith. At some point he was moved from the Counter in Poultry to the Clink on Bankside, and compared it to a move from Purgatory into Paradise. On 12 April 1597 he was shunted into the Tower, while one of his servants was held in solitary confinement in Bridewell, which sat directly west of what is now Blackfriars station and stretched all the way up to St Bride's in Fleet Street. On the evidence of his servant, Gerard, a fastidious man, called it 'the most loathsome of all the prisons'. The servant almost starved to death in a narrow cell with thick walls and no bed, so that he slept crouching on a window-ledge; he could not change his clothes 'for months', and what little straw there was on the cell floor was crawling with vermin so that he could not rest on it. 'Worst of all, they left his excrement in an uncovered pail in that tiny cell, and the stink was suffocating.' Gerard's own experience of the Counter was similar: a tiny garret for a cell, a bed that was always soaked whenever it rained, and next door the only latrine for that entire wing of the prison: 'the stench from it often kept me awake at night or even woke me up', he later wrote.

Gerard was probably transferred to the Tower as a precaution in consequence of a possible attempted escape from the Clink, and was lodged in the Salt Tower in the south-eastern corner of the Inner Ward, locked in the cell that had once been occupied by Father Henry Walpole, to whom Topcliffe had referred in his memo.

According to Gerard, the morning after his arrival he inspected his cell, and in the dim light saw the name of Henry Walpole 'cut with a chisel on the wall.' Nearby in a narrow window was Walpole's 'little oratory'. Gerard felt greatly comforted to be in a cell that he felt had been 'sanctified' by the martyr Walpole, who had been tortured as many as fourteen times. His own fate would not be quite so grim and, unlike Walpole whose signature can still be seen today where he carved it into a large block of stone, Gerard lived to tell the tale.

Father William Weston and in particular Gerard left important accounts of their stays in the Tower and of their experience of the building and all it stood for, quite different from a detached account like Platter's. It is true that Platter does refer to the big rack and its ropes in the basement of the Tower and comments briefly, but he hardly saw what Gerard did the day he was marched to the torture chamber from the lieutenant's lodgings. The details noted by the Jesuits remain one of the principal sources of information about the history of the Tudor buildings of the Tower.[1]

Gerard's fate was sealed when he refused to reveal to the Attorney-General, the Cecil protégé Sir Edward Coke, where his superior Henry Garnett was hiding. Garnett was an enemy of the state, he was told, and 'you are bound to report on all such men'; they then produced the warrant for the torture, signed by Francis Bacon among others. Gerard persisted in his silence and was therefore led away, 'in a kind of solemn procession', through an underground passage which opened into a vast dungeon under the White Tower, full of instruments of torture. They told him he would have to endure them all. He was suspended by his hands from one of the huge support pillars, but because he was so tall his feet still touched the ground, so they dug away the earth from under him. He steadfastly refused to confess in spite of the pains that started to spread through his body. He felt, he later wrote, the blood 'rush up into my arms and hands and I thought that blood was oozing out from the ends of my fingers and the pores of my skin'. His suffering was 'so intense' that he thought he could not possibly endure it. But endure it he did, and even managed, as they took him back to his cell, to pass on a message to his friends on the outside, to reassure them that he had not betrayed them.

Gerard did not fully recover the use of his hands for five months and when he did it was to carry out the most audacious prison escape in Elizabethan England, and the only successful escape of a prisoner of importance from the Tower. For a prison, conditions in the Tower of London were generally bearable. For example, though beds and linen were not provided, prisoners could pay to have such items sent in; spectacles too – Henry Garnett asked his loyal friend Mrs Vaux to let him have a new pair because he felt rather lost without his. Again, prisoners could receive visitors, who were allowed to stay until 5 p.m. when a tolling bell announced the Tower curfew and all outsiders had to leave the building or be locked in for the night. At the time of Gerard's stay there even the Warden of the Tower generally returned to his home in Charing Cross overnight; for him, the Tower was just a place of work. Nor did prisoners starve during their incarceration: they were served dinner in their cells. Gerard mentions a daily ration of 'six small rolls of very good bread' – presumably from the Tower bakery – and these could be supplemented with any other food that prisoners desired.

And this is where the oranges came in. In the summer of 1597 Gerard often sent the warder who looked after him to buy large oranges; it seems the man was partial to them and so presumably was Gerard. The warder would hardly have spent much time looking for them, so they must have been readily available from the market stalls near the Tower. They must nevertheless have been a bit of a novelty still in the 1590s, since Shakespeare first refers to orange-colour in *A Midsummer Night's Dream* and then, twice, to oranges in *Much Ado about Nothing*, a play from the late 1590s which is almost directly contemporary with Gerard's incarceration. Oranges were also finding their way to Stratford now, through Greenway, who took them up from London in 1598 for Mistress Quiney, wife of Shakespeare's friend Richard Quiney and future mother-in-law of Judith Shakespeare.[2]

Gerard's account of his life in the Queen's prisons reads not unlike a modern Cold War thriller, particularly in the reason he gives for buying oranges – that orange juice lent itself even better than lemon juice to secret writing, enabling him to communicate with his former fellow internees in the Clink. Lemon juice can be treacherous, it can be intercepted, read and resealed without the intended recipient ever knowing – but orange juice, once revealed by heat, stays revealed, 'so a letter in orange juice cannot be delivered without the recipient knowing whether or not it has been read.' It is readily apparent why the Queen's secret service thought that the Catholic priests and Jesuits were dangerous fifth columnists. This orange juice business was the kind of knowledge fully-fledged secret agents might be expected to possess, but it beggared belief that self-professed pacifist servants of Christ should just happen to have it too. His orange juice enabled Gerard to conduct a secret correspondence with a fellow prisoner that eventually gained him his freedom. If the authorities had grounds for believing that Gerard was innocent of any direct plotting against the Queen, they also knew that he had links to all the major figures in the Catholic underground, including the Arundels, Wisemans, and Vauxs, all of whom knew Garnett and all of whom were waiting in the wings, ready in the event of a political or military bid for power from within.

One day while Gerard was recovering from his terrible ordeal in the Salt Tower he spotted a man in the street outside who was repeatedly covering and uncovering his head. It was early May 1597, and hot. Given the south-easterly position of the Salt Tower, the street can only have been the wharf between Cradle and Well towers close to today's Tower Bridge Approach. In the sixteenth century the wharf ran east towards Iron Gate stairs south of St Katharine's Street, where Tower Bridge joins the northern shore of the river. Day after day he was there, pacing up and down in full view of the Salt Tower; he was of course soon arrested, and interrogated in the Tower. It turned out that his name was Francis Page, and he was a devout Catholic who had lived at the Wisemans' of Braddocks at the same time as Gerard. He had come to ask Gerard's blessing. Eventually he and Gerard were brought face to face, but there was a lot of Dogberry about the authorities, and they were outwitted by the two dissenters, and Page was released. Determined to forge his destiny in martyrdom, he grimly achieved it at Tyburn a few years later after being received into the Society of Jesus. The memory of the faithful Page elicited from Gerard one of his most poignant passages:

> 'Like gold in the furnace he was tested, and was accepted like the victim of a holocaust: he washed his robe in the blood of the Lamb.'

Now he no longer walks up and down by the waters of the Thames watching me in the Tower, but serene and happy in heaven he looks down on me, still tossed on the waters by the winds and storms. But he is, I trust, anxious still for my safety.

The waters of the Thames and the shores of biblical Babylon here merge seamlessly in the writings of a man whose fearlessness was matched by his gift for narrative and pathos. He later used much the same language about Garnett, confident in the knowledge that these newly martyred saints were guarding his path in heaven and speeding him on his way to salvation. He himself had been found unworthy of martyrdom, Gerard noted sadly many years later in his autobiography, his God choosing not to single him out.

All of London was involved in the politics of the day, and particularly in the schism of religion that divided the nation like a geological fault line. When Babington was arrested the bells of London everywhere tolled out the good news and bonfires were lit throughout the City, in Clink Street too, where William Weston was interned temporarily in a building on the river opposite the prison. As the men were transported from the Tower up-river under escort to be tried at Westminster a flotilla of small craft swarmed about them for the entire length of the journey containing the curious, the mob, and the hacks of the time. Every state success against the Catholics was publicly advertised, as when Campion was dragged through the streets with a large sign advertising his status as a recusant and traitor. Shakespeare could not have remained ignorant of it all, even if he had wanted to – neither in London nor in Stratford. But at least in Stratford there were no public executions, no grim prison fortresses, no heads stuck on spikes high above Clopton Bridge. It is impossible to know what Shakespeare really thought of it all, whether he shared the deep revulsion felt by some about the treatment meted out to recusants – when the Warden of the Tower eventually resigned it was rumoured that it was because he could no longer face supervising the maltreatment of prisoners on his watch. That in this climate of violence and state terror Shakespeare should have been writing controversial history plays is surely an indication of his own involvement in this debate about who the English people really were, or imagined that they were. Perhaps he too, like Page, wandered along the shores of the Thames and looked up at the Tower, a building he features in his plays more prominently than any other, troubled by what it hid from the people of London. He could hardly ignore the fate of the grand Ardens of Park Hall, so infamously traduced by the state, with whom he and his family had been claiming kinship to secure a coat-of-arms. Later his best friend would be imprisoned here. Every time he looked at the fortress he must have thought about whom it held. It is inconceivable that someone so deeply steeped in history was not also acutely aware of the politics of the present.

Londoners awoke on Wednesday 5 October 1597 to a proclamation about the escape from the Tower during the night of John Gerard and John Arden. What had happened was this. Gerard knew that John Arden, of whose case he was aware, was being held in the Cradle Tower under sentence of death. Arden was allowed to exercise on the roof of Cradle Tower, which was not uncommon – William Weston similarly records sitting out in the sun on another tower – and Gerard could see him from his cell, for Cradle Tower and Gerard's part of the Salt Tower were separated only by a garden, the Queen's so-called 'Privy Garden'. Noticing that Arden's wife seemed to have unchecked access to her husband, Gerard thought he might through them secure a pyx and hosts, thus enabling him to celebrate mass. By bribing his warder Gerard communicated with Arden in one of his 'orange' letters and eventually the two men were able to spend an entire day and night together. It was then Gerard realized that from Cradle Tower, hanging above the moat, they could probably cross to the outer wall of the moat with the help of a rope, and from there reach the wharf, and get away in a boat down the river.

He smuggled instructions for a rescue mission out of the Tower, and on the night of 3–4 October all was set. But as the two prisoners waited in the dark on top of Cradle Tower the three men who rowed up the river to assist in the escape were caught by the Thames tide and tossed by the current against one of the massive starlings of London Bridge, pinning the light craft against the starling and threatening to break it up at any moment. In the autumn night the crew's screams for help could be heard nearly half a mile down-river. A number of people tried to launch boats to come to their rescue, but in the end could do little more than gather in a desperate circle around the three men wedged on the pillar. Two of the men were eventually saved when a powerful sea-going launch intervened, and the third was winched up to the bridge in the nick of time. What story they told the authorities is unknown, but earlier in the evening they had pretended to be fishermen.

The following night of Tuesday–Wednesday, 4–5 October, the men were back. This time they managed to throw the rope across the moat to the tower, as agreed with Gerard, but things did not go quite as Gerard had envisaged. The outer wall was higher than he had imagined, so instead of gliding down the rope he and Arden had to cross an almost horizontal rope hand-over-hand. Worse still, the tension of the rope had slackened in the course of Arden's passage, so that Gerard quite literally faced an uphill struggle, as he hung over the moat. To spare his hands, barely recovered from his torture, he started crawling out from Cradle Tower on top of the rope, but after only a few yards his body swung round and he almost fell. The rope was now quite slack and Gerard hung suspended from it, scarcely able to make any progress. At last he got as far as the middle of the rope, then stuck again. He thought all was over, but eventually one of his friends from the boat was able to heave him up and over the outer wall to safety.

For the next nine years Gerard was a dedicated and relentless evangelist for the Catholic faith. The torturers in the Tower had not dented his faith, nor intimidated him in the slightest. His underground ministry was a thorn in their sides until he left England in 1606. It is possible that in the intervening years Shakespeare and Gerard sometimes passed one another in the Strand, a part of town where the Jesuit had probably two safe-houses, with the Arundels and the Wisemans. He was very nearly apprehended here in the summer of 1599, but while the authorities never again laid their hands on Gerard, the persecution of those who sheltered him intensified. Less than a year after his escape from the Tower his friend Jane Wiseman was facing the ultimate penalty the Elizabethan state could legitimately exact. Accused of treason for sheltering Catholic priests, to avoid forfeiting her estate Jane refused to plead, a gesture of defiance which automatically carried the severest penalty in the land: she was sentenced to be pressed to death, a barbaric punishment that was formally abolished only in 1827, by which time Dickens was already fifteen and the Great Reform Bill of 1832 was just around the corner. The sentence would be carried out in the infamous yard of the old Marshalsea prison in Southwark near Mermaid Court off Borough High Street. By the time Dickens wrote his famous Marshalsea novel *Little Dorrit* (1855–7) the prison had already closed, after first moving to its location north of St George the Martyr on Borough High Street. The old prison sat directly south of Guy's Hospital, which today straddles the backyards of some of the major mediaeval and Elizabethan inns including Chaucer's Tabard which stood in what is now Talbot Yard.[3]

That for Shakespeare this punishment epitomized the ultimate horror is suggested by his allusion to it in a flippant quip in *Measure for Measure*, when the irreverent and flamboyant Lucio declares that having to marry his pregnant, prostitute girlfriend is a fate worse than pressing to death. Perhaps flippancy was Shakespeare's way of coping with a reality that defied moral understanding, a society in which his talent was able to blossom fully but which at the same time tolerated a judicial system that retained such elements of barbarity as the punishment handed down to Jane Wiseman on 3 July 1598:

> The sentence is that the said Jane Wiseman shall be led to the prison of the Marshalsea of the Queen's Bench, and there naked, except for a linen cloth about the lower part of her body, be laid upon the ground, lying directly on her back: and a hollow shall be made under her head and her head placed in the same; and upon her body in every part let there be placed as much of stones and iron as she can bear and more; and as long as she shall live, she shall have of the worst bread and water of the prison next her; and on the day she eats, she shall not drink, and on the day she drinks she shall not eat, so living until she die.

That Elizabethan England could not, after all, quite face up to its own darker side is evident not just from a comparison between this detailed piece of sentencing and a woodcut from 1623, the year of the First Folio, in which a fully-clothed male figure looks almost relaxed with the weights sitting on top of him in a tidy box. His facial expression is abstract and detached.[4] When it came to it, the authorities did not quite dare to carry out the sentence on Jane Wiseman, and it was commuted to life in prison. In her friend Gerard's words, 'her position and her good name gave the Queen's councillors second thoughts. They did not want to shock London by their barbarity.' Perhaps the unflinching acceptance twelve years earlier of the same fate by Margaret Clitherow, who was canonized together with Campion in 1970, had proven to the authorities that proceeding in this fashion could be counter-productive.

19

The Money-lender of London: 25 October 1598

I T WAS AROUND the time of Gerard's escape from the Tower that an old acquaintance of Will's from Stratford turned up in London on corporation business. This was Richard Quiney, whose son Thomas later married Shakespeare's daughter Judith. It seems likely that the two men got together, for recent events in Stratford, particularly the death of his son and his purchase of New Place in May 1597, suggest that Shakespeare was gradually drawing closer to Stratford than he had been for over a decade; that he would see fellow Stratfordians in London can probably be taken for granted. In exchange for their news of his family and of business opportunities in Stratford, he in turn was able to show them the ropes in London.

Shakespeare and Quiney had grown up in Henley Street, and as small boys had probably walked to the King's New School together. Perhaps they shared memories of muffled walks out of Henley Street in deepest winter, each clutching a lantern to light him on his cold way through the snow. Shakespeare was rich now, and known to be so – no one in Stratford could miss the statement made by his possession of New Place, which may well be why in a letter of 24 January 1598 Quiney was urged by his fellow Stratfordian Abraham Sturley to broach the matter of the Shottery tithes with Shakespeare. Sturley pointed out to Quiney that the latter's father, Adrian Quiney, thought that 'our countryman, Master Shakespeare, is willing to disburse some money upon some odd yardland or other at Shottery or near about us.' According to Sturley, old Quiney was keen that Shakespeare should be approached about the tithes because it would procure him well-disposed business partners locally, and was bound to be to the advantage of all concerned: 'If obtained it would advance him indeed and would do us much good.'[1] It may have been Old Stratford and church tithes that many years later secured Shakespeare his posthumous space in the chancel of Holy Trinity. In Stratford there was strength in numbers and in good business partnerships, and from now on Shakespeare continued to broaden his base at home. After a decade or so in his adopted London, Shakespeare began to act as financier for transactions in Warwickshire – though he was not yet quite ready to invest in tithes.

The year 1598 marked a watershed for Shakespeare. He now drew a line under his relationship with both Emilia Bassano and the Earl of Southampton in a play in which he also paid tribute to Marlowe. Five years on from the tragic events in Deptford it was apparently safe to do so, as the publication just then of Marlowe's last work, *Hero and Leander*, suggests. The poem was published in the year of Southampton's marriage, of Shakespeare's *The Merchant of Venice*, of Meres's *Palladis Tamia*, and of Lord Burghley's death. It was dedicated to Marlowe's patron Thomas Walsingham, at whose country seat in Kent it was probably written in the spring of 1593, shortly before Marlowe's death, and at the same time as Shakespeare's *Venus and Adonis*.

Shakespeare's sonnets were now mentioned in print for the first time, and by an insider, Francis Meres, in his *Palladis Tamia*. This was entered on the Stationers' Register on 7 September, very shortly after the clandestine wedding of Southampton and the pregnant Elizabeth Vernon, which took place towards the end of August 1598. Meres refers to those sonnets at a time when the relationship between the two men had run its course, and it is hard to imagine that Shakespeare would have continued to address passionate, homoerotic love poems to a newly-married man about to become a father. Not that Southampton ceased to be prodigal and profligate after his marriage, even though he was scared enough of the Queen's wrath at his elopement with one of her Maids of Honour to try to hide in France in defiance of her wishes. As a contemporary noted in a letter of 8 November 1598, 'The new Countess of Southampton is brought abed of a daughter, and to mend her portion the earl her father hath lately lost 18,000 crowns at tennis in Paris.'[2]

By 1598 the time for sonnets had long passed. Shakespeare chose instead to write a play which pits a deviant homoerotic relationship against straight love and marriage. *The Merchant of Venice* was entered on the Stationers' Register in July 1598, just weeks before Southampton's marriage. And why Venice, if not because Shakespeare's and Southampton's mistress was a Venetian, and Venice resembled London far more then than now? There were parallels to be drawn between the Canal Grande and the busy Thames, Venetian gondolas and the ornate and elaborate Thames wherries, the Rialto and Rialto Bridge and the Royal Exchange and London Bridge. At a time when England itself was poised on the verge of empire the Elizabethan view of Venice was of a powerful marine trading empire and bulwark against the Turks. For Shakespeare the maritime republic of Venice is one not of beauty but of economic might and governance. He probably learnt about Venice above all from the Venetian Emilia Bassano, and certainly both his 'Venetian' dramas, *The Merchant of Venice* and *Othello*, may carry echoes of his affair with Emilia, quite apart from his borrowing of her maiden and first names for characters in both plays.

The only hard documentary evidence for dating *The Merchant of Venice* to 1598 is its entry on the Stationers' Register in that summer; the play was probably written shortly before then. As in *Othello*, the names in this play about Venetian Jews and gentiles appear to be entirely of Shakespeare's invention. The play concerns two Venetian men who are very close, the merchant of the title, one Antonio, and another businessman by the name of Bassanio whose economic fortunes are at a low ebb. Antonio, though this is not stated explicitly in the text, appears to be older than Bassanio, who at the start of the play is set to embark on a quest for a rich bride. Antonio's antagonist in Venice is a financier, the money-lending Jew Shylock, father of a daughter of marriageable age. These two have squared up to each other in the past, near the Rialto, Venice's traditional business centre, and now lock horns again as Antonio stands guarantor when Bassanio borrows from Shylock in order to sail in style to Belmont, home of Portia, the rich bride he hopes to win. Shylock advances the money, subject to a bizarre bond: the only security he requires from Antonio is a pound of the flesh of his body should Bassanio default on his debt. The story of the pound of flesh has a long pedigree, even though, as usual, Shakespeare makes it his so that today his version and his characters are among the most recognizably associated with it.

In *The Merchant of Venice* striking similarities echo Shakespeare's life, and particularly the story outlined in the *Sonnets*. Portia quickly realizes that her new husband had a 'bosom lover' before her, and that their feelings for each other ran deep – too deep, the play seems to suggest, as a mechanism is set in motion to rescue Antonio from the clutches of Shylock and the unbending Venetian law he is ruthlessly seeking to exploit, at the same time bringing the relationship between Antonio and Bassanio to a head in the trial scene and its aftermath. The exchange of rings between Antonio, Bassanio, and Portia suggests that whatever homoerotic subtext may linger beneath the surface, overtly Shakespeare advocates heterosexuality as the 'natural' state. The imaginative logic of the play demands that Bassanio leave Antonio behind, painful though that may be, and at the end of the play Antonio is the last character left on stage after the others have paired off. He is as solitary now as Shylock, who has lost both his daughter and ducats, and faces the prospect of a forced conversion to Christianity.

There is a point in the play at which Antonio refers to himself as 'a tainted wether of the flock / Meetest for death'. He is an outsider, melancholy at the thought of his best friend marrying a woman, yet prepared to offer his own flesh and blood to safeguard his friend's future and secure for himself a loving memory in his friend's life and marriage. Bassanio must commend him to his wife, tell her of his supreme sacrifice, that he laid down his life for his friend: 'And when the tale is told, bid her be judge / Whether Bassanio had not once a love.' If the fiction of the play is matched to the story of the life that emerges from the *Sonnets*, for Antonio read Shakespeare, with Bassanio is a version of the Earl of Southampton, who quite possibly told Shakespeare about his relationship with Essex's cousin Elizabeth Vernon sometime during the summer of 1598.

Resonating beneath the surface of *The Merchant of Venice* is Marlowe's *The Jew of Malta*, first performed at the Rose Theatre in February 1592. Shylock recalls the play in an aside in which he compares the men's eagerness to desert their wives for their friends – 'These be the Christian husbands,' he notes, and goes on to allude to

Marlowe's villainous hero Barabas: 'Would any of the stock of Barabas / Had been her husband rather than a Christian!' According to Henslowe's diary, Marlowe's dark, witty, and outrageous farce, its Prologue spoken by Machiavelli, was periodically revived, and became grimly topical in June 1594 when Elizabeth's Portuguese Jewish physician Roderigo Lopez was put to death for allegedly trying to poison her. The Queen did not believe it, and neither did informed opinion of the time, or since. But one of Lopez's own former patients, the Earl of Essex, fiercely ambitious and unscrupulous, had been pursuing a cruel vendetta against the doctor and used him to enhance his own grip on power.

For Shakespeare to evoke Marlowe in 1598, for him to write the parts of Shylock and his daughter Jessica where Marlowe had Barabas and Abigail, was deliberately to invite comparison with his scornful dead friend and rival. The fact that his play was entered on the Stationers' Register as *The Merchant of Venice, or otherwise called the Jew of Venice* renders the comparison explicit. The hard edges of Marlowe's black comedy are rounded out in Shakespeare's play, and the characters, particularly Shylock, assume a measure of humanity that invites compassion and understanding, neither a facet of Marlowe's play. As the father of a daughter Barabas is a cipher, whereas Shylock is no different from any other Elizabethan father – or from Shakespeare, now the father of daughters only.

Marlowe's play is a brilliant piece of theatre, as cheerfully anti-Catholic in its portrayal of fornicating friars and nuns as it is anti-Semitic. Shakespeare on the other hand seems to have something altogether different in mind. By combining the Jewish plot with a play about men who share an intimate sentimental bond and then find their union sundered by a young woman, he seems to commemorate his own relationship with Southampton and even, perhaps, with his Anglo-Italian, Venetian-Jewish mistress. In its mellow, faintly melancholic way *The Merchant of Venice* seems to be Shakespeare's last contribution to the battle of poetic wits so abruptly ended by Marlowe's murder in 1593. The rivalry had long since become irrelevant, but apparently Shakespeare would not let it go without proving that he too could deploy what he once called 'the proud full sail' of Marlowe's 'great verse'. Within the first few lines a fittingly marine and Marlovian chord is struck when Salerio is speculating about the reasons for Antonio's sadness:

> Your mind is tossing on the ocean,
> There where your argosies, with portly sail
> Like signors and rich burghers on the flood,
> Or as it were the pageants of the sea,
> Do overpeer the petty traffickers
> That curtsy to them, do them reverence,
> As they fly by them with their woven wings.

By returning to his old rival's play for his own sentimental leave-taking from Southampton and that entire homoerotic world, Shakespeare is paying tribute to Marlowe. Burghley's death on 4 August 1598 marked a watershed in Elizabethan England at large; for Shakespeare and the Southampton circle it seems to have signalled the end of one particular cycle of events. *The Merchant of Venice* is the final salvo in a contest between homosexual and straight sex that involved Shakespeare, Southampton, Marlowe, and Emilia Bassano, and to which Elizabeth Vernon now put a stop, Portia to Shakespeare's self-sacrificing Antonio. The sonnet writer's desire to surrender his entire self to the love of the fair youth is there too in Antonio; it is restrained at first, but becomes transcendent in the trial scene, to the point where Antonio offers up his heart for Bassanio. In the play the heart is both real and metaphorical; in the wider context of the *Sonnets* and the play it is a metaphor for adoring love. Antonio's uncovering of his chest is Shakespeare's baring his soul in the poems, and perhaps in real life.

Shakespeare was probably living and working in London in the summer of 1598. Southampton had been cavorting about with Elizabeth Vernon throughout that year and had made her pregnant as early as February or March. He had probably been lost to Shakespeare for more than a year before then, ever since the death of Hamnet. By the time of *The Merchant of Venice* Emilia Bassano was reunited with her husband, Southampton was married, and Shakespeare had in many ways 'returned' to Stratford. *The Merchant of Venice* appears to mark the end of two passionate love affairs that lasted from 1590 to, probably, the summer of 1596, proof perhaps of an almost obsessive desire on Shakespeare's part to view and understand his life through the prism of his works. He is the opposite of the most impersonal of dramatists – it is as if he felt compelled to tease his world with his life story, never quite telling it, but imparting tantalizing hints of what was going on inside him; only this dramatist could have written the *Sonnets*. The Will Shakespeare of autumn 1598 was of course a very different man from the Shoreditch playwright who had probably been Marlowe's companion. Young men grew up fast in the England of the time and Shakespeare had packed a great deal into his first ten years in London. Now it was time to take stock, and perhaps to calm down. Since May 1597 he had been a substantial Stratford burgher and property owner with a coat-of-arms and disposable cash.

The Merchant of Venice must have been the hottest ticket in town, particularly if it was suspected by those at court and by the *literati* that it was a drama with hidden codes. Perhaps it was playing at the Swan on Bankside or at the Curtain in Shoreditch when Richard Quiney of Stratford-upon-Avon sat in the Bell Inn writing a letter to his friend Will Shakespeare. Serendipitously, it was a letter requesting a loan from the author of the latest play about money-lending.[3]

Quiney's note has exceptional importance as the only letter addressed to Shakespeare to have survived; it was written, in his elegant cursive hand, on Wednesday 25 October 1598:

Loving countryman, I am bold of you as of a friend, craving your help with £30 upon Master Busshell's and my security or Master Mytton's with me. Master Ruswell is not come to London as yet and I have especial cause. You shall friend me much in helping me out of all the debts I owe in London, I thank God, and much quiet my mind which would not be indebted. I am now towards the court in hope of answer for the dispatch of my business. You shall neither lose credit nor money by me, the Lord willing, and now but persuade yourself so as I hope and you shall not need to fear but with all hearty thankfulness I will hold my time and content your friend, and if we bargain farther you shall be the paymaster yourself. My time bids me hasten to an end and so I commit this [to] your care and hope of your help. I fear I shall not be back this night from the court. Haste. The Lord be with you and with us all. Amen.

From the Bell in Carter Lane the 25 October 1598. Yours in all kindness,

Richard Quiney.[4]

The letter, addressed 'H[aste] To my Loving good friend and countryman Master William Shakespeare deliver these', is among the Quiney papers in the Stratford archives. Mytton and Ruswell were retainers of Sir Edward Greville from Warwickshire, and eleven years later were summoned on the same occasion as Gilbert Shakespeare, though on what charges is not clear from the records. It would seem that Richard Quiney, the Shakespeare brothers William and Gilbert, and some of Greville's retainers were linked closely enough to trust one another in financial affairs.

A Stratford corporation minute of 27 September 1598 instructed Quiney 'to ride to London about the suit to Sir John Fortescue for discharging of the tax and subsidy' – Fortescue was the Master of the Royal Wardrobe, next to Blackfriars. So Quiney was in the capital on corporation business, almost certainly in connection with new corn and malt legislation which restricted the hoarding by private individuals of both above a certain volume. A Stratford survey of February 1598 shows that the master of New Place himself was not as civic-minded as he ought to have been: officially, the Shakespeares were hoarders at a time of national shortages.

By October 1598 Quiney was something of an old hand at London visits, for it was more than a year since he had first appeared there as Stratford's special envoy. It is therefore somewhat surprising that within a month of his arrival this time he should have incurred such substantial expenses that he was forced to ask Shakespeare for a loan, security to be provided by the three named individuals. In the meantime he was in a hurry to get off to court about his business, and he alerted Shakespeare to the fact that he might not be back that evening. Perhaps his appointment at court was for late in the day, or perhaps it was not in Whitehall but at Greenwich; confusingly Sir John Fortescue, whom Quiney was specifically delegated to see, lived in Carter Lane, just a few doors west of the Bell Inn.

The caution itself, 'I fear I shall not be back this night from the court', is odd – it is as if he intended to tell Shakespeare not to trouble himself with turning up at the Bell that night as it might be a wasted trip. It is unfortunate that Quiney entrusted the letter to a messenger, rather than addressing it in full, which would reveal exactly where Shakespeare lived on 25 October 1598. Official documents have him still living in Bishopsgate then, but a list of debtors to the Exchequer shows that by 1599–1600 he had moved south of the river to Bankside in Southwark under the jurisdiction of the Bishop of Winchester. The Exchequer note and Malone's memo claiming to have evidence putting Shakespeare south of the river in 1596 strongly suggest that he had probably lived here for a while before October 1598. In any case, it is a reasonable assumption that any messenger setting out in search of Shakespeare on this Wednesday would have headed south of the river, and probably straight for the Swan, or else for the Curtain in Shoreditch. The fact that Quiney did not address his letter to a house or even a ward can only have one explanation, which is that the bearer knew exactly where to find Shakespeare. He did not need to know him by sight – he had only to turn up at the playhouse where the Lord Chamberlain's Men were performing, and hand it in. The carrier of Quiney's letter was probably a footman from the inn, which was much patronized by councillors and business-men from Warwickshire. A map drawn shortly after the Great Fire of 1666 shows the space formerly occupied by the Bell Inn spreading deeply into a courtyard to the south of Carter Lane, just like the big hostelries in Bishopsgate or in Long Southwark. It seems to have been run by a real-life Mistress Quickly, because one of its Stratford visitors reminded his executors to settle his debts with the landlady of the Bell, and would have employed a number of staff – London's large inns were well-appointed and comfortable places.

To muddy the waters, there was another Bell Inn nearby which also welcomed Stratfordians. It stood in neighbouring Friday Street, which runs towards the river east of Carter Lane and parallel to Bread Street. About three weeks or so after Quiney's letter to Shakespeare, Daniel Baker, future adversary of the theatre and closet Puritan, sat in Stratford writing to his 'loving friend Master Leonard Bennet at the Bell in Friday-street';[5] on the same day he dispatched another letter, 'to his loving uncle Mr Richard Quiney of Stratford at his chamber at the Bell in Carter Lane': two letters to two different men staying at distinct, though neighbouring, inns of the same name in London. There seems to be no record of a Leonard Bennet in Stratford, but he must have been a visitor to London rather than a native, or he would hardly have needed to stay at the Friday Street Bell Inn. That he was known to Baker suggests that he was probably from Stratford, or at least from the Stratford area. Daniel Baker was related to Quiney, whom he calls 'uncle', through Richard Quiney's marriage to Elizabeth Phillips, daughter of Thomas Phillips; Baker's mother was probably Richard Quiney's sister-in-law.

Quiney may have run up debts in London through circumstances he had not anticipated. His family was wealthy, after all and the borough had voted him a budget for going to London – though this may have been payable in arrears; in an emergency, lenders could supply cash-in-hand. In this period Quiney conducted a great deal of business in London. He knew the drill, but perhaps on this occasion in October 1598 he could not be fitted in when he was scheduled to be seen at court and therefore had to stay on in London, an obviously unforeseen and a potentially costly turn of events. In such a case, a fellow countryman with deep pockets would be a useful acquaintance. The fact that earlier in the same year Shakespeare had been approached by the Quineys and Sturley to underwrite the purchase of the Shottery tithes rather suggests that lending money was what he did, not unlike his *alter ego* Antonio in *The Merchant of Venice*.

That Shakespeare agreed the loan the very same day it was requested is implied in a letter sent by Abraham Sturley to Quiney on 4 November, addressed 'To his most loving brother, Master Richard Quiney, at the Bell in Carter Lane at London give these'. In it he acknowledges receipt of a letter from Quiney sent back to Stratford through Greenway, who delivered it at Sturley's house on the night of Tuesday 31 October:

> Your letter of the 25 October came to my hands the last of the same at night per Greenway, which imported . . . that our countryman Master William Shakespeare would procure us money, which I will like of as I shall hear when, and where, and how . . . now to your other letter of the 1st of November received the 3rd of the same.

When he wrote to Shakespeare Quiney seems to have been in a considerable rush ('My time bids me hasten to an end'), with scarcely time to pen another letter, and in any case he did not yet know Shakespeare's reaction. It may be that his visit to court that day was delayed or even cancelled at the last minute, after he had already written to

Shakespeare – that he either never left for Whitehall at all, or else returned early to find Shakespeare waiting for him, in emollient mood. If by any chance he did not leave the Bell Inn after writing his letter and just waited for Shakespeare to arrive there that would explain why he carried the letter home with him to Warwickshire.

Quiney and Shakespeare probably shook on the deal there and then in one of the convivial lounges of the Bell. After Will's departure, perhaps to catch a late boat home across the river, Quiney sat down, eager to impart his good news to Sturley in time for Greenway to gather it in his mailbag for Stratford. The events of 25 October 1598 had not turned out quite as planned, but he had successfully borrowed money from Shakespeare. What does not quite make sense is that in his letter to Shakespeare Quiney implied that the money was for his own personal need, that the debts that so troubled him were his own, whereas Sturley's letter suggests otherwise – that the large sum of money requested was for some joint business interest concerning Sturley and Quiney. It almost looks as though Shakespeare was effectively tricked into lending money to ease the personal need of a friend who all along and in concert with another party intended to use it for a different purpose altogether. Why else did Quiney not inform Shakespeare of the fact that he and Sturley needed the money between them? And why was the letter either never sent, or returned to Quiney? Perhaps Shakespeare returned it when he sent the money – which may or may not have been extracted under false pretences. It is worth noting that Sturley is not cited among the guarantors of this substantial loan. Possibly Shakespeare was less well disposed to Sturley than he was to Richard Quiney and the others, for Sturley had long been associated with the Lucys and was in their pay in the late 1580s, just at the time when Shakespeare probably had his brush with them. What the Quiney–Sturley correspondence does strongly suggest is that Shakespeare could be trusted to be a loyal and generous friend, that he was prepared to lend to those whom he knew well, and particularly to fellow townsmen from the same neighbourhood. Shakespeare's personal reputation has occasionally suffered from allegations that he had an appetite for litigation, but the truth is that he was no more litigious than any other bourgeois burgher of the period.

In replying to Quiney's first letter of 25 October, Sturley referred to a *second* letter posted by Quiney in London on Wednesday 1 November and received in Stratford on Friday 3 November, which proves the existence of some sort of express mail service between London and the Midlands. It cannot have been brought normally by the Stratford carrier Greenway, who had delivered *his* London mailbag in Stratford on 31 October, the bag that included Quiney's first letter. It must therefore have been someone else who brought the second letter in an expeditious two-day transfer of mail between London and Stratford. It looks as though different 'postmen' operated this route, and that even in London Shakespeare was never more than two days away from his family, by letter at least. The Quiney correspondence for this period seems to suggest that a lively epistolary exchange between Stratford and London was the norm, despite the paucity of surviving evidence.

It is almost inconceivable that during his various and prolonged spells in London between 1597 and 1602 Quiney should not have seen one of Shakespeare's plays. Shakespeare's reputation was beginning to soar, and that same year, 1598, for the second time in two years, a quarto of his brilliant *Richard II* appeared for sale. A Shakespeare quarto cost between five and eight pence; they were not particularly prestigious publications, but they brought in a little money – why else would anyone publish a play, when to do so was to court plagiarism? What renders the 1598 quarto of *Richard II* particularly significant is the fact that it had Shakespeare's name emblazoned on it – presumably in the hope that its attribution to a popular playwright of the day would help sell it. It was the first time that this had happened, and a quarto of *Richard III* bearing Shakespeare's name followed: the Stratford tearaway had now become a marketable commodity. It is a pleasant turnabout. Quiney may well have picked up a *Richard II* quarto and taken it home to Warwickshire with him. That Shakespeare himself owned quartos of his own plays can probably be taken for granted, and no doubt he showed this one to his parents, his wife, his children, and his friends. These were now *his* books. Many years later, in the sunset of his career, he paid tribute to the extraordinary power of books in the figure of Prospero.

By the autumn of 1598 Shakespeare was a man of means. When his company looked elsewhere to secure a permanent playing venue he was ready to contribute his own cash. With the expiry of the lease of the Theatre in April 1597 the Lord Chamberlain's Men had become nomads, probably playing at the Curtain and the Swan while the great Theatre lay empty. This was clearly news in London – in the words of the contemporary satirist Everard Guilpin, 'but see yonder, / One, like the unfrequented Theatre, / Walks in dark silence and vast solitude.'[6] The Burbages eventually decided to build a new playhouse on Bankside, where they owned a thirty-one-year lease on land near the Rose theatre. Giles Allen, the Shoreditch freeholder whose intransigence lay behind the original abandonment of the Theatre, persisted in his claim to the Theatre on the basis that common law entitled him to everything that stood on his plot; the Burbages and their colleagues and friends set about dismantling the building, and on 28 December 1598, a cold, snow-bound day, they took down all the timber of the building and got it ready for transporting to Bankside.

20

A Stratford Alexander in *Henry V* at the Globe: 1599

THE CARPENTER PETER Street, future builder of the Globe and the Fortune, helped in the demolition of the Theatre. He had been involved two years earlier in the proposed transformation of the Blackfriars frater that came to naught. Having grown up in the same part of the City of London as the Burbages, he probably knew the joiner James Burbage as a young man, and may have been involved in the building of the Theatre in the mid 1570s. Under his expert guidance the timbers of the old Theatre were reassembled to become the Globe. The foundations of Globe 1 (1599) and Globe 2 (1613–14) were identical.[1] Shakespeare's three main theatres were therefore to all intents and purposes the same house.

The legal saga launched by the demolition of the Theatre ran for years. Pulling down the old house was a noisy affair and, as Allen's admittedly partisan deposition makes clear, noisome for the neighbours – prolonged, too, since every single piece of timber had to be numbered ready for reassembling south of the river. Transporting the materials down to the river undoubtedly involved many cartloads. It would not have been taken across London Bridge, for it was rather narrow, charged a hefty toll for transports, and was closed at night. Much more likely is that the wagons and carts trundled through the snow-bound City down towards Peter Street's timber-yard on the wharf at Bridewell stairs, which was probably squeezed in between Watergate and the aptly named John Carpenter Street. It must always have been a timber-yard and was certainly so in the late 1550s, for the substantial timber-yards of the Bridewell district are clearly sketched in on the copperplate; Street had been operating from these particular premises since 1596. From Bridewell Stairs it was easy to ship the timber across to Bankside on barges.

The first Globe probably cost between four and five hundred pounds to build. A few months after its completion Peter Street was contracted by the Lord Chamberlain's rivals to build another theatre to almost the same specifications, but square rather than round. This playhouse, commissioned by Henslowe and Alleyn, became the Fortune, in the Liberty of Finsbury; its site commemorated by Fortune Street, directly north of the Barbican. Presumably Henslowe decided to move his operations north of the river to avoid the competition of Shakespeare's company – the Lord Chamberlain's Men enjoyed an excellent reputation and had the advantage now of playing at a brand-new theatre very close to Henslowe's Rose, a smaller house now twelve years old. And no matter how excellent the wherry service, audiences might have thought twice about crossing the river if instead they could walk to a play through the City. The outlay for the Fortune was estimated at £440 and seven months were allowed for building it, suggesting that the Globe may have taken rather less time since the numbered timbers were ready to be assembled, and indeed a reference in the lease of the ground occupied by the Globe dated 16 May 1599 describes it as '*de novo edificata*', 'newly erected': it looks as though the Globe took less than five months to complete. Once the foundations were in place it was mostly a matter of joinery. A considerable part of the money raised to pay for the Globe in 1599 was apparently borrowed. The Burbages held 50 per cent and Shakespeare, Augustine Phillips, Thomas Pope, John Heminges, and Will Kemp the rest. When Kemp left the company in 1599 his share was merged into the other players' holdings, so that after 1599 four of them held half the shares of the first Globe and the Burbages the rest. What percentage of this half Shakespeare held is not known.

When the Lord Chamberlain's Men moved there, Bankside had already become a playground *extra muros* for Londoners. As well as harbouring the Rose and the Swan theatres, it was also a popular venue for bear- and bull-baitings, favourite Sunday pastimes. The inquisitive visitor Thomas Platter once again takes us right to the heart of 1599 when he was visiting the capital. Platter was not a man to flinch at public executions in France and Catalunya, and he watched bear-baiting with detached curiosity, recording how a blind old bear was brought on and boys started striking at it with staves until the bear broke loose and fled back into its cage. Afterwards Platter and his companions went to inspect the English mastiffs that were set on the bears and counted 120 of them, as well as a number of bears and bulls. He was dismayed by the stench of the entire area of Pike Garden. The kennels, boxes, cages, and stalls for dogs, bears, and bulls lay south of the spot where nowadays the Millennium Bridge touches the Surrey bank of the Thames, occupying the eastern wing of Tate Modern.

The two bears 'Harry Hunks' and 'George Stone' were the stars of late sixteenth-century Bankside and Shakespeare would have seen them and known their names. Stews and taverns were as much a part of Bankside as cock-fighting and bull- and bear-baiting. Bankside also boasted several prisons including the Clink near the inlet of St Mary Overy's dock. It was damp and insalubrious because of the nearby Thames and the sewer which cut through Dead Man's Walk to the west of the prison; the entire area to the west of Paris Garden was known as Lambeth Marsh. The Clink was a comparatively insignificant prison, and Weston, Gerard, and others found its regime easygoing compared with other penal institutions, perhaps because so many of the inmates were prisoners of conscience rather than hard-bitten criminals. Alleyn's father-in-law Philip lived in its immediate vicinity. He did not seem to mind. His vested interests on Bankside were many and variable – he ran theatres, taverns, and whorehouses, and eventually secured the franchise to become Master of the Royal Game, which included bear-baiting. He was a formidable entrepreneur, a side of his character perhaps rather belied by the cosily innocuous domestic chit-chat of his correspondence with Alleyn.

With the building of the Globe in 1599 Southwark became Shakespeare's place of work for the next twelve years. The Globe stood near Maiden Lane. Its foundations are today marked on the pavement at Anchor Terrace, in a spot south-east from where Southwark Bridge Road crosses over Park Street. The massive fly-over disguises the fact that in the late sixteenth century the Globe stood less than 80 yards away from its competitor the Rose, which occupied the south-eastern corner of Rose Alley, a cut which has linked Maiden Lane to Bankside since the Middle Ages. The two theatres were perhaps too close together for the players' comfort, for they could undoubtedly hear one another across the distance between the houses. The Globe flew a flag or barrier, sometimes alleged to have depicted Atlas or Hercules propping up the world. If the Swan's featured a swan, it is likely enough that the Globe's emblem was the globe. The choice of the name 'Globe' may even have been Shakespeare's: 'All the world's a stage / And all the men and women merely players,' he said in *As You Like It*, only the third play ever acted at the Globe. Prospero too alludes to the Bankside theatre when he declares that 'solemn temples, the great globe itself' will dissolve alike in the end.

It is a moot point which of Shakespeare's plays inaugurated the new playhouse. The Globe and 'this wooden O' evoked by the opening Chorus of *Henry V* are probably one and the same,[2] and the excitement in the choruses of *Henry V* about the boundless possibilities the stage affords for the imaginative recreation of oceans and spaces is such that it may have been this play rather than *Julius Caesar* which launched the Globe on its trajectory of fame. In Act V Shakespeare compares the welcome extended by Londoners to Henry V with that which the Romans granted to Caesar, or that which the people of London will accord the Earl of Essex on his victorious return from Ireland:

> Were now the general of our gracious Empress –
> As in good time he may – from Ireland coming,
> Bringing rebellion broachèd on his sword,
> How many would the peaceful city quit
> To welcome him!

These triumphalist references to Essex in Act V date *Henry V* to before 28 September 1599, the day Essex rushed into the Queen's palace at Nonsuch on his return from a failed campaign in Ireland: clearly he was still in Ireland when Shakespeare wrote Act V. Similarly, Act V must date from after 27 March 1599, when Essex first left London for Ireland. The Globe seems to have been fully operational by the middle of May 1599, and a theatrically celebratory, martial, and grandiloquent play like *Henry V* looks an obvious choice for its inauguration.[3] *Julius Caesar* was certainly performed at the Globe in September 1599, because Platter saw it there on the 21st of that month. At the time it was probably a new play, and it must have taken Shakespeare some time to write such a heavily versified, marmoreal work. Most of *Henry V*, up to the end of Act IV, had probably been written during Lent of 1599. News of Essex's departure for Ireland broke towards the end of March, and Shakespeare reacted by putting him into the Chorus of Act V, apparently unable to resist the analogy between Henry's French war and Essex's Irish expedition. It seems likely, then, that *Henry V* was finished by the middle of April 1599, if not before, and that it may have been intended to coincide with the opening of the Globe theatre the following month. It is entirely probable that Shakespeare might want to pay tribute to Essex in an English war epic written at the time of the Tyrone conflict, for Southampton and Essex were the closest of allies, not only comrades-in-arms in Ireland, but related since Southampton's marriage to Essex's cousin. There is every reason for thinking that Shakespeare and Southampton continued as friends and it may have been this friendship that before long set Shakespeare and his company on a potentially deadly collision course with the Privy Council over a play involving the deposition of an English king.

The most intriguing aspect of *Henry V* from a biographical point of view is neither its link to the Globe nor its allusion to Essex and the Irish wars, but Shakespeare's extensive use of French in the fourth scene of Act III. Here the Princess of France, Katherine, and an elderly lady-in-waiting by the name of Alice, speak together in a scene abounding in *franglais* double-entendres. A thread of comedy picked up again at the very end of the play, when Harry of England woos Kate of France both in 'plain English' and artfully halting French. It was not taught in the grammar schools, and there is no way of knowing when Shakespeare became so accomplished in the language. The only plausible explanation afforded by the available facts is his friendship with Richard Field's French Hugenot family, since it was at least another three years before he moved in with the Mountjoys. If his French can indeed be traced to the Fields, it follows that Shakespeare must have seen a lot of them in their Blackfriars precinct in London; moreover his Venetian mistress was married to a French musician: the French scenes in *Henry V* may thus help to consolidate, if somewhat obliquely, Shakespeare's links to Field and Emilia.

To have acquired the knowledge of French Shakespeare displays by means of such tenuous contacts bespeaks an exceptional ear for language, perhaps bolstered by his classical grammar school education. His use of Italian is sporadic only, and it seems quite likely that he picked it up from Emilia in a similarly *ad hoc* way, but chose not to deploy it in the theatre because there was no audience for it. Where Italian settings are concerned no holds are barred after *The Taming of the Shrew*, a play which probably owes its very relocation from Athens to Padua to the Italian mistress. It has long been suspected that Shakespeare's 'ocular proof' derives from the Italian text of his source, which here has '*vedere con gli occhi*', a phrase not found in the French translation of Cinthio which some scholars argue Shakespeare used. It looks very much as though he could read Italian, and that his command of the language was good enough for turns of phrase to linger in his mind and find their way into English. If 'ocular' occurred more widely this argument in favour of his ability to read Italian would fall, but it does not; it is only in *Othello*, and at just the point where it also occurs in the Italian source. Shakespeare borrowed endlessly, his mind apparently hoovering up everything he read and storing it for retrieval. His use of 'ocular' is, remarkably, only the second recorded usage in English in this meaning.

When Shakespeare moved into New Place from his parents' home in Henley Street he acquired a new set of neighbours. One of them was the same schoolmaster and bibliophile, Alexander Aspinall, who had perhaps bought some gloves from Henley Street three years earlier. It may be that Shakespeare and Aspinall borrowed books from each other, or discussed them across the fence that separated their respective gardens as they tended their pear and apple trees. Shakespeare built up the library in New Place, and it was he who created the 'study' which existed in the house many years after his death. He probably bought his books either in St Paul's Churchyard or else in the Strand, in London. Richard Field, whose master printed Holinshed's *Chronicles* while he did North's *Plutarch* and Ovid's *Metamorphoses*, three of Shakespeare's favourite texts, probably possessed an impressive library, though strictly speaking it may have belonged to the printing company rather than him personally. It is possible to work out a list of various books that Shakespeare read and used in his works, and this is exactly what Geoffrey Bullough did in his compendious eight-volume collection of the sources that Shakespeare demonstrably drew on and used in his works, but these probably constitute a fraction only of his overall reading. The books he needed in Stratford must have come up from London, either by packhorse or in his own luggage. It may be that some of the books his friend Field printed in London found their way to his parental home in Stratford; books could also be bought in Oxford, on the route Shakespeare seems to have used more and more often – for obvious reasons, both Oxford and Cambridge supported a thriving trade in books.

Shakespeare and Aspinall were not the only book-owners in Stratford, but private libraries were all but non-existent in the Warwickshire circles Shakespeare frequented, with a few exceptions. Almost half of the estate of Master John Bretchgirdle (he had baptized Shakespeare); some £10, consisted of books. Moreover, Bretchgirdle's assistant curate, John Brownsword, master at the grammar school from 1565 to 1567 and holder of an MA from Christ Church, Oxford, seems to have owned an impressive collection of books, even though none are itemized in his inventory. Brownsword also wrote Latin verse and he is included as a poet in Meres's *Palladis Tamia*. If Meres was after all part of Shakespeare's circle, it might have been Shakespeare who alerted him to Brownsword's existence. Among Stratford inventories there is only one which features a library as such, that of John Marshall, clerk of Bishopton. Marshall's books comprised some 170 volumes, among them Latin grammars, Ascham's *Schoolmaster*, Ovid's *Tristia*, Aesops' fables, Terence's plays, Cicero, and Castiglione, as well as a number of religious texts and tracts. And then there was one Clement Swallow of Shottery, who seems to have died around 1572 because his inventory was taken that year. The last item in it consists of 'certain law-books and other books with other trifles of small value'. Perhaps Master Swallow owned law-books because he was a justice of the peace; perhaps this Swallow was a Shallow. The fact that Perkes's first name in the famous country scene of *2 Henry IV* is the unusual Catholic papal name Clement leaves one wondering whether this might not be another name that migrated from the life into the works by way of, in this case, Shottery and a man who owned books.

In Stratford Aspinall was sometimes known as 'Great Philip Macedon',[4] a sobriquet he earned because he called his son Alexander like himself. The two Alexander Aspinalls became, therefore, Alexander the Great and Alexander the Little, to Stratford's intellectual elite, the staff and students of the grammar school where Aspinall had taught for so long. It is only a short leap from the Stratford Alexanders two doors north of New Place to jokes about Alexander the Great-Big-Pig in *Henry V*. Shakespeare was always planning ahead to the next project and in the final stages of writing *Henry V* he was probably also reading Plutarch and Holinshed's British chronicles in preparation for his next play, *Julius Caesar*. The two most important Greek lives behind *Julius Caesar* are the 'Life of Caesar' and the 'Life of Marcus Brutus', and the Greek parallel life to Caesar is that of Alexander the Great.

So literature and Shakespeare's life in Stratford probably converge in the Alexander jokes in *Henry V*. In one memorable passage the Welshman Fluellen draws a witty comparison between Alexander and Henry V. What really links Macedonia and Monmouth, he explains, are their two rivers, the clincher being that 'there is salmons in both'. This is a nonsense of course, and is intended as a spoof of Plutarch. It also provides a counterpoint to the cult of heroism that permeates the end of *Henry V*, as does the young king's callous rejection of Falstaff:

> As Alexander killed his friend Cleitus, being in his ales and his cups, so also Harry Monmouth, being in his right wits and his good judgements, turned away the fat knight with the great-belly doublet – he was full of jests and gipes and knaveries and mocks – I have forgot his name.

Rousingly patriotic, *Henry V* fits in well with the bellicose mood of the first half of 1599 in London; *Julius Caesar* is a much more sceptical play about institutionalized power. The fact that it deals with Roman rather than English history affords Shakespeare more room for manoeuvre, of course, to consider the role of the people. Immediately after the stabbing of Caesar, Cassius remarks to his fellow conspirators that their 'lofty scene' will be re-enacted countless times in the future, that the Caesar whom they killed will 'bleed in sport' in countries and languages that have not yet been discovered, and every time this happens Brutus, Cassius, and the other conspirators will be called 'the men that gave their country liberty'. A more resounding endorsement of republicanism is hard to imagine. Neither is a more prophetic one about the future of this hugely popular play.

Thomas Platter's account of a performance of *Julius Caesar* in September 1599 is among the most notable contemporary eye-witness reports of a Shakespearian play. His brief diary entry, that of a perceptive tourist, records the kind of detail that might otherwise never be known. Writing up his notes some five years after the event, Platter recalled how after lunch, around two o'clock on 21 September, he and his party crossed the Thames and 'in the strewn-roof house saw the tragedy of the first Emperor Julius'. There was a cast of 'at least fifteen characters', and their acting skills impressed him greatly. The show ended with a very well executed dance, 'two in men's clothes and two in women's in wonderful combination with each other'.[5] – which must have been Brutus and Caesar dancing with Portia and Calpurnia, since the two spouses are the only two female roles in the play. It is strange to think that when Platter saw the play the number of times it had ever been performed could probably still be counted on one or two hands.

The association that began in 1599 between Shakespeare, the Globe, and Southwark extended literally beyond his death, for both his monument in the chancel of Holy Trinity and the engraving which prefaces the 1623 Folio have their origins in Southwark. In 1599 Shakespeare pitched his tent in this hybrid area of town and country, a southern mirror of Shoreditch but one that now boasted the most splendid theatre in the country. By living on Bankside he cut out the daily journey across the Thames, although this was clearly not a major issue because by 1602–3 he had moved back north of the river into the City of London. Throughout his career he rented rather than owned property in London. By the end of the century it seems likely that Shakespeare was spending a considerable part of his time in New Place in Stratford. There was perhaps a good reason for him to travel between London and Stratford with increasing frequency, because by 1600 he had probably met someone destined to play a crucial role in his life, and she had moved to Oxford.

21

Picturing a Poet and a Pantomime Rebellion:
1600–1

S HAKESPEARE'S NEXT PLAY, his third Globe drama according to this book, was *As You Like It*. The Forest of Arden is first introduced as a place where the 'penalty of Adam' has as little power to hurt 'as the icy fang / And churlish chiding of the winter's wind', and its wintry character may reflect the fact that it was finished in Warwickshire during the fiercely cold weather of Easter 1600. The spring of 1600 was desperately cold: it snowed on Easter Sunday, 23 March, and again from 4 April until well into May. The play notably contains the only part said in the seventeenth century to have been played by Shakespeare in addition to that of Hamlet's father's ghost – Old Adam. Autobiographical traces have been detected in the play's setting in the Warwickshire Forest of Arden, and in its use of a country yokel by the name of William. The fact that the play's Forest of Arden is probably intended, as in the play's source, to represent a forest in Europe, perhaps near Lyons, or possibly the Ardennes, which straddle the border country of Belgium and Luxembourg, is no bar to its essential Warwickshireness. Shakespeare was indeed pitting his two lives, London (court) and Warwickshire (forest), against each other in this play; it is a further illustration of the way he intermingles life and fiction.

As You Like It is remarkably relaxed. It is one of Shakespeare's most discursive plays. Nothing much happens, but it buzzes with dazzling chat and lightning repartee about poetry and love, men and women, and women who have to act like men to transcend the social restrictions of a male-dominated society. Shakespeare seems to have been uniquely fascinated by the boy–girl or 'female page' motif in his plays, beyond the simple necessity imposed in the theatre of the period by the injunction against women acting in plays. When the Puritans came to power later in the century they quoted the Book of Deuteronomy's injunction against transvestism – boy actors donning women's clothes – in their battle against the stage they hated, but when Shakespeare was writing they were as yet contained by Parliament and the Crown. It has become fashionable to think that a latent homosexuality attracted Shakespeare to boy–girl transvestism, and there may be some truth in this. He uses the motif in no fewer than five plays, ranging from the early *The Two Gentlemen of Verona* to *Cymbeline* twenty years later. But there may be a simpler and more obvious reason for his fascination with cross-dressing – his own twins were probably impossible to tell apart: put Hamnet in girl's clothes and you had Judith while Judith dressed as a boy was Hamnet. The inherent dramatic possibilities, in such twins fully grown, could not have escaped such a writer as Shakespeare. Perhaps it really was this simple.

In *As You Like It* Shakespeare also recalled Marlowe and *Hero and Leander* as well as his famous lyric and, probably his death too. At about the same time Marlowe's death – as well as his gifts, his atheism, and his homosexuality – were mentioned in a play put on at St John's College, Cambridge. In it, one Judicio remarks:

> *Marlowe* was happy in his buskind muse,
> Alas unhappy in his life and end,
> Pity it is that wit so ill should dwell,
> Wit lent from heaven, but vices sent from hell.

His fellow Ingenioso replies that 'Our *Theater* hath lost, *Pluto* hath got, / A tragic penman for a dreary plot.' Two references to Marlowe's death, by Shakespeare and by the anonymous author of a play put on at Burghley's and Southampton's old Cambridge college, thus appeared at more or less the same time. Perhaps censorship surrounding the Marlowe business was being relaxed now that Burghley was dead. The play was *The Second Part of the Return from Parnassus*, one of three anonymous closet dramas performed by the students at St John's. (Not only did the second play commemorate – if that is the right word – Marlowe at the same time as Shakespeare did, but the authors also cheekily suggested that Jonson might have been well advised to stick to bricklaying, because he was 'so slow an inventor'.)

Shakespeare was famous now, and the *Parnassus* plays are a powerful witness to his ascendancy. The authors allude repeatedly to *Romeo and Juliet* and quote *Venus and Adonis* and *The Rape of Lucrece*, almost always in connection with one particular character, a foolish courtier by the name of Gullio, who appears only in the second part of the trilogy. After slightly misquoting the opening two lines of *Venus and Adonis*, Gullio exclaims, 'O sweet Master Shakespeare, I'll have his picture in my study at the court' – this being the court of St John's College, Cambridge.[1] The picture of Shakespeare referred to in the *Parnassus* play may well be the same as the one used in the First Folio which seems to show Shakespeare in his mid to late thirties, as he was in 1600. Similarly, Hamlet's invitation to his mother to 'Look here upon this picture, and on this, / The counterfeit presentment of two brothers', may have been inspired by the fact that Shakespeare was drawn or painted around this time. The fact that he probably played Hamlet's father's ghost, the subject of one of the two pictures in the play, would have rendered the lines especially poignant. If a print depicting him was in circulation at the start of the seventeenth century, it seems fairly certain that Shakespeare himself would have owned a copy. A picture of oneself was surely another step on the road to gentrification.

Even if the approximate dates of these plays were unknown, it would be reasonable to guess from the reference to 'Master Shakespeare' that the *Parnassus* plays were written after October 1596, when the Shakespeares acquired their arms. The authors were clearly familiar with the personnel of the Lord Chamberlain's company, three of whose shareholders, Shakespeare, Burbage, and Kemp, feature in the plays, the two last as characters in the final instalment of the trilogy, where they discuss their peers and the demerits of academic drama. And there is more to this where Gullio is concerned. He is a bombastic fool besotted with Shakespeare whose past career bears a close resemblance to that of Southampton, particularly as regards his military service in Spain, Portugal, and Ireland, and a visit to Paris – from where Southampton sneaked back in 1598 for his underhand marriage.

Gullio also has a 'chamber', that is rooms, in Shoreditch, the heartland of the theatres before 1599, and quotes liberally from *Venus and Adonis*, which was of course dedicated to Southampton – perhaps the main reason why *Venus and Adonis* is accorded such prominence. He was also, briefly, the dedicatee of Thomas Nashe's *The Unfortunate Traveller*, and Gullio's sparring partner in *Parnassus*, Ingenioso, is based on Nashe. Little is said of Gullio's love life, but his devotion to *Venus and Adonis* might be taken to suggest that he is a narcissist, which would also fit Southampton. Such is Gullio's love of this most popular of Shakespeare's works in the period that he professes to value it above all other literature. Let the rest of 'this duncified world esteem of Spenser and Chaucer' – he is for Shakespeare and *Venus and Adonis*. Coincidences pile upon one another. Gullio's remark 'I stood stroking up my hair, which became me very admirably' can only be a reference to Southampton's much-noticed mane. It could even be argued that the name of Gullio's love, 'Lesbia', is phonetically not very different from Southampton's wife's name Elizabeth, which abbreviates to 'Lisbeth'. There is nothing here, taken on its own, to identify Gullio unequivocally with Southampton, but cumulatively they are persuasive – as is Gullio's absence from the third *Parnassus* play, by which time Southampton was serving a life sentence in the Tower of London.

Southampton was a St John's College, Cambridge man, a patron of the arts, a friend of Shakespeare's, and a soldier. Is it likely such a parody of such a man would be staged in his own college, an institution that enjoyed the patronage of the Cecils and which at that very time counted Robert Cecil's nephew among its alumni? It may be that the reason Southampton could be parodied at St John's at this time was precisely because he was safely in the Tower – in which case the second part of *Parnassus* must post-date his trial in February 1601.

The satire of Gullio is not vicious; it is as a gull and literary glutton that he is lampooned, and Southampton's easily led, foolish impulsiveness was pleaded in mitigation at his trial by Robert Cecil, who stuck by his friend, arguing that he had been led astray. It may well have been true, because Southampton was something of a hothead and, unlike Hamlet, was ever ready 'greatly to find quarrel in a straw / When honour's at the stake'. It may be that in reinforcing this generally benign picture of Southampton the *Parnassus* plays enjoyed the blessing of the Cecils, as a small cog in their machinery of propaganda.

The plays also contain what may be various clues about Shakespeare and Southampton. For instance, there are three references to

Shoreditch in the *Parnassus* trilogy: two of them flag it up as a place of debauchery; in the third Ingenioso (Nashe) reveals that he has set up a meeting 'at Gullio's chamber in Shoreditch'. This may well suggest that Southampton had rooms there. He was addicted to play-going, and after his return from Ireland in 1599 it was said that he was to be seen at the various theatres every day, with Lord Rutland, to the detriment of their duty of attendance at court. Lodgings of some kind in the Shoreditch area would certainly have been convenient, and his frequent presence would help his easy familiarity with the players, and of course particularly Shakespeare. If it was the case that he had been drawn into homosexual circles at Cambridge, it was quite likely that he would gravitate towards Shoreditch, where some of his former Cambridge companions lived in Norton Folgate.

As the century drew to a close the Queen was old and fading, and the nation and its executive were preoccupied with her lack of a direct heir. There were tensions and factions within the Privy Council, particularly between the younger Cecil and the Earl of Essex. The strains culminated in the most cataclysmic event of Shakespeare's time in London, the attempt by Essex on Sunday 8 February 1601 to seize power. Father William Weston watched the unfolding events from inside the Tower of London, where he had been transferred from Wisbech in 1598. His sight was failing, and he felt lonely and abandoned; his faith had been severely tested by solitude and despair, and there were times when he nearly lost his mind. One day, as he recalled later, he was sitting listlessly in his cell when he heard the noise of men running about and what sounded like a frenzied call to arms. Pikes, mail-jackets, and muskets appeared and there were shouts, threats, and a general panic. Something dreadful had clearly happened, and he wondered whether it might be an attempt on the Queen's life, or an attack on the Tower itself. The warder who brought him his meal that evening was fully armed. Weston asked what was going on and the warder, much agitated, replied that they were all lost and betrayed because the Earl of Essex and many nobles had risen up against the Queen. But the commotion was all over in a few hours, and not many days later Essex was beheaded not very far from Weston's window in the Tower.

The story of the Earl's erratic bid for power reads like a cross between a bad pantomime and a farce, and ended with him holding some of the country's chief law officers hostage inside his mansion off the Strand. Essex Street and Essex and Devereux Courts today recall its presence south of St Clement Danes and Temple Bar. A few yards to the east sits Middle Temple where Shakespeare's *Twelfth Night* was performed almost exactly a year later in February 1602. To judge from an eye-witness account, the conspirators' attempt to breach the gates of the City of London at Ludgate was a shambles that ended with the Essex party desperately boarding boats at Queenhythe to ferry them back to the Strand. Essex's own personal ambition seems to have been the driving force. He had been outmanoeuvred time and again by the Cecils and their allies on the Privy Council and his war against Tyrone in Ireland had ended in failure, further diminishing his influence over affairs of state. Southampton was at Essex's side throughout this turbulent day, and the two stood together on the roof of Essex House during a parley that afternoon as they tried to bargain with the Queen's forces. They were tried side-by-side in Westminster Hall on 19 February 1601, a trial that lasted exactly one day.

It is open to question whether or not Shakespeare had advance warning of the coup from his one-time boon companion. That something of significance was afoot must have been suggested to the Lord Chamberlain's Men when they were approached on the Thursday beforehand by Essex's friends and urged to perform *Richard II* that Saturday. Hauled later before Lord Chief Justice Popham, the hapless spokesman for the company, Augustine Phillips, pointed out in their defence that they had resisted the initial approach not least on the grounds that this was an old play that might leave them acting to an empty house. In the end they had given in, ostensibly in exchange for the solid financial inducement of 40 shillings above and beyond their normal fee, possibly also as a result of behind-the-scenes lobbying by Southampton. The players escaped almost scot-free from what might quite well have been construed as a grievous *lèse-majesté*, for the Queen is known from the testimony of one of her contemporaries to have seen herself as a Richard II figure, a monarch deposed by a pretender.

Barely three weeks after playing *Richard II* for the Essex cause, the Lord Chamberlain's Men performed at court before the Queen; it was Shrove Tuesday, 24 February 1601, the eve of Essex's execution and the title of the play is not known. Presumably the Privy Council intended the choice of this particular company as a symbolic gesture, keen to stress that normality had been restored, that playing had resumed, that life went on as usual. Shakespeare's friendship with Southampton quite apart, it cannot have been easy for the actors, several of whom had been close to members of the Essex circle. The ailing Queen herself was hardly indifferent to what was to happen on the morrow, when her former favourite would die a violent death. If Robert Cecil was present at the play, it would be interesting to know what he thought, having at last achieved the family's ambition of destroying the glittering Essex. The Cecils had built their lives and amassed a fortune by preying on others, and Essex had become one of their most power-ful enemies.

Lent 1601 began with the execution of Essex on Ash Wednesday. Presumably Shakespeare was in London that day, his company having acted before the Queen the previous night. It is perhaps permissible to suppose that on this morning his thoughts and his friends' must have been on Tower Hill where the hero of the Chorus of *Henry V* was to die a traitor's death. The theatres were closed during Lent, and while there is no way of knowing how Shakespeare spent the next six weeks it may be that this all-too-vivid reminder of the dangers of the court world made him feel how better by far it was to enjoy a life of quiet domesticity at home in Stratford. Lent was traditionally the playwright's long vacation, but there were plays to be written in preparation for the new season, background reading to be done, and perhaps his father and siblings to be helped in their glovers' business. In New Place Shakespeare would be comfortable, warm in front of his many large fires, with time enough despite the calls on it to play with his daughters, go for walks, and generally enjoy the life of a country gentleman. It is easy to imagine him being mobbed by his family and neighbours on his return this time, all wanting to know what exactly was going on in London, and what it was like to play before the old Queen the night preceding her favourite's beheading. No doubt he was guarded in his replies, and he may have compared notes with other

Stratfordians who knew London. It would be interesting to know how many of the good burghers of Stratford knew about the sonnets, and the fact that they were addressed to one of the two chief defendants in the most sensational treason trial of the day. As Shakespeare probably knew, for the time being the wayward earl was safe in the Tower, and quite comfortable there: Southampton had enjoyed a lucky escape.

It appears that during or after Lent 1601 Shakespeare, having lauded Essex and the heroism of war in *Henry V*, satirized the whole heroic war ethos in his play *Troilus and Cressida*. In it, Achilles and Patroclus are portrayed as both cowardly and openly homosexual. There can be little doubt that the play was inspired by the events of February 1601. The comparison of Essex with Achilles had been made very specifically by the author of the source-text for Shakespeare's *Troilus and Cressida*. In the dedication of his *Seven Books of the Iliad* (1598), George Chapman announced that in Achilles Homer had prefigured the Earl of Essex, the 'now living instance of the Achillean virtues'.[2] With Essex and Achilles so clearly linked in the contemporary mind, it would seem to follow that a similar connection can be made between Southampton and Patroclus, Achilles' lover. The railing chorus in Shakespeare's play, Thersites, spits poison at all the main characters, describing Patroclus as 'Achilles' male varlet' and 'his masculine whore'.[3]

It would seem that in writing *Troilus and Cressida* as a satire on martial values centred on two homosexuals, Achilles (Essex) and Patroclus (Southampton), Shakespeare was skating on thin ice. Robert Cecil and the Privy Council might have been pleased enough, but Essex still had many powerful allies, not least the King of Scots, James VI. As for Southampton, biding his time in the Tower, it seems hardly conceivable that Shakespeare should have betrayed his friend to the point of exploiting his homosexuality for satirical purposes in a politically angled parable. But it was not unknown for a playwright to be handed a 'plot' and ordered to fashion a play from it: Henslowe records paying Ben Jonson an advance of 20 shillings in 1597 'upon a book which he was to write for us before Christmas next after the date hereof which he showed the plot unto the company' – the 'book' being a play and the 'plot' a 'treatment', a short proposal for a script. So it is possible that someone in authority suggested a 'plot' to Shakespeare and demanded that he produce a piece of propaganda around it. The peculiar history of the text of *Troilus and Cressida* and the fact that as late as 1609 it seems not to have been acted in the theatre ('never staled with the stage, never clapper-clawed with the palms of the vulgar', according to the quarto), fortify the perception that this is distinctly odd work. It is certainly deeply cerebral and acidic, and there has long been a suspicion that it may have been written for a particular coterie, or for an inns of court audience of lawyers; if the political content was suggested by the authorities, it may be that they did not intend it for general public consumption. *Troilus and Cressida* seems a treacherous work for Shakespeare to have written of his own volition, but becomes comprehensible if the impulse for it originated with members of the Privy Council who were also busy making sure elsewhere, notably in Cambridge, that for his own safety Southampton should be seen for what he was, a fool.

The motifs of the play and the specific targets for satire may have been imposed on Shakespeare, but the skeleton story of two doomed lovers during the Trojan war had its origin in Chaucer's classic poem *Troilus and Criseyde*. The Globe theatre rose in Chaucer's own backyard of Southwark, and it is possible to trace another faint connection between Shakespeare and Chaucer at just this time. When in 1612 Shakespeare was involved in the court hearing of Mountjoy *versus* Belott, he indicated that he had come to know the Mountjoys of Muggle or Monkwell Street in or around 1602 – he said he had been acquainted with them for 'ten years or thereabouts'. This is vague enough, and it may well be that he had had lodgings in their home before 1602 after only a short stay on Bankside, whither the London tax collectors had followed him from Bishopsgate. In Muggle Street he found himself in the same neighbourhood as the best-known Chaucerian editor of the day, Thomas Speaght. Speaght's house was perched at the top of the street, up against London Wall and next to St James-in-the-Wall, while the Mountjoys' corner house stood at the north-eastern intersection of Muggle and Silver streets (it is clearly visible as a stylized building on the 'Agas' map). Shakespeare was a celebrity, and it may be that Speaght sought out his company, perhaps even suggested the story of Troilus and Cressida to him. Possibly the literary ghost of Chaucer stalked Shakespeare both on Bankside and in a north-western corner of the City of London.

Whatever inner anxieties and resentments Shakespeare's company may have harboured about the authorities and their demands, there was nothing they could do. The players had families to support and lives to live, and the company had sailed very close to the wind with that performance of *Richard II*. They could not afford another confrontation with the authorities: total compliance was in order.

As summer turned to autumn Shakespeare had an idea for a new play. *Troilus and Cressida* had perhaps been foisted on him to some extent by the Privy Council; this one was for himself only, or rather himself and his family. It was a play about twins, its title was *Twelfth Night*, and its subtitle was *What You Will*.

22

Daughters and Sons and Lovers: 1601–2

T WELFTH NIGHT WAS probably written over the summer of 1601, as it seems to echo Ben Jonson's *Poetaster*, put on by the Children of Blackfriars that spring. Shakespeare again borrows the name of a real person for one of the main characters – 'Orsino' surely derives from Virginio Orsini, the Duke of Bracciano, who was in London during the Twelfth Night celebrations of 1601, and before whom Shakespeare's company performed on at least one recorded occasion. The next year, on Tuesday 2 February 1602, the Feast of Candlemas, a performance of *Twelfth Night* was given at Middle Temple, possibly the play's first performance.[1] Happily John Manningham was there – he who was the source of the story about Burbage, Shakespeare, and the sexy citizenness. Later on that Candlemas of 1602 he noted:

> At our feast we had a play called 'Twelfth Night, or what you will', much like the Comedy of Errors . . . A good practice in it to make the steward believe his lady widow was in love with him, by counterfeiting a letter as from his lady, in general terms telling him what she liked best in him, and prescribing his gesture in smiling, his apparel, etc., and then, when he came to practise, making him believe they took him to be mad.

It was six weeks after this that Manningham recorded his anecdote about Burbage and Shakespeare. Shakespeare was probably present during this special indoor evening performance, and perhaps rumours about the players started to fly among the legal wits that very night, though it seems odd that Manningham waited six weeks to write down the Shakespeare–Burbage story.

While the senior bencher Touse is credited with passing the story to the diarist, we also need to consider John Marston. He was a

Midlander and an Oxford scholar, poet, satirist, playwright, and lawyer, who eventually became a priest. He had joined Middle Temple at just the time of the Burbage–Shakespeare caper. In the mid 1590s Marston and his father, a lawyer at the same inn of court, had jointly stood surety in Middle Temple for their fellow Midlander Thomas Greene, Shakespeare's 'cousin'. Greene kept chambers in London after being called to the bar in 1600. He probably saw the Middle Temple production of *Twelfth Night* in which case he would have been present alongside the Marstons, Manningham, Curle, and Touse.

Hamnet was dead, yet *Twelfth Night* features brother–sister twins, Viola and Sebastian. It also contains lines that are sometimes cited as proof of Shakespeare's estrangement from his own children's mother. 'Let your love be younger than thyself,' Orsino urges Cesario, because female beauty, that which holds 'the bent' of men's affections, fades all too quickly: 'For women are as roses, whose fair flower / Being once displayed, doth fall that very hour.' Orsino was no Hamlet or Lear, and unlike these two tragic heroes his views have not generally been taken as expressive of their author's. Yet there is no irony here, no feeling that in this Orsino is talking anything other than plain common sense. Orsino thinks that men should not marry women older than themselves. If Shakespeare thought so too, and Anne was indeed eight years his senior, then the lines seem to sound a note of retrospective regret.

When Shakespeare wrote *Twelfth Night* in 1601 Judith was sixteen, probably about the age of Viola and Sebastian, though this is not given; instead there is the curious detail that their father dies on the day that they turned thirteen. Perhaps something in Shakespeare died forever in the year of Hamnet's death when he wrote an elegiac play with the thirteen-year-old Juliet as its heroine. The profound longing of the two 'halves', brother and sister, to be reunited once more lends *Twelfth Night* a bitter-sweet note: perhaps Shakespeare wrote it for Judith. Sebastian uses the phrase 'deity in my nature': to reunite Judith and Hamnet would indeed have required an act of God. If *Romeo and Juliet* was written for Hamnet and Susanna, perhaps this one was for Judith. There is no way of knowing what was said between father and daughter in the privacy of New Place. Perhaps it was her idea all along, inspired by one of the early performances of *As You Like It*.

Perhaps. It might be worth recalling, however, that it was at Candlemas, 2 February 1585, that the twins Judith and Hamnet were baptised at Holy Trinity, seventeen years before the performance of *Twelfth Night* in the Middle Temple at Candlemas 1602. It might just be a coincidence, for it was the lawyers of the Middle Temple who devised the programme for that night's entertainment in 1602. But it was Shakespeare who wrote the play, the only one among all his works to be constructed around boy–girl twins, and it seems unlikely that he was unaware of the coincidence of dates. The Middle Temple performance took place two or three days after Judith's seventeenth birthday, and it would be nice to think that her father brought her down to London to see it, as a present. Whether or not this happened, there is enough to suggest that Shakespeare was rather closer to Judith than is sometimes assumed. She has been seen as the Cinderella of the Shakespeare family, but it could well be that she was immensely precious to her father, and that the young women of the last plays are at least as much her as Susanna. Viola is one of the most tenderly imagined and most feminine of Shakespeare's heroines. Whereas Rosalind in *As You Like It* is empowered by her disguise and bestrides the play with wit and mastery, Viola is trapped in her transsexuality. Rosalind seems more like Susanna Shakespeare, who was later compared favourably with her father and described as 'witty above her sex' by those who knew her, who inherited most of her father's estate after marrying well, and who may even have looked after her apparently more reticent and passive sister Judith. There is every reason for Shakespeare to have modelled his younger heroines on his own daughter, and of course the Viola–Judith daughter was the one left at home with her father at the time when he was writing the last plays.

Again and again details and events from Shakespeare's life can be traced in his plays. He seems to have written compulsively, not just to earn a living but also to control and impose meaning upon events in his own life, and the works become a way of life. In *Twelfth Night*, Shakespeare indulges in the fantasy of resurrecting a lost male twin: the play ends happily when Viola's brother turns up. The twins are reunited, and the Duke and Olivia achieve their hearts' desires when Viola appears to make 'division' of herself. Instead of one, suddenly there are two, one each of the right gender for their respective partners.

Earlier it was suggested that Shakespeare's interest in death by water might stem from his childhood and teenage years on the Avon and a connection was traced between this and drowning as a literary motif in *The Comedy of Errors*, his first so-called 'New Comedy', a classical genre that Shakespeare and his contemporaries inherited from Menander, Plautus, and Terence. At source New Comedy revolves rather narrowly around children and parents split at birth, mostly by shipwreck. The roots for this have been traced back to the late fourth century BC when the world of the Aegean basin was full of dispossessed people searching for lost families. In dealing with recurrent motifs such as drowning in Shakespeare's comedies, we are continually treading a fine line between generic convention and the possibility of genuine biographical nuggets and data. Ophelia's drowning in *Hamlet* and the twin Sebastian's presumed death by water in *Twelfth Night* feature in two contiguous plays, while also meshing intimately with particular names and aspects from Shakespeare's domestic life, particularly of course the death of Katherine Hamlet in 1579. It may just be coincidence but then again there may be more to it. We ought at least to consider the possibility, on the 'evidence' from *Hamlet* and *Twelfth Night*, that Hamnet drowned in the Avon, even if the awkward witness of *The Comedy of Errors* injects a measure of scepticism into trying to link Shakespeare's marine imagery with the boy's death, because the play of course pre-dates it by some five years. Furthermore in *Twelfth Night* and in *The Tempest*, both written after Hamnet's death, the drowned youths survive their trial by water. If the young man had died in either or both, one might feel more justified in seeing this personal tragedy echoed in the plays.

Anything is possible, of course, in literature even more so than in life, and we must not throw caution to the winds. In *Twelfth Night* the boy is resurrected and in *The Winter's Tale* the little boy Mamillius dies while his baby sister survives. It seems that Shakespeare the father of surviving daughters cannot bring himself to let a daughter perish. After *Hamlet*, fathers and daughters enjoy the most important domestic relationships in the plays.

But Hamnet was *not* Sebastian, and Shakespeare could not bring his son back from the dead the way he resurrects Sebastian in the play. It was more than five years since Hamnet's death when on 8 September 1601 Shakespeare buried his father John at Holy Trinity.

It may be that it was his father's death that prompted him to write a play named after his dead son. Shakespeare had striven hard to restore his father's fortunes. He had returned the former mayor of Henley Street once again to his position of respected citizen. Father and son may well have been close. One of the few references to John Shakespeare in the seventeenth century, by someone who apparently met him 'in his shop', describes him as 'a merry-cheeked old man that said Will was a good honest fellow, but he durst have cracked a jest with him at any time'.[2] Clearly old John Shakespeare was not intimi- dated either by his son's success or his witty way with words. Will had inherited his father's business acumen, but unlike John he never came unstuck or needed to hide away in his home from creditors; on the contrary, Shakespeare enjoyed displaying his wealth – hence his pur- chase of New Place. His father was doubtless a frequent visitor there. He would have been in his late sixties by then, and may have been Shakespeare's model for garrulous old men like Polonius. Though it has not so far been traced, the probability is that this former keeper of the borough accounts as chamberlain made his will, as a sensible man of property would. He appears to have left the bulk of his estate to William as the first-born son, probably with provision for his wife and daughter Joan to go on living in the Henley Street house; what pro- vision he made for his other three sons is not known.

It is possible that John Shakespeare made a further will, by which he entrusted his soul to the safe keeping of the Catholic church. This so- called Testament of John Shakespeare was a hand-written document of six leaves which was eventually passed to Edmond Malone by his young contemporary, the Reverend James Davenport (1787–1841); Davenport had had it from a Stratford alderman with whom it had been lodged years before by the master bricklayer who found it in the rafters of the Henley Street house on 29 April 1757, while retiling the roof. Unfortunately, the original that Malone once held in his hands is since lost. Malone initially believed the will to be genuine, but later changed his mind, promising to expose it at a later stage as a hoax. Fortunately he printed the text of the will, so its contents at least are known. It was what was called a 'Borromeo will', a Catholic 'contract and testament of the soul', drafted originally by Cardinal Carlo Borromeo of Milan in the 1570s; copies entered England with the Campion mission of 1580. These wills were formularies which allowed outwardly conformist Protestants, by the simple insertion of their names, to die in the old faith of their forefathers. The one allegedly found in the Henley Street house corresponds in all essentials with another Borromeo will in English which survives intact and which surfaced in 1966.

There is no doubt that the text of the document found in Henley Street is genuine. The workmen who discovered it are almost certainly above suspicion and no commercial gain was sought from the discovery, neither by the bricklayer nor by Thomas Hart, a direct descendant of Shakespeare's sister Joan who had commissioned the retiling, nor even by the local poet, draftsman, and amateur Shakespeare sleuth, John Jordan. However, and perhaps inevitably, it is Jordan's role in the story, his eagerness to be published and his putting forward a forged version of the missing first leaf, that have aroused suspicion and scepticism and tainted the whole document. If the testament from Henley Street was a hoax, it was a forgery by someone who had access to a genuine version of the testament, wrote it out with John Shakespeare's name inserted at every juncture, and then somehow managed to plant it in the rafters of the house in Henley Street. The question is why anyone should do such a thing. Jordan can be ruled out as a suspect, because he was only eleven years old when the testament was discovered; he copied it twenty-seven years after the event, in 1784. The fact that he later tried to fob off Malone with a forged copy of the missing first leaf of the will has no bearing on the authenticity of the original document, which Jordan never owned. On the balance of probabilities it would appear that John Shakespeare intended to die in the Roman faith. The fact that the will was not buried with him suggests either that he changed his mind or else for some reason the testament could not be retrieved for his funeral on 8 September. If anyone apart from John and Mary Shakespeare knew where in the house the formulary was kept, it would surely have been their eldest son and executor.

The odds are that John Shakespeare first received a copy of the formulary during the Campion mission, when there were Jesuits staying in

Lapworth and elsewhere in the Midlands, including at Shottery and perhaps even at the Badgers', next door to the Shakespeares, or else with the Wheelers or Whateleys. John Shakespeare probably hid the will shortly after taking possession of it. And as the 1580s became ever more violent and oppressive no doubt he signed it and then stashed it safely out of sight. No one would think to look in the roof of the house. It seems hardly likely that John Shakespeare would have forgotten about the testament, but it is certainly odd that Shakespeare and his mother should not have retrieved it to put in John's coffin or into his winding sheet. Perhaps the times were once again too dangerous. It may be that coffins were checked by the authorities for just such documents before being committed to the earth – yet so very few have come to light that it looks as though most secret Catholics of the period successfully evaded detection, and took the wills to their graves with them.

It was barely seven months since Shakespeare's friend Augustine Phillips had pleaded 'not guilty' on behalf of the Lord Chamberlain's Men in front of the Lord Chief Justice with regard to their performance of *Richard II*, so any suspicion of Catholicism attaching to Shakespeare's father might have had grim consequences. If Shakespeare and his mother knew of the will and where it was cached, it is surprising that they did not dispose of the incriminating document. Perhaps they hoped to use it for Mary Arden but then did not, and after her death Shakespeare forgot about it. Once the original house had been leased to the Hiccoxes the will in the roof was beyond the reach of the family. Did it give Shakespeare an occasional headache, after letting the house, to think that a potential time bomb, with his father's name on every page and starting each paragraph, was ticking away in the roof of his ancestral home?

Paragraph XII of the formulary is of particular interest for its doctrinal implication:

> *Item*, I John Shakespeare do in like manner pray and beseech all my dear friends, parents and kinsfolks, by the bowels of our Saviour Jesus Christ, that since it is uncertain what lot will befall me, for fear notwithstanding lest by reason of my sins I be to pass and stay a long while in purgatory, they will vouchsafe to assist and succour me with their holy prayers and satisfactory works, especially with the holy sacrifice of the

mass, as being the most effectual means to deliver souls from their tor-
ments and pains; from the which, if I shall by God's gracious goodness
and by their virtuous works be delivered, I do promise that I will not
be ungrateful unto them for so great a benefit.

The wording and sentiment are pure Catholicism, as is the plea for
intercessory prayers for a soul in purgatory. The ghost of Hamlet's
father returns to haunt his son from just such a prison house. The
confusion of doctrines observable in *Hamlet* is often seen as sympto-
matic of its period, only two generations since the Catholic faith was
the one and only faith of a spiritually united country. It seems that
Shakespeare's intensely personal stake in the play lay not just in the
fact that the old play *Hamlet* fortuitously had a hero with the same
name as his dead son. No doubt he seized on that in the first instance,
only later realizing the potential for in some way conversing with his
father across the grave. Perhaps, indeed, Shakespeare used *Hamlet* as a
way of coming to terms with his own spiritual betrayal of his father.
After all, John Shakespeare did *not* take the Borromeo testament with
him into eternity, and the reason may have been that his son William
refused to see that he did so, for ideological reasons as much as out
of political astuteness. In the play Hamlet is at 'school in Wittenberg' –
the cradle of Protestantism, where Martin Luther had nailed his
polemical theses to the door of the Schlosskirche in 1517. It may be
that John Shakespeare's faith was not shared by his son, that while
his faith put him in purgatory, his son's was more in line with the
powerful Anglican orthodoxy that prevailed in London. Doctrinally,
Hamlet and his father's ghost are utterly at odds over the hereafter, and
it is Shakespeare who has cast Hamlet and his friends as students at
Wittenberg. There is nothing of this in the source. The tragedy deliberately muddies its religious waters.

Whatever spiritual debates or even disputes he and his father may
have had in the privacy of the house in Henley Street, Shakespeare
once more revisits them in a long play's journey into night, a play
perhaps of old sorrows, writing *Hamlet* as his way of dealing with the
loss of his father, a play in which a dead father's ghost appears to a son
who is named after Shakespeare's own son in real life. That the play
was written after the summer of 1601 may be confirmed by the 'little

eyases' passage. Rosencrantz's mysterious reference to 'an aery of chil-dren, little eyases, that cry out on the top of the question and are most tyrannically clapped for' is an allusion to the competition for audiences in the summer of 1601 between the child companies and Ben Jonson on the one hand and the adult actors or 'common players' and their writers on the other, the so-called War of the Theatres, a murky spat that pitted John Marston against Ben Jonson and also involved Dekker. Shakespeare's modest contribution to it, with his 'little eyases' (fledg-ling hawks), is triggered in the play by the arrival in Elsinore of 'the tragedians of the city', who used to be Hamlet's favourites. When he enquires why they are touring, since they were better off staying put in the city (and, reading between the lines, at a permanent venue – like the Globe), Rosencrantz replies: 'I think their inhibition comes by the means of the late innovation.' Clearly he means they had been prohibited from playing at their usual venue, something with which Shakespeare was all too familiar, decrees of 'inhibition' issued by the Privy Council being rather more than a professional hazard. At the stroke of a pen the Council could theoretically strip players of their livelihood, although it rarely did so because the players were well connected at court, and the Lord Chamberlain in 1601–2 sat on the Privy Council. It is quite possible that the 'inhibition' in *Hamlet* refers to an actual 'innovation', such as, for example, the Council's attempt on 31 December 1601 to enforce its earlier statute limiting the number of playhouses to only two.

Hamlet was entered on the Stationers' Register on 26 July 1602 as 'A book called the Revenge of Hamlet Prince of Denmark as it was lately acted by the Lord Chamberlain his servants'. The second quarto, on which almost all modern texts are based, appeared in 1604, in the same year as Marlowe's posthumously published *Doctor Faustus*, a play of intellectual restlessness in tune with the moral chaos of *Hamlet*. Shakespeare's great tragedy voices a deep anxiety about the human condition and the fact particularly that all human life inextricably entails its own cessation, that death is the one and only absolute cer-tainty about life; and that death may indeed be the 'be-all and end-all', alpha and omega. While crammed with allusions to the Bible, *Hamlet* is at the same time relentlessly secular. It is a profoundly radical work, a humanist tragedy in the full sense of the word. When Hamlet mourns for his father, Claudius comforts him with the thought that the 'common theme' of humankind and nature is the 'death of fathers.' Claudius is good on the loss of fathers.

The play is full of elusive and imprecise clues about the relationship between Shakespeare and his family and other aspects of his life. The plot of the murder, for instance, the poisoning of old Hamlet in his orchard, is an echo, though perhaps not a direct echo, of the murder of the person who sold Shakespeare New Place. *Hamlet* might have been written at New Place, or in a room backstage at the new Globe theatre, or perhaps even in his lodgings at the Mountjoys. Lent 1602, which was probably when the main work on the play was done, started on Ash Wednesday, 17 February, with Easter falling on 4 April. A fortnight earlier had seen the Middle Temple performance of *Twelfth Night*, perhaps with Shakespeare playing in it, perhaps with Judith in the audience. Lent would have given him the time to complete what is a long play, its scale perhaps linked to its commemorative nature: Shakespeare had written *Romeo and Juliet* in response to his son's death, now he wrote *Hamlet* in the wake of his father's, and later *Coriolanus* followed his mother's death. Thus, three of Shakespeare's greatest tragedies were almost certainly written in response to personal family bereavements: the links between Shakespeare's life and literary productions could hardly be more direct. For him, they are the norm; his plays follow the same pattern of self-expression as the autobiographical *Sonnets*. No other writer of the period was more anxious than Shakespeare to be heard. Perhaps the sonnets and the plays were his substitute for the commonplace diary kept by his friend Ben Jonson.

It is all but impossible to realize that there was a time when the line 'To be, or not to be, that is the question' was as yet unwritten. Since it was first spoken by Burbage on the stage of the Globe it has gone round the world, and in a sense no longer belongs to Shakespeare, any more than his plays do. It would be fascinating to know exactly where Shakespeare was when he wrote that line, whether it was last thing at night by a fluttering candle, or early in the morning. But such details are lost forever. All that is known is that in 1602 Shakespeare's father had recently died, his son Hamnet was dead, and his closest friend was languishing in the Tower while that friend's master, the most glamorous soldier in the land, had lost his head on Tower Hill. Little wonder that *Hamlet* should be soaked in darkness and pain. At times it sounds like an anthem for doomed youth. When Ophelia exclaims 'O, what a noble mind is here o'erthrown' she could be referring to the young Southampton. In 1602 he was twenty-nine years old while Hamlet in the play is thirty. It is tempting to compare him to the fictional prince of Denmark. Perhaps Shakespeare was atoning for portraying his friend as a homosexual buffoon in *Troilus and Cressida*. Southampton's parents' marriage had been a traumatic one, mostly through his father's militant Catholicism which landed him in prison. He accused his wife of adultery and died when the young earl was just eight years old. Henry Wriothesley was twenty-one when his mother wed again in 1594, at the height of his friendship with Shakespeare, and twenty-five when she married for the third time. The young man probably discussed his mother's remarriages with the poet and Shakespeare may have remembered this when writing the role of Gertrude.

The play is also riven with angst about middle-aged female sexuality, particularly with regard to Hamlet's mother Gertrude. This matronly figure mysteriously marries Hamlet's uncle rather soon after her first husband's death and thus becomes the most sexually imagined woman in Shakespeare. Hamlet goes into an unsettling amount of detail about his mother's behaviour in bed, all based on conjecture. Nevertheless, in what he says to her he cruelly hits the spot with his references to wanton pinches, 'reechy kisses', paddling in necks, and terms of endearment. He urges his mother to desist from living in 'the rank sweat of an enseamèd bed', no longer to be 'stewed in corruption, honeying and making love', no more to be cooped up in 'the nasty sty' of sex that is Claudius's bed. It does not get much more graphic than the imagined middle-aged sex romp in the fourth scene of Act III. Since Shakespeare is forever crossing the boundaries of life and art, it is perhaps legitimate to wonder whether there is more to this, whether the mother of Hamlet having sex with old Hamlet's younger brother Claudius might echo a real event from the life of that other Hamlet's mother, Anne Hathaway. In other words, it is worth considering whether Shakespeare was perhaps sexually betrayed by one of his younger brothers – so that Hamlet remonstrating with Gertrude may reflect Shakespeare imagining his son arguing with Anne.

That Shakespeare committed adultery while he was in London is scarcely in doubt; that in his turn he might have been cheated on in Stratford during his long absences, and perhaps by a wayward brother, should not be ruled out. But the ghost instructed Hamlet not to hurt his mother, so perhaps a brother made a pass and was turned down. Rowe's assertion that Shakespeare played old Hamlet's ghost should not be forgotten. Whatever of his own life lay behind it, Shakespeare must have been aware of the implication of having a character called Hamlet after his own son address such devastating lines to his mother. At the same time, considerable affection for Gertrude is expressed in the play, and it must not be forgotten that her 'adultery' is so only in a strictly biblical sense, since the Bible prohibited sex with a widowed sister-in-law; it was not an offence in common law. Despite the ghost's use of the phrase 'adulterate beast' to describe Claudius, there is nothing in the play to suggest that he was previously sexually involved with Gertrude; the unexplained speed of the love affair or marriage of Claudius and Gertrude is as much one of *Hamlet's* mysteries as the obsession with sex and adultery is of *King Lear*.

After *Hamlet*, as not before, younger brothers are cast as villains. Prospero in *The Tempest*, an unmistakable *alias* for Shakespeare even after full caveats, is betrayed by a cruel younger brother who remains completely unredeemed throughout. In *King Lear*, Edgar is similarly double-crossed by a younger sibling, one who, moreover, carries the name of Shakespeare's baby brother Edmund. It is perhaps surprising that Shakespeare, as one of four brothers, should not make more, earlier, of the relationship between them. That he was close to Gilbert and delegated his business affairs to him has already been noted; Edmund, about twenty-two, may still have been living in Henley Street when *Hamlet* was written in 1602. Unlike his three brothers, Richard Shakespeare, Will's junior by ten years, has not yet been named in the London records of the period, but there is that one appearance in the so-called Stratford Bawdy Court files of 1608. Despite the court's name, his offence was probably far from titillating – not receiving the sacrament, or not ceasing to trade in time for church. He was fined 12 pence, the money to go to the poor of Stratford.

At the time of *Hamlet* Anne Hathaway was about forty-six and Richard was twenty-six. The Shakespeares had now lived in New

Place for five years, and it would not be unreasonable to think that Richard and Gilbert, and perhaps Edmund, were also living there. According to the documentary record Joan had stayed on in Henley Street, perhaps to look after her widowed mother Mary Arden as well as making a home there with her husband William Hart, whom she married some time around 1599. Her first son, another William, was born in 1600, and there were three more to come. Although Joan, her husband, and her mother lived in it, it was Shakespeare who as the eldest son inherited the Henley Street house on his father's death in September 1601. It was really too big for the few people now to be accommodated, and Shakespeare apparently decided to lease out the eastern parts of the premises (what is now called the woolshop). Before doing so, and perhaps with a future let of the west side of the house in mind, he seems to have added a house to the back of the western edge of the main rectangular frame. This is known today as Joan Hart's Cottage, and it may indeed have been intended to create a comfortable space for the remaining family, while leaving a large enough house available to the new tenants. To build, expand, or convert with a view to letting seems to have been common practice at the time.

Whatever rebuilding and partitioning Shakespeare carried out in the Henley Street house seems to have taken its time. Perhaps his mother and sister were reluctant to surrender the big house in which they had lived all their lives. What happened next was that Shakespeare let out part of the premises in Henley Street to Lewis Hiccox, whom he had already acquired as a tenant along with Thomas Hiccox when on 1 May 1602 Gilbert Shakespeare, acting on behalf of his brother William, made an expensive purchase of land and tithes in Old Stratford. As if this were not enough, Shakespeare spread his local investments further a few months later when, towards the end of September 1602, he bought a quarter-acre of land with a cottage, down from the King's New School and opposite New Place gardens. By 1603 Hiccox had been granted a licence to earn his living as publican and innkeeper in the Henley Street house. The Hiccox *établissement* was called the Maidenhead, eventually the Swan and Maidenhead – 'swan' was clearly something of a selling-point, since there seem to have been at least two other taverns or inns in the town so named. By the time Lewis Hiccox opened in Henley Street his kinsman Thomas (perhaps his brother) had moved to premises opposite. He had earlier (on 31 October 1599) been granted a lease to build 'a fair house' in this fire-ravaged area, on the ground where the Shakespeares' neighbour John Cox had lived for forty-one years, on condition that the house would be standing by the autumn of 1602. When the Maidenhead opened in 1603, Shakespeare became the owner of an inn and public house.

It would appear there had been no unseemly rush to make the most of the Henley Street house. Doubtless major alterations were needed to make it viable as an inn after years as a family home. It seems most likely that Shakespeare's brothers moved to New Place. It was a large house, but with Anne, her two daughters, and probably her three brothers-in-law – one of whom was only three years older than Susanna – and presumably a number of servants now living there, not big enough for any untoward relationship to remain hidden. In the analogy between the life and the play, it seems likely that Anne stayed loyal to her husband and family after all, for Gertrude clearly has no idea about Claudius's murder of old Hamlet.

For Shakespeare *Hamlet* seems to mark a watershed. Moving on from the 'sweet prince' who was his son, he commemorates his adored father John Shakespeare, pays tribute to the glass of fashion and nobility in the Tower, and perhaps comes to terms with a domestic drama in New Place. After *Hamlet* adultery becomes a defining feature of Shakespearian drama, particularly in *Othello*, *King Lear*, and *Antony and Cleopatra*. Shakespeare launches into a series of dark and obsessive plays in which female sexuality is confronted as something dangerous and destructive. Several plays from around this time, including *All's Well* and *Measure for Measure*, reveal a fascination with complex and confused forms of desire. The so-called 'bed trick' that is part of this involves the illicit possession of a sexually desired woman in a bed in the dark of night, but in each case the man's intended wife is substituted for the object of desire. The thrill of bad behaviour runs its course, but the sex itself is retrospectively legitimated by the marriages which conclude the plays. Sexual passion is of course a *leitmotif* of Shakespeare's comedies, and these two late works are no exception. Nevertheless *Measure for*

Measure, his last ever, is generically the most unusual of Shakespeare's comedies. Much of the action is set in a prison, and some of it in the condemned cell. It ends with a man disguised as a friar marrying a young woman who is a novice of the Clares, one of the strictest monastic orders, bound by a vow of silence; the other unions consist of the forced marriages of Lucio to his prostitute girlfriend Mistress Kate Keepdown, who 'was with child by him in the Duke's time', and of poor Mariana to Angelo, the man who first jilted her and then possessed her in a 'moated grange', mistaking her for someone else.

The main plot revolves around a young man who is sentenced to death for making a young woman pregnant before they have been married in church. They are engaged to be married, however, through what the young man, Claudio, calls 'a true contract' – that is, the two have pledged their troth to one another in front of witnesses and are therefore legally bound in marriage, though the union must be sanctioned by the church before it can be sexually consummated. As Claudio puts it, 'You know the lady; she is fast my wife, / Save that we do the denunciation lack / Of outward order.' He is sentenced to death for following natural instincts legitimized by a betrothal. This carries a strong echo of Shakespeare's own sexual life, and the question arises as to why he should have revisited it at just this time. The most likely answer is because he was almost certainly conducting a clandestine love affair, which may well have rekindled memories of an eighteen-year-old boy who years earlier had become a father before himself becoming a man.

In *Measure for Measure* there is no question that Claudio and Juliet are innocent, and deserving of compassion, particularly in comparison with the two 'absolute' characters in the play, Claudio's novice sister Isabella and Angelo, the Duke's 'precise' deputy. Both have extreme views of sexuality, Isabella's steeped in the rhetoric of Catholic martyrdom. Asked to 'lay down the treasure of your body', she replies that she will under no circumstances surrender her body up 'to shame'; rather, she would prefer to 'strip myself to death as to a bed / That longing have been sick for', and to wear as rubies 'th'impression of keen whips'. This is the rhetoric of John Gerard, William Weston, and Catholic poets like Richard Crashaw. While granting Isabella's need to preserve her dignity, Shakespeare seems profoundly suspicious of such rhetoric and the absoluteness, the rigidity of mind, it engenders. The fallible sexuality of Claudio and Juliet is much more sympathetic, acknowledging as it does inescapable imperatives of the human body.

Isabella in *Measure for Measure* is the only major character so-named in any of Shakespeare's plays, and it is not her name in the play's source. He might have plucked it from nowhere in particular – or he might have found it in his own family's history. A man as keen as Shakespeare on English history and his own family may well have been aware that towards the end of the fifteenth century at Wroxall Abbey, a few miles to the north of Stratford, there had been a prioress by the name of Dame Isabella Shakespeare; another sub-prioress of the same abbey, one Dame Joan Shakespeare, died in 1571, when he was seven years old.

23

Affairs of the Body and Heart: 1602–4

IT WAS POSSIBLY around this time that Shakespeare launched into a love affair with a woman by the name of Jane Davenant. How Shakespeare and Jane Davenant (née Sheppard) first met is not documented, but it is likely that they became acquainted while he was playing on Bankside in the late 1590s, before she moved to Oxford in 1601.[1] Jane Sheppard, or Jennet as she was also known, was not quite five years younger than Shakespeare. She was baptized at St Margaret's in Westminster on 1 November 1568. It is likely that she married her husband John Davenant, a prominent wine merchant, in around 1593, when she was twenty-five, for parish records indicate that she suffered several miscarriages between then and her eventual departure for Oxford. In the 1590s Jane Davenant and her husband lived up from the Vintry at Three Cranes Wharf, directly east of the inlet of Queenhythe which survives to this day, the prime site in London then for the unloading of barges carrying wine. A notable tavern stood here, The Three Cranes, mentioned in the same breath as the Mitre and the Mermaid by Jonson in *Bartholomew Fair*. It is possible that it was patronised by players returning home after finishing their shows in Bankside, for Three Cranes Wharf was directly across the river from the Rose and Globe. From their house near by the Davenants must have been acutely aware of the traffic across the water and any other matters relating to the Bankside playing venues. London rumour had it that the Davenants were keen supporters of the theatres, and of Shakespeare in particular.

There are two important seventeenth-century witnesses to the story of Shakespeare and Jane Davenant, John Aubrey and the antiquarian Anthony à Wood, both of whom knew the Davenants. Aubrey (1626–97) and Wood (1632–95) were, respectively, twenty and twenty-six years younger than Jane Davenant's son, the play-wright William. In 1681 Aubrey wrote that

> Sir William Davenant Knight Poet Laureate was born in . . . the City of Oxford, at the Crown tavern. His father was John Davenant a vint-ner there, a very grave and discreet citizen. His mother was a very beautiful woman, and of a very good wit and of conversation extremely agreeable . . . Master William Shakespeare was wont to go into Warwickshire once a year and did commonly in his journey lie at this house in Oxon: where he was exceedingly respected. (I have heard parson Robert D[avenant] say that Master William Shakespeare here gave him a hundred kisses.) Now Sir William would sometimes when he was pleasant over a glass of wine with his most intimate friends . . . say that it seemed to him that he writ with the very spirit that did Shakespeare, and was seemed contented enough to be thought his son. He would tell them the story as above (in which way his mother had a very light report, whereby she was called a whore).

Anthony à Wood did not disagree with much of this, although the reference to Robert Davenant's being kissed by Shakespeare may have been crossed out by Wood.[2] In his rehashed version of Aubrey he included the information that William's father John Davenant was 'an admirer and lover of plays and play-makers, especially Shakespeare, who frequented his house in his journeys between Warwickshire and London'. This may have come from one of the Davenants them-selves, since Wood later patronized the tavern that the Davenant family had owned for the first twenty years of the seventeenth century. In Jane Davenant Aubrey paints a picture of a woman of impressive personal magnetism, one who in her own way may have been as accomplished as Emilia Lanier. It was established earlier that in January 1598 she, like Emilia, sought out Forman, who was living in Lambeth then. She had recently lost a baby, and wanted to know whether or not she was pregnant again; perhaps, at nearly thirty and after several miscarriages, she was desperate to know. It is unlikely that she was seeing Shakespeare at this time, though he had by then extricated himself from his entanglement with both Southampton and the Dark Lady.

It seems reasonable to suppose that Shakespeare, having bought New Place in 1597, tried to spend as much as possible of each year there and, paradoxically, it might have been this new-found taste for domesticity that brought Jane Davenant back into his life. If his family ties and perhaps particularly at first his concern for his ailing father caused him to return to Stratford at other times apart from the Lenten break – well, he was rich now, and could afford the best horses. It was at about this time – 1601, the year of his father's death, the year the Davenants moved to Oxford – that he may have begun to favour the Oxford route between Stratford and London above all others. Seventeenth-century rumour had him putting up at the Davenants' Crown Inn on Cornmarket, and there is no good reason to doubt that he did so. The King's Men performed *Hamlet* at Oxford in 1603 and presumably the Davenants continued to support the company they knew from Bankside. It hardly required any effort on their part, indeed, for it seems that players performing at Oxford usually 'lodged at the galleried King's Head inn in Cornmarket almost opposite Davenant's tavern', staging their plays in the inn yard.[3]

It was around this time in 1602, when he was writing *Hamlet*, that Shakespeare shifted his London base to the Mountjoys' house.[4] The fact that the Mountjoys, the Davenants, Jane's family, the Sheppards, and the Fields all knew one another, that Marie Mountjoy was having an affair with one of her neighbours, a silversmith, and consulted Forman at just the time when Emilia Lanier stopped seeing him rather suggests that Shakespeare took lodgings with them because they all belonged to the same London circle of writers, actors, publishers, printers, and craftsmen attached to the court. Within a year or so Shakespeare's friend Ben Jonson was living in almost the same neighbourhood, at Blackfriars, and Shakespeare is mentioned prominently in the cast list of *Sejanus*, which dates from around 1604, and of *Every Man in his Humour* in the Jonson Folio of 1616. In the months and years after 1602, Shakespeare's journey between London and Stratford may well have assumed a cosy 'family' character, between his landlords in London and their – and his – close friends, the hosts of the Crown in Oxford.

It was while he was living with the Mountjoys that Shakespeare wrote *Othello*, his brooding tragedy about the dark side of human sexuality, and a small but significant strand of the play's plot may reach back right into his landlord's household. For once there is hard documentary evidence, Shakespeare's own testimony in a lawsuit, the papers for which survive in the Court of Requests. Ten years after the event, Shakespeare testified that he had lived with the Mountjoys in 1602 and that Marie Mountjoy had enlisted his help as a go-between in the proposed marriage between her daughter Mary and the Mountjoys' apprentice Stephen Belott. The legalese of the relevant passage is sufficiently dry:

> And further this deponent [Shakespeare] sayeth that the said defendant's wife [Marie Mountjoy] did solicit and entreat this deponent to move and persuade the complainant [Belott] to effect the said marriage and accordingly this deponent did move and persuade the complainant thereunto . . .

So here is William Shakespeare, aged thirty-eight, wooing Stephen Belott on behalf of his landlord's wife. Presumably she picked him for this delicate errand because of his way with words – and, of course, he was famous, a renowned dramatist. Their address in the City of London suggests that the Mountjoys were comfortably off, and that the master of New Place lodged not in a garret but probably on an entire floor to himself.[5] The sober language of the Belott–Mountjoy documents and their practical concern with the size of the dowry and a promissory note regarding the expected estate to be left to the young couple after old Mountjoy's death are of their time. A trained actor and intellectual magpie like Shakespeare might be assumed to have an excellent memory, but testifying ten years later he could not remember any details about the sums involved – a curious lapse, reminiscent of an apparently equally abstracted encounter with the Master of the Revels, Sir George Buc, in 1599 during which Shakespeare failed to remember the name of the author of a play about which Buc was enquiring.[6]

It is hardly befitting that a writer who passionately recycled his plays because their motifs and rhetoric stayed stored in his mind, a man with a flair for business and a good head for figures, should not have been able to cast his mind back accurately to ten years earlier, particularly when his intercessions with young Belott involved the not inconsiderable sum of £200. The fact is that the written record shows Shakespeare twice failing to provide an answer after being

The Swan Theatre on Bankside was drawn in 1596 by the Dutch visitor Johannes de Witt and copied by his friend Arend van Buchel. It may show a performance of a play by Shakespeare

A 'perspective view' by John Jordan in the eighteenth century with, on the left, New Place, the Gild Chapel, Shakespeare's school, and the medieval almshouses. Jordan's New Place dates from c.1702 when the Clopton family extensively rebuilt the old stone and timber house in which Shakespeare had lived

The same view today with the Falcon inn on the right of the picture

The inside of the Gild Chapel in Stratford with faded traces of the Last Judgement on the arch across the nave; the images had been whitewashed in the year of Shakespeare's birth when his father John served as borough chamberlain

New Place once occupied this gap, but now the well and a few foundation walls are all that remains; the neighbouring Nash house, into which Shakespeare's granddaughter Elizabeth married, is extant

Looking west towards the Gild Chapel from inside the gardens of New Place

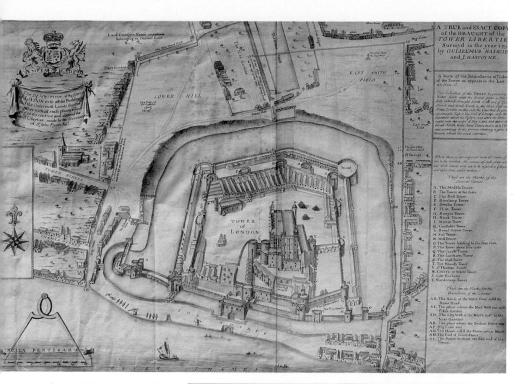

Above: The Tower of London as it was when John Gerard escaped from it in 1597

MR. WILLIAM
SHAKESPEARES
COMEDIES,
HISTORIES, &
TRAGEDIES.

Published according to the True Originall Copies.

LONDON
Printed by Isaac Iaggard, and Ed. Blount. 1623.

Right: The frontispiece of the First Folio showing Shakespeare as he was in around 1600 at the age of 36

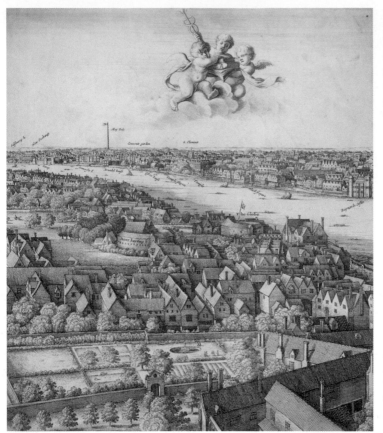

Left: Wenceslaus Hollar's view of Bankside looking towards the Strand and showing the second Globe Theatre of 1613 and the Bear Garden, with the labels reversed

Below: Hall's Croft, an impressive property which was erected in c.1614, probably by John Hall for himself and his family

Above: The chancel of Holy Trinity
in Stratford, with the Shakespeare
bust up on the left wall overlooking
the graves of Anne Shakespeare,
William Shakespeare, Thomas Nash,
John Hall, and Susanna

Right: Shakespeare's face may have
been moulded from a life or death
mask towards the end of his life; the
monument was in place by the time
the First Folio was published in 1623

Below: The inscription on
Shakespeare's grave which urges
posterity to let his bones rest in peace

GOOD FREND FOR IESVS SAKE FORBEARE,
TO DIGG THE DVST ENCLOASED HEARE.
BLESE BE Y MAN Y SPARES THES STONES
AND CVRST BE HE Y MOVES MY BONES

Above: A Stratford lithograph by C. F. Greene from 1820, showing Market Cross and the corner house in High street where Judith Shakespeare lived with her husband Thomas Quiney; it had been the town's medieval prison (hence the name 'Cage') and it still stands today

Left: Ben Jonson, painted in the year after Shakespeare's death

Below: The contrasting signatures of Susanna Hall and her daughter Elizabeth Nash, on a document of 1647

consulted for information, when his professional life for twenty years had consisted of remembering lines as well as writing them, almost suggests that he did not want to co-operate, leaving behind an uncomfortable impression of Shakespeare as someone who disengaged himself from real life when it suited him. 'What, Michael Cassio, / That came a-wooing with you?' Desdemona gently chides Othello when she is trying to coax him into restoring Cassio's command, an echo perhaps of Will Shakespeare in real life and real time wooing the man Belott on behalf of someone else, another cross-over from life into art, only detectable because Shakespeare was asked to testify in a minor law-suit a decade later. Stephen Belott married Mary Mountjoy on 19 November 1604 and no doubt Shakespeare was there, having been instrumental in their union. Belott and his new wife were eventually to be found living in the house of the same George Wilkins who later collaborated with Shakespeare on *Pericles*; he also testified during the Mountjoy–Belott suit.

The Belott–Mountjoy tug-of-war and marriage coincided almost exactly with the genesis and première of *Othello*, which was performed at court in November 1604. In the Italian source, Giraldi Cinthio's *Hecatommithi*, the blame for the tragedy is laid partly at least at the door of Desdemona's father for having 'given her a name of unlucky augury' as the name Desdemona means 'unfortunate' in Greek. This is compounded by the Italian resonance of the young Venetian's name, *démona* meaning female devil unlike Shakespeare's plangent 'demona' which seems to evoke wistfully the character of Othello's wife. Cinthio calls Othello 'the Moor' or '*il capitano Moro*', while Iago is simply 'the Ensign'; Bianca, Michael Cassio, Emilia – all are Shakespeare's. Juliet's ingenuous question about the arbitrary link between external reality and linguistic signifier, 'What's in a name? That which we call a rose / By any other word would smell as sweet', applies more widely to Shakespeare's works. Shakespeare's names of major characters, unlike those in Jonsonian comedy, are rarely generic, except for Marina (born at sea), Perdita (the lost one), and Miranda (the admired one) in the last plays. There are no Subtles, Faces, Volpones, or Corbaccios in Shakespeare as a rule. The nomenclature of *Othello*, a play in which Shakespeare invents all the names except one, may also contain clues about his life, as one would expect from a dramatist who uses the plays as vehicles for self-expression. As it happens the names in *Othello* cut both ways: on the one hand they are literary, imaginative, and internal in that the Moor and his Venetian wife seem to be doomed to tragedy by their names, while on the other hand Emilia may step into the play from the real world of Will Shakespeare and Emilia Bassano.

The most mystifying cross-over from real life, however, occurs in one of Iago's replies to Desdemona. She has asked him what praise he would heap on a deserving woman. 'She that was ever fair and never proud', he replies, then includes among the attributes of feminine virtue 'She that in wisdom never was so frail / To change the cod's head for the salmon's tail'. The fishy idiom of this passage is commonly labelled 'obscure', but it seems that a bawdy joke is involved, since 'tail' is a word Shakespeare repeatedly uses for the female genitals, as in Petruchio's 'What, with my tongue in your tail?' in *The Shrew*. Cod's heads carry a similarly specific masculine sexual meaning. At its most obvious, then, this seems to be an allusion to lesbian aberrations, the fact that fair women sometimes prefer tail to head of cod. But the word 'salmon' occurs three times only in Shakespeare, and this includes the fish in the rivers of Monmouth and Macedon in *Henry V.* Long before he was old enough to appreciate bawdy jokes, Shakespeare would have associated 'salmon' first and foremost with a part of sixteenth-century Old Stratford known as Salmon Tail and Salmon Jole, to the west of Bull Lane and verging on today's Sanctus Street. The history of these names is obscure, but they may recall mediaeval salmon ponds belonging to the monks from Old Stratford and the College near Holy Trinity. In Middle English, and still in Shakespeare's time, the word 'jole' denoted the head of a fish, and hence 'the head and shoulders of salmon, sturgeon, or ling' (*Oxford English Dictionary*). In Stratford, therefore, in Salmon Tail and Salmon Jole, the tail and head of salmon sat side-by-side.

If Shakespeare was indeed playing with the consonance between a Stratford locality and a common bawdy idiom of the period, he was presumably aware how few outside Stratford would see the joke, which suggests that it was included for his own personal satisfaction. This, in its turn, seems to suggest that he himself planned to play Iago – intellectually manipulative, ever orchestrating, pulling strings, deviously destructive, consumed alike by envy and sexual obsession. Towards the end of the play Othello realizes the enormity of what Iago has made him do, and stares down at Iago's feet: 'I look down towards his feet, but that's a fable. / (*To Iago*) If that thou beest a devil I cannot kill thee.' The devil was commonly thought to be cloven- or club-footed, and the lines suggest either that Iago has a club-foot and Othello should therefore have guessed that he was the devil, or that Othello is expecting to see a cloven foot on Iago because someone so wicked must surely be the devil incarnate. If Shakespeare was himself lame, as his Richard III can be taken to suggest, and playing Iago, Othello's bewildered remark may well have borne a resonance beyond the play: it may be that the sex-obsessed Iago's author was feeling guilt-ridden for conducting a sexual relationship with a friend's wife, Jane Davenant.

Iago is only twenty-eight to Shakespeare's forty when he wrote *Othello*, but it would be a mistake to think that Shakespeare always matched his own age to that of the character he played. On that criterion, the Moor himself would be a more fitting part than Iago for their originator; as it happens it is known from another source that the star of the company, Richard Burbage, played Othello.

Iago's latent homosexuality may also connect guiltily with Shakespeare. When Othello requests Iago to give him 'a living reason' for exposing Desdemona's betrayal, Iago relates a fantastical tale about having recently shared a bed with Cassio. 'I lay with Michael Cassio lately,' he begins, then explains how he was kept awake by toothache and thus overheard Cassio talking in his sleep. Convinced that the body lying next to him was Desdemona's, Cassio gripped and wrung Iago's hand, kissed him hard 'as if he plucked up kisses by the roots' from his lips, then laid his leg over Iago's thigh and, while sighing, kissed him and cursed the fate that had given Desdemona to the Moor. Othello's response to this perverse fiction spiced with graphic homosexuality is to exclaim 'O monstrous, monstrous!', which is indeed what it is. Heterosexual intimacy is not Iago's forte; instead, he is the chief peddler of pornographic fantasies in the play. It is significant that in Shakespeare's version his marriage to Emilia has not produced offspring, whereas in the source of the play the Iago character is the father of a three-year-old daughter whom Desdemona adores. One day the Ensign takes his daughter to her and steals her delicately embroidered handkerchief, a present from the Moor, while she presses the little girl to her breast. Iago's barren marriage and the aura of homosexuality surrounding him further set him apart from benign nature. *Othello* resembles *The Merchant of Venice* to the extent that both plays feature homosexual men who cannot move in harmony with the natural heterosexual order of being: Antonio is not allowed into the magic circle of coupledom symbolized by the rings he extracted from Bassanio, while Gratiano (who returns in *Othello* as Desdemona's uncle) has parted with Nerissa's ring to a lawyer's clerk – albeit the clerk is Nerissa in disguise. The last two lines of the play are Gratiano's 'Well, while I live I'll fear no other thing / So sore as keeping safe Nerissa's ring': he will be on guard lest someone else should get hold of Nerissa's ring (her vagina) and cuckold him. Antonio's final line in *The Merchant of Venice* is 'I am dumb' – that is, silent – while Iago's last two lines similarly promise that the rest will be silence: 'Demand me nothing; what you know you know; / From this time forth I never will speak word.' The silent stoicism of homosexual men in ordinary heterosexual cultures may be the only thing that Antonio and Iago share, except for the fact that both parts were written by Shakespeare, perhaps for himself, or inspired by his own ambiguous sexual self, or both.

If Shakespeare did play Iago, then his having given Iago's wife the name Emilia acquires a logic and momentum of its own. Notwithstanding the intrinsic circularity of such a deductive process, Emilia in *Othello* reflects aspects of the character of Shakespeare's mistress as reconstructed from the *Sonnets* and from Forman's diary. What there is of Emilia Lanier in the Forman papers from 1597 suggests that she was ambitious, ostensibly for her husband but ultimately for herself too. That she became one of the first English women poets in the seventeenth century indicates that she was independently minded, and to some extent at least lived by her own rules rather than following convention. Shakespeare's choice of Emilia as the name of Iago's wife may well have been inspired by the one Venetian woman he knew, who happened to be called Emilia and whose views on married faithfulness may have resembled those expressed by Iago's Emilia to Desdemona. It is the scene of the willow song, towards the end of Act

IV, and Desdemona has just asked Emilia whether or not she would commit adultery, 'do such a deed for all the world'. Emilia's response is that she would 'not do such a thing for a joint-ring, nor for measures of lawn, nor for gowns, petticoats, nor caps, nor any petty exhibition; but for all the whole world, ud's pity, who would not make her husband a cuckold to make him a monarch? I should venture purgatory for't.' Emilia speaks the most pragmatic lines about sex and adultery of any woman in Shakespeare.

It may be dangerous to draw close analogies between reality and fiction, but when there is reason to suspect their existence, it is at the very least interesting to acknowledge them, and ponder their implications. In the case of the two Venetian plays, *The Merchant of Venice* (1598) and *Othello* (1604), it is permissible to wonder whether Shakespeare would have chosen Venice as a setting for these plays if he had never been involved with the real Emilia, a Jewish Venetian woman – a musician whose talents may have contributed to the preoccupation with music at the end of *The Merchant of Venice*, as the lovers rest in Belmont. In the first play Shakespeare 'mapped' the marine city of Venice with regard to the Rialto and its customs, business traditions, and ethnic mix; revisiting it in *Othello*, he pays attention to social and political detail. Venice for Shakespeare is a real place, one that he appears to know, so intimately in fact that it seems as though he must have been there.

The use of Emilia Bassano's name in *Othello* and the fact that her character is married to Iago leads to further speculation about Iago. The character clearly comes from somewhere inside Shakespeare's head in the first instance, but the name is perplexing. It is notoriously hard to pronounce in English, whether as trisyllabic 'I-a-go' or as a two-syllable word starting with a contracted 'ia' diphthong. The best-known 'Iago' is of course none other than 'Santiago', as in Santiago de Compostela, the shrine in north-western Spain dedicated to the apostle St James – and the year in which *Othello* was written heralded the era of King James I. Shakespeare engaged with the Scottishness of the new Stuart dynasty in *Macbeth*, written two years after *Othello*. His use of the first name of the new king in his first play of the first full year of that king's new reign for a man who was a psychotic pornographic schemer seems almost reckless. And if Shakespeare did indeed intend

Iago to be homosexual, then his use of Iago/James becomes down-right defiant, since all the actors must have known from their contacts at court that the new king was at the very least bisexual.

Using the Spanish version of the name does of course disguise its punch, and with its awkward pronunciation it becomes, phonetically, as elusive as the character's opaque immorality. Even so, it would be interesting to know whether the King balked at the 'coincidence' when he saw the first recorded court performance of *Othello*, in November 1604. Any tendency to take exception may have been mollified by the thought that *Othello* paid homage to his poem *Lepanto*, about the famous naval defeat of the Turks in 1571, which had been published in a new edition in 1603.

Within two months of James' accession to the throne of England, the Lord Chamberlain's Men had become the King's Men, by Royal Patent. Now they were safer from the kind of heavy-handed tactics that the City of London deployed against the players from time to time. Among King James's first acts was to free the Earl of Southampton from the Tower, perhaps a further indication of a sym-pathetic disposition towards the players. Shakespeare's name is prominent on the Royal Licence of the King's Men, where he follows Lawrence Fletcher, a former 'comediane serviteur' to King James in Scotland but precedes Burbage, Phillips, and other members of the company. This may have been due to the intercession and renewed patronage of Southampton. Within less than a year the King's Men had been issued with four and a half yards of 'scarlet cloth' each, enough for a doublet and breeches in which to process in King James's coronation. In the 'Account' by the Master of the Great Wardrobe Shakespeare tops the list, ahead of Phillips and Fletcher, Heminges and Burbage. Such privileged positions in royal charters and accounts demonstrate that Shakespeare had truly 'arrived', and it seems likely that he and Southampton, both older and wiser now, picked up where they had left off. Certainly the earl's time in the Tower had not dented his enthusiasm for the players, as seems evident from a letter addressed to Robert Cecil in 1604 by Sir Walter Cope relating to a proposed entertainment to be laid on for the new Queen by Southampton. Cope sounds harassed: he had spent all morning looking for players and entertainers but with little success. Burbage claimed that the company had 'no new play that the Queen hath not seen' but offered to revive '*Love's Labour's Lost* which for wit and mirth he says will please her exceedingly; and this is appointed to be played tomorrow night at my Lord of Southampton's . . .'[7]

No retribution similar to that generated by Shakespeare's unwise use of the name Oldcastle followed upon his Iago/James 'coincidence', and *Othello* slipped comfortably and unchallenged into the Shakespeare canon and later the Folio. Whether or not Shakespeare himself under-took the role of Iago/James, the play constitutes a most intense meditation on the devastating power of human sexuality, and it is not at all clear why he should have written such a work at this time. It is not easy to see anything in Cinthio's anodyne *Hecatommithi* that might have fired his imagination, unless it was the play made of Desdemona's name in an otherwise name-free narrative. The anxieties about sexual betrayal and desire explored in *Othello* verge on mania. If Shakespeare and Jane Davenant were involved at this time, then perhaps the play reflects the moral chaos into which Shakespeare was plunged by the affair. Cassio's wooing of Desdemona on Othello's behalf and Shakespeare's acting for Mme Mountjoy in the business of Belott ran on twin tracks chronologically. Was there also another parallel between Shakespeare's life and Brabantio's? In 1604 Shakespeare's daughters were twenty-one and nineteen years old; it was a while yet before Shakespeare lost Susanna to John Hall and had to be told, like Brabantio, that she saw a 'divided duty', between him and her husband.

If Hall had not arrived in town by 1604, the Jesuits certainly had. Catholic stirrings were inevitable in the wake of the Stuart accession, and hope ran high that their cause might find a sympathetic ear in the new Scots king. Certainly it seems that they became bolder now in Stratford, which was not far from the Jesuits' regional headquarters in Worcestershire. Shakespeare would have known that something was afoot locally when in January 1604 a priest was spotted in Stratford who then bolted to safety. It was not clear to the people who encoun-tered him that he was indeed a Jesuit, but the authorities had little doubt on this point. Two local residents, 'Joan Ainge spinster' and an otherwise unidentified 'boy' who was nearly knocked over by the stranger gave statements about the incident. Both recalled that the man was wearing high shoes with stockings and green breeches, and the boy testified that he had gone up to the Reynolds house. The stranger 'had run so of knavery to overthrow him and so [the boy] gave him way, and looked after him to see whither he would, and he saw him stay his hand upon the cheek post of Mr Reynolds' door and so stand still, and so the said boy turned and went his way'. Shakespeare may not have been in Stratford at the time, but the rest of his family certainly were and he would have heard about it, the more so since the incident happened all but on his doorstep – Reynolds's large property was just a few yards north of New Place; he also owned a farm over in Old Stratford, near Holy Trinity, but it seems more likely that his foppish-looking visitor fetched up in Chapel Street. As die-hard Catholics the Reynoldses had found themselves on the same 1592 recusancy register as the Debdales and the Cawdreys, whose son George was officially listed by the recusancy commission as a 'seminary priest or a Jesuit'. They were as deeply implicated as it was possible to be.

It is unlikely that the Reynoldses' caller was George Cawdrey, for Joan Ainge would surely have recognized him, or others might have if she did not. He was probably one of the Jesuits sheltering at Hindlip Hall, across the county border in Worcestershire, the ancient manor house soon to achieve tragic fame throughout the Midlands when the head of the Jesuit mission, Father Henry Garnett, was captured in one of its priest holes. Perched on top of a hill with commanding views over the surrounding countryside, the manor of Hindlip was owned by Thomas Habington, a friend of Antony Babington's and a considerable antiquarian scholar. It was one of the safest Catholic refuges in the country. The Hall and its warren of secret passages and hiding places have long since gone and the site is now the headquarters of the West Mercia constabulary. At some time or other most of the main Jesuit players, including John Gerard, Nicholas Owen, Thomas Stanney, and Edward Oldcorne who had disembarked in England with Gerard, passed through the house. The conspicuous and inept fop from Stratford could have been almost any of these, with the exception perhaps of the elegant Gerard, who was a master of disguises. His identity will never now be known; Oldcorne certainly maintained a high profile in the Midlands, operating out of Hindlip for sixteen years; or it might have been Oldcorne's assistant, Father Thomas Lister, a wavering, neurotic and claustrophobic character who greatly tried Garnett's patience.

Whoever it was, what is really interesting is that the priest was there at all: his mission presumably was to consolidate the base of the local recusant sympathizers. It would also be interesting to know whether the mysterious stranger called on the Shakespeares when he was in Stratford. His hosts obviously included the Reynoldses, and probably also the Cawdreys, the Badgers, and other local Catholics. It is highly likely that he called too on the Debdales of Shottery, among the most stubborn of all recusant local families, and particularly since their son had been put to death in London. In all likelihood this was a mission to prepare the local faithful for the accession of a new monarch and the hopes of securing a better deal for Catholics. The Midlands were as important in this *risorgimento* as Lancashire, the traditional citadel of the Catholic high command. As for the Reynoldses, they were Catholics and on intimate terms with the Shakespeares. William Reynolds, the son of old Reynolds and eleven years younger than Shakespeare, was left a gold memorial ring in the poet's will. The Catholic missionaries were gearing up to get the new king on board. When they failed, they took another route, one that was infinitely more dangerous and violent.

Of course Shakespeare must have been aware that Jesuits were active in Stratford and the neighbouring villages, but the record shows only that in his home town he was always first and foremost a businessman. In the space of three years he parted with the considerable sum of £760 in investments. His outlay on 24 July 1605 of £440 for a share in local church tithes was the equivalent to the entire projected cost of the Fortune theatre in London. It seems certain that his father's bitter experience of overreaching himself had taught Will prudence, and that this huge sum was only part of his assets. He owned New Place and its barns and gardens, and there was his share in the Globe theatre, and presumably much other liquid cash, otherwise he could hardly have afforded his further investments and his purchase a few years later of the Blackfriars gatehouse. As ever his investments were shrewd and sound, bearing no resemblance to the redistributive and egalitarian ethos of his next play, *King Lear*.

And if Shakespeare was indeed the father of William Davenant, he managed to fit it in, business, writing, acting and family notwith-standing. Davenant was christened at St Martin Carfax in Oxford on 3 March 1606, and was therefore conceived in June or July 1605, at just the time when Shakespeare is known from his financial transaction of 24 July to have been in Stratford. There are no records to place him in Oxford for July 1605, but that he can be proved to have been in the Midlands at just the right time is enough: he would certainly have had the opportunity to see Jane Davenant. The King's Men were probably playing in London at the time, but Shakespeare seems to have had enough clout with the company to live life on his terms.

A journey into Warwickshire would probably have involved ten days or even a fortnight away; perhaps major shareholders like Shakespeare could take time off for the occasional visit home – and he was certainly the company's biggest asset. Shakespeare's company was also blessed in that their undisputed star, Burbage, was a Londoner whose immediate family lived near him: *he* was not likely to be called far away by family duties.

It may be that this year Shakespeare stayed on in Stratford until nearly the end of August, when the King went to Oxford, where on 27 August he was treated to a work called *The Three Sybils*. In it his lineage was acclaimed and his descent traced from the fruitful line of Banquo – so different from the sterile Macbeths – an obvious prompt for *Macbeth*.[8] There is no way of knowing, but it is intriguing to think that Shakespeare was in Oxford in August 1605 in the wake of the royal party. He may have been there again in October, for the King's Men performed *Othello* in Oxford on 9 October 1605, by which time Jane Davenant was four or five months pregnant. One wonders whether she and her husband saw the play, one quite possibly inspired by her relationship with the rich player and dramatist who was perhaps him-self playing Iago. If he was the father of the baby she was carrying, she may have taken the opportunity to tell him.

24

'My Father's Godson': 1605–6

IT MAY BE that Jane Davenant's information about her pregnancy triggered the writing of *King Lear*. The old *Leir* play – in which Shakespeare as a rookie in Shoreditch may have had a hand – had recently been printed. It contains some of the raw materials for the main plot of Shakespeare's masterpiece, but there is nothing of the sub-plot, that important part of the play which deals with the Gloucester family and the price they all have to pay for old Gloucester's adultery, which produced the illegitimate Edmund. Attempts to find the inspiration for the Gloucester material in texts Shakespeare knew, like Sidney's *Arcadia*, have proved fruitless, and this may well be because it came from Shakespeare's own life. There was also a real-life Lear story in the air at just that time, one that brought the Earl of Southampton emphatically back under the spotlight: the sorry tale of the Annesleys not only anticipated the main plot of *King Lear* in a number of ways but also involved Southampton and his family. Brian Annesley was a wealthy Kentish man with three daughters. The two eldest were married, and when he developed senile dementia they wanted to have him declared insane and committed accordingly. The chief harpy was his daughter Lady Wildgoose, possibly referred to by the Fool in his jingle 'Winter's not gone yet if the wild geese fly that way'. While poor fathers are despised by their offspring, rich ones will keep them dancing attendance: 'Fathers that wear rags / Do make their children blind, / But fathers that bear bags / Shall see their children kind.' After divesting himself of both authority and wealth, the Fool promises, Lear will suffer nothing but grief at the hands of his thankless daughters.

Wild geese head south when winter approaches: they will not stay behind, any more than will Lear's selfish daughters. The sight of wild geese flying in formation is impressive, and the real-life Lady Wildgoose may have been a mere coincidence; on the other hand, in the Annesley story, as also in Shakespeare's play, it was the compassionate youngest sister who would not stand to see her father abused, and petitioned Robert Cecil for help – her name was Cordell, close indeed to Shakespeare's Cordelia. When Old Annesley died in July 1604 Cordell inherited most of his estate, having been helped in her struggle by Sir William Harvey, one of the executors of her father's will. Harvey was Southampton's stepfather, his mother's third husband, and when Southampton's mother died in 1607, Harvey married Cordell Annesley, perhaps because, like Lear, he wanted to 'set his rest on her kind nursery'. Shakespeare would understandably have heard of the Annesley family saga through Southampton, and no one in authority stood closer to the Annesleys than the Southamptons.

The various strands that converge in *King Lear* are the contemporary domestic tragedy of the Annesleys, literary texts like the anonymous *Leir* play and Spenser's *Faerie Queene*, which tell versions of the story of the main plot, and events from Shakespeare's own life which probably become the blueprint for the sub-plot of *King Lear*. It seems likely that Shakespeare began to work on the play after the partial eclipse of the moon on 27 September 1605 and the total lunchtime eclipse of the sun on 12 October following,[1] for some lines of Gloucester's unmistakably refer to just these two: he says that these 'late eclipses in the sun and moon portend no good to us', but instead augurs the cooling-off of love and friendship, division between brothers, 'in cities mutinies, in countries discords, palaces treason, the bond cracked between son and father.' Those lines were probably written not too long after 12 October 1605, for there is a certain immediacy in the reference to the 'late' eclipses. A plague scare closed the theatres in July 1606, and *King Lear* was acted at court on St Stephen's Day (26 December), 1606. It is possible to narrow the time down further. There is a defining moment in the play when, on the verge of madness, Lear confronts the unleashed elements, raging against nature, asking it to flatten 'the thick rotundity of the world' and to crack its own mould and thus forever annihilate all future generations at source: 'all germens spill at once / That make ingrateful man'. Kent stands by appalled and protests that he has never seen 'Such sheets of fire, such bursts of horrid thunder, / Such groans of roaring wind and rain.' No man can endure such an onslaught, he claims.

The powerful storm scenes in *King Lear* are unequalled for sheer imaginative drive, although a few unforgettable images of perverted nature render the storm which rages during the night of Duncan's murder in *Macbeth* almost as memorable. It is surely no coincidence that Shakespeare's two plays with the most powerful storm scenes follow each other closely in 1606, for the devastating storms which hit England and northern Europe over the weekend of 30 March 1606 must have been fresh in his memory. In the words of an eye-witness account, 'The nine and twentieth, and thirtieth of March [1606], the wind was so extraordinary great and violent, that it caused great ship-wreck; it also caused the sea, and divers rivers to overflow their bounds, and drowned many people, and much cattle.'[2] What better inspiration for the storm scenes in *King Lear* and the fierce tempest during the night of Duncan's murder in *Macbeth*? It looks very much as though the third Act of *King Lear* was directly topical, written after Sunday 30 March 1606.

The problem with dating the play by means of such natural phe-nomena as the eclipses of the autumn of 1605 and the storm of the end of March 1606 is that the six months covered seem much too long, even for a complex work like *King Lear*, especially when it includes the four weeks of Lent, which Shakespeare seems so often to have exploited for a bout of concentrated writing in New Place. It may be that the reference to 'late' eclipses is more distanced than it seems, for surely in his references to the portentous character of the eclipses and their auguring 'mutinies', 'discords', and 'treason' Shakespeare can only have had in mind the so-called Powder Plot of 5 November 1605, when a group of well-connected Catholics attempted to blow up Parliament. Robert Cecil's response was swift, savage and efficient, and the fate of the chief conspirators is well known. But what was the aftermath of the plot in the Catholic Midlands and parts of Warwickshire, nearly twenty years since the Babington Plot?

News of the averted catastrophe in London reached Stratford the next day, 6 November. Posts tore through the night to alert the local authorities in Warwick, Charlecote, and elsewhere. Within hours of the discovery of the plot in London the mayor of Stratford, one William Wyatt, was leading a raid on Clopton House where one of the conspirators, Ambrose Rookwood, was hiding out. In ordinary circumstances Wyatt would have been out of his league tangling with the Cloptons and their friends and allies, for in 1605 he was a mere burgher, living in Sheep Street opposite what is now Cordelia Cottage. Clashing with a fellow citizen over the rental of a horse was more in his line, but he knew what he was looking for at the Cloptons', and he found it: vestments, chalices, chasubles, and other traces of an active Catholic cell. The bulk of the 'evidence', however, had already been successfully shifted to the Badgers of Henley Street, the Shakespeares' next-door neighbours. It had taken a few hours only for the fall-out from the Gunpowder plot to reach the Shakespeares' Henley Street neighbours.

It was all very reminiscent of the persecutions under Elizabeth, among the most prominent local victims of which had been Robert Debdale of Shottery and his and Shakespeare's mother's extended Arden family. As it happened, they featured in a tract published in 1603 when James came to the throne, its subject matter a notorious case of exorcism in Denham in Buckinghamshire, a place Shakespeare might well have passed through on his way to and from Stratford. The tract, *A Declaration of Egregious Popish Impostures*, had been commissioned by the Privy Council and its author was Samuel Harsnett, a militant, Cambridge-educated Protestant, at the time chaplain to the Bishop of London and eventually Archbishop of York. Shakespeare probably read the *Declaration* because of the attempted Fawkes coup of November, which is to say that he turned to Harsnett only after 5 November 1605. That he knew it by the time he wrote the play is plain from the fact that several of the devils in Poor Tom's catalogue of spirits in *King Lear* are straight out of Harsnett, including the famous 'foul fiend Flibbertigibbet', an evil nocturnal spirit who 'gives the web and the pin, squinies the eye, and makes the harelip, mildews the white wheat, and hurts the poor creature of earth.'

Harsnett's pamphlet is a rancorous tirade against Campion, Weston, Debdale, and other Jesuits, casting them as lecherous and obscene disciples of the devil. Luckily for the good and enlightened people of England, Harsnett notes, Tyburn has a way of dealing with them.

Never mind their blood-soaked girdles (Campion) or hoses (Debdale) on the quartering block, they are relics only to benighted fanatics. Throughout his account Harsnett hints at a devious sexual subtext, and there may have been something in this: the Jesuits certainly practised exorcisms on poor Sara Williams of Denham, who eventually testified against them, and Harsnett reports with relish Sara's claim that 'the priests did pretend that the devil did rest in the most secret part of her body' and that he would also issue that way from her. This allowed them to feel her up, Harsnett notes, or, even better, to have other women do so.

The tract teeters on the verge of pornography with unexampled savagery, thrilling to the use of the word 'tail' in a particularly poisonous swipe at the revered Campion. Everyone in Harsnett's audience would have known what was meant, since execution for high treason ordered the ripping off of the 'privy member', which would be thrown into a fire or large seething cauldron, followed by the entrails of the victim – decreed by the law to be alive and 'seeing' at that stage of the proceedings. The horror and the outrage to the dignity of the human body speak for themselves. *A Declaration* is not for the faint-hearted, a piece of vicious propaganda that carries an effective rhetorical punch. Would Shakespeare, if he were indeed a Roman Catholic, have borrowed so much from Harsnett's book?'[3] Not for the first time Shakespeare presents a paradox, in his use of a text that he must have execrated – always assuming that the ties between the Catholic Debdales, Burmans, and Hathaways, all neighbours in Shottery, also meant that Shakespeare was close to them – not least because of its treatment of the Ardens and of Debdale.

Shakespeare's parde of Harsnett's devils in his play might suggest that after the November 1605 plot his view of Catholic defiance became more hostile. In this context, his use of the word 'rip' is interesting. It is hard not to hear an echo of the treason trials in Edgar's line about reading the letter by Goneril found on the dead Oswald: 'To know our enemies' minds we'd rip their hearts; / Their papers is more lawful.' Again, in *Macbeth* Macduff reveals that he was 'from his mother's womb / Untimely ripped', and the word occurs only twice more in the rest of Shakespeare's plays. The fourteen months between 5 November 1605 and the end of 1606 were among the darkest and bloodiest in the nation's history. Guy Fawkes and a number of the conspirators were put to death on Friday 31 January 1606, when scaffolds were erected at certain key locations, notably at the western end of St Paul's Cathedral and in Old Palace Yard in Westminster, in full view of Westminster Abbey and the palace of Westminster. Londoners could choose not to attend executions at Tyburn, but it was much harder to avoid them in the hub of the city.

Already the Shakespeares' former neighbour from Henley Street, George Badger, had been taken to London for interrogation about his collusion with the Cloptons. Then, on Thursday 23 January 1606, a week before Guy Fawkes's execution, Henry Garnett, Edward Oldcorne, Nicholas Owen, and Ralph Ashley were all captured at Hindlip. Garnett and Oldcorne had been cowering in a cramped hole for seven days and nights. Garnett's legs had started to swell up badly, but there was no chance of relief – if only they could have shifted the books and other 'furniture' to gain just a little more space. In the meantime, neither of them went 'to the stool' at any point although they did pass water. Garnett claimed that they were in good heart throughout, even though they heard the searchers above them and were convinced that they would be found sooner or later. When eventually the two men emerged from their hiding hole, the stench nearly overwhelmed the searchers.

Shakespeare can have been under no illusion about the scale of local recusant involvement in these plots against the state. If he was himself perhaps shifting or realigning his allegiances at this time, as his use of Harsnett might be taken to suggest, it may be that these events consolidated his sense of a real threat to the commonwealth. Leading Jesuits repeatedly protested their aloofness from political chicanery in open letters to the Privy Council, but people found it hard to accept such protestations at face value – after all, Father Oswald Tesimond had confessed Robert Catesby's seditious intentions to Garnett only a few days before 5 November. To the new Protestant mindset under extreme political pressure just then, the seal of the confessional lacked biblical authority and credibility.

One of Garnett's various cover names was 'Farmer', and in addition to being the chief Jesuit in England he was famous (or infamous) for a treatise on equivocation written in defence of Southwell's use of it at his trial in February 1595. In Shakespeare's *Macbeth*, the drunken Porter's speech alludes both to his *alias* and to his own equivocations at his trial, staged at the Guildhall on Thursday 27 March 1606. By then one of the Jesuits' most loyal and most necessary followers, Nicholas Owen, had perished under torture in the Tower of London. The official version was that he had committed suicide, but Owen probably died on the rack. English law forbade the racking of men and women who suffered from hernias, but this appears to have been disregarded in Owen's case. In the words of his friend and sometime roommate John Gerard, 'his bowels gushed out with his life.'

He had been with Garnett for nearly twenty years. Gerard describes him as 'the chief designer and builder of hiding-places in England', and he could therefore betray more priests and their supporters than almost anyone else. He must have died in unimaginable agony, and is venerated in Catholic circles to this day as one of the true heroes of the Elizabethan underground. He was canonized by Pope Paul VI among the Forty Martyrs of England and Wales. His death must have been a desperate blow to Garnettt whose own terror at the thought of torture is well documented in his correspondence. At the time of Southwell's detention Garnett had clung to the hope that his own physical body would be able to endure what Southwell must have suffered, because it formed part of the wider mystical body of Christ: surely He would help His disciples by assuming upon Himself some of the pain inflicted on them by their blind and misguided countrymen? In the end Garnett was racked only once. When they came for him a second time he pleaded with them not to make him suffer again but promised to provide all the answers they desired, just as if he had been racked. It seems that on this occasion the Privy Council relented and listened to his pleas for justice or mercy.

While all this was going on, Shakespeare was writing *King Lear*. This play is quite as obsessed as *Othello* with adultery and female sexuality, but whereas in *Othello* adultery is a hallucinatory fiction, in *Lear* it is real, and jauntily acknowledged by the chief offender, Gloucester. The play opens with Gloucester bragging to Kent about his younger son Edmund's illegitimacy. To Kent's remark 'I cannot conceive you', Gloucester cheerfully replies:

> Sir, this young fellow's mother could, whereupon she grew round-wombed and had indeed, sir, a son for her cradle ere she had a husband for her bed . . . Though this knave came something saucily into the world, before he was sent for, yet was his mother fair, there was good sport at his making, and the whoreson must be acknowledged.

Gloucester's punishment for both his sexual *faux-pas* and his unrepentant shamelessness is swift and terrible: his illegitimate offspring betrays him and, in a singlularly violent on-stage scene in any of the plays, he is cruelly blinded. Cast on the mercy of his rightful son and heir, Edgar, he dies of a broken heart. Almost everything to do with the Gloucester plot seems to have been Shakespeare's invention – there are, at least, no known sources for it. Nevertheless, it is possible to discern a subtext of guilt, if not downright fear of retribution, which might be explicable if Shakespeare was indeed involved with Jane Davenant during the writing of the play.

The question is whether there are any clues in the play that connect it to the Davenants – and it happens that a key phrase points quite specifically in that direction. On a purely literary level it acts as a bridge between the two plots, and has dynastic implications. It occurs in the first scene of Act II when Regan and Gloucester are discussing Edgar's heinous apparent readiness to usurp his father. 'Madam, my old heart is cracked, is cracked,' Gloucester complains, to which Regan replies, incredulously, 'What, did my father's godson seek your life? / He whom my father named, your Edgar?' This is the only use of the word 'godson' in all Shakespeare's plays and poems. For it to occur in a play written at just the time when William Davenant was born, the only person on record as having passed himself off as Shakespeare's godson – someone who occasionally claimed to be his actual son – would be a most remarkable coincidence. At the very least, the claim that the dramatist Davenant was the godson of the playwright William Shakespeare must be seriously considered. There is no reason why the Davenant boys, parson Robert and dramatist William, should have lied to Aubrey or to anyone else about having known Shakespeare; the claim that Davenant was

Shakespeare's biological son is of a different order. If Jane Davenant's pregnancy was the result of a liaison with Shakespeare in the summer of 1605, he would presumably have known of it by October 1605. No wonder he has Gloucester refer to the recent solar and lunar eclipses – doubtless he was himself struck by their portent.

From the opening lines of *King Lear* it is known that Gloucester's adultery resulted in a son: if the parallels between Shakespeare's life and the play are as intimate as the various clues appear to suggest, then the writing of *King Lear* got under way after the sex of the baby was known in early March 1606. All the clues in the two plots – the storm in Act III, the sex of the illegitimate offspring, the use of the word 'godson' – push back the writing of *King Lear* to some time after 3 March 1606. The misleading immediacy of his reference to the 'late' eclipses is easily explained: he could rely on his audience remembering those eclipses because they were etched in the minds and hearts of the English by the Powder Plot that followed, which people connected directly with those omens. The day after Shakespeare may have stood godfather to William Davenant in Oxford was Shrove Tuesday, 4 March 1606. He probably planned to write the play during Lent, completing it in time for the re-opening of the London theatres after Easter (20 April 1606), hoping perhaps that it would be ready for performance by May or early June. His apparent use of the storms of 30 March in the second scene of Act III suggests a still more specific writing schedule, with the first two acts of the play completed during March 1606 and Acts III–V during April and May – timely for his reference to spring's cuckoo-flowers in mad Lear's crown of weeds, towards the end of the fourth Act.

Rumours about Shakespeare and Davenant had spread by the eighteenth century. Thus the Reverend James Davenport of Holy Trinity, who became Malone's trusted helper in Stratford, acknowledged in a letter to Malone in late May 1788 that he had 'heard . . . of the tradition that Sir William Davenant was a natural son of our poet'. Davenport's use of 'heard', so like the Reverend John Ward's, 126 years earlier, about the local tradition of Shakespeare's vast earnings, demonstrates that Stratfordians were still eagerly discussing the private life of the town's most famous son, especially in its more sensational and salacious aspects. Shakespeare certainly had at least one legitimate godson, in the person of young William Walker of Stratford, to whom he probably stood godfather in about 1609, and to whom he left money in his will. He may also, many years earlier, have been god-father to Ben Jonson's son Benjamin, whom Jonson called his 'best piece of poetry' in a poem addressed to the boy, who died aged 7 in 1603. There may have been others. Shakespeare's cousin Thomas Greene called his first two children William and Anne, possibly after the Shakespeares, but neither is mentioned as a godchild, nor remem-bered in Shakespeare's will. Nor is William Davenant, who was eleven when Shakespeare died. This does seem to argue against Shakespeare having been his godfather, but leaves open the question of pater-nity – any provision he might have made must have been done very privately, to avoid a posthumous acknowledgement of adultery.

As with *Othello* and indeed any other play performed by the King's Men, the most immediate intersection of the play with real life lay in the casting. Burbage is known to have played Richard III, Othello, Hamlet, and Lear – Edgar's godfather – and certain roles can be con-fidently pronounced to fit Will Kemp (Falstaff, Peter), Robert Armin (Touchstone, Feste), John Lowin (Henry VIII), and others. A crude matching of the cast of *King Lear* with the personnel of the King's Men might suggest that middle-aged Will Shakespeare was well equipped to play Gloucester, and perhaps he wrote the part with himself in mind, a middle-aged adulterer who had recently become the father of an illegitimate son. But it does not follow that he also assumed the role in the theatre. If he played the twenty-eight-year-old Iago with a limp or a club-foot, why would he not have played Gloucester's legitimate son Edgar, who describes himself as 'made lame by fortune's blows'?

The lack of hard evidence as to whether Shakespeare himself had a limp bedevils a fascinating line of speculation concerning the plays, and Shakespeare the player. *Othello* and *Lear* both feature a character who may limp. Othello staring down at Iago's foot may be a most important visual clue to the fact that on the stage of the Globe, Iago had a limp. If Shakespeare wrote the part of Iago for himself, and played it, it looks as though he was almost compulsively drawing attention to his disability, and generating theatrical capital from it. The part of Edgar, like that of Iago, is substantial, the second-longest in the play. If it could be proved beyond a doubt that Shakespeare played those two parts, it could then be categorically asserted that he undertook major roles in his plays, not just the bit parts usually assigned to him. If there is a direct connection between the Gloucester plot in the play and the birth of William Davenant, there is a certain odd symmetry in the boy's real-life godfather William playing the role of the godson in the play – a comparable imaginative logic to his playing the slow and limping Nurse with a lost daughter called Susan who would have been the same age as Juliet Capulet – and Susanna Shakespeare.

25

The Easter Rising of 1606:
A Little Local Difficulty

O N EASTER SUNDAY, 20 April 1606, Susanna Shakespeare refused to take the Eucharist. Her father was just then deeply into writing *King Lear*. The trial of Father Henry Garnett had taken place, but he was yet to be executed. It was not a good time for making a stand – in fact it was probably the worst time since the Armada year of 1588, and one of the most dangerous moments in English history. She was promptly cited by the local church court, popularly known as the Bawdy Court, and she was not alone when she appeared in Holy Trinity in May that year to answer a summons for non-compliance. Among others there stood with her Margaret Reynolds, the mother of Shakespeare's Catholic friend William Reynolds, Wheeler *père et fils* and their servant Alice, all three from Henley Street, Sibyl Cawdrey, Hamlet and Judith Sadler, one Thomas Stanney and his wife, and two Brooke brothers, one of whom, Robert Brooke, also lived in Henley Street, in the premises that had previously been the Badgers'. There is no mention at all in this of Susanna's mother or father, or of her sister, aunt, and uncles. She stood her ground alone, and apart from her family. Her father had probably left for London even before Easter, to help the King's Men to get the Globe ready for performances when the new season opened some time after the Lent break.

How Susanna Shakespeare came to find herself in the company of so many die-hard Catholic recusants is a mystery. The Sadlers, close friends of her parents and perhaps godparents of the Shakespeare twins, were a slightly different case: they held out briefly, pleading for time to 'cleanse' their consciences before receiving Communion; in response the court set 'a day to receive', the Sadlers accepted it, and that was that. Failure to comply would have resulted in excommunication and a regime of crippling fines. Susanna's isolation almost seems to suggest a rift between Shakespeare and his eldest daughter, presumably over religion if it culminated in her Easter defiance, and it may be that this family discord fed into the battle between father and daughters in *King Lear*. Lear's savage cursing of his eldest daughter Goneril is one of the most terrifying speeches in any of Shakespeare's plays. He prays Nature to render her sterile, but if she must have a baby then it ought to be a bitter creature that will make her weep, ravage her face with premature wrinkles and thus

> Turn all her mother's pains and benefits
> To laughter and contempt, that she may feel –
> That she may feel
> How sharper than a serpent's tooth it is
> To have a thankless child.

If Act III of the play dates from after the storm of 30 March 1606, and if Shakespeare began with Act I and wrote on to the end, then these lines in the first Act were written several weeks before Susanna's defiance of the ecclesiastical authorities. Perhaps she and her father were already at odds earlier in the spring of 1606 – about the time, say, of the birth of William Davenant. If she had found out about his affair with Jane Davenant, that would be explanation enough for difficulties between father and daughter. It is difficult to see what else might lie behind the heart-felt vehemence of those lines and in this fierce attack on the father–daughter relationship, a bond usually so strong and so benign in Shakespeare's plays.

It may be that Susanna was every bit as headstrong and rebellious as her father. On her grave in the chancel of Holy Trinity she is praised for being 'witty above her sex' and 'wise to salvation', the last sentence noting that 'Something of Shakespeare was in that'. People who knew her thought she resembled her father, that like him she was bright, funny, witty, and spirited; why not also headstrong and defiant? There may be echoes of early battles of will between father and daughter in old Capulet's onslaught on Juliet when she begs him not to marry her off to Count Paris. Capulet's furious 'Thank me no thankings, nor proud me no prouds . . . Out, you green-sickness carrion! Out, you baggage, / You tallow-face!' is the reaction of an irate patriarch whose daughter dares to cross him. In *Romeo and Juliet* the audience is on Juliet's side, because Shakespeare wants them to be. Possibly his own personal experience of a moody, truculent thirteen-year-old girl is more widely reflected in the play, one of intimate domestic tragedy. The pain that the tyrannical Capulet unjustly causes his child may reflect a burden of guilt on Shakespeare's part, in a portrait perhaps tinged by his own self-loathing for having been too heavy-handed with his children.

On Easter Sunday 1606 Susanna Shakespeare, twenty-three and unmarried, apparently ranged herself with the recusant Catholics. Unlike the Sadlers she did not petition the court for more time to consult her conscience, but seems to have conformed after making her point. It rather looks as though her defiance was only a gesture – but gestures of this kind could be very costly. Would a young, single woman, apparently unsupported by her family, be so daring? It may be that by Easter 1606 Susanna had already met John Hall and was now sufficiently committed to him to embrace his strict Protestantism which perhaps saw the Eucharist as too Romanist – though he was not among those reported for failing to take communion, possibly because he was not yet settled in Stratford. Within little over a year of her bold gesture of defiance, Susanna was married to him. Receiving the Eucharist was mandatory on the main religious holidays, like Easter and Christmas, and Susanna obviously did so at Christmas 1605, suggesting that her relationship with John Hall developed during the spring of 1606, just at the time when the birth of William Davenant may have revealed her father's closeness to Jane Davenant.

The eighteen months from July 1605 to the end of 1606 thus appear, from Shakespeare's perspective, to have been packed with incident. He may have been involved with Jane Davenant and made her pregnant; he was certainly planning the biggest financial investment of his career. His company played *Othello* in Oxford that October, possibly with him in the role of Iago. On 5 November 1605 the Powder Plot was discovered, and Shakespeare read Harsnett; he was able to enjoy again the patronage and friendship of Southampton. Susanna was probably being courted by her John. He was a physician, and in time he too, like his more famous father-in-law, became something of a local legend. His earlier encounters with Shakespeare may perhaps have been rather rocky, particularly if his zeal for his religion led Susanna to deviate from the Shakespeare family's policy of conformism – perhaps, like Desdemona, Susanna faced 'a divided duty', between her father's careful, diplomatic Anglicanism and her future husband's tougher Protestantism. Like Desdemona, she may have wanted to be something more than a mere 'moth of peace' – to do her bit, as it were. *King Lear* carries what may be echoes of a serious falling-out between father and daughter. Between March and December of 1606 Shakespeare wrote *King Lear*, *Macbeth*, and *Antony and Cleopatra*, a prodigious output presumably made possible in part at least by the closure of the theatres from July 1606, which set Shakespeare free to concentrate on his writing.

These were difficult times for the Catholic Midlands. Like all of London, Shakespeare probably heard of the arrest of Father Garnett at Hindlip Hall; unlike most Londoners, he would have known all about Hindlip. He may have been a witness to Garnett's execution, which took place on Saturday 3 May 1606 outside the western porch of St Paul's, within less than ten minutes' walk of where he lived in Muggle Street. After a day-long sham of a trial Garnett had been sentenced to death a month later. The person who faced the London crowd on the scaffold on that day had been publicly 'proclaimed' five months before, along with others, just like Edgar in *King Lear*. 'I heard myself proclaimed, / And by the happy hollow of a tree / Escaped the hunt. No port is free, no place / That guard and most unusual vigilance / Does not attend my taking.' In the words of the actual proclamation, Garnett, the once slender Wykhamist who had worked for Tottel, was now 'a fat man' of medium height aged between fifty and sixty, with a high forehead, a thin and greying hairline, and a closely trimmed beard on his cheek and chin. Shakespeare would have known all about his reputation for running the spiritual sector of the Catholic underground.

By the insistence of a sympathetic crowd, Garnett was spared the horror of vivisection. When his head was cast into the boiling cauldron 'it received no alteration at all; as neither it did after it was placed upon London Bridge, and set up there upon a pole.' It refused to wax 'black, as usually all heads cut from the bodies do', and became the focus of great curiosity. It was thought to be a 'miracle', and people flocked to the Bridge to see it; the magistrates thereupon ordered the head to be reset, to make it face upwards and away from the crowds below – or so John Gerard's report of the death of Henry Garnett claims. Gerard had his stories of Garnett's death from Catholics who were present, and desperate to collect a relic. This usually meant gathering blood from the victim in a handkerchief, or retrieving a blood-stained item of his clothing, as had happened with Campion's girdle and Debdale's hose, those articles of attire that so irritated Harsnett. According to Gerard, an ear of corn from one of the baskets into which the hangman had flung Garnett's quarters started showing the Jesuit's face when the authorities turned the real one on London Bridge, becoming one of the most famous Catholic relics of the age. It had been gathered by a devout Catholic who had squeezed in under the scaffold while Garnett was being quartered. Here 'he received the blood which streamed down through the chinks of the boards, upon his hat and apparel, and dipped such linen as he had prepared in the same.'

Little wonder that the colour of *Macbeth* should be red as blood, that after the murder of the king and his grooms Macbeth should speak of having blood-stained hands like a hangman's, that Lady Macbeth should exclaim 'Yet who would have thought the old man to have had so much blood in him?' Shakespeare's audience would have been fully alive to the event that lay behind these references. We can thankfully only imagine such butchery. Were it not for the imaginative sympathies of plays like *King Lear*, we could dismiss such horrors as belonging to a benighted past. But Shakespeare tells us otherwise. He was present and his plays testify to the fact that another way was available, even if it was not taken. The execution of law and justice in Shakespeare's real world morally lagged far behind the humanity and compassion of his greatest plays.

John Gerard had good reason to recall the fate of his Father Superior, his mentor and friend, for on this very same 3 May 1606 he slipped quietly out of the country and crossed to the Continent. He was free now. He had been nearly eight years on the run since his flight from the Tower. He was convinced that the spirit of Henry Garnett guided him to safety on the day of his death in May 1606, and particularly when at the very last moment his escape almost went wrong. Gerard died peacefully in Rome in 1637, having outlived his contemporary Shakespeare by twenty-one years. By an odd coincidence, his final days in England were probably spent in the very same gatehouse over Ireland Yard that Shakespeare bought about eight years later. Around the time of the Gunpowder Plot Gerard turned up at the gatehouse and asked its then owner to shelter some of the chief conspirators – Catesby, Wintour, Percy, and Digby, 'famous and noble men'. The lady of the house at the time dared not admit them in the absence of her husband John Fortescue, nephew of the powerful Master of the Wardrobe across the road, Sir John Fortescue. So the conspirators lodged instead in the nearby house of a die-hard recusant, Robert Dormer. Dormer's residence lay downhill from the gatehouse, and waiters from a tavern next to the cut of Ireland Yard testified to having seen these men come and go at Dormer's on a daily basis. When the plot was exposed, Gerard was proclaimed throughout the kingdom. Subsequently he appeared again out of the blue at the Blackfriars' gatehouse to seek refuge, wearing a false beard and a wig. He pleaded with Fortescue to take him in, because he knew not where to hide: 'the Lord Fortescue looked at him with deep sorrow and said "You have no one now to lose other than me and my family."'[1] The Catholic cause was exhausted.

The crack-down after the Gunpowder Plot marked a turning-point in the country's history. The King survived his Catholic enemies, and it was the Puritans who forty-four years later dragged his son King Charles I to the scaffold. Charles was five years old in 1605, and during the early interrogations of Guy Fawkes King James repeatedly asked him whether he felt no qualms at the thought of the death of the innocent royal children. Fawkes remained defiant.

Topical allusions abound in *Macbeth*, which portrays the murder of a Scottish king by a regicide whose erstwhile companion Banquo was an ancestor of the Stuarts – but does it contain other encoded references? It was written immediately after *King Lear*, therefore probably during June and July in time perhaps for a first performance before the King in Oxford on 1 August 1606.[2] *Macbeth* is sometimes said to be about the dangers of ambition, and ambition is certainly a motif. What is more striking, however, is the extent to which this play is child-obsessed. No other Shakespeare text features so many children, and at every level: actual children, like little Macduff, Fleance, and even young Siward, but above all in metaphor, simile, and symbol, as in the bloody apparitions, one of which features 'a child crowned, with a tree in his hand'. One of Shakespeare's best-known lines is Lady Macbeth's 'I have given suck, and know / How tender 'tis to love the babe that milks me' – which she then swears she would kill to validate her oath. When Macduff learns the dreadful news of the slaughter of his entire family, one of his first baffled reflections is 'He has no children'.

The portrayal of the Macbeths as a doomed but devoted and guilt-ridden couple who cannot reproduce is disturbing. Their infertility signals nature's intervention against them. The murder of the king makes Macbeth the most unnatural of men, a deadly traitor to the social concordat which echoes the ordained order of the natural universe. In depicting Macbeth as childless – unlike his wife – Shakespeare inflicts on him a symbolic version of the ritual punishment of traitors: the official doctrine to justify the barbaric ripping-off of a traitor's 'privy member' held that traitors were freaks of nature and therefore must never again engender offspring. As a most unnatural man, Macbeth will never have progeny: his wife has not only had a baby in the past, but signally fails to become a monster. Guilt drives her to madness, and her haunting jingle about Lady Macduff, 'The Thane of Fife had a wife, where is she now?' is as evocative as her compulsive, futile washing of her hands.

The many children in *Macbeth* are all male, and even the women in the play, with the exception of Lady Macduff, are either half-male or try desperately to pervert their feminine nature: the weird sisters have beards, and Lady Macbeth summons the spirits of darkness to descend on her and turn her milk to gall. Much has been made of Shakespeare having had a difficult relationship with women, but at the same time it is clear that he associated the feminine with benign nature, with caring for, loving, and protecting the vulnerable, particularly children, other women, and parents. Few of his lines are more revealing in this respect than Lady Macbeth's about the wife of the Thane of Fife, but almost equally telling is her protest that she would have killed Duncan herself if only he had not looked like her father: 'Had he not resembled / My father as he slept, I had done't.' For a moment there is a glimpse of Lady Macbeth's past, of a time when she was a little girl, perhaps, and watched her father sleeping. By anchoring her moral nature in this kind of image Shakespeare roots her firmly in a kinder, gentler self. The Folio text is the only source text for the play, and in it Shakespeare never actually refers to the character 'Lady Macbeth': She is only ever 'lady' and 'Macbeth's wife', just as Lady Macduff is called 'Macduff's wife' and 'wife'.

Nature and time are great healers in Shakespeare's plays. For all the weird sisters' promises, Macbeth would prefer *not* to have to act to become king, and at first steps back from the prospect of achieving power. After all, if it was written that he would be king, then he will be king: 'If chance will have me king, why chance may crown me / Without my stir.' The line and a half which immediately follow on are among the most comforting Shakespeare ever wrote: 'Come what come may / Time and the hour runs through the roughest day.' This is Shakespeare's version of a comforting cliché – 'this too will pass', he might have written today. Like everyone, Shakespeare too needed metaphorical crutches to get through life. He knew full well that there is no such thing as total evil. Macbeth is almost a good man gone bad, rather than a bad man becoming very bad.

Macbeth is dyed red in blood, more so than any other Shakespeare text, from the bloody sergeant of the first line of the second scene to the blood on Macbeth's hands that will 'the multitudinous seas incarnadine', the bloody child, and, finally, the man who kills the killer, Macduff, who probably killed his mother at his birth, because he was delivered by Caesarean section, which was almost invariably fatal to mothers in Shakespeare's time. If Shakespeare was involved with Jane Davenant and had fathered her child, new-born babies and the dangers of childbirth may have been on Shakespeare's mind at just this time. In Macbeth's exhortation to his wife to 'bring forth men children only', Shakespeare may have had in mind the 'man child' who was his son or godson. None of Jane Davenant's London babies survived, and the reason for the Davenants' move to Oxford, leaving behind a prospering business in the Vintry, has been attributed to just this; certainly, after the move she went on to carry another seven children, including William and Robert, who lived to adulthood. The many children in *Macbeth* may perhaps, in part at least, owe their lives to Shakespeare's sense of finally having a son restored to him – not Hamnet, but another William.

At the same time, it may be that one of the metaphorical children in *Macbeth* conceals a more profound and dangerous gesture of allegiance. Shortly before the murder of the king, Macbeth is pondering the moral implications of his planned assassination. He starts with a number of evasive euphemisms which circle around the act of murder without actually naming it: 'If it were done when 'tis done, then 'twere well / It were done quickly.' Then, and seemingly from nowhere, images of 'angels, trumpet-tongued' and of heavenly babies surge through the verse:

> And pity, like a naked new-born babe,
> Striding the blast, or heaven's cherubin horsed
> Upon the sightless couriers of the air,
> Shall blow the horrid deed in every eye
> That tears shall drown the wind.

These are images that at first seem to sit incongruously with the king of the 'barren sceptre' – unless, that is, the 'new-born babe' refers to another baby that featured in the poetry of the period, the infant Christ in Father Robert Southwell's vision of the night before Christmas, 'The Burning Babe':

> As I in hoary winter's night stood shivering in the snow,
> Surprised I was with sudden heat, which made my heart to glow,
> And lifting up a fearful eye, to view what fire was near,
> A pretty babe all burning bright did in the air appear;
> Who, scorched with excessive heat, such floods of tears did shed,
> As though his floods should quench his flames, which with his tears
>   were bred . . .
> With this he vanished out of sight, and swiftly shrunk away,
> And straight I called unto mind that it was Christmas Day.

The imagery and resonances are close enough to suggest that at the very least Shakespeare remembered Southwell's poem when he wrote the play. If the similarities were intended as a deliberate tribute to the dead Southwell, it could be suggestive about the way Shakespeare positioned himself with regard to the Catholics. On the other hand, it was probably quite characteristic of Shakespeare that he should pay homage to Southwell's poetic genius while at the same time – in the Porter's lines on equivocation – ridiculing his and Garnett's tactics.

The plague struck London again during the summer of 1606, when Shakespeare was probably finishing *Macbeth*. The theatres closed as usual and there followed an interminable period of interdiction which lasted throughout 1607 and stretched on into April 1608. Even then there was only a short remission from closure. Effectively, there was a crippling 30-month moratorium on acting. It is hard to gauge the extent of the havoc this caused. The actors were compelled to tour to earn a living. It must have been tough, and probably made the company value their footing at court more highly. In a work printed in 1609 Shakespeare's contemporary, the playwright Thomas Dekker, fed up with it all, lamented the closure of the playhouses, standing now like empty taverns 'that have cast out their masters, the doors locked up, the flags, like their bushes, taken down; or rather like houses lately infected, from whence the affrighted dwellers are fled, in hope to live better in the country.' There is little to do now, he notes, but to stroll idly through the fields or else 'to drink up the day and night in a tavern, loathsome, to be ever riding upon that beast with two heads, lechery, most damnable'. And all this time the bear- and bull-baiting venues continued to operate their business: 'the company of the Bears hold together still; they play their tragicomedies as lively as ever they did; the pied bull here keeps a tossing and a roaring when the Red Bull dares not stir.'[3]

Shakespeare, however, was a wealthy man now. He may have worried about the loss of profits while the Globe was closed, but he seems to have been far from fed up: in the teeth of the closure of the theatres and immediately following on from *Macbeth*, he wrote his rhetorically most spectacular play, *Antony and Cleopatra*. No other play in the canon is so insouciantly inventive: Shakespeare has let rip his incomparable command of the language to celebrate the historical adultery between the famous Roman commander and the legendary Egyptian queen. In *Antony and Cleopatra* the traditional boundaries between language and its referent are almost elided as the language of the play becomes pure rhetorical theatre. While *Romeo and Juliet* is suffused with tenderness and a lyricism that aims to capture in language the poetry of a teenage relationship, the pulse of *Antony and Cleopatra* beats in the sounds of English itself. When Cleopatra conjures up in her mind's eye her past with Antony, she finds that 'Eternity was in our lips and eyes, / Bliss in our brows' bent, none our parts so poor / But was a race of heaven.' Her staged appearance in death provokes from Octavius the phrase 'strong toil of grace', and Charmian claims that in death there now lies 'a lass unparalleled'.

The play cuts loose from both conventional morality and also, or so it would appear, from the physical theatre. It is an odd fact that this undoubted masterpiece of Shakespeare's maturity has yet to enjoy a truly outstanding success in performance. Perhaps, while the theatres were closed, Shakespeare wrote a play that was essentially not actable, a drama of utter exuberance and imaginative freedom, a text best read aloud for the sheer magic of its words. But his plays were the shared property of the entire company, and on them depended the welfare of the shareholders: when the plays were great theatre, they filled the house; when they were not, the company lost out. It is unlikely that Shakespeare deliberately wrote a play that would not translate well on to the stage.

After the bleakness of *King Lear* and *Macbeth*, the luminosity of *Antony and Cleopatra* comes almost as a shock. Something must have happened in the autumn of 1606 to brighten Shakespeare's mood. If the middle-aged Gloucester suffered dreadfully for his adultery, Antony enjoys his to the full. The ground has of course shifted, from the essentially Judaeo–Christian worlds of *King Lear* and *Macbeth* to the classical age, with very different concepts of sexual morality. At the beginning of the play's ten-year action Antony is forty-three years old, Cleopatra is twenty-eight – the ages given by Plutarch, whose biography of Antony Shakespeare follows very closely. In late 1606 when Shakespeare was writing *Antony and Cleopatra* he was himself in his forty-third year and Jane Davenant was thirty-eight, exactly Cleopatra's age at the end of the play. Antony and Cleopatra openly celebrate their 'mature' adultery. Cleopatra airily dismisses any comparison between her affair with Antony and her youthful fling with Caesar – back then she was, in her own words, in her 'salad days'; now she is with 'Phoebus' amorous pinches black, / And wrinkled deep in time' and Antony, her 'man of men', is the better for loving the older her.

Cleopatra's darkness as an Egyptian Greek, 'a tawny front' in the disparaging words of the Romans, is an issue in the play and in Shakespeare. At three key points in his career – in the *Sonnets*, *Othello*, and *Antony and Cleopatra* – Shakespeare explicitly connects sexuality and skin colour. It seems probable that all three can be traced back to Emilia Lanier, and that Shakespeare was writing about Cleopatra at this point in his life because he himself made a connection between his two illicit affairs, with Emilia and Jane – just as he may have done in *Othello*, in calling one of his characters Emilia. Less than a year separates the guilt-ridden world of Gloucester and the celebratory sex of *Antony and Cleopatra*. If the works do indeed reflect Shakespeare's moods closely it seems reasonable to conclude that by late 1606 or early 1607 his relationship with Jane Davenant had settled into something far more relaxed than is suggested by the earlier works. It is interesting that Shakespeare gives the children of Antony and Cleopatra short shrift, while they figure prominently in the source. In his drama Shakespeare gets away with it – he has to, if he wants his audience to stay focused on the lovers: children would be a distraction. To that extent *Antony and Cleopatra* is antithetical to *Macbeth*: from a child-obsessed play he has moved to a play in which children are discarded so that the two seasoned middle-aged lovers can enjoy their relationship to the full. Here then may be Shakespeare having his fill, at almost the same time that his daughter Susanna was preparing to marry John Hall.

What Shakespeare and the company actually did during the closure is a matter for guesswork only. There may have been some playing in London in late 1607–8, for Shakespeare is known to have been there to play at court – which was extremely lucrative, netting the company up to £130 in just one Christmas season. An extensive tour seems the obvious answer yet, surprisingly, no known records place them in any given parish on any given date. But if they did not tour, how did they survive, and how was it that Shakespeare, for example, continued both to write, and to make enough money during this period to fund future substantial investments? The year 1606 had started darkly for Shakespeare. Its ending with *Antony and Cleopatra* suggests that he had found peace if not happiness, and had risen above moral sanctions about adultery. As an Anglican, Will Shakespeare was guilty of offending against one of the Ten Commandments; as Antony, he was a free classical spirit. The continuing closure of the theatres meant that Shakespeare was almost certainly spending more time in the Midlands, and it would have been comparatively easy for him to see Jane Davenant in Oxford – an ease perhaps reflected in the guilt-free sexual bliss of *Antony and Cleopatra*. If Southampton, Shakespeare, and Emilia Bassano-Lanier had their counterparts in Bassanio, Antonio, and Portia, it may be that Antony and Cleopatra were Will Shakespeare and Jane Davenant.

26

A Wedding and a Funeral: 1607

SUSANNA MARRIED JOHN Hall in Holy Trinity on Friday 5 June 1607. Since there was no playing in London, her father was almost certainly present to give her away. As Susanna and John Hall plighted their troth to each other during the wedding ceremony of the Book of Common Prayer, presumably Anne Hathaway stood next to Will. There is no way of knowing what she made of his many absences, or whether (or what) she may have known or suspected about her husband's life in London and, latterly perhaps, in Oxford. Perhaps she sought comfort and solace in her daughters who seemed to have adored her, as their stirring tribute to Anne after her death seems to indicate. In what might be Shakespeare's home-coming play, *The Winter's Tale* (1611), the mother, Hermione, is rejected by her husband Leontes in a temporary fit of insane jealousy. She is a model of virtue and nine months pregnant, while he is a domestic tyrant. At the end of the play she seems to remain unmoved by his pleas for forgiveness and does not talk to him, but addresses her daughter instead. If Shakespeare had wrongly accused Anne of disloyalty at the time of *Hamlet*, it may be that they had reached a similar point in their marriage by 1611. If Leontes and Hermione evoke Will and Anne in middle age, then Shakespeare must have felt desperately sorry for what he had done to her.

After her marriage the bride usually moved into the house of the bridegroom and his family, just as Anne had twenty-five years earlier. But there were no Halls in Stratford before John Hall's arrival there, and it is likely therefore that he and Susanna moved into New Place first before eventually settling into the premises now known as Hall's Croft in Old Town. It seems probable that John and Susanna, unlike Will and Anne, did not have sex until they were married. It may be that his Puritan backbone led him to master desire – or perhaps his knowledge of human biology was simply better than his father-in-law's. Whatever the reason, it was not until 21 February 1608, almost nine months to the day since their wedding on 5 June 1607, that a child was born to the Halls. They named their daughter Elizabeth, after the old Queen, or the new King's daughter.

At some point Shakespeare made his way to London again. He was now a freeholder, a landlord, a tithe collector, a Globe and Blackfriars shareholder, and a land speculator in Welcombe to the north of Stratford. He no longer lived alone in London; his youngest brother Edmund, who was twenty-seven in 1607, was there too. It is impossible to know just when he had left Stratford, but as an aspiring player he would hardly have headed for London after the closure of the theatres in July 1606. He may have gone after his father's death in late 1601. The most plausible reason for Will and Edmund to be together in London in late autumn 1607 was for a performance at court during the Christmas 1607–8 season. A year earlier the King's Men had performed *King Lear* before the King on Boxing Day. Perhaps there is a connection between the fact that Shakespeare's villain in *King Lear* is called Edmund and the presence of Edmund Shakespeare – though it is true that the name occurs prominently in Harsnett, having been chosen by Weston in honour of Campion. It is inconceivable that Will would not have wanted to further his younger brother's career. It has already been argued that Shakespeare may have played the role of a limping Edgar in *King Lear*; it would perhaps be quite like him to cast his brother Edmund as Edmund in the play, a younger brother wanting to usurp the position of his elder sibling. Will as Edgar and Edmund as Edmund Gloucester would have invested the part of the Bastard with a piquant immediacy, at least as far as the Shakespeare brothers were concerned, at the same time affording the young man a superb dramatic vehicle in one of his brother's masterpieces.

Edmund Shakespeare's triumphs, if any, were short-lived. While Susanna was burgeoning in Stratford, Edmund buried his illegitimate baby in London and then himself succumbed to sickness or plague towards the end of December 1607. It was a bitter winter, even for the times when winters generally were harsher in the south of England than they are now. It was a small Ice Age, and the Thames froze over repeatedly. On 8 December 1607 a severe frost set in. By Boxing Day parts of the river were covered in ice and a few days later Londoners were crossing the Thames on foot 'at every ebb and half flood . . . in divers places'. The severe cold continued in this fashion until the middle of January 1608.[1] Whenever the Thames froze over, market stalls sprang up on it as soon as the ice could bear them. London traders then as now were quick off the mark, but perhaps the most imaginative response to the severe frosts was that of a woman who lay down on the ice for a glacial cuddle with the river. She wanted, she said, to be able to say that she had lain with Old Father Thames.

Such a light-hearted note would have been alien to Shakespeare on 31 December 1607, for on that New Year's Eve he buried his younger brother in St Saviour's in Southwark. Edmund was sent off in some style with, as the fee-book of St Saviour's notes, 'a forenoon knell of the great bell'. For the considerable sum of twenty shillings Shakespeare ensured that Edmund was buried in the church and not in the church-yard outside. He seems to have been almost as solicitous about his brother's remains as he later was about his own. The relevant entry in the registers of St Saviour's for Thursday 31 December 1607 reads: 'Edmond Shakespeare, a player: in the church.' Shakespeare himself was of an age when he must have begun to expect losses among those he loved, though his father had lasted well and he, Gilbert, Joan, Richard, and Edmund, like their mother, had survived until now. Edmund was Mary Arden's first child to die since little Anne, twenty-eight years before; the fact that he was the youngest must have been hard on her, and perhaps contributed to her own demise nine months later.

The burial of Edmund's baby in St Giles Cripplegate in the Barbican suggests that he lived in Shoreditch at the time, perhaps even in one of the Burbages' rooms in Holywell, but Shakespeare probably chose St Saviour's for Edmund's burial because it was the Bankside players' church as well as the parish church of Southwark.[2] Nearly half the names listed in the 1623 Folio under 'principal actors' also appear in its registers. The funeral service for Edmund was probably held in St John's Chapel, off the north transept of St Saviour's. Three hundred years later this side chapel was renamed Harvard Chapel in honour of

John Harvard, who was baptized here barely a month before Edmund Shakespeare's funeral. Shakespeare almost certainly knew Harvard's grandfather Thomas Rogers from Stratford, and might even have known of John Harvard's baptism in St Saviour's. As he sat in the chapel mourning his brother, a monument next to the altar seems to have caught Shakespeare's eye. It was the tomb of Chaucer's great fourteenth-century contemporary, his friend the poet John Gower, author of, among others, the well-known poem *Confessio Amantis* which includes tales from Shakespeare's favourite writer Ovid. The monument is still in the church and still bears the legend that was on it when Edmund Shakespeare died, even though it migrated to the north side of the main nave long ago.

Shakespeare refers to the poet Gower only in *Pericles*, and since the play was written in the spring of 1608 it seems probable that seeing Gower's tomb in St John's Chapel set off a train of thought in the echo chamber of his imagination. Perhaps he comforted himself with the Christian promise that the dead would be resurrected, that his brother would live on in eternity, and that all losses would be restored. Something like this seems to lie behind the words of the Prologue of *Pericles*, when he imagines Gower risen from 'ashes ancient'. As a writer he could and did wake the dead: he had already used Gower's *Confessio Amantis* as a source for one of his earliest plays, *The Comedy of Errors*. He also used precisely that language of resurrection when writing about his own creative genius in *The Tempest* and casting himself as Prospero.

The loss of his brother must have been a blow to Shakespeare, the *pater familias* mourning now not his own child Hamnet but his mother's child, the family's baby brother. Under the circumstances the closure of the theatres was probably a blessing, leaving Shakespeare free to go home to comfort his mother and to find solace himself with his family. Presumably another and happier reason for wanting to be home in Stratford in the spring of 1608 was the arrival of his first grandchild, on 21 February 1608. Perhaps this lay behind Shakespeare's intense focus in *Pericles* on a mother giving birth. In this play, both mother and daughter are lost before they are found again. Whereas in *King Lear* a daughter dies in the arms of her despairing father, in *Pericles* a father so grief-stricken that he becomes mute is reunited with 'a beloved daughter and a wife', and thus learns to speak again.

Pericles was entered on the Stationers' Register on 20 May 1608, suggesting that the play was finished in time for the reopening of the theatres in April 1608 – as to which the company's friends on the Privy Council had perhaps tipped them the wink. But after nine long months the London theatres reopened only to close again three months later, in mid-July. It may have been this which made George Wilkins, Shakespeare's collaborator on *Pericles*, publish a novel closely based on the play that same year. Even if Shakespeare did not write the first two acts of the play, he may have had a revising hand in them, since some of the writing seems unmistakably his. The three undoubted Shakespearian Acts, III–V, move the imaginative action on to a different plane, away from the stylized plot about incestuous potentates to the birth of a baby girl, the 'death' of her mother at sea, and the restoration of the entire family through good fortune as well as the offices of a brilliant physician.

Gower enters as the Prologue to Act III to alert the audience to the forthcoming arrival of a baby. She is born during a storm at sea, hence her name, Marina. Her mother Thaisa dies during the birth, or so everyone assumes. Before entrusting her body to the sea, Pericles bids farewell to his seemingly dead queen: 'A terrible child-bed hast thou had, my dear, / No light, no fire.' The phrase 'child-bed' occurs three times only in Shakespeare, twice here in *Pericles* and once in *The Winter's Tale*, when Leontes's wronged wife Hermione complains bitterly that she was 'the child-bed privilege denied, which 'longs / To women of all fashion.' The appearance of the phrase now in *Pericles* can surely not really be separated from Susanna's very recent experience of giving birth. It provides as much of a bridge between Shakespeare's life and his drama as his use of 'godson' in *King Lear*.

Almost immediately after Thaisa's premature committal to the sea Cerimon makes his appearance, the only doctor outside *All's Well*, *Macbeth*, and *Cymbeline* with a significant speaking part. It is hard not to think of Dr John Hall when Cerimon introduces himself in lines written within weeks of Hall and Susanna becoming parents. He always, he claims, preferred 'virtue and cunning' to fame and wealth, because they are not subject to mutability and instead can make a man a god. What he calls the 'secret art' of the physician and the exercise of his craft have led him to an understanding of nature's 'blessed infusions' and thereby the gift of cures. To be a healer confers true pleasure and peace of mind, whereas a desperate ambition for honour or money pleases only 'the fool and death'. The way Cerimon contrasts virtue and skilled knowledge ('cunning') with social standing and wealth sounds a Calvinist note worthy of John Bunyan. Here, in the middle of *Pericles*, the audience seems to be eavesdropping on Hall talking to Shakespeare about his medical expertise and his idealistic dedication to it. Cerimon's contempt for 'tottering honour' found a remarkable parallel in 1626, when Hall refused a knighthood. Hall may have had other reasons for turning it down, but if Cerimon is his mentor, it cannot be thought unexpected.

Cerimon restores Thaisa to life from near death: perhaps Hall did the same for Susanna – perhaps things went badly wrong during Elizabeth's birth, and she remained an only child because her mother suffered complications that rendered future pregnancies impossible. Should the first volume of John Hall's medical journal ever come to light, it might reveal much; the extant second volume only covers the years 1617 to 1635, plus a handful of earlier cases but not, unfortunately, Shakespeare's last illness. Hall records treating his wife and daughter at different times but he makes no mention anywhere of obstetrics – not unexpectedly, since this was the preserve of midwives. However, if something went wrong during Elizabeth's birth it may be that John Hall was able to restore Susanna to life when the midwives had given her up as lost. Perhaps that is why Shakespeare has Cerimon declare that his medical skills make him a god.

Pericles boasts the most visceral brothel scenes in Shakespeare and is one of only two plays to use the word 'prostitute', the other one being *All's Well*. Although his co-author Wilkins lived at the corner of Turnmill and Cowcross, a notoriously louche area of town, the brothel scenes are strictly Shakespeare's. If Shakespeare's collaborator on *Pericles* had inside knowledge of the world and language of London's fleshpots, he also knew the Mountjoys and Belotts: he testified in their lawsuit, and the newly-wed Belotts eventually boarded in his house.[3] It seems that Wilkins and Shakespeare both lodged at the Mountjoys' for a while, hence their acquaintance. Whatever dramatic ambitions Wilkins may have harboured, his collaboration with Will Shakespeare availed him little, since the theatres stayed resolutely shut after their brief reopening. Wilkins could not really connect with the idiom of Shakespeare, resonating with the most intense lyrical yearning. If ever there was a drama of wish-fulfilment, the last three acts of *Pericles* are it. On being reunited with his daughter, Pericles urges Helicanus to give him a gash, 'Lest this great sea of joys rushing upon me/ O'erbear the shores of my mortality / And drown me with their sweetness.' In a scene in which a dream does indeed come true, Shakespeare is at his most mature and expressive: Pericles is having 'the rarest dream that e'er dulled sleep / Did mock sad fools withal'. Shakespeare could conjure up harmony and happiness in his plays, but not of course in his own life. He had not been able to bring back his son from the dead, he could not spare his daughter a difficult childbed. But if perhaps John Hall did just that, coaxing Susanna back from the abyss, it accounts for the emotional charge of *Pericles.*

Shakespeare was probably in London, appearing in the first performances of *Pericles,* when in Stratford – and on his forty-fourth birthday, no less – a murder took place. It was the night of 22 April 1608, and in the Swan down on Bridge Street a row broke out between two men. They were Richard Waterman *alias* Dixon, the landlord's brother, and a butcher by the name of Lewis Gilbert. There had been bad blood between them for a while before they clashed in a downstairs parlour in the tavern part of the inn. Waterman tried to evict Gilbert, but the latter obstructed the door. Two of Waterman's daughters and their mother witnessed all this, and one of them screamed, 'He will spoil my father, he will murder my father.' Presumably Gilbert had at this point drawn what was later described as his 'long knife'; he was, after all, a butcher. Upon this the landlord, who was sitting by the fire next door talking to a friend, rushed in to help. He forced open the door and grabbed Gilbert by the collar of his doublet to throw him out. Gilbert there and then stabbed him 'in the right side of the navel' and ran off. Thomas Waterman died the same evening and the following day the inquest jury returned a verdict of murder against Gilbert. His subsequent fate is not known, but if he was caught he would have been hanged. Shakespeare undoubtedly knew the dead landlord and his family because the Watermans were local glovers turned publicans. Not only that, but it is possible that many years earlier John Shakespeare had been apprenticed to Waterman's grandfather, whose wife hailed from the wolds south of Snitterfield and knew Will Shakespeare's grandfather Richard.

By the time of Waterman's murder in 1608 Shakespeare was a grandfather and surrounded by women – his mother, his wife, two daughters, and a granddaughter. But he also had a son-in-law, who was becoming a friend and confidant. Happiness over the baby's arrival and her mother's survival may well be reflected in the joyous reunion scenes in *Pericles*. Yet the still-recent death of Edmund must have tempered the family's cheer, and what Pericles calls 'the shores of my mortality' were becoming all too transparent to Shakespeare.

His whereabouts in the spring and summer of 1608 are uncertain but, remarkably, in August 1608 the King's Men expanded their operating base in London, taking possession of the Blackfriars theatre as a playing space. A seven-strong syndicate set up by Richard Burbage consisted of himself and his brother Cuthbert, Shakespeare, Heminges, Condell, William Sly, and Thomas Evans. This last was presumably the son of the Henry Evans who had led the boy players in the Blackfriars from 1596 until the spring of 1608, when they were dissolved after a performance of a play by Chapman upset the French ambassador.[4] It was twelve years since old James Burbage had first acquired these premises, and the opposition which had then blocked playing in the precinct had died down. Perhaps the company sought to repossess the Blackfriars theatre now because they needed a smarter venue, somewhere less public, where plague would not routinely 'stop play'. It is difficult to see any other reason for them to move just then when they already had the Globe, which had now been lying empty for two years. The Blackfriars stage was to be very different, no longer a theatre in the round but a much smaller, rectangular indoors space, a precursor to the modern proscenium-arch theatre. Some tickets cost seven times their equivalent at the Globe. The Blackfriars aimed for a very different audience, and was effectively a halfway house between the Globe and the court.

It is inconceivable that Shakespeare should not have been involved in these Blackfriars negotiations; he was too important in the company, and then there was his business flair. It seems safe to assume that he was in London during August 1608, and that he had probably been so at least since April that year, when the theatres reopened. The fact that the boy players were acting during March suggests that Blackfriars may have enjoyed certain privileges, perhaps even an occasional exemption from the ban on performances, making it doubly desirable. The King's Men saw their opportunity, and seized it. It was now or never. Big profits loomed on the horizon. But no sooner were they installed at Blackfriars than the theatres were closed again, for another indeterminate period.[5]

27

Losing a Mother and a Daughter: 1609–11

THE MOVE TO Blackfriars coincided with the death of Shakespeare's mother, nearly seven years to the day since his father's death. They buried Mary Arden on 9 September 1608. The register of Holy Trinity does not reveal whether she rests inside the church or in the churchyard, but the funeral arrangements made for Shakespeare's brother Edmund at St Saviour's nine months earlier suggest that, where possible, Shakespeare preferred interment somewhere inside the church. Though he may have been back in the same church five weeks later for the baptism of his godson William Walker, remembered in his will, it was 'things dying' rather than 'things living', to borrow his own words from *The Winter's Tale*, that preoccupied him. That the outcome was a tragedy about a mother and a son is further proof of Shakespeare's obsessive need to write, and to write about his own life above all. The death of his father resulted in *Hamlet*, in which he seems to have worked through various obsessions and anxieties about his mother, his brothers, his dead son, and the Earl of Southampton. In the play triggered by his mother's death the hero was not a version of Southampton or young Hamnet but perhaps of the middle-aged Shakespeare whose wife, like the chaste Virgilia of the play whom her husband Coriolanus calls 'my gracious silence', may have been similarly silenced by her husband.

Mary Arden had lasted well into her late sixties, supposing her to have been eighteen or so when she married in 1557 or 1558. She had lived through the early triumphs, trials, and tribulations of John Shakespeare's twin business careers of glover and wool trader. Presumably she enjoyed the trappings of honour that came with John holding office in the town, particularly when he became mayor. The middle years, when John was in disgrace and went to ground in

Henley Street, would have been hard, particularly when her eldest son William got into trouble. His subsequent successful London career could not have been anticipated, but the fruits were there for all to see in the amount of wealth he accumulated in a short space of time, enough to recover the family fortunes and to fund a successful application for a coat-of-arms.

The treatment of mothers in his last plays suggests that the relationship between Shakespeare and Mary Arden was never resolved, that all his life he was closer to his father. Shakespeare's preferred solution for the mothers of his heroes and heroines is to have them disappear: the boy–girl twins in *Twelfth Night* no longer have a mother, nor do Desdemona, the daughters in *King Lear*, Innogen in *Cymbeline*, or Miranda in the *Tempest*. When a mother appears in *The Winter's Tale* she becomes metaphorically a statue, her son having died already, and in *Coriolanus* the mother destroys her son. *Coriolanus*, featuring Volumnia, a formidable and destructive mother, followed almost certainly in the wake of Mary Arden's death and is arguably Shakespeare's most disturbing tragedy. It must have been written after the great frost of 1607–8 which sealed the Thames in sheets of ice, hence no doubt the phrase 'the coal of fire upon the ice'. If this provides an earliest possible date in the winter of 1608, an important clue in the play suggests a specific later date. In Act III Coriolanus berates the patricians for having granted 'Hydra here to choose an officer' who will turn their 'current in a ditch, / And make your channel his'. In short, the people, a multi-headed snake, should not be represented by their tribunes because they will eventually push them to abuse the patricians' privileges. The image of ditches and channels seems to evoke Sir Hugh Myddleton's ambitious project for supplying London with spring water from Hertfordshire by cutting a four-mile long special trench. There may be a more specific allusion to the profiteering aspect of this new project, not publicly funded but a private venture that pledged water only to paying customers. Work on the Myddleton project started in February 1609 so that Shakespeare was probably writing *Coriolanus* around then.

Coriolanus portrays a mother–son relationship that is suspect and destructive. Volumnia is an overpowering figure who sees her son primarily in martial terms, at the expense of both his and her humanity.

He is rumoured to have become an engine of war 'to please his mother' and he is lost when she disapproves of his decision to spurn a popular plebiscite. In the end Volumnia persuades him not to sack the city of Rome out of revenge for its treacherous treatment of him. He knows that to obey her will mean certain death to him, but does so anyway. Before parting from her he asks, 'O mother, mother, / What have you done?' There is no recognizable maternal warmth in Volumnia, who sees her son as a warrior hero to the exclusion of all else. When she asserts that the breasts of Hecuba suckling Hector did not look lovelier than his forehead 'when it spit forth blood / At Grecian sword, contemning', it is a long distance from the tenderness of the baby at Lady Macbeth's breast.

While Volumnia is fiercely ambitious for her son in war and in peace, his love for her is unqualified and unquestioned. All his achievements, it seems, have been only to please her. If Shakespeare's relationship with Mary Arden was anything like this, then perhaps he also stood at his mother's graveside in Holy Trinity saying to himself 'O mother, mother, what have you done?' It is possible that Shakespeare had striven ceaselessly to please Mary Arden above all, but felt that she never quite reciprocated his devotion. Earlier in the year he had had to break to her the news of her youngest child's death. If the expensive funeral at Southwark is any indication, Shakespeare must have done his utmost by Edmund. What he could not do of course was to save him. Perhaps Mary Arden blamed her eldest son for taking the baby of the family with him to London and exposing him to the dangers of the plague.

Coriolanus is the most austere and masculine play in Shakespeare's canon, as well as the most morally opaque, unmistakably hostile, uncomprehending, and alienated. In similar vein, Shakespeare now did something which must have deeply upset his wife: he published his *Sonnets*. A loving and devoted husband would surely not have released poems which implicated him in at least two extra-marital liaisons. It seems clear that he did not censor the poems before publication, and he was probably responsible for the narrative sequence – after all, only he knew the plot of his own sentimental life. His decision to publish now may have arisen partly out of frustration with the continuing closure of the theatres. Years earlier he had published *Venus and*

Adonis and *The Rape of Lucrece* during a similarly prolonged break in playing; now he had written *Macbeth*, *Antony and Cleopatra*, *Pericles*, and *Coriolanus* with never a chance of putting them on. Nor could he print them, because to do so would jeopardize his company's future investment in these scripts.

Presumably Shakespeare decided to issue the *Sonnets* – his only work not so far exposed to the public – because he wanted the money. Either the need was pressing by 1609, or he had delayed publication to spare his mother the truth about his relationship with Southampton and his affair with Emilia Bassano. To the very end he may have been reluctant to offend or upset her. Now she was gone, and he felt no such scruples as regards his wife, his children and siblings, or indeed the Dark Lady and Southampton.

The fact that the poems were not reprinted after 1609, and the dedication of the First Folio fourteen years later to Pembroke and Montgomery, may point to a temporary coolness between Shakespeare and Southampton over publication of the sonnets. On the other hand, the *Sonnets* may themselves have been a peace-offering to the earl. Relations may in any case have been strained at this time because on 28 January 1609 *Troilus and Cressida* was entered for publication on the Stationers' Register and then printed in quarto. It is hard to believe that Shakespeare would have been a happy party to this reopening of old wounds, but the continued period of interdiction was bound to cause the company to generate income where it could. The satirical portrayal of Southampton as Achilles' male whore may well have come about through political pressure in the first place, but it was still a slur. As a slur in a hitherto unpublished play it had long been forgotten, with no life beyond the spoken word and, if the address to the reader which follows the substituted second title-page of *Troilus and Cressida* is to be believed, was only ever seen by a small, select audience. But printing it was a very different matter. Now everyone who could read could discover the sexual proclivities of two of the country's best-known grandees, with the added innuendo that the real bond between Southampton and Essex eight years earlier may have been their sexual perversion. The history of the publication of *Troilus and Cressida* is notoriously tricky to unravel down to its inclusion, at the last minute and anomalously, in the First Folio, hence its absence

331

from the Folio contents page. Shakespeare probably had no veto over the printing of the play – but only he could have initiated publication of the *Sonnets*, and if it was not because he needed the money, perhaps his aim was to counteract the damage done to his friendship with Southampton by the publication of the quarto of the play. If so, he may have done more harm than good, because rather than assuaging them the poems further consolidated suspicion about Southampton's sexual tendencies.

If Shakespeare kept copies of his sonnets, including the early so-called 'Hathaway' poem, it is hard to imagine that he would not also have owned quartos of his plays and poems in his 'study of books', as his son-in-law John Hall called it. The same study probably contained sets of Holinshed and Plutarch. During the long enforced sabbatical from playing that started towards the middle of 1606 Shakespeare may well have been rewriting plays in his study at home, using his own printed quarto versions. The 'revised' Folio text of *King Lear* probably originated with Shakespeare himself annotating one of his own 1608 quartos of the play during the interminable break from playing.

That Shakespeare's 154 sonnets are in some kind of order seems unarguable, and this apparent chronology immeasurably enhances the narrative. In offering the poems to the printer Shakespeare could presumably have taken the opportunity to revise them and perhaps reshape the story, but he seems not to have done so to any extent. The one thing a middle-aged grandfather might have been most concerned to excise, the homosexual subtext of his 'book', he emphatically did not. He may well have been reluctant to censor his own writing because there were other copies of the poems in circulation, making it difficult for him to depart from them at whim. Two of the most scandalous had in any case already been published in the best-selling *The Passionate Pilgrim* in 1599, including 144, about the poet's two loves. All literary London must have known. The association of the *Sonnets* with one of the most prominent noblemen in the land presumably enhanced their saleability and therefore he had to publish the real thing. Perhaps Shakespeare was prepared to sacrifice his wife's sensibilities to pecuniary considerations.

Thomas Thorpe published the first quarto of the poems in 1609 under the title *Shakespeare's Sonnets. Never before Imprinted*, with his famously delphic dedication 'To the only begetter of these ensuing sonnets, Mr W. H., all happiness and that eternity promised by our ever-living poet wisheth the well-wishing adventurer in setting forth', signed 'T[homas].T[horpe].' It is one of the most teasing literary mysteries of all time, and the identity of 'Master W. H.' remains elusive. Shakespeare himself might be meant, since as the author he could be thought to be 'the only begetter' of the sonnets, and this would account for the use of 'Master' ('Mr'), which is hardly a suitable form of address for the other obvious candidate, 'the Right Honourable Henry Wriothesley, Earl of Southampton, and Baron of Titchfield', to give him his full title as it is used in the dedications of both *Venus and Adonis* and *The Rape of Lucrece*. But if Shakespeare is intended by the 'only begetter', then 'H' for 'S' is a mistake of surprising magnitude in this otherwise elaborate and carefully crafted if maddeningly over-punctuated dedication, whereas it is temptingly easy to see 'W. H.' as the transposed initials of one H. W., Henry Wriothesley.

It has been argued that 'W. H.' should be read as William Herbert, who shares the dedication of the 1623 Folio with his brother Philip. But both were Knights of the Garter, and properly identified in the Folio as 'William Earl of Pembroke and etc. Lord Chamberlain to the King's most excellent Majesty' and 'Philip, Earl of Montgomery, and etc. Gentleman of his Majesty's Bedchamber'. It is hard to imagine either being addressed simply as 'Master', and Pembroke was only ten years old in 1590, when the first seventeen sonnets were probably written.[1] Furthermore, the *Sonnets* were not included in the first Folio dedicated to Pembroke; nor were the two longer poems, already dedicated to Southampton. It seems arguable therefore that the *Sonnets* were also addressed to him, and that this was known at the time. The Pembrokes would hardly have welcomed the inclusion in a volume inscribed to them of a work originally offered to someone else. Southampton seems to have been displeased by the entire venture of the *Sonnets* and probably disowned a dedication clear enough to his contemporaries though rendered ever more discreet by the passage of time.

There were many channels by which copies of the printed poems could easily reach Stratford, not least through Richard Field, who was flourishing in London and still had many family connections in Stratford. It is hard to believe that Field did not know about the *Sonnets*, or that he would not have read them – but why did he himself not print or publish them? There may be more than just a coincidence to that famous mention he gets in Shakespeare's *Cymbeline* which was written in 1610, the year after the publication of the poems. Even if one does not subscribe wholeheartedly to the view that Shakespeare was a misogynist, the *Sonnets* make painful reading for the Shakespeare marriage and may suggest that he cared little for the hurt they might cause to his wife.

The theatres reopened in the autumn of 1609. The King's Men had several new plays on their stocks, and two different venues for their performance. As always they hit the ground running, and playing allout at Blackfriars at last must have been exciting. Countless evening performances at court had given the company plenty of experience of staging plays at night, but to perform here was different. It would have been characteristic of Shakespeare to try to capitalize on the new stage, the sophisticated audience, and the potential for another kind of theatre. Shakespeare was surely part of the team that regrouped in London, but where he lived after 1609 is unknown.

A letter written by Shakespeare's 'cousin' Thomas Greene, lawyer and Stratford town clerk, survives from this time. He was living at New Place, having perhaps moved in with his wife after Mary Arden's death. On 9 September 1609 Thomas Greene wrote to a Stratford correspondent from whom he was trying to buy a house. He was intending to move into St Mary's House over in Churchway, close to Holy Trinity and directly east of a barn belonging to the Catholic diehard Reynolds. In a memorandum about the impending move, Greene mentions that he had cut down the walnut trees with his vendor's agreement, then notes that the vendor, George Brown, had in turn asked Greene's permission to 'sow his garden', which Greene readily granted 'because I perceived I might stay another year at New Place.' It is clear that the Greenes and the Shakespeares were close, not only from the fact that the Greenes appear to have named two of their children after Will and Anne and another one after the Halls' daughter Elizabeth: there is a sense of complete ease in his current situation in Greene's letter to his vendor. The Greenes must have moved out of

New Place in the course of the early summer of 1611, because in June that year the corporation minuted its decision 'to repair the church-yard wall at Master Greene's dwelling house'. Quite how substantial their new house was, with its barns and stables, is plain from Greene's offer of it and his tithes to the corporation for sale; the year after Shakespeare's death the whole estate fetched £640, considerably more than the total cost of the first Globe in London eighteen years earlier. At the time it was described as 'a pretty neat gentlemanlike house with a pretty garden and a little young orchard standing very sweet and quiet; the place and building within this 6 years cost above 400*l*.' Patently Greene was a rich man. His involvement with the Shakes-peares was obviously of a privileged nature, living as he did with them on a semi-permanent basis at just the time when Shakespeare was writing *Cymbeline* and *The Winter's Tale*. He was a man of some *gravitas* in Stratford, where he held the office of town clerk for four-teen years from 1603 on.

The Greenes were followed to Old Town not long afterwards by the Halls, and so in 1611 Judith was left behind alone at New Place, now indeed all the daughters of her father's house and all the brothers too, to paraphrase her alter ego Viola from *Twelfth Night*. The year 1611 is not a blank page in the life of Judith Shakespeare as far as the records are concerned. On the contrary, a document dated 4 December 1611 shows Judith's 'signature', and not just once but twice. The circumstances and people involved in the document suggest that Judith was moving away from the influence and tutelage of her father. In itself the document is unremarkable, merely the conveyance of a house in Wood Street. What is interesting about it is that Judith Shakespeare witnessed the transaction, 'signing' the deed of sale with a mark alongside that of Lettice Greene, the wife of the same Thomas Greene who had until recently lived at New Place.

The house in Wood Street was sold on behalf of the Quineys, Judith's future husband's family, the vendor Elizabeth ('Bess') Phillips-Quiney widow of Richard Quiney, twice mayor of Stratford. The Quineys were among the richest families in Stratford, but Bess Quiney had been left to provide for a horde of children following her hus-band's untimely death nine years before. In early May 1602 he had walked into a drunken tavern brawl in the course of which some of Sir Edward Greville's men were threatening the landlord with drawn daggers. Quiney had tried to quell the riot but 'had his head grievously broken' by one of Greville's retainers. A month later he was dead, presumably from his injury. Gilbert Shakespeare and Quiney had numbered some of Greville's men among their friends, but they were not friendly on this occasion – perhaps drink was to blame, or bad blood between Quiney and Greville, who had started to enclose the Bancroft with hedges in spite of strong protests from the corporation. Several stand-offs had ensued between him and the townspeople and mayor. At the time of the affray neither the Shakespeares nor the Quineys could have anticipated that their two families would one day be linked by marriage. The sale of the Wood Street property may have been intended to set up Thomas Quiney in business, for two days after it went through he bought a twenty-one-year lease of a house in High Street, the so-called Atwood tavern on the west side of High Street, north of the Harvard house, described in the lease as the house where 'Thomas Rutter now dwelleth'. He may well belong to the same Rutter family who eventually purchased the Maidenhead (the east wing of the Henley Street house) from the Hiccoxes and whose inventory has survived along with theirs.

The most obvious reason for Judith Shakespeare and Lettice Greene being called upon to act as witnesses would be that the Quiney and Shakespeare families were in the process of becoming still more closely linked. They had long been friends, and neighbours for even longer. And it was about this time that Judith's father wrote a play about a father surrendering his daughter to a young man: *The Tempest* may be even more about Judith than the comedy about twins a decade earlier, though Judith was of course twenty-six in 1611 whereas Miranda in the play is fourteen, and Judith was not motherless, unlike the princess in the play.

The first contemporary news of the play is of a court performance of 1 November 1611, possibly its first ever performance. This is so close in time to Judith's witnessing of a Quiney deed that the temptation to view them as somehow linked is hard to resist. It may be that Judith was being wooed in the summer or autumn of 1611, it would seem with Shakespeare's blessing, though it meant that he stood to lose his daughter. Since the proceeds went to Thomas Quiney, perhaps Judith signed the deed of sale as an interested party: it may be that she was betrothed to Quiney as early as the winter of 1611–12. But why did she not marry for another five years? It may be that she could not leave her parents' home because her services were still required to look after her mother. It is also possible, of course, that Judith held out against marrying Quiney, and that her decision to marry him was prompted by her father's illness. That would certainly account for the couple's failure to observe proper ecclesiastical procedure in 1616: they may have been hurrying to marry so that Shakespeare could give away his daughter before dying.

The daughter behind Miranda, Marina, and Perdita was probably Judith rather than Susanna, married mother of three-year old Elizabeth Hall. And if the literary magician from New Place is Prospero on his island, who might Ariel, Caliban, Ferdinand, and Antonio be? Clearly Shakespeare did more than just import his own household into this archly self-conscious play, which almost from the first was seen as his most personal work. He is undoubtedly both more and less than Prospero, as his friends clearly thought in placing the play right at the front of the commemorative 1623 Folio. Not only is it a defining work in its poetic brilliance and self-advertising artfulness, but it marks his formal leave-taking of the stage.

It is hard to doubt that Shakespeare saw himself as a wizard of language and books, who had for twenty years created airy nothings out of his imagination and become rich by it. The thought of Shakespeare, in contemplative retirement like Prospero, with every third thought of his grave, does not quite fit, however, for documentary and 'anecdotal' records both suggest otherwise. That said, there remain broad similarities. Shakespeare was retiring from the stage, entailing a physical move from one location to another, from London to Stratford; he was a wordsmith; he was a father with an unmarried daughter. Did he also have his Antonio, a brother who betrayed him and remained resolutely unrepentant? If so, it might have been Richard, as was noted earlier.

The Tempest hints at a thaw or rapprochement between Shakespeare and Southampton by 1611. The only known source for the plot of the play is an unpublished account of the Virginia expedition and the shipwreck in 1609 of the company's flagship, the *Sea-Adventure*, in the Bermudas, Ariel's 'still-vexed Bermoothes'. It is likely that Shakespeare learnt about this from Southampton who would have had a copy of William Strachey's pamphlet relating the tribulations of the *Sea-Adventure*. The ship went aground but the crew reappeared in May 1610 after what seemed like a miraculous drowning and rebirth in Bermuda, known at the time as the Isle of Devils. The much-feared islands in fact provided food, timber, and everything else the crew required to build two small pinnaces in which they were able to sail to Jamestown, their original destination. Caliban probably owes as much to the Virginia colonizers as to Montaigne's well-known essay on cannibals, called 'Of the Cannibals' in John Florio's translation.

While Shakespeare was writing about retirement, the Halls were planning to set up on their own somewhere in Old Stratford. The first rent return for Hall, dated 1612, does not reveal where he lived, but returns for the following three years, all for eightpence, place him in a close by Evesham or 'Easome' way, at the southern-most edge of seventeenth-century Stratford. A 1611 rent return notes a levy of eightpence 'for a close by Evesham way' on one Abraham Sturley – so perhaps Hall took over Sturley's home in 1612. This would be of some interest because Sturley, a Puritan of an earlier generation, may have had a hand in bringing Hall to Stratford in the first place. Thirteen years earlier the same Sturley had corresponded with Quiney about Shakespeare's readiness to invest in the Shottery yardlands. Before that and after leaving Cambridge, he had worked for the Lucys of Charlecote. Another possibility concerns Susanna's uncle, Shakespeare's brother Gilbert, whose death in his forty-sixth year was recorded on 3 February 1612 in the Holy Trinity registers where he was called '*adolescens*', meaning 'bachelor'. He had been Shakespeare's trusted lieutenant for many years. There is always the possibility that at some point he had moved out of New Place – supposing he ever lived there – to set up on his own as a corporation tenant in Old Town, and that it was *his* residence that the Halls now inherited.

28

'Do not go Gentle into that Good Night':
1612–15

ON MONDAY 11 May 1612 Shakespeare appeared as a witness in court at Westminster to testify in the Mountjoy–Belott case. The court records identify him as 'William Shakespeare of Stratford-upon-Avon', which seems to prove that by then he was no longer officially resident in London. He had probably left the Mountjoys' lodgings when the closure of the theatres in 1606 was prolonged, but may have returned between the autumn of 1609 and the end of 1611. The winter of 1612–13 was warmish and wet, with freak gales and severe storms. Four centuries ago, when its impact on farming and crop yields was more keenly felt than now, the weather was a perennial cause of concern. Memories harked back to the blighted years of the mid 1590s when the summers were cold and wet and the corn rotted where it stood, and the stark contrast with the intense cold of 1607–8, when thick snowfalls and severe frosts almost paralysed the country. But Shakespeare's company was busier than ever. In the run-up to the wedding of Princess Elizabeth to the Elector Palatine on 14 February 1613 they appeared twenty times at court, and on eight of those occasions they put on plays by Shakespeare.[1]

Ten days before the wedding Shakespeare had buried his brother Richard. Of Mary Arden's eight children only he and Joan now survived. Neither Gilbert nor Richard apparently made a will, and they left few traces on Stratford's civic life. This seems surprising when their cousin, the town clerk Thomas Greene, not only held one of the most important offices in the corporation but was also living at New Place. For some unknown reason, neither one of the town's richest and most literate men nor his brothers were called upon to serve. The fact that Shakespeare was 'retired' is not pertinent, as it was not unknown for members of the borough to serve until they dropped. When he was away from home for extended spells Will Shakespeare clearly could not be expected to sit on the town council, but after 1611 he was settled more or less permanently at New Place, with only occasional forays to London. It is an abiding mystery that while the Shakespeares advanced socially and materially, and clearly thought of themselves as a Stratford family above all, yet only the patriarch of the family, John Shakespeare, ever served the town in an official capacity.

In early spring of 1613 Shakespeare probably ceased to be actively involved with the King's Men. At the very least he was retrenching by then. His acquisition of a grand London property a few weeks later may further point in that direction. What better way of making ends meet as a grandfather in retirement than as a wealthy landlord collecting money from tenants? This was Shakespeare's first ever investment in London real estate. 'The gatehouse' straddled a passage on the eastern boundary of Blackfriars, opposite the Royal Wardrobe and just up from the church of St Andrew's, masking one of several gateways into the former monastery. The Cockpit inn today occupies the southern wing of the property Shakespeare bought in 1613. Shakespeare no doubt knew the precinct well, and probably acted at Blackfriars when the King's Men resumed playing in 1609. With his penchant for English history he was perhaps acutely conscious of the spirit of place of the old frater. It had been one of Henry VIII's favourite venues and had served as a parliament chamber; it was here that the legatine trial to do with the King's divorce from Katherine of Aragon had taken place, as Shakespeare would have known from Holinshed, this the very place where the cardinals had sat, the same 'great hall' wherein 'was preparation made of seats, tables, and other furniture, according to such a solemn session and royal appearance.' According to the chronicler, the frater had been 'platted in tables and benches in manner of a consistory, one seat raised higher for the judges to sit in'.[2] The Blackfriars great hall was famous for its hammerbeam roof, said to be similar to the one in Westminster Hall. It is easy to understand how the King's Men could ask seven times more at the Blackfriars box office than at the Globe; and why shares in the Blackfriars in the long run proved so much more lucrative than those in the public venue in Southwark.

Wolsey as Lord Chancellor and his fellow cardinal Campeggio had presided over the divorce hearings at Blackfriars, a fact that may have inspired Shakespeare to write about Henry VIII which included a scene set exactly where its historical counterpart had taken place eighty-four years earlier. The disputations of the trial still hung in the air, or so it must have seemed to Shakespeare. A similar frisson can be experienced in the Jerusalem Chamber, setting of the momentous death-bed scene in Part 2 of *Henry IV*. Bolingbroke's nobles are ready to rebel against him, the illegitimate king, and he has attempted to distract them with a crusade to the Holy Land, where he also hopes to expiate his usurpation of King Richard by dying in Jerusalem. In a way he does, but his Jerusalem lies in the heart of Westminster, and he suffers usurpation in his turn when his son snatches the crown from his pillow while the old man is still alive. In the Jerusalem Chamber, art and history seamlessly converged. They did so again in *Henry VIII*.

Along with the gatehouse came 'all that plot of ground on the west side of the same tenement which was lately enclosed with boards on two sides thereof by Ann Bacon widow . . . and being on the third side enclosed with an old brick wall.'3 The land west of Shakespeare's gatehouse had been carved out of the old Prior's garden. Shakespeare's property occupied the northern wing of the gatehouse and rooms across Ireland Yard which cut through to the western range of the monastery and from there connected with Playhouse Yard.4 Shakespeare signed the deed of purchase on 10 March 1613. The cost was £140, of which he paid £80 cash on that day; the following day he mortgaged the property back to the vendor for the outstanding £60, which fell due on 29 September. Shakespeare had three trustees and joint signatories; one was his fellow player John Heminges, another William Johnson, probably the landlord of the Mermaid tavern, and one John Jackson not positively identified. The trustees are a puzzle, and it has been argued that they were a device to deprive Shakespeare's wife from her share of it in the event that he predeceased her. It is possible, but there is no other evidence in Shakespeare's will to suggest such an aim, and it may rather be that the decision to involve trustees was more to do with the fact of it being his first London investment. He no longer had London-based brothers to

look after his business affairs while he was in Warwickshire, as increasingly he was, and perhaps felt the need to have friends in an official
capacity on the spot. It was not necessarily a sign of a deteriorating
relationship with his wife.

Shakespeare seemed to favour rolling investments, and probably
bought the gatehouse to spread his portfolio of houses, barns,
orchards, and tithes. His acting days were almost certainly over and his
writing career was drawing to an end. His last solo work, *The Tempest*,
already lay two years in the past. London's rising middle class might
not be able to purchase mansions in the Strand, but they could afford
Blackfriars, where the houses, unusually for London, enjoyed fresh
running tap water. The man who had bought the largest house in
Stratford was ever conscious of status and rarely shied away from new
ways of making money. Perhaps he had got wind through his friends
the Combes that they were planning to enclose at Welcombe near
Stratford and realized that his Warwickshire revenues might decrease
in the future; or thoughts of bad weather, crop failures, and further
corn and malt shortages might have directed his thoughts to sources of
revenue less closely tied to the land, and the vagaries that could afflict
an agrarian society. The proximity of a theatre in the Blackfriars
evidently bothered Shakespeare no more than it did the Burbages: it
was, after all, the shared property of the King's Men. Shakespeare
in fact left no shares in either the Globe or the Blackfriars, and presumably decided to get rid of them sometime after 1613.

If Shakespeare had hoped for a quiet summer in 1613, a time to
relax among his orchards in Stratford and enjoy a life cushioned by
shrewd investments, he was in for a rude awakening. In early June that
year a young man by the name of John Lane alleged that Susanna Hall
had contracted gonorrhoea from a casual sexual encounter with the
haberdasher Rafe Smith in the house of one John Palmer. In the
idiom of the action brought in court by Susanna as plaintiff on 15 July,
'about five weeks past the defendant [Lane] reported that the plaintiff
[Susanna] had the running of the reins and had been caught with Rafe
Smith at John Palmer.' It is not clear who John Palmer was, but the
most prominent Palmers in the Shakespeare story were his mother's
neighbours in Wilmcote, and the house thought for more than two
centuries to be Mary Arden's home is now known to have belonged

to the Ardens' neighbour Adam Palmer. It is possible that Lane's allegation was that Susanna had been surprised with Smith in the proverbial
hay at one of those Palmers. It seems rather too modern – a love-nest
in Wilmcote where the thirty-year-old mother of a five-year-old
daughter has trysts with a lover while her husband is out and about
curing the sick.

Far-fetched the idea may be, but it is not beyond possibility, for
Susanna and Rafe Smith almost certainly had something in common
that was far more important then than it would be now: they had
been brought up in the same neighbourhood. Rafe Smith was
probably a scion of the house of Smith & Co., haberdashers of Henley
Street, the first house on the north side's town end. He was five years
older than Susanna. If there was an affair, it might have originated
back in the days when they were growing up in Henley Street. Shades
of her father, if he did indeed meet Anne Hathaway in Henley Street.
What put John Lane of Alveston near Stratford in a position to gossip
about the Halls' household was probably the fact that his sister
Margaret was married to John Greene, the brother of Thomas
Greene of New Place. She is his most likely source of rumours
about any goings-on in the Hall household, now moved to Old Town,
with Thomas Greene not far away near Holy Trinity. Such was the
closeness between the Greenes and the Shakespeares that it might even
have been Thomas who had gossiped with Manningham about
Shakespeare's sex life in London when he and Manningham were
at Middle Temple together. Though Greene himself kept a diary, he
may not have known that Manningham did too, and in it recorded
the tantalizing glimpse of Shakespeare's behaviour in London passed
on by Greene.

By 1613 the Lanes were wealthy, living in the manor of Alveston
which they had bought from the vile Sir Edward Greville. The effigies
of Nicholas Lane and his son John, the libeller of Susanna, can be seen
in the local church. John Lane's first cousin was one Thomas Nash, a
neighbour of the Shaws and Shakespeares of Chapel Street: in 1626 he
married the Halls' only child, Elizabeth. There was a dynastic logic to it.
This was new bourgeoisie money marrying more money, and it seems
likely that Shakespeare would have approved. It may seem odd that the
Lane–Nash–Hall links were forged despite young Lane's defamation of

Susanna, but time had passed and, as Shakespeare well knew – after all, he opened his country play *2 Henry IV* by referring to 'rumour painted full of tongues' – rumour and her many tongues (heard as a literary motif in Virgil's *Aeneid*) were an all-too-common fact of life. Susanna had sued and won and Lane, who did not appear to defend his slander, was excommunicated: the *affaire* Hall–Smith may have been a storm in a teacup, but in a small town like Stratford Susanna had a reputation to protect, as daughter, wife, and mother.

The case of Susanna Hall *versus* John Lane had not even come to court when disaster struck again, this time in London, where the King's Men were putting on a Shakespeare–Fletcher collaboration, *All is True*, known by its First Folio title, *Henry VIII*. It was Tuesday 29 June 1613. The performance, which started at 2 p.m., had reached line 49 of the fourth scene of Act I. At this point the stage direction '*Drum and trumpet; chambers discharged*' provokes from Cardinal Wolsey the question 'What's that?' It heralds, of course, the landing of the King's barge and his imminent entry. The actors did not get much further because a spark from the firing of the 'chambers' or cannon ignited the thatched roof of the Globe, and within less than an hour the theatre had burnt to the ground. Miraculously no one was injured, and the company's losses were, apparently, minimal, apart from the fabric of the theatre itself. In the words of an eye-witness, 'This was the fatal period of that virtuous fabric wherein yet nothing did perish but wood and straw, and a few forsaken cloaks; only one man had his breeches set on fire that would perhaps have broiled him, if he had not by the benefit of a provident wit put it out with bottle ale.'[5] If the company had lost their costumes and playbooks, as happened to the poor players of the Fortune in 1621, they would have been indeed 'undone'.

Within twenty-four hours the fire at the Globe was the subject of London ballads, among them a brilliant anti-theatrical satire entitled 'A Sonnet upon the pitiful burning of the Globe playhouse in London', written by someone who, if he had not been there, knew people who had. He crows about how the 'reprobates, though drunk on Monday, / Prayed for the Fool and Henry Condy', and comically evokes the bolting from the burning Globe of 'knights' and 'lords' as well as Burbage. He singles out Shakespeare's friend Heminges for special mention: "Then, with swollen eye, like drunken Flemings, / Distressed stood old stuttering Heminges.' He was 47, it was true, but proved to have plenty of mileage left in him, and can scarcely be blamed if he stood and wept as the Company's playhouse burnt to the ground. The weather for once was too good to be true for *All is True* on this day. Not even the ale-house next door could save it, the satirist remarks gleefully, although if the fire had 'begun below, sans doubt, / Their wives for fear had pissed it out.'

It was left to the shareholders to pick up the bill for rebuilding the Globe. Now more than ever must the Blackfriars frater have seemed an excellent investment: for the next few months they probably shifted their centre of gravity entirely north of the river – they could after all only ever play at one venue. It is less likely that by June 1613 Shakespeare had sold his shares in the Globe and Blackfriars to finance his purchase of the gatehouse than that he had agreed to collaborate with Fletcher in one or two more plays and use the extra box-office income. For much the same reason probably Shakespeare just then collaborated with Burbage on a commissioned *impresa* or emblem for the Earl of Rutland, with Shakespeare writing the lines and his friend Burbage, a keen painter, executing the drawing.

In the end the company stumped up the £1,400 required for the new house. When the second Globe rose phoenix-like on the same spot, but with a tiled roof, it was thought to be 'the fairest that ever was in England'.[6] Shakespeare would hardly be said to have deserted his friends and former partners in the company even if he had now stopped playing: his works remained, after all, the cornerstone of their repertoire. Their loyalty to him would in return extend well beyond the grave into the production of the First Folio in 1623, a Herculean task that was both commemorative and money-making. The signs are that Shakespeare never cut loose from friends like Burbage, Heminges, and Condell, all of whom are remembered in his will.

Perhaps in the summer of 1614 Shakespeare could at last plant and prune in his orchards. He had always been keenly interested in gardens and now he had the leisure to attend to his passions. But on 9 July 1614 another fire swept through Stratford, with 'the wind sitting full upon the town', as the council's petition to the Privy Council put it.

The blaze ravaged some fifty-four houses as well as barns and stables; the total damage amounted to an estimated £8,000. It was the third such disaster in the space of ten years but again, mercifully, all the Shakespeare properties were spared. The £8,000 needed to make good the losses would come in part out of local coffers and in part from national reserves, and it may have been in this connection that Shakespeare and his son-in-law John Hall made their way to London towards the middle of November. It seems almost inconceivable that the borough council of Stratford would not have taken the opportunity to send two of its foremost citizens as delegates to London, particularly when Shakespeare was known to be well connected to the Privy Council. But although councillors on corporation business in London usually had their expenses defrayed by the borough (and itemized by the chamberlains), there is no record of such payments to Shakespeare and Hall; perhaps they waived their fees, because they were combining private and borough business.

Shakespeare and Hall are known to have been in London on Wednesday 16 November 1614. Thomas Greene was there too just then, hoping to catch William Combe about something bad that was brewing in Stratford. He failed to find Combe, but caught up with Shakespeare instead, noting in his diary: 'At my cousin Shakespeare coming yesterday to town I went to see him how he did.' The business he wanted to raise with Shakespeare concerned the proposed enclosures in the Welcombe hills directly north of Henley Street. This was the first time the welfare of Stratford's citizens had been threatened by enclosure since Greville's designs on the Bancroft twelve years earlier. There had long been a pen here for sheep and swine, but that was quite different from a full-scale enclosure, and Greville had at the time been implacably opposed by the corporation and its mayor Richard Quiney.

On that occasion the burghers of Stratford won, although the mayor may have paid a heavy price for his courage and civic leadership, if he was indeed killed over it. Shakespeare's biographers may well wish that Greene had been more forthcoming about Shakespeare's health and appearance, when he saw him 'how he did', but of course his primary interest was the exact state of affairs over the boundaries at Welcombe. Business is business, after all, and that is what this was about, hence his writing down, probably verbatim, what Shakespeare and Hall said – the fact that Shakespeare was accompanied by Hall may suggest that he was no longer in robust enough health to travel alone.

In the absence of more directly relevant material, the well-documented Welcombe enclosures have gained considerable prominence in biographies of Shakespeare. Greene's account of his meeting with Shakespeare and John Hall that day in London suggests that Shakespeare was so relaxed about the whole business that both he and Hall assumed that no surveying, let alone any active digging of a trench and drawing of hedge mounts, would start before April 1615: 'He told me that they assured him they meant to enclose no further than to Gospel Bush . . . and that they mean in April to survey the land and then to give satisfaction and not before and he and Master Hall say they think there will be nothing done at all.' They were wrong. William Combe and his enforcer Arthur Mainwaring meant to dig all along the moment it thawed, which happened within weeks of Shakespeare's and Hall's visit to London.

What enabled Shakespeare to appear almost casual about what was clearly a matter of urgency and importance to his fellow Stratfordians was a deal for compensation he and Greene had struck three weeks earlier with one William Replingham, acting on behalf of the enclosers. The precipitate survey of Welcombe which took everyone by surprise was carried out around 10 December. There could be no doubt now about the imminence of enclosure. Greene sought out Replingham in a hurry, noting in his diary that he 'came from Wilson to look Master Replingham at the Bear and at New Place, but missed him'.[7] It seems that Combe's man could usually be found at either of these two places. There is not necessarily any suggestion that Shakespeare and the Combes were in cahoots here, but it is clear from Combe's will and the Stratford oral tradition that Shakespeare was friendly with the family, and it may be that he was reluctant to be drawn against them. As a businessman Shakespeare was possessed of plenty of acumen, as was proved in the Welcombe affair after his death: perhaps he was mistaken, or misled, about the timing of Combe's survey.

The Welcombe boundaries proposed by Combe can still be traced on the Ordnance Survey maps for the area, as can the track towards the former hamlet of Welcombe and Clopton House. Had the area been successfully enclosed and turned into sheep pastures, it would undoubtedly have been a financial boon for Combe and Mainwaring. The battle of wills over enclosure intensified however when that winter of 1614–15 the women and children of Stratford joined the fray by taking up shovels and filling in the new Welcombe trenches, at considerable risk to themselves. At the start of 1615 things turned ugly when in one of the ensuing skirmishes two Stratfordians were assaulted by Combe's men. Then both sides lost their appetite for a fight when on 17 January 1615 there 'began a great frost with extreme snow, which continued until the 14 of February'. This spell of intense wintry weather dragged on until 7 March, thus causing significant losses among livestock and posing a severe risk to travellers.[8] Everything was paralysed. Nature, it appeared, did not want to see Welcombe enclosed, and eventually even Combe had to admit defeat when the Lord Chief Justice, Sir Edward Coke, ruled in favour of Stratford corporation. The battle for Welcombe constituted a real victory for the men, women, and children of the borough who rose against a rapacious local grandee. Shakespeare had not done much to help.

29

Shakespeare Dies: 1616

PRESUMABLY THE ONLY two members of the original Henley Street
family now alive, William and his sister Joan, saw each other regularly, and presumably Shakespeare called whenever he could on the
Shakespeare-Harts, who lived less than ten minutes away from New
Place. Then, too, there was business to conduct in Henley Street,
where the bulk of the Shakespeare home had now metamorphosed
into Lewis Hiccox's Maidenhead. In the meantime the Halls were
doing well in their splendid house near Holy Trinity. They were rich
in their own right, Shakespeare having conferred on Susanna a dowry
of 107 acres when she married. In 1614–15 the Halls are recorded
for the last time in Evesham Way. It rather looks as though they were
building themselves a house, the one known as Hall's Croft, which
dendochronology places authoritatively in 1614. The coincidence of
timing between the last record of the Halls in Evesham Lane and the
building of Hall's Croft is irresistibly seductive, and fits in with the
Stratford tradition of placing Susanna and the doctor at Hall's Croft.
Perhaps they moved into their new home in the course of 1615, and
might have stayed there had Shakespeare not been taken ill in early
1616, thus precipitating their move back to New Place. Perhaps they
kept Hall's Croft on and leased it out, continuing the association with
their name; or it may simply have kept the name it was known by
from the start after its builder and first owner. It does not, however,
feature in either Hall's will or his daughter's: if it had belonged to the
Halls, it must have been sold before Hall died in 1635.

In a small-town agrarian society like that of early seventeenth-
century Stratford, everyone felt they knew everyone else's business,
and rumour – as Shakespeare well knew – was the very stuff of life.
Sometimes (to the delight of scholars) it can be shown to contain

more than a grain of truth. Stratford had its share of sexual scandals, the one involving Susanna a case in point; another was that of the play-hating Puritan Daniel Baker, forced to admit to an affair and accept paternity of illegitimate offspring. It was a pity, then, that Judith Shakespeare apparently did not have her ear close enough to the ground when she was being courted by Thomas Quiney. Judith's junior by four years, he was probably named after his grandfather Thomas Phillips of Henley Street, one of the elder statesmen of the borough and father-in-law of Richard Quiney. Thomas and Judith must have known each other almost all their lives, since the Quineys and Shakespeares were originally neighbours in Henley Street, living more or less opposite each other. Henley Street was Judith's playground for the first twelve years of her life, and here she would have met the Quiney children. She must have known little Tom Quiney from across the road; she could hardly have avoided him.

One or two houses up westward from the Quineys lived Master John Wheeler; like them he had been expanding in Henley Street and eventually consolidated his stake in as many as four properties in the street through a combination of ownership and leasing, in addition to holdings in Windsor and Greenhill Streets. The council grumbled about the run-down state of his leasehold property at the far corner of Henley Street: it ran back all the way to the orchard of the White Swan, which by 1598 was owned by Perrott's son-in-law, Master Richard Woodward of Shottery. The Wheelers were recusants and had been so in 1606 when they appeared on the same list as Susanna Shakespeare. Their children would have played with the Quiney and Shakespeare children; one of them, a grandchild of the John Wheeler who had served on the borough council years earlier with John Shakespeare (they left at the same time in 1586), was probably Margaret Wheeler. In the glorious summer of 1615 she and Thomas Quiney started an affair and Margaret became pregnant shortly afterwards.

At the best estimate Quiney behaved very badly; if it was the case that he had been engaged to Judith for several years already, his behaviour was even more reprehensible. Judith was certainly a better prospect than her rival. Their recusancy laid the Wheelers open to a string of heavy penalties if they persisted in it, while the Shakespeares were not only rich but also it seemed conformist, Dr Hall's Puritanism notwithstanding. Judith and her family were obviously unaware of Quiney's affair as late as January 1616 when Shakespeare first drafted his will. He may have been feeling unwell, and anxious to ensure that Judith would be properly provided for now that she was getting married.

One of the puzzles about Judith's marriage is that it took place on Saturday 10 February 1616, the weekend before Ash Wednesday. Marriages were technically forbidden during the pre-Lent period which began with Septuagesima Sunday (on 28 January 1616). Judith and Quiney did not (as far as is known) have the Bishop of Worcester's dispensation and therefore ought not to have been allowed to marry at Holy Trinity when they did. What sort of strings were pulled locally cannot be known, but the Shakespeares and Quineys commanded plenty of clout in the town. The couple were subsequently excommunicated, but only briefly, and it is probable it did not worry them unduly. An otherwise illegitimate child was the usual reason for such haste, but Judith and Thomas's child was born almost exactly nine months after the marriage like its cousin Elizabeth Hall. What is much more likely is that Judith wanted to marry while her father was still alive. Defiance of canonical law was a small price to pay for being given away by one's father. What should have been a happy time for all concerned could hardly be so with a dying father – and the groom's heavily pregnant girlfriend out there in the streets of Stratford.

Within six weeks of the Quiney–Shakespeare marriage Margaret Wheeler died while giving birth to Thomas Quiney's child; mother and baby were buried on 15 March 1616. It seems almost impossible that Judith should have been unaware of the affair, and yet that appears to have been the case, though Stratford was surely not large enough for the successful conduct of a clandestine liaison. Clearly Shakespeare knew nothing of it when he first drafted his will in January 1616 and none of the family seem to have known then either; maybe the Shakespeares, Halls, and Harts were all too preoccupied with William's illness to look sideways. It is tempting to join up the trail of dots suggested by the documentary record and to visualize Shakespeare rewriting his will within weeks of Judith's marriage, in response to the scandal that had since broken over Quiney's affair. He redrafted his will on Monday 25 March, and the following day his new son-in-law appeared before the consistory court in Holy Trinity. Thomas 'admitted that he had had carnal copulation with Wheeler' and was sentenced to do 'public penance in a white sheet on three Sundays in the church of Stratford'. He pleaded for a lesser sentence, and got off rather more lightly than he deserved; in the end he paid five shillings for the relief of the poor of Stratford and confessed his fault, in his own clothes, to the minister of the chapel of Bishopton. If Shakespeare had planned for a serene retirement, Prospero relaxing in his gardens rather than languishing in a monastic cell, he had reckoned without the hot-blooded younger generation.

It is possible that Shakespeare had a hand in securing the remission in Quiney's punishment. It is generally taken for granted that, as Judith's father, he must have been outraged by Quiney's behaviour. No doubt – but there was the small matter of his own past behaviour and his premarital sexual encounters with Anne Hathaway. Or perhaps Judith may have interceded with him on behalf of her husband, guilty as he was; it may be that Shakespeare had ever loved her most, never mind the will granting Susanna and her family the bulk of his estate. For the last eighteen years of his life Judith had been all that was left of the twins; her father probably saw Hamnet's face every time he looked at hers. She may have been Viola, and all the daughters of the last plays. Perhaps she should have married sooner, but it may be that her father could not bear to let her go, or she may have felt that she could not leave him or her mother. Perhaps Judith had been her father's muse ever since *Twelfth Night*; now that he was leaving her behind, he would have wanted to do whatever he could for her.

A story was current in Stratford in the middle of the seventeenth century about the way Shakespeare met his death. It was first recorded in 1662, coincidentally the year in which Judith Shakespeare-Quiney died, at the age of seventy-seven. The Reverend John Ward lived in Stratford and knew its people well; it was he who had referred to the gift of a thousand pounds allegedly bestowed on Shakespeare by Southampton. As far as it is possible to judge, Ward is a fairly reliable witness to what was being said about Shakespeare in Stratford in the late 1650s or early 1660s: his repeated use of the phrase 'I have heard' suggests a strong local oral culture. Something else Ward 'heard' was that 'Shakespeare, Drayton, and Ben Jonson, had a merry meeting, and it seems drank too hard, for Shakespeare died of a fever there contracted.' Might this 'merry meeting' have been Judith's wedding feast of 10 February 1616? If so, it would suggest that Shakespeare, far from being unwell a few weeks before when he first drafted his will, may have been in good and festive form. The people of Stratford knew about Drayton, of course: he too was a Warwickshire lad, frequently visiting nearby, and at some point Shakespeare's son-in-law John Hall treated him, calling him 'poet laureate' in his case notes. Apart from Ward's diary entry there is no other known record of Shakespeare and Drayton ever meeting in Warwickshire – but why should there be? If they had met regularly at New Place once a month, there would be no record of such private, social calls. Wining and dining the Lucys or the Earl of Warwick at the Bear or Swan at corporation expense was another matter altogether, and of course would be recorded.

A meeting between Shakespeare and Drayton is plausible, as is the notion that Jonson should have called on his friend in the Midlands. This after all was what Jonson did, visit friends in the country. By 1616 he was a fêted literary figure, and when he stayed with his friend Drummond of Hawthornden at the latter's castle in the Pentlands south of Edinburgh he was lionized in the Scots capital. If he could heave his girth all the way to Scotland in 1618, he could certainly get as far as Stratford-upon-Avon, and where Ben was, excess of conviviality was never far away. Awkwardly, however, there is reason to be sceptical about Ward's report, for on this visit to Scotland – two years later – Jonson confided to Drummond that he and Drayton were enemies: 'Drayton feared him, and he esteemed not of him,' Drummond recorded. Jonson alleged, moreover, that 'Sir W. Alexander was not half kind unto him, and neglected him, because a friend to Drayton.' If there was such hostility between Jonson and Drayton, they were scarcely likely to converge upon Stratford for a reunion with their mutual friend Shakespeare. It may be significant that Nicholas Rowe, although he noted that Shakespeare enjoyed the conversation of his friends in retirement at Stratford, did not repeat the rumour of a drunken literary symposium on the Avon. It is of course not impossible that whatever animosity lay between Jonson and Drayton first arose at just this party.

Whether or not Jonson and Drayton called on Shakespeare together on this particular occasion, they and others assuredly did visit him in Stratford. He may have lived in deepest Warwickshire after *The Tempest*, but not, it would appear, in isolation from his circle of friends, whether from London or Warwickshire. Surely Burbage, Heminges, and Condell also called in or stayed at New Place from time to time, enjoying the gardens and orchard and walks by the Avon. As for his other 'family' in Oxford, according to William Davenant, Shakespeare frequently called on his parents in Oxford, even after young William was old enough to know the meaning of the word 'godfather'. He probably saw them in late November 1614 during his last recorded journeys to London, and may have continued to do so until he apparently began to fail in late 1615 or January 1616.

The 'fever' Ward reported Shakespeare having contracted following a drinking bout might, after all, have been connected with the wedding of Thomas Quiney and Judith Shakespeare – with family and friends gathered in honour of the occasion, infections would be easily spread. A particularly virulent disease had recently hit Warwickshire: typhoid. At the time it was called the 'new fever' or the 'spotted fever', after the pink spots which appear on the chest and abdomen of the infected person. It is plain from John Hall's diary that typhoid was rampant in south Warwickshire just when Shakespeare died. The year 1616 was a busy one for the grim reaper in Stratford, the higher than usual tally of deaths pointing to a small local epidemic. Blaming typhoid for Shakespeare's death has a number of implications, not the least of which concerns the timing of his will. After first contracting the fever a patient would be seriously ill within a week and probably – but not necessarily – dead within another three weeks. Typhus, which is transmitted through water contaminated by raw sewage or by flies and lice from human waste was almost eradicated in the twentieth century by antibiotics. The span of the disease, from infection to death or recovery, is about a month, which corresponds almost exactly to the time that elapsed between Shakespeare's final will of 25 March and his death on 23 April.

If Shakespeare died of typhoid, it seems unlikely that the January draft of the will was triggered by the illness that killed him towards the end of April. Very likely it was no more than precautionary, an initial attempt to sort out his affairs and provide for his family in the light of his last child's forthcoming marriage. The poet and dramatist who had looked so deeply into the seeds of things, who had given such extraordinary expression to suffering and to happiness, who had as if by magic made life-enhancing public entertainment and great art from the profoundest dilemmas of mankind, now faced his own extinction. Above all as he lay dying, surely he must have known that he had written works that were peerless. Perhaps the knowledge of his achievements was a source of comfort in this extremity. It has been argued that in his thirties he had probably been very sick, perhaps even with the plague. He had survived then, and might do so again. He had often thought about death, and one of his least distinguished characters speaks of it memorably as the common lot of all humanity – poor Feeble, in *2 Henry IV*, a victim of the abuse of the King's levy by Falstaff and Shallow. 'A man can die but once', he remarks stoically, and continues: 'We owe God a death . . . he that dies this year is quit for the next.' Julius Caesar agrees. In bullish vein he asserts that Caesar will not be cowed by auguries of doom and death, since in life death is a necessary certainty:

> Cowards die many times before their deaths;
> The valiant never taste of death but once.
> Of all the wonders that I yet have heard,
> It seems to me most strange that men should fear,
> Seeing that death, a necessary end,
> Will come when it will come.[1]

What Caesar glosses over is the chasm between the intellectual knowledge of death as a biological reality, and a reluctance to believe that it applies to oneself. The truth is that mankind cannot bear too much reality, to echo T. S. Eliot, and nothing is more real than the cessation of being – unless death is seen as a rite of passage to a life after death. In 1 Corinthians 55 St Paul asked 'O death, where is thy sting? O grave, where is thy victory?', and John Donne borrowed his words for his sonnet celebrating the death of death. There is a distinctly religious strain in Shakespeare's last plays, whether in Prospero's meditations on his grave or in the emphasis on 'faith' in *The Winter's Tale*, with a character named Paulina after, it seems, St Paul. On the other hand, there is little evidence of Shakespeare practising his faith in any everyday sort of way – there is no record of him ever having served as churchwarden, for example, unlike his friend Heminges in the City of London, so possibly he should not be imagined seeking comfort in his faith as death approached. Even in the last plays, the role of the Deity seems merged into the human characters. Prospero may come to regret his usurpation of the Almighty's role, but it is hard to imagine him in a monastic retreat. The end of *The Tempest* has almost the air of a gesture, as if this were something Shakespeare thinks Prospero ought to do by way of penance. Prospero's Catholic cell in Milan carries as little imaginative conviction as Chaucer's retraction at the end of his great erotic love poem *Troilus and Criseyde*, when the dead Troilus surveys his past life of love and sex, of *eros* (romantic love) and *thanatos* (death), from the elevated sphere of *agape* or divine love. Having achieved a true perspective, Troilus now laughs at the absurdity of human love, but readers of the poem rarely laugh with him.

There is nothing in the later plays to suggest that in his last days Shakespeare discovered in himself enough faith to echo Troilus; nor is it clear which faith he might have sought. Richard Davies's assertion in the seventeenth century that Shakespeare 'died a papist' continues to intrigue biographers, in particular because of the ongoing debate about the testament later found in the rafters of the house in Henley Street. None of the many letters he must have written – like Quiney, and Sturley, and others – have so far come to light. Some among his friends and acquaintances kept diaries, notably his cousin Thomas Greene, but he neglected to record anything of interest about Shakespeare. Similarly, the lawyers in the Mountjoy suit never asked their witness the most important question – who he really was. But after all, how could they have known that the vaguely abstracted gentleman from Warwickshire who appeared before them with rather deficient powers of recall regarding the matter in hand would, four hundred years later, be esteemed the most talented person of his generation. In the nature of things, Shakespeare's own claim to immortality went unrecognized at the time, but at least he enjoyed wealth and success in his day, probably above anything that he himself ever imagined during those long hours at school in Stratford or in the early years of his father's disgrace.

Shakespeare scholars would have written a very different will from the one he left. It would be bursting with information about his family, his friends, perhaps his lovers, and about the vast amounts of money he must have squirrelled away; there would be provision made for his godson Davenant. Clues to his true faith would abound, and he might refer lovingly to his wife, or long to be buried near his dead son – in 1630 his friend John Heminges asked to be buried as closely as possible to his adored wife Rebecca. At the very least the will would convey a strong sense of the man, his family, his circle of acquaintances; it would provide a digest of his life towards the end of it; the man and the work might come together at last.

The legendary dramatist would surely leave behind instructions about his work, perhaps about possible publication. As for the rest of his library, his books were presumably a precious commodity, probably left to John and Susanna Hall (both could read, and John at least could write). From their use as source material it seems likely that he owned Holinshed, Plutarch, Ovid, and Virgil, but there must have been many other volumes. It would have been usual to take an inventory of New Place at his death and this may yet come to light; the Hiccox and Rutter inventories of the Henley Street home surfaced only comparatively recently. Three volumes from Shakespeare's library in different national collections have already been tentatively identified.

But Shakespeare did leave a last will and testament. It is not a short document, but a detailed parcelling-out of his estate; as a piece of writing, it is also singularly dull and elusive. Had he deliberately designed it to throw the inquisitive off the scent, he could not have done so more effectively. In spite of all the unpicking over the years it has yielded little, except for one tantalizing bequest on the final sheet of the three-sheet will dictated by Shakespeare to his solicitor Francis Collins: 'Item I give unto my wife my second-best bed with the furniture.' He does not mention her by name, as he does his 'niece' (he means his granddaughter) Elizabeth Hall, and his daughters, but this may mean no more than that, as he had only one wife, there could be no confusion about who is meant. Had he called her 'my wife Anne', it would hardly have been more reassuring.

Shakespeare's bequest to Anne of his 'second-best bed' suggests that his best bed had already been disposed of as part of the bequest of New Place to the Halls, with the exception of certain specifically listed items such as his plate (to Elizabeth) and his silver goblet (to Judith). Since John Hall presumably looked after Shakespeare in his final illness, he and his wife and daughter had almost certainly removed to New Place by early spring 1616. Perhaps he and Susanna now occupied the main bedroom containing the best bed, possibly upstairs, as in the Henley Street house, with Shakespeare in a room downstairs during his last weeks. Equally, Anne Shakespeare may have asked specifically for 'the second-best with the furniture' because it was an heirloom and 'had come from her old home at Hewland'; and she perhaps asked for it when the draft will was read out, hence the interlineation of the bequest in the final draft.[2] The beds belonging to Anne's home at Hewland Farm feature almost as intriguingly in her father Richard Hathaway's will of 1581 as does Shakespeare's second-best bed in his. Her father stipulated that the 'two joint-beds in my parlour shall continue and stand unremoved during the natural life of . . . Joan my wife and the natural life of Bartholomew my son and John my son.' This would seem to rule out 'the second-best bed' in New Place having migrated there from Shottery – but only if Richard Hathaway's wishes were strictly honoured. Perhaps the surviving Hathaways wanted Anne to have a bed, so she took one with her to Henley Street; perhaps it was usual for the bride to bring a bed with her – the rich brewer Robert Perrott declared in his will that among others he was leaving his widow Elizabeth 'the bed which she brought unto me with all furniture thereunto belonging'. And in 1608 Thomas Combe left his widow all 'tables, bedsteads . . . except the best bedsteads which I will give and bequeath unto my said son William with the best bed and best furniture thereunto belonging to have to his own use . . .'[3]

So that was the second-best bed, perhaps a Hathaway bed from Hewlands originally, perhaps William and Anne's marriage-bed. If there was a 'second-best bed', there must have been a 'best bed', possibly Shakespeare, as the master of New Place, acquired a new bed on his return home in 1597 – it is tempting to envisage it with the newly acquired Shakespeare arms carved on it. This crested bed would naturally supersede the one Will and Anne had shared during the early years of their marriage over in Henley Street.

Shakespeare's apparent disregard of his wife in his will is sometimes held to be related to common law, which supposedly guaranteed a widow one-third of her husband's estate and continued residence in the family home; in such a case there would have been no need for him to make additional provision for her, and the written will's sole function would be to dispose of the remaining two-thirds of his estate. It is impossible to determine how far the will is a declaration of Shakespeare's total assets; it must be assumed that he and Francis Collins would have done what they could to minimize any liabilities arising on his death.

Shakespeare left £10 to the poor of Stratford, a fair if not overly generous provision. Names glaringly absent from the will hint at other stories. The Hathaways are nowhere mentioned, though Shakespeare's brother-in-law Bartholomew Hathaway of Tysoe and other members of Anne's family were alive at the time. Then there are the missing Globe and Blackfriars shares. It seems most likely that Shakespeare sold them, sometime in the course of 1613, perhaps in the summer of that year in time to pay off the outstanding £60 mortgage on the gate-house that fell due in September 1613. They would have been difficult to shift after the fire at the Globe on 29 June 1613, though any buyer prepared to take the long view and accept the expenses involved in rebuilding the theatre would have had his reward, since the Globe continued trading successfully for twenty-nine years after the fire.

The absence of the Greenes from the will is striking: it is as though they had never featured in the poet's life. Not even a ring for mourning or another symbolic token is left them, though the links between the Greene and Hall-Shakespeare families endured well beyond April 1616. Thus it was Thomas Greene's brother John of Clement's Inn who acted on Susanna's behalf in 1618 as a trustee of the Blackfriars gatehouse after her father's death. Thomas himself left Stratford in 1617, and in a letter written that year described his time in Stratford as 'golden days'. With his beloved wife Lettice he went to London to pursue a career as a barrister, having it seems kept chambers there throughout his Stratford years. Eventually he became Reader and Bencher, as befitted a man of his considerable gifts.

Thomas Combe, the brother of the Welcombe encloser, features somewhat surprisingly in the will, as does Shakespeare's recusant neighbour from Chapel Street, William Reynolds. Combe's appearance may be little more than a quid pro quo: John Combe had left Shakespeare £5 in his will. There is no reference to Shakespeare's friend and boon companion Ben Jonson, but Burbage, Heminges, and Condell are each left the considerable sum of twenty-six shillings and eightpence to buy mourning rings. Richard Field of *Cymbeline* and long poems fame is missing, and Shakespeare removed 'Master Richard Tyler the elder' from the draft will and replaced him with Hamlet Sadler, thus left money for a mourning ring. Hamlet Sadler was probably the godfather of Shakespeare's dead son, so this may have been the substitution of one godfather for another, lending weight to the supposition that the Tylers had stood as godparents to one of the Shakespeare children. Now there was a rift, and in the few weeks which separate the January and March drafts of the will Tyler had disgraced himself in Shakespeare's eyes. The fact is that a whiff of corruption had gathered around Tyler after he and others were delegated by the borough to collect money in other counties of England for relief from the conflagration of 1614. In March 1616 Tyler and his companions were censured for 'everyone preferring his own private benefits before the general good' and for claiming expenses in excess even of what they gathered. It looks as though Tyler was struck out of Shakespeare's will in a fit of moral indignation. It did not, however, prevent the Shakespeare estate requesting Tyler's co-operation shortly afterwards in a transfer of the deeds of the Blackfriars gatehouse.

Shakespeare's will contains not one allusion to his hidden London past. It is a strikingly Stratford-centric document for someone who spent the best part of his life elsewhere. There is no mention of Southampton, the Davenants, Emilia Lanier – of anyone whose name could cause grief or hurt to his family. If Shakespeare did make any arrangements for Davenant, he did it privately and well before his illness. The will does feature his 'godson William Walker', an eight-year-old Stratford boy who is left twenty shillings in gold. If Shakespeare set the house of his hidden life in order at all, it must have been done before he fell ill, leaving only the bland dispositions of his public will for posterity to pore over.

The sole frisson provided by the extant will is the notion that it was revised in late March 1616 to take account of the Quiney débâcle.

Certainly on the first sheet, concerning Judith's inheritance, the word 'January' has been deleted and replaced by 'March'. The phrase 'son-in-law' (i.e. Thomas Quiney) has been crossed out and replaced with 'my daughter Judith', suggesting that this part of the will was being rewritten to bypass Quiney, with Judith's share of the estate to devolve directly to her. The bulk of the Shakespeare inheritance – New Place, the Blackfriars gatehouse, and all his local holdings from the Manor of Rowington – passed to Susanna and her family, who thus received the lion's share of her father's possessions. Even eight-year-old Elizabeth Hall is separately and impressively provided for – perhaps she and her grandfather got on well.

As well as providing for Judith financially Shakespeare also left her his 'broad silver gilt bowl', presumably an object of sentimental value to him. Shaken though he might have been by Quiney's disgrace, Shakespeare would not therefore turn on his daughter Judith; rather, he may have thought that she now needed his help more than ever, hence his careful ring-fencing of her share of his estate. Quiney could only get at her considerable additional cash reserve of £150, due to her three years after the drafting of the will, in March 1619, by providing land to the same value as collateral. Here Shakespeare shrewdly took the long view, no doubt hoping the carrot of this large sum of money would spur Quiney on to accumulate land-holdings. Their value was the equivalent roughly of twice Shakespeare's own official outlay for New Place. The sum left in escrow (that is, as security) to Judith was considerable and sent a clear signal to Quiney that, like fortune, Shakespeare favoured the brave and enterprising in business.

Shakespeare did not forget his sister and her three sons, though he apparently failed to recall the name of one – William and Michael Hart he was sure of, but Thomas eluded him; he was nonetheless left £5, like his brothers, and their mother was left £20 as well as 'the house with the appurtenances in Stratford [Henley Street] wherein she dwelleth for her natural life under the yearly rent of 12 pence'. She was charged the ground rent for an entire burgage, to be paid to the Shakespeare estate; this was to be administered after his death by John and Susanna Hall as executors, with Thomas Russell and Shakespeare's solicitor Francis Collins acting as overseers of the will. By now the house in Henley Street included an attached wing, Joan

Hart's cottage, projecting into the back garden, an annexe, modest only by comparison with the frontage of the Henley Street house as a whole. The Harts had probably moved into the annexe after John Shakespeare's death. The levy of twelve pence stipulated by Shakespeare in his will suggests either that he charged his sister a burgage rate for the cottage, as a kind of long-range mortgage, or else that Joan retained ownership of the outer western bay of the Henley Street house and the cottage together. The latter is more likely. Shakespeare probably left his sister the outer western bay of the house and the annexe, which together may have added up to a burgage, since garden cottages in Stratford were counted into ground rent. Thus in 1555 Thomas Patrick of Henley Street was instructed by the council to pay '2d a year to the chief rent roll for his hovel in the street in the backside of his tenement in Henley Street, or else that he do take down his hovel and pale again.' The odds are that Joan Hart and her family lived in the cottage, with access to the gardens at the back, while leasing out the western-most bay of the main house. The entire original three-bay rectangle of the Henley Street house must therefore have constituted the Maidenhead inn; only that way can the number of rooms that made up the Hiccox (1627) and Rutter (1648) inventories be accounted for. Support for this hypothesis may lie in the fact that in the eighteenth century the Harts *reclaimed* the western-most bay as living quarters: they could only have done so if they had leased them out in the first place, and that may have been as long ago as the time of William Shakespeare.

Shakespeare left £5 and his ceremonial sword to Thomas Russell, a token of friendship perhaps as well as a vote of confidence in this executor. Russell, born in 1570, was a substantial local landowner who lived on the Stour at Alderminster, less than five miles to the south of Stratford, clearly a trusted friend of the poet's although the details of how long they knew each other remain shrouded in mystery. Russell was connected to the Willoughbys of Wiltshire, and in 1594 the younger son of his friend Henry Willoughby had published *Willobie his Avisa*, which contains what may be an allusion to Shakespeare's involvement with Southampton; his sister-in-law had married the elder brother of the author of *Avisa*. After his first wife's death Russell married in 1603 the wealthy widow Anne Digges through whom he also inherited two sons, one of them being the Leonard Digges who wrote a prefatory poem for the first Folio; Digges was twelve years older than his new stepfather.

There are no hidden clues to Shakespeare's religion in the will. If he ever put his name to a secret spiritual testament on the lines of the one alleged to be his father's, it has not survived – or not come to light. If it was indeed John Shakespeare's that was hidden in the rafters of the Henley Street house; but if a similar document was concealed in New Place, subsequent rebuilding and demolition must have lost it to posterity. The only clue to Shakespeare's faith is that in the later plays faith itself emerges as an important concept. Shakespeare's extant will covers the religious spectrum, from militant recusants like Reynolds to his Protestant son-in-law John Hall, and any number of apparently middle-of-the-road local Anglicans. As far as religion is concerned he seems to be even-handed, guided not by sectarian ideas but by friendship and family.

William Shakespeare died on St George's Day, Tuesday 23 April 1616; he was buried in Holy Trinity two days later, on 25 April. A precise roll of those who attended his funeral cannot be drawn, but it seems safe to assume that the mourners in Holy Trinity on that April day in 1616 comprised his wife and daughters, his granddaughter, his sister and her family, John Hall and Thomas Quiney, the executors and witnesses of his will, Francis Collins, Thomas Russell, friends and neighbours like July Shaw, the Sadlers, Richard Field, Robert Whatcott (who may have lived at New Place since he testified on Susanna's behalf in 1613), and others. It was most likely the grandest funeral since Combe's, two years earlier. Because Shakespeare's interment involved the digging of a grave in the very chancel of the church, members of the town council and the mayor were probably present too. Some of his London friends may have attended, and he left mourning rings for Burbage, Heminges, and Condell.

Probably the chief mourner among the crowd that processed back from Holy Trinity into Stratford after this particular funeral was Shakespeare's widow Anne Hathaway. Grief-stricken, heavy-hearted, and solemn they doubtless all were during this return to New Place for the 'funeral-baked meats' that would have been laid on there.

Perhaps they derived comfort from the thought that their husband, father, friend was now 'with God', as Nurse had remarked about her daughter Susan in *Romeo and Juliet*, or with Hamnet, or both. William Shakespeare was no more. His fifty-two years of life on earth had been fulfilling and busy, and there may have been some comfort in that. Perhaps the prospect of the monument in the chancel was something to look forward to, even in this extremity. At some point in the future they would once again be able to gaze upon his features on Sundays in their parish church. Death and funerals were much more part of the fabric of everyday life then than now, but the pain of bereavement would have been the same. It was inside the family that Anne and her daughters would have sought solace and comfort. Perhaps it was hardest for Judith, surely even then aching from the humiliation inflicted on her by the wretched Thomas Quiney; particularly if, as seems possible, she was her father's favourite daughter, loved even more than her elder sister.

Since the end of the seventeenth century rumour has had it that Shakespeare himself wrote the words engraved on his gravestone:

> Good friend for Jesus' sake forbear,
> To dig the dust enclosed here!
> Blessed be the man that spares these stones,
> And cursed be he that moves my bones.

The grave does not have a name on it, and it is impossible to know for sure whether Shakespeare wrote these words – but almost certainly he did. They achieved their purpose: Shakespeare's grave has never been opened, his bones never moved across into the charnel house. Nor were any members of his family subsequently interred *with* him – next to him, yes, and there they still rest. It was a rare honour to be interred in the chancel rather than buried in the churchyard, and probably required some kind of special dispensation, perhaps from the Bishop of Worcester. Shakespeare was of course a senior collector of what in the days before the Reformation had been the tithes of the College with responsibility for Holy Trinity, and it may be that this entitled him to burial in the chancel. If so, the £440 he spent in 1605 on acquiring the collection of tithes was an investment in eternity as well as good secular business.

London may have had a hand in the burial in the chancel. Shakespeare inspired loyalty and affection. As Rowe remarked, 'everyone who had a true taste of merit, and could distinguish men, had generally a just value and esteem for him'. He was echoing Hamlet's words of friendship to Horatio, that ever since his 'dear soul was mistress of her choice' and thus 'could of men distinguish her election', she had chosen him. These words, among the most powerful Shakespeare ever wrote about friendship and loyalty, further testify to the importance he attached to bonds between men. And this held good across the board – there was mutual esteem, for example, between various of the players, Shakespeare included, and some of the most powerful people in the land. No doubt helping hands were given, favours done. Southampton survived Shakespeare by eight years, but it is clear from Pembroke's heartfelt response to Burbage's death in 1619 that Southampton was not the only influential patron to be devoted to the players: Pembroke felt he could not attend an after-dinner play laid on for the French ambassador because it was too 'soon after the loss of my old acquaintance Burbage'. Shakespeare demonstrably enjoyed the patronage of the two Herberts at some point later in his life, although he himself never addressed anything to them.

It is possible that a poem from the period throws an interesting light on the grave in the chancel. It was written by one William Basse from neighbouring Oxfordshire, in time to be echoed by Jonson in his elegy to Shakespeare in the First Folio of 1623, and urges Spenser, Chaucer, and Beaumont (who died the month before Shakespeare) to make room for Shakespeare in Westminster Abbey. If they cannot do so, however, Shakespeare is told he may have to sleep serenely alone 'under this carved marble of thine own' and rest in 'unmolested peace' as a lord in his 'unshared cave'. Since the bust is not of marble, Basse's poem probably refers to the tombstone in the chancel floor rather than the monument up on the wall. The use of marble was not uncommon: the inscription on the tombstone of Judith Combe in the chancel of Holy Trinity is framed by white marble and constitutes a perfectly preserved example of 'carved marble', 'carved' referring to the inscription. The Basse poem may support the contention by the famous Stratford antiquarian Halliwell-Phillipps that the original slab on the Shakespeare grave was moved in the middle of the eighteenth century, to the extent that the original stone was perhaps framed with marble like Judith Combe's. The stone now in place faithfully reproduces the curse on the original, as recorded by several seventeenth-century visitors long before the stone could have been changed. Shakespeare's name is not on the stone, and the grave looks foreshortened and recessed into the communion rail. It can hardly have been so in April 1616: probably the name on the gravestone was swallowed when the communion rail was drawn across the top of it. This had happened by 1737, when Vertue sketched the chancel, because even then Shakespeare's tomb was shorter than Anne's.

Since Shakespeare left no money in his will for either his grave or his bust, the assumption must be that the arrangements were made before he died, probably during the last four months of his life when it became clear to him that he might not recover. The drafting of the inscription on the stone may have been done at the same time. Shakespeare's 'ten in the hundred' friend John Combe, who predeceased him by two years, left the princely sum of £60 for a monument to himself in Holy Trinity, in an alcove in the northern corner of the east wall. The monument was the work of a Southwark stonemason by the name of Gerard Johnson or, to give him his real name, Gheerhart Janssen; he had earlier worked on a Lucy grave at Charlecote, but how he came to be active in the Midlands is not clear. Shakespeare may have been familiar with this workshop from his London days, and presumably saw Combe's completed monument; perhaps he commissioned Janssen to do his memorial too. It is on a smaller scale than Combe's, but still cannot have been cheap. A highly professional piece of work, it shows Shakespeare as he appeared towards the end of his life, a solid middle-aged pillar of the community. The upper body and head are perfectly proportioned, and the expression of the face so realistic that it probably derives from a life mask, which would seem to suggest conclusively that the idea for a bust originated before Shakespeare's death and that he himself was consulted about it. This in turn lends further weight to the suggestion that the verses on the slab are his, that he wanted to rest inside the church in full view of his monument on the north wall. The face looking out from its niche is that of William Shakespeare as he was in the last few weeks of his life, the face his family were familiar with as they sat with him during the winter and early spring of 1616.

Leonard Digges knew Shakespeare in the last years of his life, perhaps from as early as 1603 when his mother married Thomas Russell, one of Shakespeare's executors. He was an avid fan: on the flyleaf of a copy of Lope de Vega's poems, published in 1613, Digges compared them to those of 'our Will Shakespeare'.[4] He knew the monument in the chancel of Holy Trinity, and his and Jonson's testimonies in the First Folio establish beyond a doubt that this bust and the portrait in the Folio are authentic portraits of the man. In his paean to the memory of Shakespeare Digges apostrophizes the poet and then vows that through the Folio his works will live on forever: 'When that stone is rent, / And Time dissolves thy Stratford monument, / Here we alive shall view thee still.'

The monument to Shakespeare was in place by the time the First Folio appeared in 1623. According to the Reverend Joseph Greene the bust and the cushion on which the poet's hands rest were all 'one entire lime-stone, naturally of a blueish or ash-coloured cast, yet of a texture and solidity almost equal to common marble, which could be had from no quarry in our neighbourhood except from a village called Wilmcote.' Greene was writing in 1749, the year of the monument's one and only major restoration. In general a scrupulous and honest reporter, he stresses that nothing was changed except the architraves, where marble was substituted for the original alabaster. What really seems to leap off Greene's page is the fact that the limestone came from Wilmcote, Shakespeare's mother's home village. It would appear that Shakespeare had a say over where Janssen procured his materials as well as how his bust should look. The masons may have come from Southwark, but the stone would be Warwickshire lime-stone.

It has not proved possible to date the construction of the bust with certainty any more precisely than between 1616, when Shakespeare died, and 1623, when Digges referred to it in the First Folio. The personal interest Shakespeare seems to have taken in it would suggest an immediate start – except for the fact that the chancel was in a parlous state. By 1618 it was decayed, ruinous and damp, requiring urgent attention. In March 1619 the council decided to fund the necessary work by cutting down and selling 'all the trees in the churchyard' of Holy Trinity. The repairs were carried out during 1621–2, the only major overhaul of the church between the year in which Shakespeare was born and 1763, when its wooden steeple was replaced with the current stone spire. By what seemed a miracle, the destructive flood of 1588 had not invaded the chancel – no miracle, but a testament to the sense of the original builders in choosing a gravel terrace some seventeen feet above the Avon, providing maximum visibility as well as maximum safety from the river. The twenty-six misericords in the chancel dating from the fifteenth century must have suffered grievously from any prolonged submersion but remain perfectly preserved. Their vivid, exquisitely carved motifs include one of a scold grabbing her husband by the beard with one hand while thumping him with a ladle or pot with the other.

With the chancel very obviously in a poor state of repair, followed by a schedule of planned renovation, it would have made good sense for Shakespeare's executors to stay their hand with the monument. But it was surely completed by the summer of 1622, for it was then that Shakespeare's troupe, the King's Men, paid a visit to Stratford. Possibly to their amazement, they were paid a fee of six shillings 'for *not* playing in the [gild] hall'. This was Stratford's first sight of the London source of Master Shakespeare's wealth, and the players' first time in Stratford as a company. What better explanation for their descent on the Midlands than that they were come to witness the inauguration of a recently completed memorial to their friend and fellow player. Since it was a Southwark firm of stonemasons who were carrying out the commission, the players on Bankside may well have known as much about its progress as the people of Stratford. It was no small matter, after all, for them to take time out from lucrative performances at the Globe and Blackfriars; perhaps they were able to combine the journey to the Midlands with playing Oxford or Banbury.

It would have been a melancholy journey west since the players' friends Jane and John Davenant had both died that spring. Jane was buried at St Martin Carfax in Oxford on 5 April 1622 and her husband followed within less than three weeks, on 23 April, exactly six years after Shakespeare's death. John Heminges had very likely met them two years earlier when he contributed ten shillings towards 'the clock and chimes' of St Martin Carfax. He was the only non-parishioner to do so, and his name is added on at the end of the churchwardens' accounts. The links between the Davenants and Shakespeare's circle obviously extended beyond his death, although it is not at all clear why Heminges should take an interest in St Martin Carfax. He was of course a Midlander just like Shakespeare, but he had put down roots in London. His reason for being in Oxford, and probably at the Davenants, was perhaps to inform them that he and Condell were then collecting the scripts and securing publication rights in readiness for the First Folio. There were pressing reasons for Shakespeare's friends to get on with these preparations, because in 1619 a less than scrupulous London printer by the name of Thomas Pavier had attempted to publish an unauthorized collection of Shakespeare's works.

When the King's Men entered the chancel of Holy Trinity in 1622 work on the Folio was well under way. From the injunction not to play, it seems that the men were not made particularly welcome – yet they were paid a fee that compared well with the usual fees of players. All is very obscure. It might be supposed, for example, that the Puritan rector Thomas Wilson would give all Shakespeares a wide berth, since Puritans execrated the theatre and how could the family of the play-wright *extraordinaire* not be tainted? But he and John Hall were close friends. With Wilson's arrival in 1619, the Protestant Daniel Baker's ascendancy on the council, and Hall's undisputed pre-eminence as the chief physician of the county, the Puritans were ruling the roost. Nevertheless, it was probably at the height of their dominance that Shakespeare's elaborate bust was erected in Holy Trinity, and Anne Hathaway interred in the chancel beneath it. Probably it was Hall's long reach that did it. It looks as though he assumed the reins of the clan after his father-in-law's death. He had been Shakespeare's *de facto* lieutenant since his marriage to Susanna, and in business matters like the Welcombe enclosures the two men spoke with one voice. The scale of Shakespeare's legacy to his daughter and son-in-law makes it plain that Hall was seen by Shakespeare as the new head of the family.

The Shakespeares continued to go about their business unhindered, therefore, even to the point of burying their dead in the chancel and commemorating them by means of images. It may be that the surviving family was more put out by the council's impromptu prohibition than the players. Would Anne and her daughters not have wanted to see the King's Men perform one of Shakespeare's great works in Stratford? It would have been something quite unprecedented, and it may well have been the men's intention to celebrate the unveiling of Shakespeare's monument with a performance of one of his plays, so that his literary voice resounded for the first time in his own particular corner of England. But it never happened, and there is no way of knowing which play they would have chosen. *The Tempest* does however seem a likely contender, since apparently for Heminges and Condell it distilled above all others the quintessence of their friend's work.

Dating the monument in Holy Trinity to the summer of 1622 may explain the relationship between the bust, Shakespeare's grave, and Anne Shakespeare's grave. Anne's sits to the left of Shakespeare's and directly underneath the bust. If the sculpture and Shakespeare's grave had been contemporary, it seems likely that they would have been placed close together; but they may be separated in time by as many as six years, whereas there is little more than a year between Anne's grave and the bust. She died on 6 August 1623, three months before the First Folio appeared. The proximity of Anne's grave to her husband's bust may suggest that as she was dying in the summer of 1623 she decided that when the end came, she wanted to rest in full sight of him. Perhaps in her final moments Anne Hathaway felt that after all she and William Shakespeare did belong together in all eternity: she had been his wife for nearly thirty-four years, and his widow for seven.

Shakespeare's two daughters, speaking as one, bade farewell to their mother Anne Hathaway in a poignant intercessory prayer in Latin – just the kind of thing the Reformed Church had tried to eradicate. Nothing much has ever been made of the apparent Catholicism of Anne Hathaway's funerary inscription, yet few educated contemporaries could have missed the significance of these lines carved on the stone in the chancel of Holy Trinity in 1623. In English the inscription reads:

Oh Mother, you fed me with the milk from your breasts and you gave me life. Woe is me then that I have to return a tombstone for such gifts! How dearly I yearn for a good angel to remove this stone and release into the light your soul, the image of the body of Christ. But my prayers are to no avail. Come quickly, oh Christ; set free my mother from her prison tomb and let her rise to the stars.

It would be interesting to know what John Hall, tolerant and non-sectarian though he was, as a doctor, treating Protestants and Catholics alike, made of his wife and sister-in-law thus apparently praying openly for their mother in frankly Catholic vein, and how the zealous Protestant vicar Thomas Wilson came to permit the inscription in the chancel of his church. Perhaps Anne Hathaway's daughters offered this prayer to their dead mother because no more than her father-in-law John Shakespeare had she never shed her Catholic faith. They obviously adored her and probably suspected that she had suffered from their father's infidelities and prolonged absences in London; the depth of the bond between them would have been enhanced by the fact that she had brought them up mostly on her own. It is highly unlikely that either Susanna or Judith provided the Latin text, but they may well have sought the help of George Quiney, Judith Shakespeare's young brother-in-law. He had returned to Stratford from Balliol College, Oxford in 1621 and at the time of Anne's death was helping out both at the grammar school and as curate at Holy Trinity, where he was a 'reading-minister' – that is, he read the lessons and sermons but did not preach.[5] Quiney died at the age of twenty-four, probably of tuberculosis. He was attended by John Hall, who wrote in his case notes that Quiney 'was a man of a good wit, expert in tongues, and very learned'.

30

Life after Death

ANNE HAD SURVIVED her husband long enough to witness the love and loyalty borne him by his friends in the royal company of players. Doubtless she knew of the plans for the First Folio, and it may be that she and her family saw an advance copy. It can scarcely be doubted that the Halls owned a copy, and there may have been a handful of others in Stratford. The first intimation of what has become one of the most famous books in English literature was a mundane note in a Frankfurt book fair catalogue of 1622 advertising it as one of the books to be printed during April and October that year. Certainly the printing at Isaac Jaggard's press in London seems to have started early in 1622, but it was the best part of two years before it appeared in November 1623. The impact of the First Folio must have been considerable. Such was the status of the book and its commercial success that it was reissued within eight years. This Second Folio of 1632 was sumptuously printed on the best available paper and provoked from the Puritan William Prynne the comment that 'Shakespeare's plays are printed in the best crown paper, far better than most Bibles'.

In their prefatory exhortation 'to the great variety of readers' the editors, who spell their names 'John Heminges' and 'Henrie Condell', urge the public to buy the book. The fate of all books, they remind us, depends 'not of your heads alone, but of your purses . . . and you will stand for your privileges, we know: to read and censure. Do so, but buy it first.' And an elite public seems to have done just that. It has been estimated that as many as a thousand copies of the First Folio were printed.[1] The scale of the book and its price put it beyond the range of all but the wealthy – it cost about a pound, at a time when, it will be recalled, the head teacher of the Stratford grammar school was very well paid on £20 a year.[2] It was clearly a luxury item.

Sir Thomas Bodley in 1610 had obtained a grant from the Stationers' Company of a copy of every book printed in the country to be made to the Oxford library bearing his name. The Shakespeare Folio was eagerly consulted by Oxford students. During its first four decades in the Bodleian the tragedies in the First Folio were the most widely read, while the histories were the least popular plays in the collection. The favourite of all was *Romeo and Juliet*, followed by *Julius Caesar*, *1 Henry IV*, and *Macbeth*.[3] Other owners must surely have included Jonson, the Burbages, the dedicatees, Southampton, and of course the editors and heads of the syndicate, Heminges and Condell. The closest link with the original story of the Folio is provided by the widow of Henry Condell, Elizabeth. He married her in 1596, so presumably she must have known Shakespeare for at least twenty years. When she died she left 'all her books' to one of her executors, Thomas Seaman; it is all but inconceivable that there was not a First Folio among them. The Lord Chamberlain, the Master of the Revels, and various other panjandrums associated with the theatre probably also bought it. Certainly it must have been assumed that there was a ready market for it, otherwise Jaggard would scarcely have been employed for nearly two years in printing it: the staff and wage bills involved would have required that there be a substantial return. The reprint of 1632, with a new prefatory poem by one John Milton, a budding genius just hitting his stride, suggests that it had sold well.

As a book, Shakespeare's brilliant plays reached out into the whole country in a way they could not while they were confined to performances in the London theatres. The First Folio includes as a frontispiece an engraving of Martin Droeshout's portrait of Shakespeare; this was seen by contributors to the First Folio who had known Shakespeare for many years and clearly approved it as a true likeness just as Shakespeare's family must presumably have approved his bust. Martin Droeshout the younger was but twenty-two years old when Shakespeare died and could not have drawn the Folio frontispiece from life, since it shows Shakespeare some fifteen or so years before his death. But Droeshout could easily have copied an earlier depiction of Shakespeare like the one that was available to 'Gullio' in Cambridge around the time of *Hamlet*. It is now thought by some, however, that the picture was done by Martin Droeshout, Sr, who was only a year younger than Shakespeare: it could therefore be a portrait from life, since Droeshout might easily have met Shakespeare – in 1604 he lived in Crutched Friars in Aldgate ward, not very far from Shakespeare in Muggle Street.

The man in the Folio picture is the author in his late thirties, and there would seem to be artistic as well as practical reasons for believing that behind the Folio portrait there lies a sketch or 'limning' of Shakespeare. The reference in *Parnassus* (*c*.1601) to a picture of Shakespeare may be to this, of which there were probably multiple copies available, not least perhaps in the Shakespeare household. If it had been sketched from life, then Shakespeare probably saw it, and presumably he approved it. The Folio portrait is not a great picture, and it is tempting to think that the original might have been drawn by Burbage.[4] If not Burbage, there is an outside chance that it could have been someone like Hilliard, acting on behalf of Shakespeare's friend Southampton, the subject of one of Hilliard's best-known miniatures – though surely Hilliard would have produced a more accomplished matrix? Perhaps after all Richard Burbage was the source of the picture, his posthumous contribution to the Folio. The two editors would have had ready access to any sketches or drawings by their friend, through Burbage's widow and surviving family.

A copy of the original may yet turn up, closely resembling the engraving in the 1623 Folio but probably with a different ruff and clothing. In the engraving, the head looks as though it has been superimposed on a rather too opulent costume, more fitting perhaps for the Earl of Essex than for Shakespeare. But of course Shakespeare's status had changed between the time of the original drawing – around 1600 – and the publication of the Folio in 1623. It is true that he was a recognized gentleman with a coat-of-arms, but he was not as yet the man eulogized by Jonson as the paragon of dramatists, with a monument in the chancel of his parish church. It was a time when men were acutely conscious of status and the manifestations thereof – the Shakespeares demonstrably so – and it is therefore quite likely that the editors of the Folio prevailed on Droeshout to superimpose a copy of the likeness on a more aristocratic ruff costume, to signal to the world at large that William Shakespeare was indeed a gentleman. The result was unfortunate, however, a head-on-platter effect, with head and torso not fully joined up, nor in correct proportions. Nevertheless, despite the years that separate the two likenesses of the Folio and the bust in the chancel of Holy Trinity, it is not difficult to recognize that they show the same man at two different stages of his life.

The so-called 'Chandos' portrait, in which the subject provocatively establishes eye contact with his audience, is another with a long-standing claim to portray the true likeness of Shakespeare. It dates from the first decade of the seventeenth century, and the publisher Jacob Tonson put a version of it on the cover of Rowe's 1709 edition of Shakespeare. Betterton, who had been Rowe's most important source for his early biography of Shakespeare, was rumoured to have acquired the picture from Davenant, but it is known that Betterton purchased it at a sale and not from Davenant, who died intestate. In the eighteenth century it was alleged that the picture had once been owned by one John Taylor – but Shakespeare had no known associate of that name. 'John' may however be a mistake for *Joseph* Taylor (*c*.1586–1652), one of the twenty-six 'principal actors' listed in the First Folio. Edmond Malone credited him with having painted the picture; the evidence on which he based this claim is no longer extant, and Joseph Taylor seems too young to have painted the star of a company he only joined until after that star's death. Yet it may be that Taylor eventually came to own the Chandos portrait – an entirely different matter. Indeed, his track record in the company and his contacts with people from the time of Shakespeare to the Restoration both seem to point in just that direction. After Burbage's death in 1619 Joseph Taylor succeeded him in the King's Men and eventually he and John Lowin headed the company for seventeen years, up to the closure of the theatres at the outbreak of the Civil War in 1642. Lowin apparently shared his knowledge of Shakespeare's directions for *Henry VIII* with Davenant, as Taylor did for the much bigger part of Hamlet: '*Hamlet* being performed by Master Betterton, Sir William Davenant, having seen Master [Joseph] Taylor of the Blackfriars Company act it, who being instructed by the author Master Shakespeare, taught Master Betterton every particle of it.'[5] Taylor and Lowin died in 1652 and 1653 respectively; Lowin is known to have acted with Davenant, and it seems inconceivable that Taylor would not have known Davenant.

If Taylor owned the Chandos portrait, he could easily have passed it on to Davenant as its obvious heir (like Davenant, he died without leaving a will). The same eighteenth-century source which attributes the Chandos picture to John Taylor also reports a rumour that the artist instead might have been Richard Burbage:[6] in this case, the Chandos would seem to have passed from Richard Burbage, who painted it, to his successor in the company, Joseph Taylor, and thence to Davenant and, indirectly, to Betterton, who let Rowe reproduce it in 1709. If the Chandos was indeed by Burbage it would of course be contemporary – though not necessarily of Shakespeare; or it might show Shakespeare in a particular dramatic role, perhaps one he had made his own – and which required an earring: Iago in *Othello* perhaps? There are superficial similarities between the Chandos, the Folio engraving, and the bust, though the Chandos is of an older man than the Folio engraving, and the physical characteristics of the head itself seem too different for them to be of the same person. Even supposing Burbage to have painted and drawn Shakespeare on more than one occasion, it is unlikely that his head changed shape as he aged, from the oblong 'egg' of the Folio to the rounded, broader and receding features of the Chandos.

A further twist concerns the Chandos picture and its contorted relationship with the bust in Holy Trinity, involving the artist and engraver George Vertue, responsible for the image of New Place. Commissioned by Jacob Tonson in 1723 to engrave the bust, Vertue produced what he affirmed to be a true copy. And so it is, compared to the bust, except for one important detail: Shakespeare's head, which is that of the Chandos portrait.[7] What probably happened is that Tonson wanted to re-use the Chandos plate, which he still had from printing Rowe's Shakespeare in 1709, absolutely convinced that the Chandos showed the real Shakespeare. Vertue himself seems to have shared this view, jotting down in his notebooks in 1719 that the Chandos portrait had been 'bought for forty guineas of Master Betterton, who bought it of Sir William Davenant, to whom it was left by will of John Taylor, who had it of Shakespeare; it was painted by one *Taylor*, a player and painter contemporary with Shakespeare and his intimate friend.' In the left-hand margin the name Richard Burbage has been crossed out: clearly Vertue had heard about Burbage's draftsmanship, and considered the possibility that he might have been the painter. Vertue and Tonson were obviously of one mind: that the real Shakespeare was the face of the Chandos portrait. By superimposing the Chandos head on the Holy Trinity bust, Tonson and Vertue aimed to give their readers the authentic look of both poet and monument.

For the monument itself, Vertue followed a highly accurate drawing by someone else – perhaps Betterton, though Betterton must have been a superb draftsman to capture the detail shown in Vertue's 1723 engraving. Whoever was responsible would undoubtedly have drawn the correct head. Not until Vertue finally went up to Stratford in 1737 did he have an opportunity to draw the bust and monument himself. Yet even as he sketched it, in its evocative setting in the chancel of Holy Trinity, he could not resist the temptation to conflate the head he saw before him with the Chandos portrait: the Shakespeare in Vertue's drawing 'from life' of 1737 is a wispy hybrid of the chancel bust and the Chandos portrait. Vertue can hardly have been stunned or mortified to discover that the head he had drawn for Tonson in 1723 was not the one before him on the monument, for the head before him in 1737 must have been in the drawing he had used for the monument. What they thought they knew of the pedigree of the Chandos portrait had persuaded him and Tonson to override the evidence provided by the drawing. With the actual bust before him, however, Vertue's certainty seems to have wavered. Perhaps he was now too much the professional artist to repeat the benign fraud of 1723 – and yet after all, he was not sketching the chancel of Holy Trinity as a commission for a book: he wished only to convey a sense of its atmosphere. So he decided, it seems, to err on the side of truth, but only up to a point.

It is impossible to establish whether or not it was Betterton who drew the original on which Vertue based his plate for Tonson in 1723. Whoever it was, he was meticulous and connected to London publishing circles. If it was indeed Betterton, and if he was as scrupulous in gathering his oral history as he was in delineating Shakespeare's monument, then his credibility is immeasurably enhanced. To this day the fashionable Chandos portrait remains the most popular of all the

Shakespeare pictures, albeit there is no certainty that it – unlike the other two – depicts William Shakespeare.

The monument in Holy Trinity was touched up once in 1748 and again in 1793, when Malone had it whitewashed. In 1861 the white-wash was stripped off and the colours beneath were restored. However it came to pass, the quirks of history allow us to travel back in time, to see the thirty-eight-year-old author of *Hamlet* in the First Folio and the fifty-two-year-old solid Stratford burgher in Holy Trinity, where we gaze on William Shakespeare, husband, lover, father, and friend. This is what his contemporaries saw four hundred years ago, the human face of the imagination that dreamt up *Romeo and Juliet*, *King Lear*, *Antony and Cleopatra*, *The Tempest*, and many others.

At the end of March 1625 King James I died and shortly afterwards Shakespeare's granddaughter, Elizabeth Hall, left Stratford for London. The timing was probably fortuitous, but it may be that she had been invited to enjoy the festivities that accompanied the accession of Charles I. She was only seventeen, and despite the complication of her father's entry in his case notes she can hardly have travelled on her own; at the least an older woman must have accompanied her, possibly male members of the family too, or others from Stratford. It is not known where she stayed during her fortnight in London: perhaps a room had been set aside for her in the Blackfriars gatehouse, or perhaps she lodged with family friends.

John Hall was clearly counting Elizabeth among his success stories when he wrote up her case history in his medical diary, beginning vaguely enough with the information that 'in the beginning of April she went to London'. After 'returning homewards the 22nd of the said month', she suffered fierce pains on the right side of her face; three months earlier her left side had been similarly afflicted, her mouth had convulsed and her periods were blocked. Her father had repeatedly purged her, and eventually she had recovered fully, as she did this time: by his skill and 'by the blessing of God she was cured in sixteen days.' It is perhaps significant that Elizabeth was back in Stratford by the 22nd, that her father mentioned this date specifically, having been vague about her departure: it may, after all, have been something of a red-letter day in the family's year – Shakespeare's birthday. Elizabeth and her grandfather seem to have been close. She was the only daughter of his beloved Susanna, and his only grandchild, and she may have nearly lost her mother at birth. Shakespeare remembers her prominently in his will. She was eight when he died, and throughout the rest of her life she lived with the memory of her grandfather, the famous 'London' writer whose bust graced the chancel of Holy Trinity and whose very large book, the First Folio of 1623, she may well have read. The daughter of the renowned physician John Hall and the granddaughter of the much-honoured Shakespeare was undoubtedly literate as we noted when discussing her exquisite italic signature.

It was perhaps because it was her grandfather's birthday that the next year, 1626, Elizabeth chose 22 April on which to marry her parents' neighbour from Chapel Street, Thomas Nash. Thomas de Quincey was the first to connect the wedding day with Shakespeare's birthday. Shakespeare's monument reads 'OBIT ANO DOI 1616 AETATIS 53 DIE 23 April' – that is Shakespeare, who was baptized on 26 April, must have been born *on or before* 23 April 1564, since otherwise he would have been fifty-two years old at the time of his death, not fifty-three. Had Shakespeare's birthday fallen on St George's Day itself Elizabeth Hall would, presumably, have rushed at the chance to marry on that day, although this point is skewed by the fact that 23 April 1626 fell on a Sunday. One could be born and die on a Sunday but not marry on one. As it happens, 22 April 1564 was a Saturday and so was 22 April 1626. If Elizabeth Hall married on Shakespeare's birthday in 1626 (our 2 May), she may have done something similar again when she married for a second time in 1649, barely a month before her mother died. Perhaps she did not wish to replicate the time of her first marriage of twenty-three years earlier. It may all have been too painful. Perhaps she just wanted to do things differently, but this time she chose Billesley chapel, a place with which neither she nor her new spouse had any obvious connection but which, as we saw, may have some claim to being the chapel in which William Shakespeare married.

By the time of John Hall's death in 1635 Shakespeare's fame had spread throughout the land, and beyond the rich. Ordinary people up and down the country knew about him and Stratford. Only the year before a visitor with no known connections to Stratford had gone with two fellow travellers to inspect Holy Trinity, where among others they saw 'A neat monument of that famous English poet, Master William Shakespeare, who was born here.'[8] The visitor, one Lieutenant Hammond, about whom nothing is known, also noticed the Combe memorial, and spotted Shakespeare's 'witty and facetious verses'. Lieutenant Hammond matters because he was just an ordinary visitor whose knowledge of Shakespeare must have been derived exclusively from the dramatist's spreading fame.

It would appear John Hall left unsettled debts, because in 1637 New Place and its study were raided by some ruffians at the behest of Baldwin Brooks, who claimed to be owed money by the Hall estate. Brooks's men forced their way into New Place, breaking down doors, and carried off 'divers books' and 'other goods of great value' – so Susanna and her son-in-law Thomas Nash alleged in the suit they brought against Brooks in Chancery. Whether or not Brooks was right to claim that the Halls were trying to forfeit their debt to him, breaking and entering was scarcely something he could hope to get away with. Nevertheless, he went on to enjoy a civic career in Stratford and indeed to become mayor, suggesting that he and the Hall-Nash families eventually came to an accommodation.

In his will John Hall had casually referred to his books as items of no particular value that could be disposed of by burning – a ruse, perhaps to duck creditors like Baldwin Brooks? Like the Burbages, and perhaps like Shakespeare, Hall had drafted a will that deliberately underplayed the true value of his estate. Or perhaps by books he meant his own handwritten manuscripts. Nearly four centuries later one of these may hold the key to how Shakespeare died. This is the first volume of Hall's medical diary, the one that has not been found and which may languish unrecognized in a collection somewhere. It left New Place at the same time as its twin (now in the British Library).[9] It is a Latin text which, unusually for early seventeenth-century England, is written in a clear italic hand and consolidates the notion that Hall had studied medicine in France after Cambridge, since European writers used italic rather than secretary. In the seventeenth century the lost manuscript volume looked identical to the one that has survived. James Cooke (1614–88), himself a surgeon and the translator eventually of Hall's diary, knew Hall's longhand. He had been taken to New Place by a friend of Hall's who knew the family well enough to invite a stranger into their home to inspect Hall's books; perhaps he was another doctor or surgeon, perhaps even one of the two physicians who had treated Hall when he was seriously ill in 1632. Writing in 1658, Cooke remembered his encounter with Susanna:

> Being in my art an attendant to parts of some regiments to keep the pass at the bridge of Stratford-upon-Avon, there being then with me a mate allied to the gentleman that writ the following observations in Latin, he invited me to the house of Mrs Hall, wife of the deceased, to see the books left by Master Hall. After a view of them, she told me she had some books left, by one that professed physic with her husband, for some money. I told her, if I liked them, I would give her the money again; she brought them forth, amongst which there was this with another of the author's, both intended for the press. I being acquainted with Master Hall's hand, told her that one or two of them were her husband's and showed them her; she denied, I affirmed, till I perceived she begun to be offended. At last I returned her the money.[10]

What happened on this day at New Place was that Cooke and his companion were shown John Hall's study, which must formerly have been Shakespeare's. The study contained a library, and it was these books that Susanna exhibited proudly. It was quite possibly the only such library in Stratford. Here among 'the books left by Master Hall' would have been Shakespeare's Ovid, Plutarch, Holinshed, and other works, including, perhaps, quartos of his plays, a 1623 Folio, and even first draft manuscripts. The library of New Place presumably enjoyed a certain celebrity in the town in which everyone by now knew that William Shakespeare was famous. Susanna's proprietorial attitude to her 'books' suggests that these were big books with leather bindings, items that she was proud to show off to a stranger. Had Cooke not been a doctor she would never have thought of producing Hall's manuscripts. This act seems to have been an afterthought triggered by the profession of her visitor. After Cooke and his friend had finished admiring the books in the study, Susanna indicated that she had more books left. It is fairly clear from what followed that she meant a separate cache and that these were medical manuscripts or treatises. They had been written, she said, by someone who worked alongside her husband as a doctor. Who this was we do not know, but Susanna brought several manuscripts to show to her visitors. It seems that the Halls had paid for some of these papers. Or so she claimed. The point about money changing hands is made three times.

Among these new papers there were 'one or two' in Hall's hand-writing. Cooke was of course right – they were – but Susanna was now upset. She was adamant that these papers belonged to her husband's colleague and that the Halls had paid for them. She would not accept that any of them were Hall's. It beggars belief that she would not know her husband's handwriting, the more so since she clearly could herself write as her two signatures of 1639 and 1647 demonstrate. The truth is that Susanna probably only pretended to believe that these papers had been written by Hall's friend and bought by her husband for a sum of money. She must have known full well that they were Hall's but she wanted or needed cash and saw a chance of making some from Cooke. Hence perhaps the afterthought in the phrase 'by one that professed physic with her husband, for some money'. When she realized that Cooke had recognized Hall's distinctive italic long-hand, she must have felt acutely put on the spot. In the end Cooke paid up and acquired the two manuscripts.

As he walked away from New Place he carried with him John Hall's complete medical case studies. Left behind was the mistress of the house. She had received her money, of course, but it had been a bruising encounter.

Perhaps Susanna was short of ready money, possibly because of the impact of the Civil War on the local economy, but even in such straits she did not part with any of the printed books from her father's library; medical manuscripts were clearly a different matter, and though she initially appeared reluctant – to raise the price, perhaps? – in the end she did not scruple to sell some to another member of the medical fraternity. It does seem unlikely that she would not have known her husband's distinctive handwriting, but again this may have been part of a desire to make them seem more desirable.

Though John Hall kept Shakespeare's books and papers in trust as part of the family's heritage, one volume found its way into the pos-session of Colonel Richard Grace, who was with Queen Henrietta Maria in July 1643 when she stayed two nights at New Place. The

Marvellous Discourse upon the life of Katherine de Medicis, by Henri
Estienne, carries on the title-page the inscription 'Liber R: Graeci ex
dono amicae D. Susanne Hall' – 'the book of Richard Grace, as a gift
from his friend D. Susanne Hall'.[11] The handwriting dates from the
seventeenth century, but is not Susanna's. The use of the 'D.' in the
inscription may serve to identify Susanna as the wife of Dr John Hall
('D.' for 'doctor'), a bit perhaps like calling her 'Mrs John Hall' today.
There is no way of knowing why, or precisely when, Susanna presented him with the book. Perhaps he was at New Place as part of the
Queen's bodyguard in July 1643 or perhaps like Cooke the next year,
he visited at New Place simply because it was famous, and ended up
walking away with the gift of a book. It is tempting however to imagine Henrietta Maria browsing through the books in Hall's study and
stumbling across this one, her attention caught perhaps by the fact that
the subject was, like herself, a Medici – Henrietta being a daughter of
Maria de'Medici, who had died the year before her visit to New Place.
The fact that the inscription recalls Susanna rather than her father rather
suggests that the point of the gift was that it came from Susanna, and
that it was not seen as a trophy from William Shakespeare's library. It
is not known why the Queen elected to spend two nights at New
Place, but William Davenant was her protégé, so perhaps she had
heard of the house and its connection with Shakespeare, and was
simply satisfying her curiosity. As for Davenant himself, there is no
record of him meeting up with Susanna and Judith Shakespeare
during one of his periodic visits to Oxford where his parents were
buried. Stratford was a day's ride away and it is hard to believe that
Davenant would not have visited Holy Trinity and the Shakespeare
graves and perhaps even called in on the surviving Shakespeares. If,
though, his and Shakespeare's daughters' paths did not in fact cross, at
the very least they would have heard about Davenant from the Queen
when she lodged in New Place.

Susanna died on 11 July 1649, just over a month after her daughter
Elizabeth's second marriage on 5 June 1649. Perhaps she was already
dying, and Elizabeth brought forward her wedding to be sure of her
presence, just as her aunt Judith seems to have hurried to marry
Quiney when Shakespeare was near death.

Judith outlived her father by forty-six years. Her marriage had its shadows – the ghost of poor Margaret Wheeler and her dead baby, perhaps? In May 1617, barely a year after her father's death, her first-born, a baby called Shakespeare Quiney, died. Her other two children with Quiney died at nineteen and twenty-one, long before either of their parents. There must have been times when Judith felt that they were all paying for her husband's sins; his various attempts at business in Stratford only further exposed him as feckless or otherwise inadequate. From John Hall's records, it seems that he never treated his sister-in-law or any of her children. Over the years the chancel of Holy Trinity became crowded with her relatives, and in 1662 Judith joined them in her late seventies, the last of the Shakespeares of Stratford. Her niece, Elizabeth Hall-Nash had left the town years earlier and her aunt, Joan Hart-Shakespeare from Henley Street, had died in 1646. In her twenties, Judith may have been her father's Miranda; in her seventies, she was a childless old lady surrounded by memories and the ghosts of her father and mother, her sister – and above all perhaps, of the twin brother who had died so many years before.

It may be that she was still saddled with her husband Thomas Quiney when she died – he is known to have enjoyed a long life, but his death is not recorded. He could at best have been a shiftless companion. Quite apart from his early betrayal of Judith, his civic record in Stratford was unimpressive: neither the corporation nor Judith's family seem to have trusted him. Unlike other graves in the chancel Judith's is not marked, but in the Shakespeare row and to the right of her sister Susanna are two further graves. The pattern of the gravestones before the altar rail would seem to indicate that these are all the graves of those who married into the Shakespeare family: Anne Hathaway, John Hall and Thomas Nash, spouses of William, Susanna, and Elizabeth respectively. Judith and Thomas should be here too, and the two additional graves next to Susanna are probably theirs, though the names on them now belong to a couple who were buried within thirty and forty years of Judith's death. Susanna's grave suffered a similar fate in the early years of the eighteenth century, when it was opened to receive another tenant.

It would be nice to know whether John Ward spoke to Judith, as he intended, in the very year of her death. Among a list of tasks he jotted down in his diary in 1662 was 'to see Mrs Quiney', perhaps related to another memo to himself to 'Remember to peruse Shakespeare's plays and be versed in them, that I may not be ignorant in the matter.' Mrs Quiney – Judith – lived about five minutes' walk away from Ward's home. She was then seventy-seven, and may have been ailing, so possibly his visit to her was pastoral rather than literary. If he did see her, he left no record of what she said.

Like her mother Susanna and indeed her great-aunt's household in Henley Street, Elizabeth Hall-Nash experienced some privations during the billeting of troops in the town in the 1640s. The Harts had to part with some of their silverware, for which their lawyers sought compensation; Elizabeth's husband Thomas Nash demanded to be indemnified for his wife's loss of her 'scarlet petticoat and lacework' – surely not looted by soldiers? It does seem a frivolous loss, compared with others, but at the same time it is heartening to know that the daughter of 'Puritan' John Hall affected beautiful undergarments. As long as the children of Puritans wore scarlet petticoats, Stratford's policy of sensible religious compromise was secure. Where scarlet petticoats were worn, there was no need for scarlet letters. But it may be that there was more to those scarlet petticoats than meets the eye. Forty-odd years earlier, Elizabeth's grandfather had been issued with scarlet cloth for the coronation of King James. Presumably it was made up, and Shakespeare wore it on the day, and then never again. This was not a 'throwaway' society: such wonderful fabric would assuredly have been saved, and sooner or later re-used in some way – but would there have been enough for a luxury petticoat? Such a garment would give pleasure in itself, and probably as a commemorative gesture too. It was perhaps not entirely respectful to wear such 'royal' fabric as an undergarment, but it might have been considered imprudent to rework it for external, public wear. As a prestigious petticoat, it could have been passed from Anne Hathaway to her daughter and then to Elizabeth, like a royal talisman.

Along with her mother Susanna and her aunt Judith, Elizabeth carried the glorious burden of direct descent from William Shakespeare. Since her early teens she had seen her grandfather's effigy in the chancel of her parish church, and she cannot have doubted his standing in the community and the scale and nature of her heritage. In

1742, as Malone recorded, Sir Hugh Clopton told the actor Charles Macklin that when Elizabeth left New Place after her second marriage, to live on her husband's estate in Abington in Northampton, there was 'an old tradition that she had carried away with her from Stratford many of her grandfather's papers'. (This is the same Hugh Clopton who spoke to Joseph Greene about the Shakespeare daughters' graffiti in the leaded glass of New Place.)

It is not in the least surprising that Elizabeth Barnard should have taken with her all the family papers, including her father's and Shakespeare's – not just books and manuscripts either, but such important family papers as the grant of the coat-of-arms to John Shakespeare. The College of Arms has its copy in London, but the Shakespeares' own has not as yet come to light. Since it was probably drawn up on parchment, its chances of survival are excellent. Any papers Elizabeth moved out of New Place would almost certainly have been stored at Abington, and a search behind the panelling there was first suggested by Malone and Halliwell-Phillipps – but there is no reason why Elizabeth Barnard should have hidden them. On the contrary, her grandfather's library and coat-of-arms must have been prized possessions, to be willed down in the Barnard family.

In 1670 Elizabeth Hall, now Lady Barnard, died in Abington. Among the most significant features of her will is the fact that, unlike her grandfather, she left bequests to descendants of the Hathaways of Shottery and Stratford. Susanna Hall had made two of them trustees of her estate, and so did her daughter Elizabeth. It would seem that towards the end of her life Susanna sought to make her peace with her mother's family, and Elizabeth followed suit. In 1661 John Barnard had been knighted for services to the Crown during the Civil War. How that sat with John Hall's daughter it is impossible to know. Four years after his wife, Barnard himself died, and New Place was sold to Sir Edward Walker. He left it to his daughter, who married John Clopton. And so, after a century and a half, the house was back in Clopton hands. It is as if they had only ever let out this *domus* before repossessing it.

The inventory taken after Barnard's death included, in 'the study' of the house, 'desks, chests, cabinet, trunks, and boxes' to the value of more than £5, as well as the family 'plate' at around £29, 'rings, jewels and a watch' for £30 and, finally, 'all the books, £29 11.0'.[12] The value put on the books is impressive – the equivalent of the Barnard 'plate' and of all their jewels. One of these books may survive in the Bodleian. It is by Ovid, Shakespeare's favourite author, an Aldine edition of the *Metamorphoses* dating from 1502. On the fly-leaf opposite the title-page is written 'This little book of Ovid was given to me by W. Hall who said it was once Will Shakespeare's'. The writer of the note signs himself TN and dates the inscription '1682'.[13] The initials TN may belong to the noted antiquary and Anglo-Saxon specialist Edward (known as 'Neddy') Thwaites of Queen's College, Oxford, who shared a passion for Shakespeare with William Hall of Lichfield. If the copy of Ovid was indeed given to Thwaites, it would explain how it came to be preserved in the Bodleian, as his entire estate, including his books, was claimed by his college after his death. The question is whether it had ever reposed on a shelf in Shakespeare's library at New Place.

In 1682 Thwaites and William Hall, Jr were both still at school; later they were contemporaries at Queen's College, Oxford, from where they both graduated in 1694. Since Hall was described as junior, his father was probably also William Hall. The Shakespeare scholar E. K. Chambers deciphered Hall's father's first name as 'G<ul?>', which may stand for 'Guillaume', the French for William. By an odd coincidence, William Hall, Jr of Lichfield fetched up as rector in Acton, the very place where the father of Shakespeare's son-in-law John Hall had lived; and John Hall's father, a physician like himself, had been yet another William Hall. In his will of November 1635 John Hall left his father's house in Acton to his daughter Elizabeth; John Hall himself came from Carlton in Bedfordshire. It looks as though the Halls of Lichfield, Acton, and Carlton were all somehow related, and that 'William' was a Hall family name. The fact that at least one of these various Halls was apparently called 'Guillaume' rather than 'William' may suggest that the Halls were of Huguenot descent, hence perhaps their Protestantism; they may have been immigrants.

A French family connection might account for John Hall's odd educational progress: after Cambridge he disappeared from view to train as a doctor somewhere on the Continent, probably in France. If the various Halls are all related, then the William Hall on the fly-leaf of the Aldine Ovid probably inherited this book after Lady Barnard's death in 1670, or her husband's in 1674. Elizabeth's remembrance in her will of Hathaways descended from her grandmother's brother suggests a strong family feeling, which may have extended to her father's family. That someone named Hall should possess a book from Shakespeare's home makes perfect sense.

Thwaites and Hall move the story forward to the end of the seventeenth century, with William Hall of Lichfield possibly one of the last tangible links with the Halls of New Place. In 1735 the Reverend Joseph Greene took up his duties as Master at the grammar school. From then until the middle of the next century the Shakespearian treasures of Stratford were guarded locally by Greene (1712–90) and the Reverend James Davenport (1787–1841) and by Robert B. Wheler (1785–1857). And a principled guardianship was needed as the poet's fame grew, particularly in the wake of the publicity generated by Garrick's Jubilee in 1769, when the risk of forgery and false rumour must have reached a peak. With the arrival of Halliwell-Phillipps (1820–89), the founding of the Shakespeare Society in 1840, and the creation of the Shakespeare Birthplace Trust in 1847, legal guardianship of the Shakespeare heritage was officially assumed by the nation.

The days are long gone since Greene was able to discover Shakespeare's will to please a wealthy patron, or Wheler to trace the bond for the Shakespeare marriage because it was there waiting to be found. Yet though Stratford may have yielded all its main secrets, significant local discoveries about Shakespeare can still be made. Mary Arden's house was only correctly identified in the year 2000, for the first time since the late seventeenth century. The house on the green at Wilmcote had been there for hundreds of years, but it took some brilliant archival detective work by Nathaniel Alcock to reunite it to Mary. Similarly, Catharine and Ronald Page discovered the exact site of Shakespeare's grandfather's home in Snitterfield in 1982, while Jeanne Jones recently unearthed the important Hiccox and Ruttery inventories for the Henley Street house. The rooms described cannot easily be related to the interior as it is currently arranged, but the evidence they afford can only add depth to attempts to understand the building Shakespeare knew. As increasing numbers of manuscripts and

documents become readily accessible through electronic archival data-
bases, serendipitous finds of materials relevant to Shakespeare should
not be ruled out.

Henry James wisely cautioned: 'Never say you know the last word
about any human heart.' The infinite complexity of Shakespeare's
mind and personality can only be guessed at, but his life and his writings may well be intimately linked. Keats thought so, and he is
arguably Shakespeare's finest reader to date. These pages have
attempted to convey one sense of who Shakespeare was. From them
emerges a restless character, a contrary, turbulent, and impetuous
youth. Adolescent boys and girls have always found ways around the
mores and sexual sanctions of their time, and Shakespeare had sex
before he was married. He celebrates the power of sexuality in his
works: it is one of his enduring themes. At the same time his plays are
touchingly ingenuous about the romantic convergence towards marriage of young men and women, leading to speculation about him and
Anne, and how they might have felt about the baby girl who arrived
in 1583. If the literary and documentary records seem to show that
Shakespeare adored his children and that he enjoyed a lifelong close
and affectionate relationship with his daughters, with his wife, things
are more complicated.

What Shakespeare may not have known until he went to London
was that there existed another kind of sexual love, one no more
acceptable then than in later centuries. If Shakespeare slipped into
homosexual practices, it was likely to have been among the acting
community in Shoreditch. He was a country boy with a past – perhaps a convicted felon from Charlecote was more likely to experiment
with forbidden sex than a sober glover from Henley Street. Not only
had Will Shakespeare poached, it seems; he had retaliated against the
lord of the manor by satirizing him in verse, and it was this above all
that caused his disgrace. Here was someone to match Kit Marlowe,
the dare-devil author of the best-known play in the land, *Tamburlaine*.

There can be little doubt that a homosexual strain runs through
Shakespeare's plays and poems – particularly the *Sonnets*, which are
addressed to a beautiful young man, a young nobleman so androgynous in appearance that an early picture of him was long assumed to

be that of a young woman with delicate and refined features. He and Shakespeare may not have been involved sexually, but the bond between them was deep. At the same time, Shakespeare had a wife and family in Warwickshire to support: every gesture of love and every tenderness granted to the young man was a betrayal of them. Then Shakespeare trespassed further on his trothplight by taking a mistress.

It seems that he was no more to be contained by social conventions than Marlowe, except in the dark, forbidden place that was sectarian politics; here, he and Marlowe parted company. Whatever temperamental bonds may have existed between them, Shakespeare was politically always more guarded. That which perhaps propelled him towards Marlowe – a run-in with the authorities – may also have made him instinctively more careful. He had probably come close to losing everything in Charlecote: finding success in London, he would not run the same risk again – the more so since with his father in financial difficulties it fell to him to fend for his entire family. His love of his father was perhaps the overwhelming emotion of his early life. In committing a felony at the Lucys', young William may have felt that he had compounded the family's disgrace, that he was doubly implicated in the misfortunes of the Shakespeares of Henley Street.

It is one of the mysteries of the Shakespeare story that it cannot be determined where he stood on the greatest national issue of the day, the Catholic question. It is not that there are no clues: there are plenty, but they pull in opposite directions. The Borromeo will in the rafters of Henley Street would appear to be a gift to the Catholics, as might his purchase of the Blackfriars gatehouse, which had associations with the core of the recusant underground. His apparent abuse of the revered proto-Protestant Oldcastle in the *Henry IV* plays would tie in with this, since lampooning the Lollard hero would seem to be the act of a Catholic fellow-traveller. The rousingly anti-Popish *King John* points in the other direction, however, as does Shakespeare's use in *King Lear* of a cruel anti-Catholic tract condemning 'egregious popish impostures'. Even if his sympathies appear on balance to lean towards the Catholics – which would not be surprising, in view of his mother's links with the ancient and grand Catholic Ardens of Warwickshire – nothing is certain.

He might not have deemed it prudent to commit himself politically, but writing was a different matter. Shakespeare could not help it: he wrote because he had to. Thus it was with the Lucy ballads in the 1580s, and thus he continued throughout his life. While it is clear that he sometimes composed with his source text propped up on the desk before him, as in *Romeo and Juliet*, *Henry V*, and *Antony and Cleopatra*, his highly wrought metaphors and similes flowed from the heart and the soul, in no way affected by the bookishness of the writing process. *Romeo and Juliet* is a case in point. If indeed this play commemorates Shakespeare's dead son, it must be the most painfully personal in the canon – yet its literary source is a moralizing poem called 'The Tragical History of Romeus and Juliet' that Shakespeare follows closely, sometimes dramatizing it almost line-by-line. In him the 'scholar' and the creative artist go together in a way that is rare for the period. Beneath Shakespeare's iambic pentameters the drum that is the private self beats with percussive ardour.

The memorial bust and the Folio portrait convey some idea of what Shakespeare looked like, and it seems safe to assume that in conversation he was funny, witty, charming, and deep – someone who had thought profoundly about the human condition. It is tempting to suppose that he must have been irresistible to women, this man who loved women and who never lost his sense of wonder at female beauty and sheer feminine otherness. His view of women, Tamora, Goneril, and Regan notwithstanding, is that they are kind and gentle, 'tender-hefted', and endlessly desirable. Such was his imaginative gift for creating women that it is easy to forget that Juliet, Rosalind, Viola, Desdemona, Cleopatra, and all the young women of the last plays were played by boys and young men. But of course they were inspired by his knowledge of real women, his wife and his two mistresses, the Dark Lady and the English Lady, his own daughters above all.

It is no surprise to find that the writing life of the author of the *Sonnets* can be understood as being rarely separable from his life as he lived it – he can seem almost compulsively subjective. He reverts to limping time and again possibly because of a personal affliction. Similarly with Hamnet and *Hamlet*: the similarity of naming between his most ambitious tragedy and his own dead son surely reveals how deeply affected Shakespeare was by the loss of Hamnet. In following *Hamlet* with *Twelfth Night*, a play about twins miraculously reunited by means of dramatic orchestration, he appears to be trying to create a counter-reality in which he is king of all that he surveys. For Shakespeare his art was ever an extension of his life. *The Tempest* makes just this point, with William Shakespeare as Prospero, creator of heaven and earth, lording it over life and death. The fact that his people are puppets, mere characters in a play, is almost forgotten. There is a supreme confidence, perhaps even an arrogance, about the Shakespeare of that last great play about death and resurrection. He knew this, of course, and so Prospero returns to Milan to seek forgiveness in prayer and retreat. Prospero's world in *The Tempest* may have been the stuff of dreams, but the author of the play knew full well that no amount of make-believe or play-acting could alter the facts of life and death.

Shakespeare communicates through the English language, his appeal stretching well beyond the bounds of English to become as universal as it is possible to be outside the international medium of music. The scale and intelligence of the moral and philosophical questions posed in his works must have something to do with it. Shakespeare looked deeply into the seeds of things. He tried to understand life, to see whether it had a meaning or not, at the same time refusing the consolations afforded by traditional religion. His is the most articulate voice from a time when the deity of the western world was first unthroned, when the certainties of the godhead became the doubts of ordinary men and women. Shakespeare was steeped in the Bible as he was in the classics, but while they honed his language and imagination, neither had as deep an impact on him as the death of his son, his love for his father and his daughters, his involvement with a feckless young man, or indeed his successful womanizing, based perhaps on charm rather than obvious good looks. He was a man of prodigious energy, always writing, acting, and transacting: he never stopped. While travelling regularly and increasingly often between London and Stratford, he always remained a Warwickshire man at heart – there is something peculiarly modern about the picture of Shakespeare the successful London playwright commuting to cultivate his gardens and orchards in Stratford. As son, husband, and father his concerns were the same as everyone else's, and in wanting to make good he was no different from others among his contemporaries. An ordinary man, therefore – but an ordinary man with an extraordinarily timeless voice that fuels an unceasing desire to know ever more about its possessor.

Main Characters

Edward Alleyn starred in Marlowe's plays, notably *Tamburlaine*; he made a fortune and married the stepdaughter of the wealthy entrepreneur Henslowe and, after her death, John Donne's daughter.

Edward Arden was the head of the ancient Arden family of Park Hall with whom the Shakespeares claimed kinship. The Arden family were broken by the alleged Somervile plot.

Alexander Aspinall taught at the King's New School in Stratford for many years and resided close to New Place; he may have received gloves from Shakespeare along with a posy of verses.

John Aubrey was a seventeenth-century biographer and antiquary who left us tantalizing glimpses of Shakespeare's life.

Anthony Babington was a young Catholic nobleman and follower of Mary Stuart; he and others were found guilty of conspiring to overthrow Queen Elizabeth I.

The Badgers were recusant neighbours of the Shakespeares in Henley Street; they were arrested in the aftermath of the Gunpowder Plot.

Daniel Baker was a play-hating Puritan relative of the Quineys.

John Barnard married Shakespeare's granddaughter Elizabeth Hall in Billesley in 1649.

Emilia Bassano, the daughter of talented musicians of Venetian Jewish extraction, married Alfonso Lanier in 1592 after becoming pregnant by her aristocratic lover Henry Carey Hunsdon. At some point she may have become Shakespeare's mistress and therefore the so-called Dark Lady of the *Sonnets*.

Stephen Belott was apprenticed to a family of Huguenots with whom Shakespeare lodged; Shakespeare seems to have successfully interceded on their behalf with Belott.

Thomas Betterton, a famous Restoration actor, was the main source for Nicholas Rowe's biography.

Richard Burbage of the Lord Chamberlain's and King's Men played a number of the most important Shakespearian roles, including Hamlet, Othello, and King Lear.

Edmund Campion, a charismatic Jesuit who had been a renowned student at Oxford, led the 1580 mission to England which culminated in his martyrdom.

Henry Carey, first Baron Hunsdon, acted as patron of the Lord Chamberlain's Men, Shakespeare's company, until his death in 1596; Emilia Bassano had been his mistress.

The Cawdreys were Stratford recusants and George Cawdrey, a near contemporary of William Shakespeare's at school, trained as a Jesuit at Rheims.

William Cecil (father) and **Robert Cecil** (son) were courtiers *par excellence* and the most skilful and powerful members of the Privy Council for most of Shakespeare's life.

Henry Chettle, playwright and printer of Robert Greene's polemic against Shakespeare and Marlowe; he subsequently apologized for libelling Shakespeare.

The Cloptons were one of the grandest Warwickshire Catholic families and were the chief benefactors of Stratford-upon-Avon for several centuries.

Lord Cobham (Sir William Brooke) was the father-in-law of Robert Cecil; he was briefly Lord Chamberlain at just the time when Shakespeare called his fat knight Oldcastle, a historical character who had been an illustrious ancestor of Cobham.

William Combe of the powerful Combe family was the son of Shakespeare's friend John Combe; William tried to push through enclosures in Welcombe in the teeth of fierce local opposition and a ruling by the Lord Chief Justice.

Henry Condell of the King's Men joined forces with John Heminges to produce the 1623 commemorative Folio of Shakespeare's plays.

James Cooke was an army surgeon who bought John Hall's medical diaries off Susanna.

The Cottoms were a recusant family from Lancashire; one of their sons, John, became a teacher at Shakespeare's school while the other one, Thomas, joined Campion as a Catholic priest.

Jane Davenant was the wife of a play-loving, wealthy London merchant; she may have become Shakespeare's lover after she moved to Oxford.

William Davenant was born in 1606 and was reputedly Shakespeare's son or godson.

The Debdales were an 'obstinate' Catholic family from Shottery who must have known Anne Hathaway's family well. Their son Robert was a Jesuit and a friend of Campion's.

Robert Devereux, second Earl of Essex was a powerful courtier and the

Queen's favourite until his disastrous Irish campaign; in the end he rose up against her, dragging the young Southampton down with him.

Leonard Digges was the stepson of one of Shakespeare's executors and wrote a prefatory poem for the First Folio in which he refers to the monument in Holy Trinity.

Martin Droeshout the younger is usually credited with the frontispiece of the First Folio, which he may have copied from an earlier drawing of Shakespeare.

Guy Fawkes was the most famous participant in the Gunpowder Plot.

Richard Field, a London printer and publisher, came from Bridge Street in Stratford; he probably knew Shakespeare at school and the two men seem to have stayed friends all their lives.

John Florio was Southampton's Italian tutor and a translator of Montaigne.

Simon Forman, astrologer and alchemist, was a quack who was consulted by, among others, Emilia Bassano-Lanier, Jane Davenant, Winifred Burbage, and Marie Mountjoy, Shakespeare's landlady in the early seventeenth century.

Henry Garnett was a former printer turned Jesuit; he succeeded William Weston as the movement's Father Superior in England and remained so until his arrest in 1606.

John Gerard was a tall and aristocratic Jesuit who pursued his apostolate even after his capture, torture, and escape from the Tower.

Robert Greene was a Cambridge-educated dramatist and author of a notorious pamphlet in which he warns his fellow players against Shakespeare.

Thomas Greene and his brother John seem to have been cousins of the Shakespeares. Thomas trained as a lawyer at Middle Temple and lived in New Place for a while; he served on Stratford borough council for a long time.

William Greenway was a Stratford carrier with business premises in Henley Street; he operated some kind of shuttle between London and the Midlands.

Elizabeth Hall was Shakespeare's granddaughter.

John Hall married Susanna Shakespeare and went on to become the most renowned physician in Warwickshire.

Samuel Harsnett was the author of a virulent anti-Catholic tract called *Popish Impostures* which Shakespeare, surprisingly perhaps, used in *King Lear*.

John Heminges played in Shakespeare's troupe and, together with Henry Condell, headed up the syndicate that oversaw the publication of the First Folio.

Philip Henslowe was a London businessman who owned theatres, brothels, and bear-baiting venues.

William Herbert, third Earl of Pembroke, godson of Queen Elizabeth I and nephew of Sir Philip Sidney, has sometimes been thought to be the W.

H. of the dedication of the *Sonnets*. Heminges and Condell dedicated the 1623 Folio to him and his younger brother Philip

Lewis Hiccox became Shakespeare's tenant in the house in Henley Street after John Shakespeare's death.

Richard Hornby was the Henley Street blacksmith whose forge stood just up from the Shakespeares' home.

Simon Hunt would have taught Shakespeare between the ages of seven and eleven; Hunt may have left the grammar school to become a Jesuit.

Thomas Jenkins probably taught Shakespeare at school in his early teens and seems to have provided the model for Sir Hugh Evans in *The Merry Wives of Windsor*.

Davy Jones was a Stratford impresario who staged the town's Whitsun play in 1583; he was the brother-in-law of Shakespeare's friend and correspondent Richard Quiney.

Ben Jonson was a brilliant playwright and poet who knew Shakespeare well.

Edmund Lambert was married to one of Shakespeare's mother's sisters; after his death the Shakespeares litigated against his son over property.

John Lane of the Lanes of Alveston spread unsubstantiated rumours about Susanna Hall's sexual behaviour.

Francis Langley was a shady London businessman who owned the Swan theatre on Bankside and was implicated in the unsavoury affair of the *Madre de Dios* diamond.

Sir Thomas Lucy of Charlecote welcomed Queen Elizabeth to his home when Shakespeare was a little boy and may have been the Justice of the Peace before whom the young Shakespeare was arraigned for poaching.

John Manningham was training as a lawyer when he saw *Twelfth Night* performed at Middle Temple.

Christopher Marlowe was the author of *Tamburlaine* and *Dr Faustus* and may have been the rival poet of the *Sonnets*.

John Marston was a playwright and, like his father, a member of Middle Temple.

Francis Meres wrote *Palladis Tamia* in which he acclaims Shakespeare as the heir to Ovid and refers to his 'sugared sonnets among his private friends'.

The Mountjoys were a Huguenot family with whom Shakespeare boarded and whose domestic dispute about a dowry he helped resolve.

Thomas Nash was Shakespeare's neighbour at New Place and the first husband of the poet's granddaughter Elizabeth Hall.

Thomas Nashe, poet, playwright, and pamphleteer, overlapped with Marlowe at Cambridge; he dedicated his novel *The Unfortunate Traveller* to the young Southampton.

Edmund Neville was related to the great Warwickshire family of Edward Arden and staged several spectacular, if futile, attempts to escape from the Tower.

Nicholas Owen built the Catholics' hiding places and was himself an aspiring Jesuit; he died under torture in the Tower of London.

Robert Perrott, a wealthy Puritan landowner and brewer at Luscombe near Stratford, was the grandfather of Susanna Woodward of Shottery.

Augustine Phillips was an actor in the Lord Chamberlain's Men; he was summoned before the Privy Council to explain the company's putting on *Richard II* the Saturday before the Essex rebellion.

Thomas Platter, a Swiss visitor to London and a diarist, recorded seeing a production of *Julius Caesar* at the newly opened Globe in the autumn of 1599.

Richard Quiney was a friend and neighbour of the Shakespeares from Stratford and wrote the only surviving letter addressed to the dramatist; his son Thomas married Judith Shakespeare.

William Replingham was one of the Combes' lieutenants and an occasional guest in Shakespeare's New Place during the proposed Welcombe enclosures.

The Reynolds family lived up from the Shakespeares in Chapel Street and were deeply recusant.

John Rigby had been converted to Catholicism by John Gerard and was cruelly executed in the Old Kent Road.

Walter Roche from Lancashire may have been the infant William Shakespeare's first teacher at the King's New School in Stratford.

Nicholas Rowe, Shakespeare's first biographer, had access to information from seventeenth century Stratford and is the main source for the Charlecote poaching story.

The Sadlers were a rich Stratford family with close links to the Shakespeares, who may have named their twins Judith and Hamnet after the Sadlers.

Rafe Smith was a haberdasher with whom, it was alleged, Susanna Hall had an affair which left her with a venereal infection.

William Smith from Henley Street served alongside Shakespeare's father John on the town council; he may have stood as godfather to William.

John Somervile was Edward Arden's son-in-law. On his way to London from Warwickshire he publicly proclaimed his intention to kill the Queen, thus bringing about the perdition of himself and of the Ardens.

Robert Southwell was a Jesuit and poet who perished at Tyburn; his best-loved poem is recalled in *Macbeth*.

Abraham Sturley was a Puritan businessman and bailiff in Stratford who urged Richard Quiney to get Shakespeare to invest in the Stratford area.

Thomas Thorpe published Shakespeare's *Sonnets* in 1609, perhaps in close collaboration with their author.

Richard Topcliffe was the regime's cruel and loathed inquisitor-in-chief.

Richard Tyler, husband of Susanna Woodward, may have acted as god-parent to the Shakespeares' first-born; he was crossed out in the final draft of Shakespeare's will.

William Tyler was a butcher in Sheep Street and served with John Shakespeare on the borough council.

George Vertue, an engraver, sketched Shakespeare's New Place, the chancel of Holy Trinity, and the Shakespeare bust in the eighteenth century.

John Ward reported rumours about Southampton's munificence towards Shakespeare and about the dramatist's earnings that were circulating in Stratford in the middle of the seventeenth century.

William Wedgewood was a bad-tempered and bigamist tailor in Henley Street.

William Weston spent many years in prison in Wisbech and London after a brief spell as Father Superior of the Jesuits in England.

The Whateleys were a rich family of glovers from Henley Street with roots in Henley-in-Arden; their allegiances were suspect as they had 'unsound' Catholic priests in the family.

Margaret Wheeler was probably related to the Wheelers of Henley Street; she conceived an illegitimate child from Thomas Quiney, who was engaged to be married to Judith Shakespeare.

George Wilkins was Shakespeare's collaborator on *Pericles*.

Robert Willis, a Puritan, recorded how his father took him to see a play in Gloucester Town Hall.

Thomas Wilson became the Puritan rector of Holy Trinity in 1619; he was friends with John Hall.

The Woodwards, who resided at Shottery Manor, had a daughter called Susanna. She married Richard Tyler and may have been a lifelong friend of Anne Hathaway to whose first-born she may have stood as godmother.

Henry Wriothesley, third Earl of Southampton, was the young man to whom the *Sonnets* may have been addressed. He had been a ward of Lord Burghley but became a close friend of the Earl of Essex with whom he stood trial for treason.

Richard Young was chief justice of Middlesex and a close collaborator of Topcliffe.

Appendix
Two Stratford maps

Stratford-upon-Avon in Shakespeare's Time

After Samuel Winter 1768 and Fripp, showing the population and housing density of Stratford in the middle of the eighteenth century. This was not very different from Shakespeare's time.

Henley Street in Shakespeare's Time

The detailed information for the Henley Street map is provided by a combination of borough and corporation levies and by an important list of manorial tenants from 6 October 1590. The list contains all the freeholders or *liberi tenentes*, notably the Borough, the College, and Crown, and a number of named individuals, who answered directly to the Lord of the Manor. For the borough and corporation tenants the Rent Rolls help determine who lived where, although this is not always an entirely reliable guide. Also properties changed hands repeatedly during Shakespeare's lifetime, a process that may have been accelerated by the various fires that affected Henley Street.

Using the twelve-pence per burgage ground rent as a guide (one burgage = 57.75 feet frontage and 198 feet depth) I have drawn the fronts of the houses proportionately. Thus a four-pence house like Combe's, for example, on the north side near the town end of Henley Street, measures one third of the twelve-pence property of George Whateley next door. Things are, however, rarely clear-cut since not all the ground rents are levied for houses. Gardens and barns are also counted in; they probably did not attract the same levy. There may have been as many as five gardens on the north side, including one between John Shakespeare and his neighbour Badger.

Again several freeholders are also borough tenants. John Wheler leased two properties from the corporation while also owning two. The ever-expanding Robert Johnson, vintner and innkeeper, was in a similar situation. In 1591 he acquired the large Ichiver property which eventually became The White Lion and is now the site of the Birthplace archives. Johnson also leased a large barn from John Shakespeare, and in 1599 he successfully bid to the borough to redevelop the fire-damaged site of the Cawdrey house a few yards across from the Birthplace. His empire was spreading at the same rate as the Hiccoxes', who were becoming his neighbours on both sides of the street.

In order to match borough tenants, who paid rent, to unidentified borough property addresses in the 1590 survey, the frontages of the houses and the rents recorded in the various Rent Rolls need to be correlated. It appears to be the case that one burgage at twelve-pence may entail a rent of 18 shillings so that $1s. = 0.66d.$, $6s. = 4d.$, and so on. The resulting matches can then be cross-referenced to the borough Rent Rolls. Since the rent collectors did not follow a standard topographical template when recording their levy, it is not always clear whether their ledger entries start at the east end or west end of Henley Street, or indeed on the north or south sides. Also their entries sometimes criss-cross the road without signalling that they are doing so. There was, of course, no need for this since they knew exactly who was who and where everyone lived in sixteenth-century Stratford.

The anomaly of the Hart and Hiccox rates at the Birthplace is discussed in the main text. The 1590s levy of nineteen-pence ground rent suggests that the western wing of the Birthplace attracted over twice the ground rent of the east house. But the two smaller bays are not twice the size or width of the substantial east house. The reason why the separate levy for the west wing of this unified structure is so high must mean that either the cottage at the back was already there in 1590 after all, and was included in the estimate for the west wing, or else the levy was for the west wing without the back extension, but with a garden between John Shakespeare and George Badger.

Notes

CHAPTER 1: STRATFORD, 1564

1. I am indebted to Paul Edmondson for this reference.
2. 26 April 1564 corresponds to modern 6 May since the Elizabethans computed the year by the antiquated Julian calendar. This was eventually superseded by the reformed Gregorian calendar which we still use today.
3. This note was written into the register at a later date. The records of Holy Trinity are undoubtedly authentic, but it is worth noting that they are a parchment copy of a paper originally made in 1600 when Richard Byfield was vicar, on the order of the ecclesiastical authorities. It is not known what happened to the original Holy Trinity register, nor is it certain that the transcripts are entirely accurate, since there seem to be inexplicable gaps – for instance, the marriage of Anne Hathaway's father to his second wife Joan. All pre-1600 parish registers theoretically exist in two copies, one the original paper version and the other the parchment copy.
4. The Smiths of Henley Street should not be confused with a family of the same name who were mercers and owned shops in Middle Row, the central reservation of houses, shops, and taverns that divided Bridge Street into Fore Bridge Street (south) and Back Bridge Street (north). This William Smith lived on the western edge of High Street, in a place called 'The New House'. He had a son by the name of William who proceeded from Stratford King's New School to Winchester because his mother Alice Watson's brother was the same John Watson who became Bishop of Winchester. At Winchester the boy William Smith was registered as 'William Smith of Stratford-upon-Avon'. From here he went up to Exeter College in Oxford in 1583 while his likely schoolmate, the glover Will Shakespeare, was learning about fatherhood. The younger Smith has been dubbed 'the aptest scholar of Shakespeare's class', which may or may not be true.

5. SBTRO BRU 15/2/4.
6 Caraman 1964: 90.

CHAPTER 2: WILLIAM SHAKESPEARE'S SCHOOLDAYS

1. Pinder was born in March 1566 and was the son of the John Pinder who was Stratford parish clerk in 1583. There is no record in the Stratford parish registers of the baptism of either Joyce Cowden or Elizabeth Evans, although several other daughters of William Evans are listed. If Elizabeth was entered under another name she might, just possibly, be the Joan Evans who was baptized on 20 September 1579. It is possible that Pinder misremembered her first name or that she refused to give it. The reason for preferring Joan to the other sisters is because her date of birth fits with the only other woman who could be 'Joyce Cowden', and that is Joan Cowell, who was baptized 4 March 1579 (assuming that Cowden/Cowell is her maiden name, like Evans'). That makes the two of them contemporaries at school and around 25 at the time of their arrests. Shakespeare might not have known them but he was bound to know their parents if he got to hear of them, as he probably did.
2. Wells 2002: 11.
3. Fripp 1928: 49.
4. Jones 2002: no.92.
5. In a letter of 12 December 1566 Jenkins was described by Sir Thomas White of St John's College, Oxford as the son of one of his servants in London, but this does not mean he was not Welsh.
6. 'Sir' here means a parson or priest. For half a century one 'sir' William Gilbert was a Stratford relief teacher. He was also a curate (Sir Hugh Evans is a parson) and taught as under-master in the 1560s and 1570s. He could well have taught the infant Shakespeare. He wrote out the will of Shakespeare's father-in-law Richard Hathaway in 1581, the year before Will and Anne married.
7. *Henry VIII* 3.2.358–64.

CHAPTER 3: MEETING THE
NEIGHBOURS IN 1582

1. *MA* iii.24.
2. The full extent of John Shakespeare's financial troubles is charted in a study by Robert Bearman, 'John Shakespeare: A Papist or Just Penniless?' in *Shakespeare Quarterly* 2006.
3. Shakespeare's Stratford had *apothecaries; bakers; blacksmiths; brewers; bricklayers; butchers; button-makers; carpenters; chandlers; clock-makers; coopers; corvisors* or *shoe-makers; curates; cutlers; drapers; dyers; fish-mongers; glovers* and *whittawers; glaziers; goldsmiths; haberdashers; hatters; husbandmen; iron-mongers; linendrapers; masons; maltsters; mercers; midwives; millers; painters; plumbers; publicans; rough-masons; saddlers; shearmen; solicitors; street cleaners; surgeons; tailors; tanners; teachers; tinkers; vintners; weavers; wheelwrights; wooldrivers; woollendrapers.* It would be easy to pair almost every one of these with multiple names from the extensive Stratford corporation records. What this miniature survey of arts, crafts, trades, and professions demonstrates is quite how diverse the town was.
4. *MA* i.61.
5. 'Greeneway' in the originals, which Wells and Weis read as 'Greenway'. Shapiro and Jones have 'Greenaway'.
6. *MA* i.103.
7. Fripp 1928: 16. Fripp (1861–1931) was a great Stratford antiquarian and life trustee of the Birthplace.
8. The Bradley house had been in the occupation of the whittawer William Wilson since at least 1574, if not since 1563 when Bradley's lease expired (SBTRO: BRU 8/8/4).
9. *MA* i.124.
10. *The Black Book of Warwick.*
11. *MA* iv.40n.3.
12. Some Stratford historians, notably Fripp and Jones, place him on the site of the present 46–49, in which case his property would have stood opposite the Shakespeares.

CHAPTER 4: ENTER WIFE AND DAUGHTER

1. Chambers 1930 ii.41–2.
2. The entry is a clean transcript and fair copy and one not made on the

day but written up later (Brinkworth 88), although Schoenbaum disagrees. Following J. W. Gray's classic 1905 study of the Shakespeare marriage, Schoenbaum notes that 'The clerk, one suspects, was copying from a hastily written temporary memorandum, or from an unfamiliar hand in an allegation; he had just been dealing with Whateley [William Whateley], and by a process of unconscious association made the substitution' (Schoenbaum 71).

3. Occasionally biographers have implied that Betterton journeyed to Warwickshire at Rowe's behest. While there is nothing contentious about that, it would push back in time the date of Betterton's journey, as does the *ODNB* entry which notes that 'Late in his life Betterton journeyed to Stratford-upon-Avon to do research on Shakespeare . . .' But Halliwell-Phillipps argues that Betterton, who died in 1710, is not likely to have undertaken his trip to Stratford towards the end of his life but rather earlier.

4. These terms derive from the inventories of Lewis Hiccox (1627) and John Rutter (1648), who both later occupied the Birthplace. During Hiccox's time there Shakespeare's sister and her family inhabited a wing of the house, and when the Rutter inventory was drafted Joan Shakespeare-Hart had been dead for only two years. Both her nieces were alive, and Judith lived until 1662.

The Hiccox and Rutter inventories mirror each other quite closely – unsurprisingly, as they show the same house a mere twenty years apart; what differences there are arise from the different terminology deployed by different inventory-takers. Hiccox acquired his lease on the property from Shakespeare himself, so this was the house that Shakespeare had lived in, although the cottage at the back was not there when he moved out in 1597. Hiccox turned the house into an inn and in his inventory no fewer than thirteen discrete spaces are listed and their contents are itemized. These include the kitchen and the brewhouse as well as the cellar (similarly in Rutter), plus something like another ten rooms. It is not surprising to find from the inventory that they were stuffed with beds, for the purpose of an inn was of course to accommodate as many people as possible overnight.

The 1627 and 1648 inventories are tantalizing documents, teasing in the amount of detail they provide about the Shakespeare house(s) (the plural is used in Hiccox which makes it clear that the entire house minus the back cottage is meant), but silent of course on the subject of how John Shakespeare and his family lived. Nor is it clear whether the terms used to describe the rooms date from the Shakespeares, or were invented by the two publicans. After all, rooms in inns *did* have names, as Shakespeare's *Henry IV* plays or indeed the huge inventory for the Swan Inn down near Stratford Bridge affirm.

5. Burgages were calculated at 3.5 perches by 12 perches with a perch measuring 16.5 feet. In other words a full burgage would have a frontage of 57.75 feet and a depth of 198 feet, and yield an annual rate of 12 pence.

6. *MA* iii.129,137.

CHAPTER 5: POACHING FROM THE LUCYS

1. Halliwell-Phillipps 1887: i.xii–xiii; The chorus of voices approving of Rowe was joined by J. W. Gray in his ground-breaking study of the Shakespeare marriage in 1905. Rowe's sources and his researcher in Stratford did not realize that another John Shakespeare with children had lived there at the time. He was a shoemaker or 'corvisor' from Bridge Street and does not seem to have been related to the poet. Rowe's most striking omission was Shakespeare's son Hamnet. We will never know for certain now, but the absence of Hamnet from Rowe may be deliberate on the part of one of his main sources, Davenant. Perhaps it suited him to 'forget' about Shakespeare's son. Why this might be so we will see later.

2. *MA* v.31.

3. Chambers 1930: ii.289–90.

4. *MA* iii.170: 6 September 1586.

CHAPTER 6: BOUND FOR LONDON

1. Harrison 397–406.

2. Fripp (*MA* iii.55). See also Chambers 1930: ii.149ff. on Thomas Greene for a full and intelligent discussion of his possible links with the Shakespeare family. Fripp (*MA* i.xxxii) also writes that a sister or a daughter of Shakespeare's grandfather Richard may provide the link with the Greenes: 'A sister of Richard Shakespeare may have been the mother, or his daughter may have been the wife of Thomas Greene of Warwick . . . who died in July 1590, and whose son, afterwards Town Clerk of Stratford, and a friend of William Shakespeare, called himself Thomas Greene *alias* Shakespeare'.

3. *Buckinghamshire Record Society Publications* ed. John Wilson no. 21 (1983).

CHAPTER 7: EARLY DAYS IN SHOREDITCH

1. Caraman 1965: 81.
2. Challoner: 244–5.
3. This is John Shakespeare *versus* William Burbage. In 1589 the two liti-gants had sought judgement by appearing before the notoriously conservative Sir Edmund Anderson 'and his fellow justices' of the Queen's bench. (*MA* iv.151) Anderson had become chief justice of the court of common pleas in 1582, coincidentally the same year that this lawsuit was apparently settled with an injunction to John Shakespeare to repay Burbage 'at the sign of the Maidenhead in Stratford aforesaid between the hours of one and four o'clock in the afternoon' (*MA* iv.59). Anderson had prosecuted Campion in November 1581 and during the trial had addressed to Campion a phrase Shakespeare later immortalized in *Hamlet*: '. . . Had you come hither for love of your country, you would never have wrought a *hugger-mugger*, had your intent been to have done well, you would never have hated the light; and therefore this budging deciphereth your treason.' If John Shakespeare harboured the least Catholic sympathies, he found himself before an old judge with Catholic blood on his hands from his recent clash with the saintly Campion. Anderson adjudicated against John Shakespeare, but the glover was back in court in 1592.
4. Stow 1603: ii.78.
5. Caraman 1964: 68–9.
6. Challoner 135, 150.

CHAPTER 8: LIKELY LADS

1. Eccles 1934: 126.
2. It is known that the play was in existence by the summer of 1587, because in a letter dated 16 November 1587 a law student named Philip Gawdy reported home to his father that a child and a pregnant woman in the audience were killed when a live musket used on stage was acci-dentally discharged into the crowd during what was probably a scene from the sequel to *Tamburlaine*.
3. Our source is a remark of Lucifer's in Thomas Middleton's *Black Book*, when he refers to one of his 'devils in *Dr Faustus* when the old Theatre cracked and frightened the audience.'

4. Greenblatt 256–7.

5. E. K. Chambers long ago suggested a date of around 1589, since lines from the play seem to be parodied by Robert Greene in his 1589 romance *Menaphon* and in its prefatory epistle by Nashe. Chambers noted further that the play imitated passages from *Tamburlaine* (*c.*1587) and *Dr Faustus* (*c.*1588) and then wrote that Shakespeare was often credited with a hand in the old play. (Chambers 1923: ii 48–9.)

6. Thus, for example, a character by the name of Polidor quests for 'those lovely dames' who to him seem 'Richer in beauty than the orient pearl / Whiter than is the Alpine crystal mould, / And far more lovely than the Tyrian plant, / That blushing in the air turns to a stone.' Again, phrases like 'heaven cristalline', 'liquid gold', 'precious fiery pointed stones of Indy', the 'azure down, / That circles Citherea's silver doves', the 'crystal Hellespont' which yields rich coffers of 'wealthy mines' in which 'millions of labouring Moors' seek for rare stones, the 'topless Alps', all unmistakably evoke the famous topless towers of Ilion from *Dr Faustus*. Marlowe's *Dr Faustus* is echoed again in 'Grecian Helena / For whose sweet sake so many princes died, / That came with thousand ships to Tenedos', and when Philema proposes to freight ships 'with Arabian silkes, / Rich affrick spices Arras counterpoines . . . sweet smelling Ambergreece . . .' we are transported by her rhetoric into a world of language that yearns to be Marlowe.

7. Gurr 1996:271: 'I am almost convinced that Shakespeare was with his plays in Pembroke's Company at the Theatre in 1592 and 1593.' The fate of Pembroke's Men may well have been sealed by the onset of the plague in midsummer 1592.

8. Bullough i.58.

9. *Henry 6* was played 14 times, with 'large takings', at the Rose, between 3 March and 20 June 1592 according to Henslowe's *Diary*. Michael Wood calculates that the audience figures may have been over 32,000. (Wood 142).

CHAPTER 9: LIVING THE SONNETS

1. The so-called first part of *Henry VI* is probably a collaborative work. Vickers 2002: 148–243 makes the strongest case yet for George Peele as Shakespeare's collaborator in *Titus Andronicus*.

2. Ward 183–4.

3. Shapiro 2005: 150.

4. Southampton was still exhibiting a long mane during the two years he spent in the Tower before his release on 10 April 1603. A few years earlier it had suffered indignity at the hands of one Ambrose Willoughby, a gentleman of the Queen's Chamber, during an altercation between him and Southampton. The source for this information about a real-life version of Pope's mock-epic *The Rape of the Lock* is Rowland Whyte, who relates how Southampton, Ralegh, and one Parker were at primero (a gambling card game of the time) in the Presence Chamber. When they were asked by Willoughby to give over and retire since the Queen had gone to bed, they at first refused. Willoughby threatened to call the guard, at which point they relented: 'But my lord Southampton took exceptions at him between the tennis court wall and the garden, struck him and Willoughby pulled off some of his lock' (Akrigg 68).

CHAPTER 10: THE RIVAL POET

1. By a strange twist of fate Parsons was visited in Madrid in the late 1590s by the eventual publisher of Shakespeare's sonnets, Thomas Thorpe, who may have been a Catholic sympathizer.
2. Schoenbaum 1975: 116.
3. After writing this I discovered that Fripp makes much the same point in *MA* iv. xlviii when talking about Shakespeare and Greene. I entirely concur with Fripp's refusal to separate the plays and life artificially even if he takes this further than I do.
4. Akrigg 181–2 reports that during the Irish campaign Southampton was seen hugging and playing 'wantonly' with Piers Edmond, Corporal-General of Horse.

CHAPTER 11: A TWENTY-FIRST BIRTHDAY POEM

1. Wood 131.
2. For a cogent and invigorating exposition of the European and British climate during just this period, see Le Roy Ladurie 246ff. and 248.

CHAPTER 12: TAMING THE DARK LADY

1. One of the best-informed discussions of the Dark Lady and Emilia Bassano is in Lasocki and Prior.
2. Chambers disagreed with Halliwell-Phillipps over Wilmcote. He preferred Wincot at Clifford Chambers-Quinton, a few miles south of Stratford, because the name Hacket is actually recorded here, though only once, with reference to the baptism of one 'Sara', daughter of Robert Hackett on 21 November 1591. Since there are no more Hacket(t)s recorded in the Quinton register little Sara's parents may not have been married in this parish. The name Hacket(t) does occur in Stratford, but it is not common, even if we accept that the parish registers of the area are neither complete nor wholly reliable. The scene is set in Gloucestershire and since the nineteenth century it has been argued that the two litigants of *2 Henry IV* may have lived in Gloucestershire in the area around Dursley and the adjoining Stinchcombe Hill. The name Visor was common in the region at the time, but Perkes is seldom found here. Stinchcombe Hill affords a good view right across to Berkeley castle on a hill four miles away so that the phrase 'by yon tuft of trees' in *Richard II* may be evidence of Shakespeare knowing this area. Wood makes the same point and connects it back to John Shakespeare's illegal trading (brogging) in wool.
3. *MA* iii.60–1.
4. Although it omits the *Henry VI* plays and *The Merry Wives of Windsor*. Since *The Merry Wives of Windsor* appears to have been commissioned for a court performance in the first instance Meres may not have been aware of its existence when he wrote *Palladis Tamia*, although if he was in the know anyway, as has been suggested, he would not need to depend on outside information. It is worth noting that in the past scholars used to argue for a rather later date, one after 1598.

CHAPTER 13: A WILL 'MADE LAME BY FORTUNE'S BLOWS'

1. Chambers 1930: ii.289.
2. The poem has been known as the Anne Hathaway poem since Gurr 1971.

CHAPTER 14: THE CATHOLICS AND OLDCASTLE

1. Kermode 2004: 129.
2. Quoted in Caraman 1965: 278.
3. From the chamberlains' yearly accounts it appears that the Underhills of Stratford owned or leased property in Wilmcote. This might mean that they and the Ardens knew one another and that in the mid-1590s Shakespeare may have had privileged information about their intentions to sell New Place.

CHAPTER 15: FROM BLACKFRIARS TO BANKSIDE

1. Chambers 1923: iv.319–20.
2. Chambers 1923: ii.362.
3. Chambers 1923: iv.312.
4. Halliwell-Phillipps 1887: ii.298.
5. Chambers 1930: ii.88 reports Malone.

CHAPTER 16: WEDNESDAY 11 AUGUST 1596: 'ALACK MY CHILD IS DEAD'

1. For the raid on John Danter's press see Levenson 107–11.
2. The story of the fate of the great diamond is related by Ingram 98ff.

CHAPTER 17: 'MERRY WIVES' AND NEW PLACE

1. Schoenbaum 1975: 80.
2. Fripp claims that it cost twice that, £120. The official amount is so low that scholars have tended to discard it as notional, arguing that the real price must have been considerably more than the sum declared in the so-called foot of the fine.
3. Chambers 1930: ii.96.
4. Halliwell-Phillipps, who misread 'near the Chapel' for 'next' and wrote

'where' instead of 'when', noted that the main entrance to the house 'was then in Chapel-lane'. This is highly unlikely in itself as well as incompatible with the Vertue sketch which clearly shows the courtyard giving on to Chapel Street which is exactly where one would expect to find it. The transcripts of Greene in Fox 1964: 159 and Chambers 1930: ii.99 are accurate, Halliwell-Phillipps 1887: ii.120 is not.

5. Fox 1956: 81. New Place returned to the Cloptons through the daughter of Sir Edward Walker who bought it from the estate of Lady Barnard: Chambers 1930: ii.98–9.

6. Lewis 595.

7. Lasocki and Prior 104.

8. Throughout this period of looking after women or at them, Forman was involved in a passionate and violent love affair with a married Catholic woman by the name of Avis Allen. In chronicling this affair in some detail in his diary he deploys an obscure coded language including the bizarre coinage 'halek' for having sex. The record of his adulterous relationship with Avis Allen and his callous treatment of his young wife Anne Baker expose Forman as an amoral chancer. Avis Allen died in June 1597 from puerperal fever at just the time when he was seeing Emilia Bassano.

CHAPTER 18: FLIGHT FROM THE FORTRESS

1. Anna Keay notes that 'The building was also used, on occasion at least, for the torture of prisoners: John Gerard's account of his incarceration describes his torture in a large dark room with "wooden posts which held the roof of this huge underground chamber", all of which is consistent with the basement of the building before the insertion of the brick vaults in the eighteenth century' (Keay 41).

2. Shapiro 261. An entry in the Stratford archives suggests that oranges were around almost a hundred years before Gerard, something which the *Oxford English Dictionary* supports by citing a usage from 1490. The Stratford reference comes from the 'Masters' and proctors' accounts 1500-1501' and reads 'Expenses of the Feast: 5 qrs. of malt; 2s for brewing the same; 12s for 5 calves; 7s paid to the cook from Coventry; 7s paid for fish and "oranges"', the word itself being thought bizarre enough to require quotation marks (SBTRO: BRT 1/3/110).

3. Chaucer's famous inn was called the Tabard because of its sign, which was a 'tabard', that is a jacket or sleeveless coat. Its 'gallant host' in the late

fourteenth century was Harry Bailey, who choreographed the pilgrims' journey from London to Canterbury. Rather like Shakespeare, Chaucer felt relaxed about importing real people into his fiction, for in a poll tax return of 1381 for twenty-two hostellers from Southwark we find one 'Henry Bailif', none other than Chaucer's host (Carlin 1996: 48).

4. The woodcut is the title-page of a pamphlet called *The life and Death of Grifin Flood Informer* 1623. (*Riverside*, 583)

CHAPTER 19: THE MONEY-LENDER OF LONDON

1. Chambers 1930: ii.101–2.
2. McClure i.52.
3. The Bell Inn stood in Carter Lane, a London street which runs on an east to west trajectory between St Paul's Cathedral and the river. Like so much else of Shakespeare's London the Bell Inn vanished in the Great Fire of 1666, and now, at the time of writing, the entire block south of Carter Lane is being redeveloped.
4. Chambers 1930: ii.102. Richard Quiney's first-born Adrian married Eleanor Busshell in 1613 so that particular friendship at least endured beyond Richard Quiney's death. Richard Quiney, Jr married Eleanor Sadler the same year and Thomas Quiney married Judith Shakespeare in 1616.
5. 'Daniel Baker to his kind and loving friend Mr. Leonard Bennet at the Bell in Friday Street in London, asking him whether he has paid iiij.li. vij.s to Mr. Edward Kympton, draper, at the sign of the Black Boy in Watling Street, and requesting him to leave x.li with Mr. Thomas Hacket, draper, at the sign of the ij. cats in Canninge Street' (Stratford, 26 October 1598) (SBTRO: BRU 15/1/127).
6. Chambers 1923: ii.398.

CHAPTER 20: A STRATFORD ALEXANDER IN *HENRY V* AT THE GLOBE

1. Chambers 1923: ii.426.
2. Another school of thought including Shapiro 2005: 99 maintains that the O of *Henry V* is the stage of the Curtain in Shoreditch.
3. Shapiro 2005 argues the case for *Julius Caesar* and a later opening of the

Globe, while Gurr 1996: 291 notes that '*As You Like It* was almost certainly the first play Shakespeare wrote for the Globe.' Henslowe's receipts (Foakes 2002: 92, 120) do not help, even though there is some evidence to suggest that they dipped considerably in the autumn of 1599 when the Globe was fully operational.

4. Fripp 1924: 63.
5. Chambers 1923: ii.365.

CHAPTER 21: PICTURING A POET AND A PANTOMIME REBELLION

1. Leishman 185: 1032-33. Stanley Wells has called this 'Shakespeare as pin-up' (Wells, 68). He reminds us of the fact that a portrait of Ben Jonson had been issued as an independent print in the 1620s and was later used as the frontispiece to two of his books.
2. Quoted in Bevington 12.
3. The play was entered on the Stationers' Register in 1603, but it is usually dated to late 1601 because another one of its spoofed characters, the bombastic Ajax, may be Ben Jonson. Between September 1600 and May 1601 Jonson was writing for the Children of the Queen's Chapel in Blackfriars and by so doing seems to have given offence to some of his fellow writers for the adult companies.

CHAPTER 22: DAUGHTERS AND SONS AND LOVERS

1. In the best single study of the play to date, Edmondson (2005:1) disagrees and notes 'Although almost certainly not the play's premiere, it [the Middle Temple performance] was no doubt an evening of high spirits.'
2. Chambers 1930: ii. 247.

CHAPTER 23: AFFAIRS OF THE BODY AND HEART

1. Although this was long before Shakespeare moved in with the Mountjoys, he may already have known them through Richard Field, and he may have met Jane through them.

2. Chambers 1930: ii.254.
3. Edmondson 23.
4. Malone notes that he had 'Another curious document in my possession, which will be produced in the History of his Life [Malone's projected biography of Shakespeare], affords the strongest presumptive evidence that he continued to reside in Southwark to the year 1608' (Chambers 1930.ii.88). Unlike Malone, however, we know from Shakespeare's own testimony given during the Belott–Mountjoy lawsuit that he lived at the Mountjoys' in the City of London by probably 1602. Malone was unaware of any documents placing Shakespeare in the City of London in the early seventeenth century because the Mountjoy dispute only came to light in the National Archives in 1910. The findings of the Belott–Mountjoy case do not impugn Malone's integrity. Instead we should seriously consider the likely existence in the eighteenth century of a document that placed Shakespeare in Southwark, even though he may not have lived there. Perhaps it was another set of tithe requests, or perhaps a 'token' book that listed the names of those in the borough who were expected to attend church.
5. For the kind of house that Shakespeare may have lodged in while at the Mountjoys, see Wood 249.
6. Shapiro 2005 215–16.
7. Chambers 1930: ii.332.
8. Fraser 161.

CHAPTER 24: 'MY FATHER'S GODSON'

1. Respectively at 03.37am and 13.06pm: NASA Eclipse homepage:http://sunearth.gsfc.nasa.gov/eclipse.
2. Stow-Howes 1631: 883.
3. Bullough vii: 419.

CHAPTER 25: THE EASTER RISING OF 1606

1. For an account of this, see an odd, but authentic, note from 1631 in Chambers 1930: ii.168. Wilson 258–9 provides highly suggestive details of Dormer's connections and the ancient underground passages of the precinct. Gerard does not mention any of this in his autobiography, probably to protect the people who had sheltered him. This account is

almost certainly true, even though the record of tenancy at the gate-house suggests that Fortescue may no longer have lived there at the time of the Gunpowder Plot. In 1604 its owner Mathias Bacon sold it to Henry Walker who in turn parted with it to Shakespeare in 1613. Walker may of course have allowed Fortescue to stay on, although it is known that he issued a lease to one William Ireland. Similarly, Shakespeare bought the gatehouse and immediately, the day after, leased it back to the vendor.

2. There are several indicators to the closeness of these two texts, notably Shakespeare's use of the phrase 'lily-livered' as in 'a lily-livered, action-taking, whoreson' (*King Lear*) and 'thou lily-livered boy' (*Macbeth*). Shakespeare had already used 'white-livered' in *Richard III* and *Henry V*, and it appears in Harsnett's *Declaration* (Bullough viii: 415). As a more practised writer now he probably used 'lily-livered' in *Othello* because it was phonetically so much more effective, gliding down the tongue on 'l's, chiming the single vowel sound in the two halves of the compound while alliterating its liquid consonant. Shakespeare clearly enjoyed his new compound so much that he re-used 'lily-livered' in *Macbeth*. It was too good to throw away, particularly in an art-form that was intrinsically oral. A masterly account of the enduring links between recusants and the Blackfriars precinct is given by E. K. Chambers in an article in *The Times* of 23 April 1928, 'A Blackfriars House, Shakespeare's investment, hiding holes'.

3. Barroll 176.

CHAPTER 26: A WEDDING AND A FUNERAL

1. Stow-Howes 1631: 891.
2. The entry in the Register of St Giles Cripplegate reads '1607 August 12 B[urial] Edward son of Edward Shakespeare, player: base-born' (Chambers 1930: ii.18).
3. This is the 'Turnbull' of Justice Shallow's lecherous feats 'about Turnbull Street'.
4. The play was George Chapman's *The Conspiracy of Charles Duke of Byron*.
5. The uncertain times may have prompted Shakespeare's legal action against his former neighbour Richard Hornby's son Thomas, who had stood as guarantor for one of Shakespeare's debt defaulters. The amount of money involved was £6, a not inconsiderable sum. It certainly was not the kind of money that as a businessman Shakespeare was prepared to forfeit. The action lasted from August 1608 to June 1609. It cannot

have made the master of the grand *domus* at Chapel Lane very popular in Henley Street where his sister Joan still lived with her family, but lawsuits of this nature were par for the course in sixteenth- and seventeenth-century Stratford and there was not usually anything personal about them. It was really just a hard-nosed extension of business. By then the Hornbys had diversified, and the blacksmith had apparently doubled up as the owner of a tavern or ale-house called the Bell. In this the Hornbys may have been trend-setters, because in the next century Henley Street would acquire several more inns and taverns.

CHAPTER 27: LOSING A MOTHER AND A DAUGHTER

1. Elizabethan records tend to be more scrupulously accurate about social rank than about anything else; when Leland visited Charlecote in 1542, however, he refers to Lucy as 'Master' thus demonstrating clearly that the word could be applied to the highest in the land; *ergo* the dedication of the *Sonnets* to a 'Mr. W. H.' does not necessarily exclude aristocracy as is sometimes erroneously assumed.

CHAPTER 28: 'DO NOT GO GENTLE INTO THAT GOOD NIGHT'

1. The plays were *Much Ado About Nothing* (twice, and variously called 'Benedict and Beatrice'), *The Tempest, The Winter's Tale, 2 Henry IV* ('Sir John Falstaff'), *Othello, Cardenio* (twice), and *1 Henry IV* ('The Hotspur'): see *Dramatic Records in the Declared Accounts of the Treasurer of the Chamber 1558–1642*, Malone Society 1961 (1962) vol. 6, pp.55–6.
2. Holinshed, in Bullough iv.466.
3. Chambers 1930: ii.155.
4. On the Copperplate neither Ireland Yard nor either of the two passages from Water Lane are marked, but John Leake's post-Great Fire survey of the City of London 1666 as well as Ogilby's 1675 map show their exact positions. Ogilby in addition shows New Street which cut across Prior's Garden as a run-on from Creed Lane. It is possible that New Street marked the western boundary of Shakespeare's plot, unless the plot extended all the way west to the old Prior's lodging at the end of Ireland Yard.

5. Letter by Sir Henry Wotton of 2 July 1613.
6. McClure i.544 (30 June 1614).
7. Chambers 1930: ii.143.
8. Stow-Howes 1631: 1023.

CHAPTER 29: SHAKESPEARE DIES

1. These are the very lines that more than any others of Shakespeare's comforted Nelson Mandela on Robben Island. He wrote his name in the margin of them in 1979, on p. 980 of the Alexander Shakespeare. A copy of this book circulated clandestinely at the time among the ANC internees and has in it the signatures of a number of them. It is currently (May 2006) the centre piece of the Complete Works of Shakespeare exhibition in Nash House, which today guards the entrance to the magnificent gardens of New Place.
2. Chambers 1930: ii.177.
3. Chambers 1930: ii.136.
4. Digges's reference to Shakespeare in the context of his visit to Spain and Lope de Vega is quoted by Jonathan Bate in Nolen 117.
5. Fripp 1928: 73.

CHAPTER 30: LIFE AFTER DEATH

1. Of these perhaps 1,000, 228 are currently known; some seventy have surfaced in the twentieth century alone, so it seems likely that others remain to be traced. Presumably a number have been lost in domestic and other fires, such as the Great Fire of London – but apart from any that may have been held in private hands and perished, as far as is known none of the copies identified by Sidney Lee in 1902 were lost during the Second World War.
2. If his modern opposite in 2007 earned a pre-tax salary in the region of £55,000 a First Folio would cost £2,750. In real life of course a 1623 First Folio now fetches vast sums. The latest Folio to be auctioned at Sotheby's on 12 July 2006 was valued at £3 million.
3. In the twentieth century, after an absence of two and a half centuries, this volume finally returned home to the Bodleian. It had probably been sold by the library in 1664 as part of a consignment of 'superfluous library books', the First Folio being deemed superfluous because of the

Third Folio of 1663–4. In the end, after a fierce fund-raising campaign that became national news, Oxford retrieved her treasure on 31 March 1906 for the then enormous sum of £3,000, beating the Folger library to it. The volume is badly damaged, but it survives in its original University of Oxford calf binding of 1624. It is a unique piece.(West 2003: 20, 111–14; Duncan-Jones 283–4).

4. In the most brilliant essay ever written on the Shakespeare portraits it was argued from the play of light and shadow on the face that 'the artist worked not from an oil painting, but from an existing 'limning' of the poet – a portrait consisting of an outline drawing, with perhaps delicate flat washes of colour – as in a Hilliard miniature' (Spielmann 3).

5. According to John Downes, who was a professional prompter in the London theatres between 1662 and 1706: Chambers 1930: ii.263.

6. William Oldys, quoted in Schoenbaum 1970: 281.

7. As the foremost authority on the Shakespeare portraits put it, 'the deadly thing is that this engraving . . . presents that monument to us pretty well *exactly as it is to-day* – all except the head' (Spielmann 22).

8. Chambers 1930: ii.243.

9. BL Egerton MS 2065.

10. From the first English edition of Hall's casebook, quoted in Schoenbaum 1975: 291.

11. The *Marvellous Discourse* was bought at Sotheby's in 1973 by the Shakespeare Birthplace Trust, and is now back in Stratford.

12. 1674 Abington inventory (Fripp 1928: 79). The Barnard inventory was published in the *New Shakespeare Society Transactions 1880–5*, pt. ii.

13. Just above the Aldus *impresa* of a dolphin wrapped around an anchor is the signature 'W.^m Sh.^e'. It resembles those in the will but has been suspected of being a forgery, a copy of an eighteenth-century reproduction of one of the signatures. The 1682 date was queried in 1917 along with just about everything about the inscription by the distinguished palaeographer E. M. Thompson. But he was mistaken, as Falconer Madan, a painstakingly scrupulous librarian at the Bodleian, demonstrated conclusively the year after. Madan matched every detail of the handwriting queried by Thompson with Bodleian manuscripts from the same year 1682. He even made a strong case for the authenticity of the Shakespeare signature above the emblem, while acknowledging that this would fly in the face of expectation (*The Library*, 1917–18). As Fripp remarks in his discussion of the pedigree of the Aldine Ovid, 'Foolish legends but not forgeries had begun in 1682' (*MA* iii.xxvi).

Bibliographical Note

SBTRO = Shakespeare Birthplace Trust Record Office
MA = *Minutes and Accounts of the Corporation of Stratford-upon-Avon, and other records*, 1553–1598, 5 volumes (1921–90)

All quotations from Shakespeare are from the Oxford *Complete Works*, (1986), edited by Stanley Wells and Gary Taylor, unless otherwise indicated.

The most influential biography of the twentieth century was undoubtedly Samuel Schoenbaum's *William Shakespeare: A Documentary Life*, which first appeared in 1975 and has since been issued in various revised versions. It was preceded by *Shakespeare's Lives* in 1970 in which with consummate brilliance, bringing a razor-sharp intelligence to the project, Schoenbaum surveyed the whole field of writing biographies about Shakespeare. *Shakespeare's Lives* is a lucid and stylish exposition of the problems encountered by generations of Shakespearian biographers. In the folio-size first edition of the *Documentary Life* Schoenbaum also made a vast amount of primary material available to the wider public for the first time; at the same time, however, he erected barriers where there had been none before and need not be now. When he could not triangulate his information he chose to query it rather than letting the matter rest, or disposed of it in a manner which impressed by its urbane wit and acuity if not invariably by its accuracy. Thus Schoenbaum won his verbal fencing match with A. L. Rowse from All Souls College, Oxford over the 'mistress' of the *Sonnets*, but as a historian Rowse was more sure-footed when it came to archives and coal-face research, even if his palaeography was not always as good as it ought to have been. Schoenbaum's cool positivism carried the day during their public spat, yet at the same time Schoenbaum relied on Rowse's *Times* essay on Shakespeare's landlady, Madame Mountjoy, and her affair with another shopkeeper. Moreover Rowse may well have been right about the Dark Lady whom he identified as Emilia Lanier.

Schoenbaum stood on the shoulders of E. K. Chambers and J. O.

Halliwell–Phillipps. Chambers's two volumes dealing with the facts and problems of Shakespeare's life (1930) are the bible of all the poet's biographers. They accumulate a great many of the essential materials for a biography, and Chambers's notes are informative and reliable; his was one of the most acute and discriminating minds ever to survey this field. Behind Chambers lies Halliwell–Phillipps, and not just Halliwell–Phillipps's own attempt at a biography but also the two indispensable volumes, *Outlines* (1887), which offer fascinating and still unparalleled insights into the physical places associated with Shakespeare in Stratford, in addition to a wealth of other information. And there is more. One of Halliwell–Phillipps's most brilliant contributions, and for the researcher arguably the most important of all, is his 1863 *A Calendar of Stratford Records* or, to give it its full title, *A Descriptive Calendar of the Ancient Manuscripts and Records in the Possession of the Corporation of Stratford-upon-Avon.* For anyone researching Shakespeare's Stratford and the wealth of documents at the Shakespeare Birthplace Trust, this is a seminal volume. Chambers and Halliwell–Phillipps are usefully supplemented by R. B. Lewis's magnificent two volumes, *The Shakespeare Documents* (1940); its copious notes are endlessly suggestive of new directions.

There has been a remarkable surge of activity in recent years in the field of Shakespearian biography, including a brand new entry in the *Oxford Dictionary of National Biography*, the first new national essay on the poet since Sidney Lee's original of 1897. A gradual recession of the long shadow cast by Schoenbaum is one reason for this renewed confidence that the project is once more worth undertaking; his biographical studies nevertheless retain their freshness and validity. Furthermore, national and international projects to digitize local archives, including the collections of the Shakespeare Birthplace Trust, have opened up new vistas barely tapped as yet. The more documents become available online, the more likely it must be that sooner or later an important new Shakespeare find will emerge. Another rich seam is the matter of Shakespeare's spiritual allegiances, about which questions are increasingly being asked, while his works and the broader environment of the period are alike scoured for traces of a hidden trail that might (or might not) end up in the rafters of the house in Henley Street, where a workman once found a handwritten Catholic testament.

My most pressing debts in this book are to the archives of The Shakespeare Birthplace Trust in Stratford-upon-Avon. These are readily available to the general reader thanks to the superb work of Richard Savage, Edgar Innes Fripp, and, latterly, Levi Fox and the present team of archivists. Fripp wrote with unmatched expertise about Shakespeare's Stratford, its streets and houses, and its surrounding villages. He was the author also of an important study of the way in which Shakespeare's life and plays converge; this was published posthumously and, though flawed, remains a treasure trove of information. Fripp's studies provide the basis for Mark Eccles's sound but austere survey of Shakespeare's Warwickshire connections, which in turn becomes the source for Schoenbaum's pages on Shakespeare's home county. I have learnt much from Robert Bearman's articles on the Shakespeare homes, on John Shakespeare, and on the testament in the rafters of Henley Street. A number of other useful publications about Stratford include among others an edited collection of bench-mark essays by different hands, *The History of an English Borough: Stratford-upon-Avon 1196–1996*. In addition to this my main sources of information on matters relating to Stratford-upon-Avon have been, above all, *The Minutes and Accounts* of the borough edited by Fripp and Savage, Halliwell-Phillipps's *A Descriptive Calendar* (1863), and Philip Styles's classic account of Warwickshire and Holy Trinity Church, in the third volume of the *Victoria County History*.

I have been inspired by a number of recent biographers of Shakespeare, notably by Katherine Duncan-Jones, Stephen Greenblatt, Anthony Holden, and Park Honan, as well as by James Shapiro's *1599: A Year in the Life of William Shakespeare*, Stanley Wells's wide-ranging *Shakespeare for All Time*, and Michael Wood's impressive *In Search of Shakespeare*, written to accompany his evocative and moving BBC series on Shakespeare's life. The *Oxford English Dictionary*, the *Oxford Dictionary of National Biography*, and the masterly *Oxford Companion to Shakespeare*, edited by Michael Dobson and Stanley Wells, were constantly to hand, as were Weinreb's and Hibbert's *The London Encyclopaedia,* John Stow's *Survey of London*, and, latterly, Andrew Dickson's inspired *Rough Guide to Shakespeare*.

For information on the personnel of Shakespeare's company and the theatre of his time I am indebted above all to Chambers's four volumes on the Elizabethan stage and to the work of Andrew Gurr. The Catholic background of Elizabethan England and how it affected the Shakespeare family has proved one of the most productive lines of inquiry since Schoenbaum's day. Among the many to enhance an understanding of this important topic are, most recently, Richard Wilson on the Catholic ghosts at Blackfriars, Gerard Kilroy on the indelible literary presence of Edmund Campion, and Clare Asquith on how the Catholic underground negotiated literary symbols. Greenblatt's superb meditation on what made Shakespeare Shakespeare fully acknowledges the significant burden that the sectarian divide in the country placed on its citizens, as does Wood's book. The autobiographies of two Jesuits, John Gerard and William Weston, brilliantly translated and annotated by Philip Caraman, SJ, provide indispensable information about Elizabethan culture, and particularly its grim underbelly of prisons and torture.

The list which follows contains a selection of the books and articles I have found particularly useful during the writing of this book; it is not intended to be exhaustive.

Akrigg, George Philip Vernon, *Shakespeare and the Earl of Southampton* (Hamish Hamilton, 1968)

Alcock, Nathaniel (with Robert Bearman), 'Discovering Mary Arden's House: Property and Society in Wilmcote, Warwickshire', in *Shakespeare Quarterly* 53 (2002), 53–82

Asquith, Clare, *Shadowplay* (Public Affairs, 2005)

Baker, Oliver, *In Shakespeare's Warwickshire and the Unknown Years* (Simpkin Marshall, 1937)

Baldwin, T. W., *William Shakspere's Small Latine and Lesse Greeke* (University of Illinois Press, 1944)

Barroll, J. Leeds, *Politics, Plague, and Shakespeare's Theatre* (Cornell University Press, 1991)

Bate, Jonathan, *The Genius of Shakespeare* (Picador, 1997)

Bearman, Robert, *Stratford-upon-Avon: a history of its streets and buildings* (Nelson, 1988)

—— (ed.), *The History of an English Borough: Stratford-upon-Avon 1196–1996* (Sutton, 1997)

——, '"Was William Shakespeare William Shakeshafte?" Revisited' (*Shakespeare Quarterly* 53, 2002) 83–94

——, 'John Shakespeare, a papist or just penniless?' (*Shakespeare Quarterly 2*, 2006) 411–33

Bevington, David, (ed.), *Troilus and Cressida* (Arden 3, 1998)

Bloom, Harold, *Shakespeare: the invention of the human* (Fourth Estate, 1998)

Braines, W. W., *The Site of the Globe Playhouse* (Hodder & Stoughton, 1924)

Brinkworth, E. R. C., *Shakespeare and the Bawdy Court of Stratford* (Phillimore, 1972)

Brock, Susan and Honigmann, E. A. J. (eds), *Playhouse wills, 1558–1642* (Manchester University Press, 1993)

Bullough, Geoffrey, *Narrative and Dramatic Sources of Shakespeare*, 8 vols (Routledge, 1957–75)

Caraman, Philip, *Henry Garnet 1555–1606* (Longmans, 1964)

——, (2nd ed.), *John Gerard. The Autobiography of an Elizabethan*, translated by Philip Caraman, with an introduction by Graham Greene (Longmans, 1956)

——, *William Weston: The Autobiography of an Elizabethan*, translated by Philip Caraman, with a foreword by Evelyn Waugh (Longmans, 1955)

Carlin, Martha, *Medieval Southwark* (Hambledon, 1996)

Challoner, Richard, *Memoirs of Missionary Priests* (1741)

Chambers E. K., 'A Blackfriars House, Shakespeare's investment, hiding holes', *The Times*, 23 April 1928

——, *William Shakespeare: A study of facts and problems*, 2 vols (Oxford, 1930)

——, *The Elizabethan Stage*, 4 vols (Oxford, 1923)

Cressy, David, *Birth, Marriage, and Death* (OUP, 1997)

Davidson, Clifford, *The Guild Chapel Wall Paintings at Stratford-upon-Avon* (AMS, 1988)

Dickson, Andrew, *The Rough Guide to Shakespeare* (Penguin, 2005)

Dobson, Michael and Stanley Wells, *The Oxford Companion to Shakespeare* (OUP, 2001)

Duncan-Jones, Katherine, *Ungentle Shakespeare* (Arden, 2001)

Dutton, Richard, *Mastering the Revels* (Macmillan, 1991)

Eccles, Mark, *Christopher Marlowe in London* (Harvard University Press, 1934)

——, *Shakespeare in Warwickshire* (The University of Wisconsin Press, 1961)

Edmond, Mary, *Rare Sir William Davenant* (Manchester University Press, 1987)

Edmondson, Paul, *Twelfth Night: a guide to the text and its theatrical life* (Palgrave, 2005)

Edmondson, Paul, and Stanley Wells, *Shakespeare's Sonnets* (OUP, 2004)

Elton, Charles Isaac, *William Shakespeare: His Family and Friends* (John Murray, 1904)

Foakes, R. A. (ed.), *Henslowe's Diary* (2nd ed, CUP, 2002)

Fox, Levi, *The Correspondence of the Reverend Joseph Greene* (The Dugdale Society, 1964)

——, *The Shakespeare Birthplace Trust: A Personal Memoir* (The Shakespeare Birthplace Trust, 1997)

Fraser, Antonia, *The Gunpowder Plot* (Phoenix, 2002)

Fripp, Edgar Innes, *Master Richard Quyny* (OUP, 1924)

——, *Shakespeare's Stratford* (OUP, 1928)

——, *Shakespeare's Haunts near Stratford* (OUP, 1929)

——, *Shakespeare, Man and Artist* 2 vols (OUP, 1938)

Gray, J. W., *Shakespeare's Marriage* (Chapman & Hall, 1905)

Greenblatt, Stephen, *Hamlet in Purgatory* (Princeton University Press, 2001)

Greenblatt, Stephen, *Will in the World* (Jonathan Cape, 2004)

Gurr, Andrew, 'Shakespeare's first poem: Sonnet 145', in *Essays in Criticism* 21 (1971), 221–6

——, *The Shakespearian playing companies* (OUP, 1996)

Halliwell-Phillipps, James Orchard, *A Descriptive Calendar of the Ancient Manuscripts and Records in the Possession of the Corporation of Stratford-upon-Avon* (1863)

——, *The Life of William Shakespeare* (1848)

——, *Outlines of the Life of Shakespeare*, 2 vols (1887)

Harrison, William, *The Description of England,* ed. Georges Edelen (Cornell University Press, 1968)

Harsnett, Samuel, *A Declaration of egregious popish impostures* (1603)

Holden, Anthony, *William Shakespeare: his life and work* (Little, Brown and Company, 1999)

Holinshed, Raphael, *The Chronicles of England Scotland and Ireland,* 2nd ed, (1587)

Honan, Park, *Shakespeare: a life* (OUP, 1998)

Hotson, Leslie, *The First Night of Twelfth Night* (Hart–Davis, 1954)

Hyde, Ralph, *The A to Z of Restoration London,* with an index compiled by John Fisher and Roger Cline (London Topographical Society, 1992)

Ingleby, C. M., *Shakespeare and the Enclosure of Common Fields at Welcombe being a fragment of the private diary of Thomas Greene, town clerk of Stratford-upon-Avon* (1885)

Ingram, William, *A London Life in the Brazen Age: Francis Langley, 1548–1602* (Harvard University Press, 1978)

Jackson, Peter, *London Bridge* (Cassell, 1971)

Jones, Jeanne, *Stratford-upon-Avon Inventories 1538–1699,* 2 vols (The Dugdale Society 2002; 2003)

Kastan, David Scott, *Shakespeare and the Book* (CUP, 2001)

Keay, Anna, *The Elizabethan Tower of London* (London Topographical Society, 2001)

Kemp, Thomas, *The Black Book of Warwick* (1898)

Kermode, Sir Frank, Shakespeare's Language (Allen Lane, 2000)

——, *The Age of Shakespeare* (Weidenfeld and Nicolson, 2004)

Kilroy, Gerard, *Edmund Campion: Memory and Transcription* (Ashgate, 2005)

Kirkwood, A. E. M., 'Richard Field, Printer, 1589–1624', in *The Library* pp. 1–35 (1931)

Kuriyama, Constance Brown, *Christopher Marlowe. A Renaissance Life* (Cornell University Press, 2002)

Lane, Joan, *John Hall and his Patients* (The Shakespeare Birthplace Trust, 1996)

Lasocki, D. and R. Prior, *The Bassanos* (Scolar Press, 1995)

Leishman, J. B. (ed.), *The Three Parnassus Plays (1598–1601)* (Nicholson & Watson, 1949)

Leland, John, *The Itinerary of John Leland . . . 1535–1543* ed. Lucy Toulmin Smith, Vol. 2 (George Bell & Sons, 1908)

Le Roy Ladurie, Emmanuel, *Histoire humaine et comparée du climat* (Fayard, 2004)

Levenson, Jill L. (ed.), *Romeo and Juliet* (OUP, 2000)

Lewis, B. Roland, *The Shakespeare Documents,* 2 vols (Stanford University Press, 1940)

Macdonald, Màiri, 'Not a Memorial to Shakespeare, but a place for divine worship: The Vicars of Stratford and the Shakespeare phenomenon, 1616–1964', in *Warwickshire History,* Vol. 9 (2001–2)

Madan F. W., 'Two Lost Causes', in *The Library*, pp. 97–105 (1918)

Meres, Francis, *Palladis Tamia, Wit's Treasury* (1598)

Minutes and Accounts: Fripp, Edgar Innes and Richard Savage, *Minutes and Accounts of the Corporation of Stratford-upon-Avon, and other records, 1553–1592.* Transcribed by Richard Savage . . . With introduction and notes by Edgar Innes Fripp, 4 vols (The Dugdale Society, 1921–29); vol. V (1593–98), ed. Levi Fox (The Dugdale Society, 1990)

McClure, Norman E., *John Chamberlain: Letters*, 2 vols (American Philosophical Society, 1939)

Nicholl, Charles, *The Reckoning: The Murder of Christopher Marlowe* (Jonathan Cape, 1992)

Nolen, Stephanie (ed.), *Shakespeare's Face* (Knopf, 2002)

Ogilby, John, *Britannia: or an illustration of the kingdom of England . . . by a geographical and historical description of the principal roads thereof . . .* (1675)

Orrell, John, *The Quest for Shakespeare's Globe* (CUP, 1983)

Page, Catharine and Ronald, 'The location of Richard Shakespeare's farm in Snitterfield', in *Warwickshire History*, Vol. 3 (1982)

Platter, Thomas, *Thomas Platter's Travels in England* (translated by Clare Williams, Jonathan Cape, 1937)

Prockter, Adrian and Taylor, Robert, *The A to Z of Elizabethan London* (London Topographical Society, 1979)

David Riggs, *The World of Christopher Marlowe* (Faber & Faber, 2004)

The Riverside Shakespeare 2nd ed., G. Blakemore Evans (Houghton Mifflin, 1997)

Rowe, Nicholas, *Some Account of the Life . . . in Shakespeare, Works* (1709)

Rowse, A. L., 'Secrets of Shakespeare's Landlady', in *The Times*, 23 April 1973

——, *Simon Forman: sex and society in Shakespeare's age* (Weidenfeld and Nicolson, 1974)

Rutter, Carol Chillington (ed.), *Documents of the Rose Playhouse* (Manchester University Press, 1984)

Schoenbaum, Samuel, *Shakespeare's Lives* (OUP, 1970)

——, *William Shakespeare: A Documentary Life* (OUP, 1975)

——, *William Shakespeare: A Compact Documentary Life* (OUP, 1977)

Schofield, John, *The London Surveys of Ralph Treswell* (London Topographical Society, 1987)

Schofield, John and Ann Saunders, *Tudor London: A Map and a View* (London Topographical Society, 2001)

Shapiro, James, *1599: A Year in the Life of William Shakespeare* (Faber & Faber, 2005)

——, *Shakespeare and the Jews* (Columbia University Press, 1996)

Shell, Alison, *Catholicism, Controversy, and the English Literary Imagination, 1558–1660* (CUP, 1999)

Sisson, C. J., 'Shakespeare's Friends: Hathaways and Burmans of Shottery', in *Shakespeare Survey* 12 (1959) 95–106

Slater, T. R., 'Domesday Village to Medieval Town: the Topography of Medieval Stratford-upon-Avon', in Bearman 1997

Smith, Bruce, *Homosexual Desire in Shakespeare's England: A cultural poetics* (University of Chicago Press, 1991)

Smith, Irwin, *Shakespeare's Blackfriars Playhouse* (Owen, 1966)

Sorlien, R. P. (ed.) *The Diary of John Manningham of the Middle Temple* (University Press of New England, 1976)

Spielmann, M. H., *The Title-page of the First Folio of Shakespeare's Plays* (Humphrey Milford, 1924)

Stopes, Charlotte M., *Shakespeare's Warwickshire Contemporaries* (Shakespeare Head Press, 1907)

Stow, John, *A Survey of London . . . 1603*, ed. C. L. Kingsford (OUP, 1908)

Stow-Howes, *Annals, or a general chronicle of England . . . by John Stow and Edmond Howes* (1631)

Styles, Philip, *The Borough of Stratford-upon-Avon and the Parish of Alveston* (OUP, 1946)

Sugden, Edward H., *A topographical dictionary to the works of Shakespeare and his fellow dramatists* (Manchester University Press, 1925)

Thomas, David, *Shakespeare in the Public Records* (HMSO, London, 1985)

Traister, Barbara Howard, *The Notorious Astrological Physician of London: Works and Days of Simon Forman* (University of Chicago Press, 2000)

Vickers, Brian, *Shakespeare, Co-author, A Historical Study of Five Collaborative Plays* (OUP, 2002)

Wallace, C. W., *The First London Theatre: Materials for a History 1913* (Nebraska University Studies xiii, 1913)

Ward, John, *Diary of the Rev. John Ward, A. M., vicar of Stratford-upon-Avon, extending from 1648 to 1679 . . . edited by Charles Severn* (1839)

Weinreb, Ben and Christopher Hibbert, *The London Encyclopaedia* (Macmillan, 1983)

Wells, Stanley, *Shakespeare for All Time* (Macmillan, 2002)

West, Anthony James, *The Shakespeare first folio: the history of the book*, 2 vols (OUP, 2001; 2003)

Wheler, R. B., *A Guide to Stratford-upon-Avon* (1814)

Wilson, Richard, *Secret Shakespeare* (Manchester University Press, 2004)

Wood, Michael, *In Search of Shakespeare* (BBC, 2003)

Woodhuysen, H. R. (ed.), *Love's Labour's Lost* (Arden 3, 1998)

Index

The use of bold denotes an entry in the list of *Main Characters*